THE NEW
CAMBRIDGE MODERN HISTORY

ADVISORY COMMITTEE

SIR GEORGE CLARK   SIR JAMES BUTLER   J.P.T. BURY
THE LATE E.A.BENIANS

VOLUME XIV

ATLAS

D0081368

THE NEW CAMBRIDGE MODERN HISTORY

VOLUME XIV
ATLAS

EDITED BY

H. C. DARBY

Professor of Geography in the University of Cambridge

AND

HAROLD FULLARD

Cartographic Editor, George Philip & Son Ltd

CAMBRIDGE
AT THE UNIVERSITY PRESS
1970

Published by the Syndics of the Cambridge University Press
Bentley House, 200 Euston Road, London, N.W.1
American Branch: 32 East 57th Street, New York, N.Y. 10022

Maps © George Philip & Son Ltd 1970
All other material © Cambridge University Press 1970

Library of Congress Catalogue Card Number: 57-14935

Standard Book Number: 521 07708 7

Printed in Great Britain
by George Philip Printers Ltd, London

CONTENTS

LIST OF MAPS

THE WORLD

WARS AND TREATY SETTLEMENTS

EUROPE

LIST OF MAPS

THE BRITISH ISLES

FRANCE

ix

LIST OF MAPS

CENTRAL EUROPE

NORTHERN EUROPE

THE NETHERLANDS

LIST OF MAPS

SWITZERLAND

ITALY

IBERIAN PENINSULA

THE BALKANS AND THE NEAR EAST

EASTERN EUROPE AND RUSSIA

LIST OF MAPS

NORTH AMERICA

xii

LIST OF MAPS

LIST OF MAPS

AFRICA

INDIA AND THE FAR EAST

LIST OF MAPS

PREFACE

The making of any atlas is an exercise in compromise—between, amongst other things, the scales of maps, the choice of names, the availability of information and the cost of production. This is especially true of a historical atlas. The present atlas has been designed with the aim of making it easily portable, convenient for frequent use and able to stand upon a bookshelf. Even so, the scales of the majority of the maps compare favourably with those of atlases of a much larger format because there are many double-page maps and because insets have only rarely been included on a page.

In planning the atlas we have tried to balance the amount of space given to maps of Europe by nearly as many maps dealing with non-European lands—with North America, Latin America, Africa, the Far East, Australasia and the world as a whole. A substantial number of maps showing economic and social conditions has been included. We wish we could have included even more, but, only too often, we have drawn a blank in our search for reliable economic information for some areas at a number of periods. To have increased such economic maps by even a small number would have involved extensive research programmes impossible within the limits within which we worked. Maps showing exploration, major wars and treaty settlements have also been included.

Some historical atlases have adopted a basic chronological plan; others have grouped maps of similar areas together. Each method can be defended, but we have followed the latter method in the belief that it facilitates reference to individual areas at different periods. The maps within each group, so far as is possible, have been arranged in chronological sequence and have been produced on the same scale to enable easy comparison between them.

Instead of a topographical index of names, a subject index has been assembled based mainly upon area and chronology. The treatment of place-names always presents difficulties to atlas makers because spellings so often change with shifting political boundaries. We have tried to follow the spellings generally in use in English historical writing. Each map has been newly compiled and has been reproduced using the latest cartographic techniques; type-faces and colours have been selected with the aim of presenting information in as clear a manner as possible. Although designed to serve the needs of readers of *The New Cambridge Modern History*, the atlas is also intended to illustrate school or university courses on modern history.

PREFACE

We are grateful for advice at various stages of the work to the editors of, and contributors to, *The New Cambridge Modern History*. Professor R. M. Hatton and Professor D. B. Horn have very kindly given us help over specific maps. We also owe warm thanks to the cartographic staff of Messrs. George Philip and Son Ltd. Finally, we are greatly indebted to Mr G. R. Versey who has given much general assistance in the preparation of the maps and index.

H. C. DARBY
HAROLD FULLARD

King's College, Cambridge
Michaelmas, 1969

ACKNOWLEDGEMENTS

Among the works consulted in the preparation of this
atlas, the following have been especially useful.

J. T. Adams, *Atlas of American History* (New York, 1943).

H. Ammann und Karl Schib, *Historischer Atlas der Schweiz* (Aarau, 1958).

АТЛАСЬ АЗІАТСКОЙ РОССІИ [*Atlas of Asiatic Russia*] (St. Petersburg, 1914).

Atlas Narodov Mira (Moscow, 1964).

Official Year Books of the Commonwealth of Australia (Melbourne, 1901-8).

J. N. L. Baker, *A History of Geographical Discovery and Exploration* (London, 1931).

J. G. Bartholomew, *The Survey Atlas of England and Wales* (London, 1903).

——*Atlas of the World's Commerce* (London, 1907).

——*A Literary and Historical Atlas of Asia* (London, 1913).

I. Bowman, *The New World* (Yonkers, N.Y., 1921).

H. Butterfield, *et al.*, *A Short History of France* (Cambridge, 1961).

The Cambridge Modern History, 14 vols. (Cambridge, 1902-12).

Atlas of Canada (Ottawa: Dept. of Interior, 1915).

Ceskoslovenský Vojenský Atlas (Praha, 1965).

J. W. Chalmers, W. J. Eccles and H. Fullard, *Philip's Historical Atlas of Canada* (London, 1966).

Chambers's Encyclopaedia (London, 1959).

J. H. Clapham, *An Economic History of Modern Britain*, 3 vols. (Cambridge, 1926-38).

The Columbia Lippincott Gazetteer of the World (New York, 1962).

H. C. Darby (ed.), *An Historical Geography of England before A.D.* 1800 (Cambridge, 1936).

I. Darlington and J. Howgego, *Printed Maps of London c.* 1553-1850 (London, 1964).

C. C. Davies, *An Historical Atlas of the Indian Peninsula* (Oxford, 1949).

АТЛАС ИСТОРИИ ГЕОГРАФИЧЕСКИХ ОТКРЫТИИ И ИССЛЕДОВАНИЙ [*Atlas of the History of Geographical Discoveries and Explorations*] (Moscow, 1959).

G. Droysen, *Allgemeiner Historischer Handatlas* (Leipzig, 1886).

Encyclopaedia Britannica, Eleventh Edition (New York, 1910-11).

J. Engel (ed.), *Grosser Historischer Weltatlas*, Teil III (Neuzeit) (Munchen, 1962).

J. D. Fage, *An Atlas of African History* (London, 1958).

T. W. Freeman, *Ireland* (London, 1950).

——*The Conurbations of Great Britain* (Manchester, 1959).

H. Fullard and H. C. Darby, *The University Atlas* (London, 1967).

The Geographical Journal (London since 1893).

The Geographical Review (New York, since 1916).

M. Gilbert, *Recent History Atlas* (London, 1966).

Greek Refugee Settlement (League of Nations, Geneva, 1926).

Helmut Haufe, *Die Bevölkerung Europas* (Berlin, 1936).

A. Herrmann, *Historical and Commercial Atlas of China* (Harvard-Yenching Institute, 1935).

——*An Historical Atlas of China* (Chicago, 1966).

W. A. Heurtley, *et al.*, *A Short History of Greece* (Cambridge, 1965).

Historical Atlas of the Muslim Peoples (London, 1957).

Historical Atlas of the U.S.S.R. for Secondary Schools, 3 vols. (Moscow, 1949-52).

Keith Johnston, *A Sketch of Historical Geography* (London, 1909).

C. Joppen, *Historical Atlas of India* (London, 1928).

C. Joppen and H. L. O. Garrett, *Historical Atlas of India* (London, 1938).

H. H. Kagan, *The American Heritage Pictorial Atlas of United States History* (New York, 1966).

Julius Klein, *The Mesta: A study in Spanish Economic History* (Harvard, 1920).

E. Kremling, *IRO Weltwirtschaftsatlas* (Munchen, 1961).

E. Lehmann, *Historisch-Geographisches Kartenwek* (Leipzig, 1960).

P. I. Lyashchenko, *History of the National Economy of Russia to the 1917 Revolution* (New York, 1949).

B. R. Mitchell and P. Deane, *Abstract of British Historical Statistics* (Cambridge, 1962).

R. Muir and George Philip, *Philip's Historical Atlas Medieval and Modern* (London, 1927).

G. P. Murdock, *Africa: Its Peoples and their Culture History* (New York, 1959).

Naval Intelligence Division, *Geographical Handbooks:* Belgium, China Proper, France, Germany, Greece, Netherlands and Yugoslavia (London, Admiralty, 1942-5).

H. Newbolt, *The Year of Trafalgar* (London, 1905).

A. E. Nordenskiöld, *Facsimile Atlas to the early History of Cartography* (London, 1889).

C. Oman, *Nelson* (London, 1947).

C. O. Paullin and J. K. Wright, *Atlas of the Historical Geography of the United States* (Washington and New York, 1932).

A. Petermanns, *Mitteilingen* (Gotha, since 1855).

Philip's Atlas of Modern History, prepared under the direction of the Historical Association (London, 1964).

Philip's Chamber of Commerce Atlas (London, 1912).

K. Ploetz, *Auszug aus der Geschichte* (Wurzburg, 1960).

R. L. Poole, *Historical Atlas of Modern Europe* (Oxford, 1902).

F. W. Putzger, *Historischer Weltatlas* (Bielefeld und Berlin, 1961).

E. Reich, *A New Student's Atlas of English History* (London, 1903).

W. Van Royen and O. Bowles, *The Mineral Resources of the World* (New York, 1952).

F. Schrader, *Atlas de Géographie Historique* (Paris, 1907).

W. R. Shepherd, *Historical Atlas* (Pikesville, Maryland, 1956).

W. Smith, *An Economic Geography of Great Britain* (London, 1953).

Axel Sømme, *A Geography of Norden* (Oslo, 1960).

O. H. K. Spate, *India and Pakistan* (London, 1954).

L. Dudley Stamp and S. H. Beaver, *The British Isles* (London, 1954).

The Statesman's Yearbook (London, since 1864).

League of Nations, Statistical Yearbooks (various titles), (United Nations, New York).

A. J. Toynbee and E. D. Myers, *Historical Atlas and Gazetteer* (Oxford, 1959).

R. F. Treharne, *Bibliography of historical atlases and hand-maps for schools* (London, Historical Association, 1939).

R. F. Treharne and H. Fullard, *Muir's Historical Atlas Medieval and Modern* (London, 1962).

United Nations Yearbooks.

United States Census of Population, 1960 (U.S. Department of Commerce).

E. W. Walker, *Historical Atlas of South Africa* (Oxford, 1922).

Weltatlas: Die Staaten der Erde und ihre Wirtschaft (Gotha, 1964).

Westermanns Atlas zur Weltgeschichte (Braunschweig, 1956).

LIST OF ABBREVIATIONS

Abp.	Archbishopric	**Helv.**	Helvetia
Arch.	Archipelago	**Hung.**	Hungary
Arg.	Argentina		
Aust.	Austrian	**Indep.**	Independent
Austral.	Australia	**I, Is**	Island, Islands
Auton.	Autonomous	**Ital.**	Italian, Italy
B.	Bay, Bight	**Jap.**	Japan
Bdy.	Boundary		
Bech.	Bechuanaland	**K.**	Kingdom
Belg.	Belgian, Belgium		
Bol.	Bolivia	**L.**	Lake, Lordship
Bp.	Bishopric	**Ld.**	Land
Br.	Britain, British	**Ldg.**	Landgraviate
Bran.	Brandenburg	**Liech.**	Lichtenstein
Brun.	Brunswick	**Lux.**	Luxembourg, Luxemburg
Bulg.	Bulgaria		
		Mand.	Mandate
C.	Cape, County	**Mar.**	Margraviate, Marquisate
Cent.	Central, Century	**Mass.**	Massachusetts
Chin.	Chinese	**Md.**	Maryland
Co.	Company	**Mex.**	Mexico
Col.	Colony	**Mod.**	Modura
Conf.	Confederation	**Mont.**	Montenegro
Conn.	Connecticut	**Mt.**	Mount
Courl.	Courland	**Mts.**	Mountains
Cz.	Czechoslovakia		
		N.	North, Northern
D.	Duchy	**N.C.**	North Carolina
D.C.	District of Columbia	**N.H.**	New Hampshire
Del.	Delaware	**N.J.**	New Jersey
Den.	Denmark	**N.Y.**	New York
		N.Z.	New Zealand
Ec.	Ecuador	**Neth.**	Netherlands
El.	Electorate		
Eng.	England, English	**Occup.**	Occupation, Occupied
		Ottom. Emp.	Ottoman Empire
Fr.	France, French		
		P.	Pass
G.	Gulf	**Pal.**	Palatinate
Ga.	Georgia	**Par.**	Paraguay
Geb.	Gebirge	**Pen.**	Peninsula
Gen.	Genoa	**Pol.**	Poland, Polish
Ger.	Germany	**Pom.**	Pomerania
German C.	German Confederation	**Port.**	Portugal, Portuguese
Gr.	Grand	**Pr.**	Principality, Prince
Gr. D.	Grand Duchy	**Prot.**	Protection, Protectorate
Gr. Pr.	Grand Principality	**Prov.**	Province
Gt.	Great	**Pruss.**	Prussia
		Pt.	Port.
Habsb.	Habsburg		
Han.	Hanover	**R.**	River

LIST OF ABBREVIATIONS

Rep.	Republic	**Sw.**	Switzerland
R.I.	Rhode Island	**Swiss C.**	Swiss Confederation
Rum.	Rumania		
		T.	Treaty
S.	San, Seigneurie, South	**Terr.**	Territory
Sa.	Sierra	**Trib.**	Tributary
Sav.	Savoy	**Turk.**	Turkey, Turkish
Sax.	Saxon, Saxony	**Tusc.**	Tuscany
S.C.	South Carolina		
Scot.	Scotland	**U. of S.A.**	Union of South Africa
Sd.	Sound		
Serb.	Serbia	**Va.**	Virginia
Sp.	Spain	**V.C.**	Viscounty
Span.	Spanish	**Ven.**	Venice
St.	State	**Vt.**	Vermont
St. Sta.	Saint, Santa		
Str.	Strait	**Yug.**	Yugoslavia

THE WORLD, 1459
(after a Map by Fra Mauro)

THE WORLD, 1492
(after a Globe by Martin Behaim)

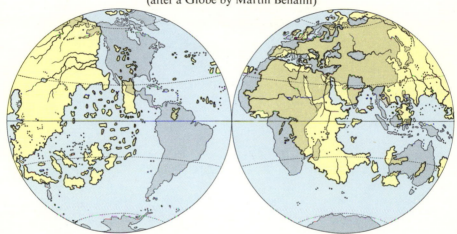

THE WORLD, *c.*1530
(after an anonymous Globe, probably made at Nuremberg)

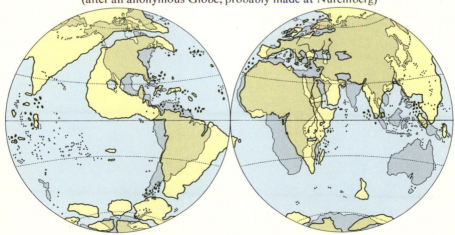

The World as known today is superimposed in grey

COPYRIGHT. GEORGE PHILIP & SON. LTD.

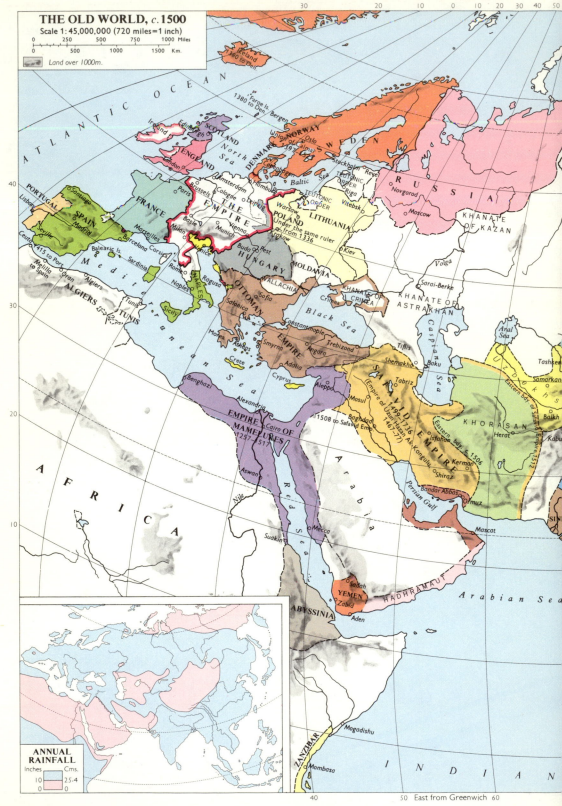

THE OLD WORLD, *c.*1500

Scale 1:45,000,000 (720 miles=1 inch)

250 500 750 1000 Miles
500 1000 1500 Km.

Land over 1000m.

ATLANTIC OCEAN

Iceland 1380 to Den.

Faroe Is. 1380 to Den.
Bergen

Ireland
Edinburgh
SCOTLAND
London ENGLAND
Paris
PORTUGAL
Lisbon
Santiago
SPAIN
Seville Madrid
Ceuta 1415 to Port.
Melilla to Spain
Oran to Spain
ALGIERS
TUNIS
Balearic Is.
Barcelona Corsica
Sardinia
FRANCE
Marseilles
Milan
Basle
Vienna
Munich
Brussels
Cologne
Amsterdam
Leipzig
THE EMPIRE
Romne
Venice
Ragusa
Naples
Sicily
MALTES
Crete
Morea
Athens
North Sea
Hamburg
Copenhagen
DENMARK
Union of Calmar 1397
Oslo
NORWAY
SWEDEN
Stockholm
Baltic Sea
Reval
Riga
TEUTONIC ORDER
TEUTONIC ORDER
Warsaw
Krakow
POLAND
Under the same ruler from 1336
LITHUANIA
Vitebsk
Kiev
Buda Pest
HUNGARY
WALLACHIA
MOLDAVIA
Sofia
OTTOMAN
Salonica
Constantinople
EMPIRE
Smyrna
Angora
Trebizond
Adalia
Aleppo
Cyprus
Black Sea
KHANATE OF CRIMEA
Crimea
RUSSIA
Novgorod
Moscow
Volga
Sarai-Berke
KHANATE OF KAZAN
KHANATE OF ASTRAKHAN
Tiflis
Shemakha
Baku
Caspian Sea
Aral Sea
Tashkent
Samarkand
Eastern bdr. of Safavid Empire, 1512
UZBEKS
Tabriz
Mosul
Baghdad
1508 to Safavid Emp.
SAFAVID EMPIRE
(Empire of Uzun Hasan 1467-36 1736)
Eastern bdr. c.1506
Isfahan
Kerman
Shiraz
KHORASAN
Herat
Balkh
Kabul
Mediterranean Sea
Alexandria
Cairo
EMPIRE OF MAMELUKES 1257-1517
Aswan
Nile
Red Sea
Mecca
Suakin
Arabia
Persian Gulf
Bandar Abbas
Ormuz
Mascat
SIN
Benghazi

AFRICA

Tunis
Algiers

Sadah
YEMEN
Zabid
Aden
HADRAMAUT
ABYSSINIA
Zanzibar
Mombasa
Mogadishu
Arabian Sea
INDIAN

East from Greenwich

ANNUAL RAINFALL

Inches Cms.
10   25.4
0   0

EQUAL AREA PROJECTION

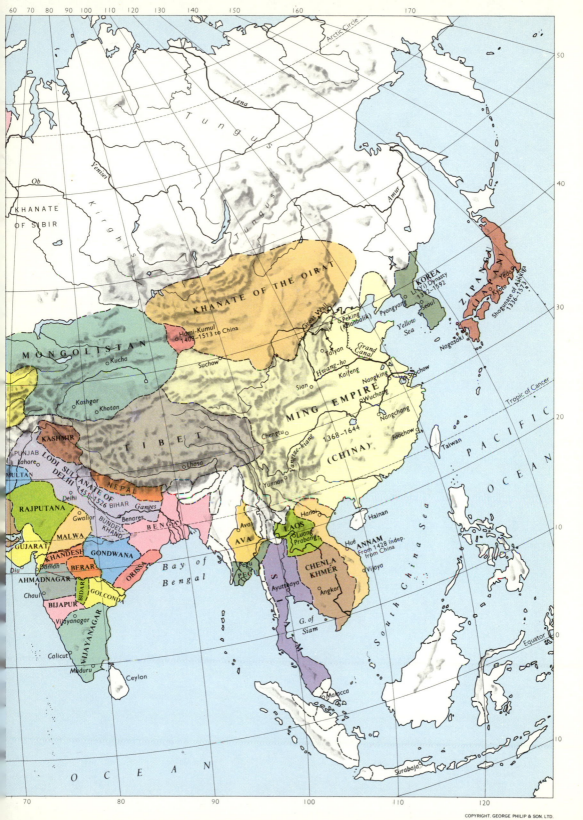

60 70 80 90 100 110 120 130 140 150 160 170

Arctic Circle

50

Lena

Tungus

40

KHANATE
OF SIBIR

Ob

Yenisei

Amur

K i r g h i s

T u n g u s

30

KHANATE OF THE OIRAT

Great Wall

Peking
(Khanbalik)

Pyongyang

KOREA
(Yi) Dynasty
1392-1592

Yeddo

J A P A N

Kyoto
Shogunate of Ashikaga
1336-1573

Z I P A N S U

Hami-Kumul
1403-1513 to China

M O N G O L I S T A N

Kucha

Taiyan

Yellow
Sea

Seoul

Nagasaki

Suchow

Kashgar

Khotan

T I B E T

Hwang-ho

Kaifeng

Sian

Nanking

Wuchang

Suchow

20

Tropic of Cancer

MING EMPIRE

KASHMIR

PUNJAB

Lahore

MULTAN

LODI SULTANATE OF
DELHI 1451-1526

NEPAL

BIHAR

Chengtu

Yangtze-kiang

1368-1644

Nangchang

Foochow

(CHINA)

P A C I F I C

Lhasa

Yunnan

Taiwan

Delhi

RAJPUTANA

Gwalior

BUNDEL
KHAND

Benares

Ganges

B E N G A L

Hanoi

Ava

LAOS

Luang
Prabang

Hué

ANNAM
From 1428 indep.
from China

Hainan

O C E A N

10

MALWA

GUJARAT

KHANDESH

GONDWANA

AVA

CHENLA
KHMER

Vijaya

Diu

Daman

BERAR

ORISSA

Pegu
PEGU

S

Ayuttaya

Angkor

South China Sea

AHMADNAGAR

Chaul

BIJAPUR

BIDAR

GOLCONDA

Bay of
Bengal

G. of
Siam

Equator

0

Vijayanagar

VIJAYANAGAR

I

A

M

Calicut

Maduru

Ceylon

Malacca

10

O C E A N

Surabaja

70 80 90 100 110 120

COPYRIGHT. GEORGE PHILIP & SON. LTD.

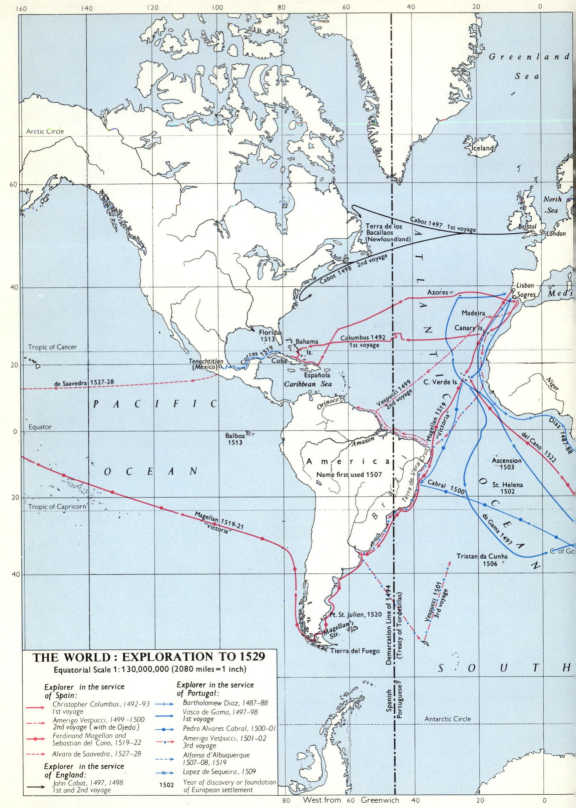

160   140   120   100   80   60   40   20   0

Greenland Sea

Arctic Circle

Iceland

60

North Sea

Cabot 1497 1st voyage
Terra de los Bacallaos (Newfoundland)
Bristol
London

Cabot 1498 2nd voyage

40

Azores
Lisbon
Sagres
Medi

Madeira
Canary Is.

Tropic of Cancer

Florida 1513
Bahama Is.
Columbus 1492 1st voyage

Cortes 1519
Tenochtitlan (Mexico)
Cuba
Española
Caribbean Sea

de Saavedra 1527-28

20

C. Verde Is.

Niger

Vespucci 1499 2nd voyage

Magellan 1519 *Victoria*

Orinoco

P A C I F I C

Balboa 1513

del Cano 1522

Diaz 1487-88

Ascension 1503

0 Equator

Amazon

A m e r i c a
Name first used 1507

St. Helena 1502

Cabral 1500

O C E A N

Tristan da Cunha 1506

da Gama 1497

C. of Go

20 Tropic of Capricorn

B r a z i l

Magellan 1519-21 "Victoria"

Tierra de Vera Cruz

Cabral 1500

Demarcation Line of 1494 (Treaty of Tordesillas)

Vespucci 1501 3-rd voyage

40

Pt. St. Julian, 1520
Magellan's Str.
Tierra del Fuego

S O U T H

Spanish
Portuguese

Antarctic Circle

THE WORLD: EXPLORATION TO 1529

Equatorial Scale 1:130,000,000 (2080 miles = 1 inch)

Explorer in the service of Spain:
→ Christopher Columbus, 1492-93 1st voyage
--→ Amerigo Vespucci, 1499-1500 2nd voyage (with de Ojeda)
◆→ Ferdinand Magellan and Sebastian del Cano, 1519-22
--→ Alvaro de Saavedra, 1527-28

Explorer in the service of England:
→ John Cabot, 1497, 1498 1st and 2nd voyage

Explorer in the service of Portugal:
→ Bartholomew Diaz, 1487-88
→ Vasco de Gama, 1497-98 1st voyage
•→ Pedro Alvares Cabral, 1500-01
·→ Amerigo Vespucci, 1501-02 3rd voyage
--→ Alfonso d'Albuquerque 1507-08, 1519
×→ Lopez de Sequeira, 1509
1502 Year of discovery or foundation of European settlement

80 West from 60 Greenwich 40 20 0

MERCATOR'S PROJECTION

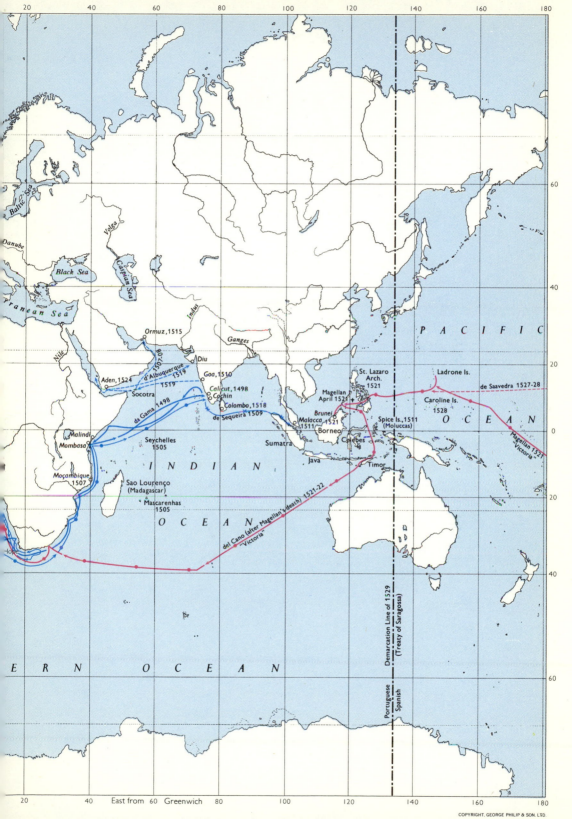

20 40 60 80 100 120 140 160 180

60

Baltic Sea

Volga

Danube

40

Black Sea

Caspian Sea

ranean Sea

PACIFIC

20

Ormuz, 1515

Ganges

Nile

Diu

Aden, 1524

d'Albuquerque
1519

Goa, 1510

Ladrone Is.

de Saavedra 1527-28

St. Lazaro
Arch.
1521

Socotra

Calicut, 1498
Cochin

Magellan
April 1521

Caroline Is.
1528

OCEAN

da Gama 1498

Colombo, 1518

de Sequeira 1509

Brunei
Malacca
1511
Borneo

Spice Is., 1511
(Moluccas)

0

Malindi

Seychelles
1505

Sumatra

Celebes

Magellan 1521
Victoria

Mombasa

INDIAN

Java

Moçambique
1507

Sao Lourenço
(Madagascar)

Timor

20

Mascarenhas
1505

del Cano (after Magellan's death) 1521-22
Victoria

OCEAN

ope

40

ERN OCEAN

Demarcation Line of 1529
(Treaty of Saragossa)

60

Portuguese
Spanish

20 40 East from 60 Greenwich 80 100 120 140 160 180

COPYRIGHT. GEORGE PHILIP & SON, LTD.

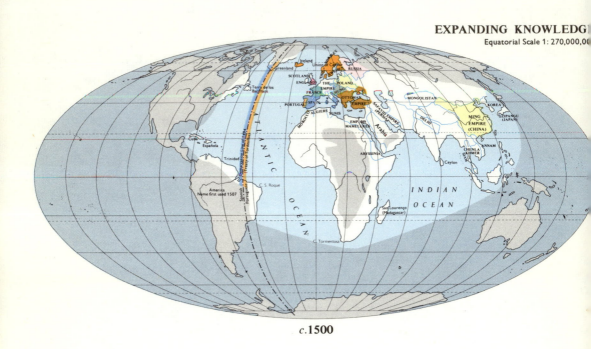

*c.*1500

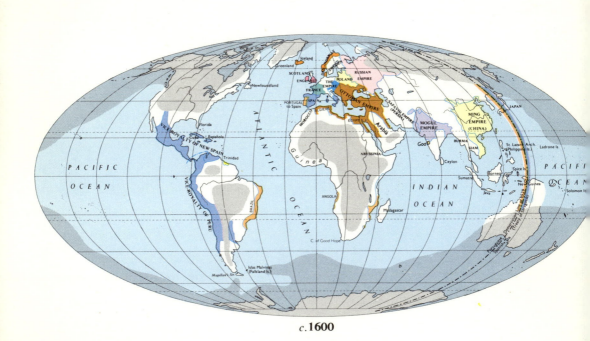

*c.*1600

OF THE WORLD
(4320 miles = 1 inch)

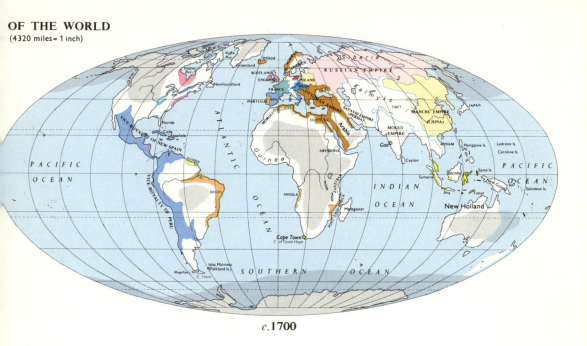

*c.*1700

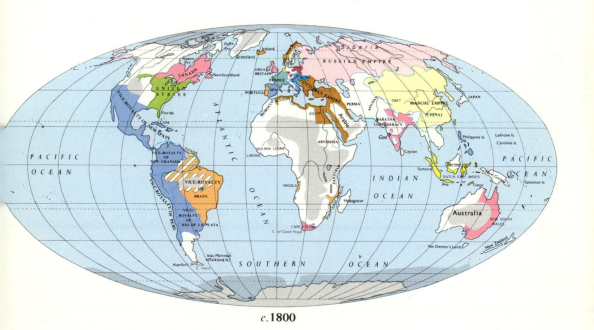

*c.*1800

COPYRIGHT. GEORGE PHILIP & SON. LTD.

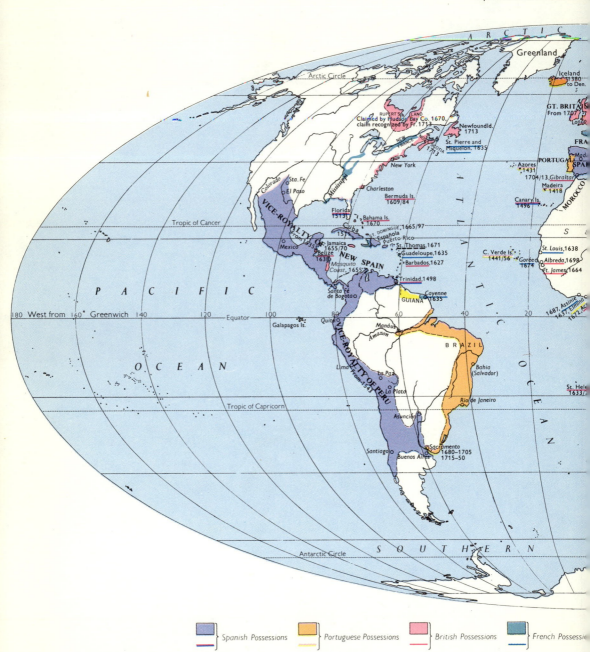

A R C T I C

Greenland

Arctic Circle

Iceland
1380
to Den.

GT. BRITAIN
From 1707

RUPERT'S LAND
Claimed by Hudson Bay Co. 1670,
claim recognized by Fr. 1713

Newfoundld.
1713

St. Pierre and
Miquelon, 1635

NEW
FRANCE
1713

Azores
1431

PORTUGAL

Mgd.
SPAIN

FRA

New York

1704/13 Gibraltar

Colorado

Sta. Fe

El Paso

Madeira
1418

Canary Is.
1496

MOROCCO

Charleston

VICE-ROYALTY OF

Tropic of Cancer

Bermuda Is.
1609/84

Florida
1513

Bahama Is.
1670

NEW SPAIN

Cuba

St. Louis, 1638

DOMINGUE 1665/97
Española
Puerto Rico

C. Verde Is.
1441/56

Mexico
1535

Jamaica
1655/70

St. Thomas, 1671

Goreé
1677

Albreda, 1698

Belize
1638

Guadeloupe, 1635

Ft. James 1664

Masquito
Coast, 1655

Barbados, 1627

Santa Fé
de Bogota

Trinidad 1498

P A C I F I C

Cayenne
1635

GUIANA

Assini
1687, 1637, 1672, Ac

West from   Greenwich

Equator

Galapagos Is.

Quito

Mandus

Amazon

La Paz

A T L A N T I C

O C E A N

Lima
From 1543

VICE-ROYALTY OF PERU

B R A Z I L

Bahia
(Salvador)

St. Hele
1633/

La Plata

O C E A N

Tropic of Capricorn

Asunción

Rio de Janeiro

Santiago

Buenos Aires

Sacramento
1680–1705
1715–50

Antarctic Circle

S O U T H E R N

Spanish Possessions   Portuguese Possessions   British Possessions   French Possessio

OVERSEAS, 1714

(2080 miles = 1 inch)

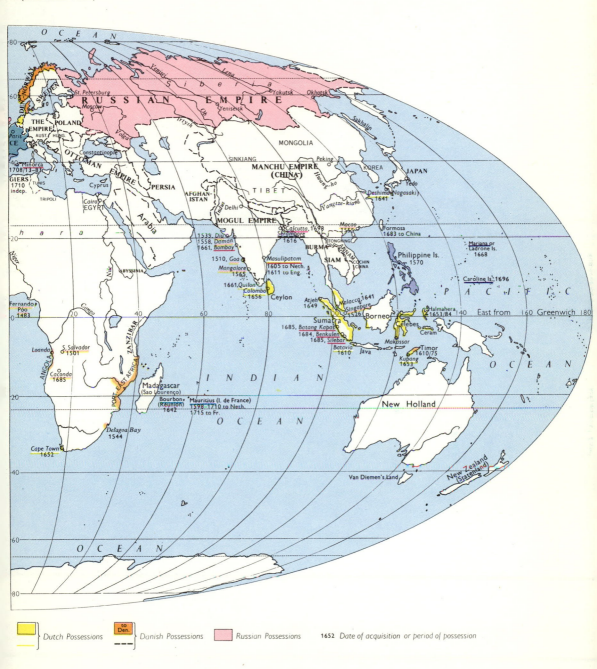

O C E A N

80

NORWAY DENMARK

SWEDEN

60 St. Petersburg

Moscow

RUSSIAN EMPIRE

S i b e r i a

Yenisei   Lena   Yakutsk   Okhotsk

Sakhalin

Paris
FRANCE

THE
EMPIRE
AUST. HUNG.

POLAND

OTTOMAN EMPIRE

Constantinople

Volga   Irtysh   Ob   Yenisevsk

MONGOLIA

SINKIANG   Peking

Heang-ho

KOREA   JAPAN

Yedo

40 Minorca
1708/13-83

GIERS
1710
indep.

TUNIS

TRIPOLI

Cyprus

PERSIA   AFGHAN-
ISTAN

MANCHU EMPIRE
(CHINA)

T I B E T

Yangtze-kiang

Deshima Nagasaki
1641

Cairo
EGYPT

Arabia

Delhi

MOGUL EMPIRE

Calcutta, 1698
Serampore
1616

Macao
1557

Formosa
1683 to China

h a r a

1539, Diu
1558, Daman
1661, Bombay

1510, Goa

Mangalore
1565

Masulipatam
1605 to Neth.
1611 to Eng.

TONKING

BURMA   COCHIN
CHINA

SIAM

Mariana or
Ladrone Is.
1668

Philippine Is.
1570

Fernando
Poo
0 1483

ABYSSINIA

Niger   Nile

1661, Quilon
Colombo
1656   Ceylon

Atjeh
1649

Malacca, 1641
Singapore
1526

Caroline Is. 1696

P A C I F I C

Loanda

S. Salvador
1501

Congo

ZANZIBAR

PORT. EAST AFRICA

Sumatra
1685, Batang Kapas
1684, Benkulen
1685, Silebar

Batavia
1610   Java

Borneo

Halmahera
1653/84 140   East from   160 Greenwich 180

Celebes   Ceram

Makassar

Timor
1610/75

Kupang
1653

O C E A N

ANGOLA

Coconda
1685

Madagascar
(Sao Lourenço)

I N D I A N

New Holland

20

Delagoa Bay
1544

Bourbon
(Reunion)
1642

Mauritius (I. de France)
1598, 1710 to Neth.
1715 to Fr.

O C E A N

Cape Town
1652

40

Van Diemen's Land

New Zealand
(Statenland)

60

O C E A N

80

▨ Dutch Possessions	to Den. ▨ Danish Possessions	▨ Russian Possessions	1652 Date of acquisition or period of possession	

COPYRIGHT. GEORGE PHILIP & SON. LTD.

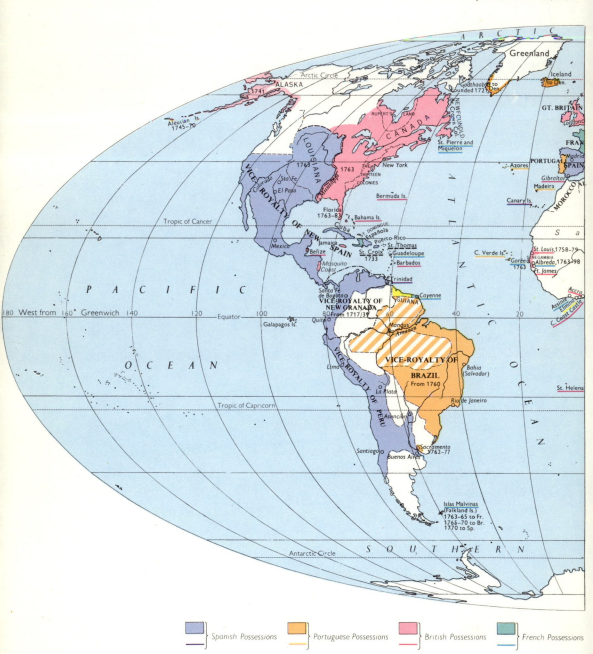

ARCTIC

Greenland

Arctic Circle

Iceland

to Den.

ALASKA

1741

Godthaab founded 1721 to Den.

GT. BRITAIN

London

Aleutian Is. 1745–70

RUPERTS LAND

NEWFOUNDLAND New Col

CANADA

St. Pierre and Miquelon

FRAN

Azores

PORTUGAL SPAIN

Madrid

Gibraltar

Madeira

MOROCCO

LOUISIANA

Colorado

Sta Fe

El Paso

1763

1763

THE THIRTEEN COLONIES

New York

A T L A N T I C

Canary Is.

Sa

VICE-ROYALTY OF NEW SPAIN

Tropic of Cancer

Florida 1763–83

Bermuda Is.

Bahama Is.

Cuba

ST. DOMINGUE Española

Puerto-Rico

C. Verde Is.

St. Louis 1758–79

Mexico

Jamaica

Belize

Masquito Coast

St. Thomas

St. Croix 1733

Guadeloupe

Barbados

Gorée 1763

NEGAMBIA

Albreda 1763–98

Ft. James

Santa Fe de Bogotá

Trinidad

O C E A N

Assini

Elmina

Accra

C. Coast Castle

VICE-ROYALTY OF NEW GRANADA

From 1717/39

80

Cayenne

GUIANA

Quito

Galapagos Is.

Equator

100

Manaos

Amazon

VICE-ROYALTY OF BRAZIL

From 1760

Bahia (Salvador)

St. Helena

P A C I F I C

Lima

VICE-ROYALTY OF PERU

La Plata

Rio de Janeiro

Tropic of Capricorn

Asunción

Santiago

Buenos Aires

Sacramento 1762–77

Islas Malvinas (Falkland Is.) 1763–65 to Fr. 1766–70 to Br. 1770 to Sp.

Antarctic Circle

S O U T H E R N

MOLLWEIDE'S EQUAL AREA PROJECTION

180 West from 160° Greenwich 140 120 100 80 60 40 20

Spanish Possessions   Portuguese Possessions   British Possessions   French Possessions

OVERSEAS, 1763

(2080 miles = 1 inch)

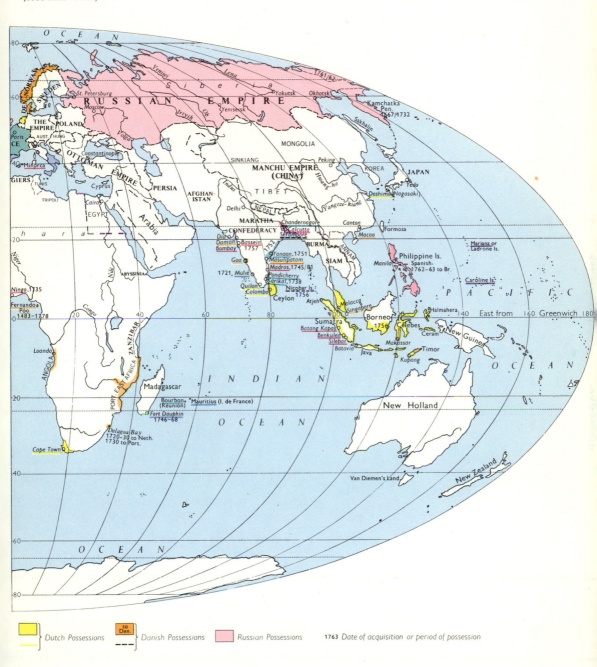

| | Dutch Possessions | | Danish Possessions | | Russian Possessions | **1763** Date of acquisition or period of possession |

COPYRIGHT. GEORGE PHILIP & SON. LTD.

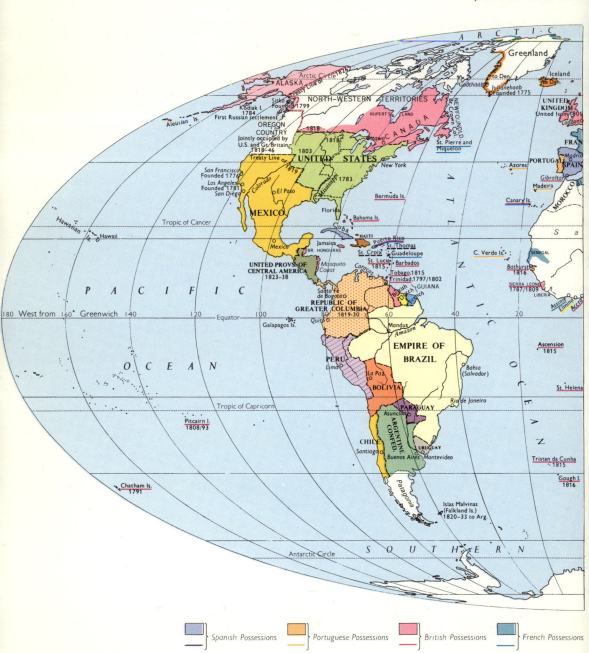

THE WORLD: EUROPEAN POSSESSIONS

Equatorial Scale 1:130,000,000

Greenland

Iceland

ALASKA

Arctic Circle 1812

NORTH–WESTERN TERRITORIES

Godthaab

To Den.

To Den.

Julianehaab
Founded 1775

UNITED
KINGDOM
United from 1801

London

Sitka
Founded 1799

First Russian settlement

Kodiak I.
1784

Aleutian Is.

RUPERT'S LAND

NEWFOUNDLD
BE Crown Col.

CANADA

Ottawa

St. Pierre and
Miquelon

FRA

OREGON
COUNTRY
Jointly occupied by
U.S. and Gt. Britain
1818–46

Treaty Line of

1818

1818

1803

UNITED   STATES

New York

PORTUGAL

Azores

Madrid

SPAIN

Gibraltar

San Francisco
Founded 1776
Los Angeles
Founded 1781
San Diego

Treaty Line

1819

Colorado

El Paso

Mississippi

1783

Bermuda Is.

Madeira

MOROCCO AL

Tropic of Cancer

MEXICO

Florida

Bahama Is.

Canary Is.

S   a

Mexico

Cuba

HAITI

Puerto Rico

Jamaica

BR. HONDURAS

St. Croix

St. Thomas
Guadeloupe

C. Verde Is.

SENEGAL

UNITED PROVS. OF
CENTRAL AMERICA
1823–38

Mosquito
Coast

St. Lucia
1815

Barbados

Bathurst
1816

Caracas

Tobago 1815
Trinidad 1797/1802

GUIANA
French

SIERRA LEONE
1787/1809

LIBERIA

Santa Fé
de Bogotá

REPUBLIC OF
GREATER COLUMBIA
1819–30

Quito

Galapagos Is.

180   West from 160°   Greenwich   140

120

100   Equator

80

60

40

20

Assinie
Elmina

Acco

ATLANTIC   OCEAN

Mandus

Amazon

P   A   C   I   F   I   C

PERU

Lima

La Paz

EMPIRE OF

BRAZIL

Bahia
(Salvador)

Ascension
1815

BOLIVIA

O   C   E   A   N

Tropic of Capricorn

PARAGUAY

Asunción

Rio de Janeiro

St. Helena

Pitcairn I.
1808/93

ARGENTINE
CONFEDN.

URUGUAY

Tristan da Cunha
1815

CHILE

Santiago

Buenos Aires

Montevideo

Gough I.
1816

Chatham Is.
1791

Patagonia

Islas Malvinas
(Falkland Is.)
1820–33 to Arg.

Antarctic Circle

S   O   U   T   H   E   R   N

Hawaiian
Is.

Hawaii

Spanish Possessions

Portuguese Possessions

British Possessions

French Possessions

1815 *Date of acquisition*

MOLLWEIDE'S EQUAL AREA PROJECTION

AND STATES OF EUROPEAN ORIGIN, 1830

(2080 miles = 1 inch)

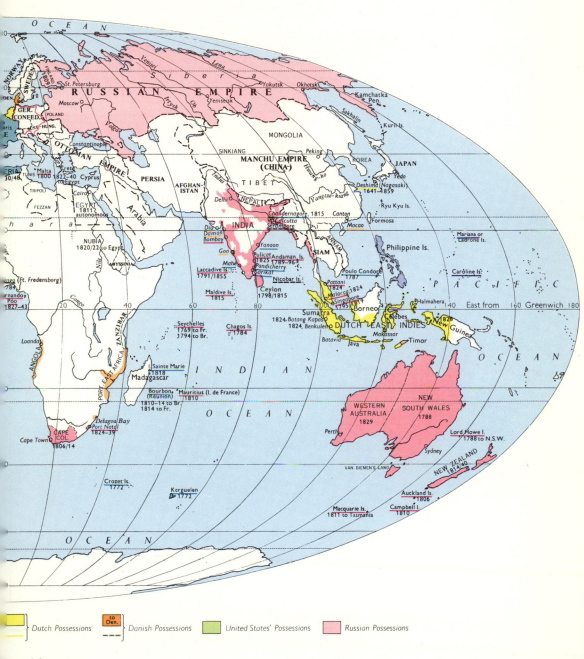

OCEAN

NORWAY
SWEDEN
FINLAND 1809
DEN.
GER. CONFED.
POLAND
AUSTRIA-HUNG.
Paris
E
30/48
OTTOMAN EMPIRE
RIA
TUNIS 1800
Malta 1822-40
Crete
Cyprus
Constantinople
Moscow
St. Petersburg
Volga
Irtysh
Ob
Yenisei
S i b e r i a
Lena
Yenisersk
Yakutsk
Okhotsk
Kamchatka Pen.
Sakhalin
Kuril Is.

RUSSIAN EMPIRE

TRIPOLI
FEZZAN
EGYPT 1811 autonomous
Cairo
Arabia
PERSIA
AFGHAN-ISTAN
Indus
SINKIANG
MONGOLIA
MANCHU EMPIRE (CHINA)
Peking
TIBET
Hoang-ho
KOREA
JAPAN
Yedo
Deshima (Nagasaki) 1641-1859
Ryu Kyu Is.

Sahara
NUBIA 1820/22 to Egypt
Nile
ABYSSINIA
Delhi
NEPAL
Yangtze-kiang
Formosa
Mariana or Ladrone Is.

mga (Ft. Fredensborg) 1784
rnando Póo 1827-43
Congo
20
40
60
ZANZIBAR
PORT. EAST AFRICA
Diu
Daman
Bombay
INDIA
Goa
Mahe
Laccadive Is. 1791/1855
Calcutta
Serampore
Chandernagore 1815
Yanaon
Pulicat 1825
Pondicherry
Karikal
Ceylon 1798/1815
Maldive Is. 1815
Canton
Macao
SIAM
ANNAM
Andaman Is. 1789-96
Nicobar Is.
Pattani
Malacca 1824
Singapore 1795
Poulo Condore 1787
Philippine Is.
Caroline Is.
Sumatra 1824, Batang Kapas 1824, Benkulen
DUTCH EAST INDIES
Borneo
Celebes
Makassar
Halmahera
New Guinea 1828
P A C I F I C
East from 160 Greenwich 180

Loanda
ANGOLA
Seychelles 1769 to Fr. 1794 to Br.
Chagos Is. 1784
I N D I A N
Batavia
Java
Timor
O C E A N
O C E A N

Sainte Marie 1818
Madagascar
Bourbon (Réunion) 1810-14 to Br. 1814 to Fr.
Mauritius (I. de France) 1810
WESTERN AUSTRALIA 1829
NEW SOUTH WALES 1788
Delagoa Bay Port Natal 1824-39
Perth
CAPE COL. 1806/14
Cape Town
VAN DIEMEN'S LAND
Sydney
Lord Howe I. 1788 to N.S.W.
NEW ZEALAND 1814/40

Crozet Is. 1772
Kerguelen 1772
Macquarie Is. 1811 to Tasmania
Auckland Is. 1806
Campbell I. 1810

O C E A N

COPYRIGHT. GEORGE PHILIP & SON. LTD.

Dutch Possessions
to Den. Danish Possessions
United States' Possessions
Russian Possessions

r period of possession

THE WORLD: EUROPEAN POSSESSIONS

Equatorial Scale 1:130,000,000

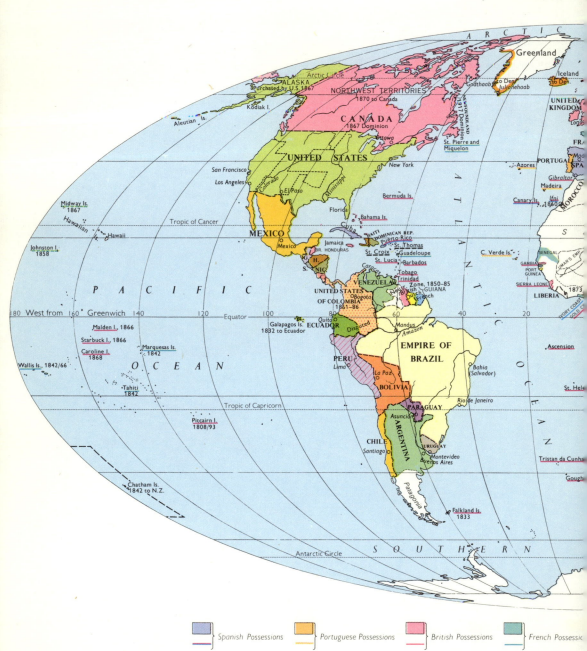

Greenland

Iceland

ALASKA
Purchased by U.S. 1867

NORTHWEST TERRITORIES
1870 to Canada

Godthaab
Julianehaab o Den

UNITED
KINGDOM

Kodiak I.

Aleutian Is.

CANADA
1867 Dominion

NEWFOUNDLAND
1917 to Canada

Ottawa

St. Pierre and
Miquelon

Azores

PORTUGAL

FR

Mo
SPA

UNITED STATES

New York

San Francisco

Los Angeles

Colorado

El Paso

Mississippi

Bermuda Is.

Madeira

Gibraltar

MOROCCO

Ifni
1860

Midway Is.
1867

Tropic of Cancer

Canary Is.

Hawaiian

Hawaii

Florida

MEXICO

Cuba

Bahama Is.

Mexico

Jamaica
BR. HONDURAS

HAITI
DOMINICAN REP.
Puerto Rico

St. Thomas

C. Verde Is.

SENEGAL

Johnston I.
1858

H.
S. NIC

St. Croix
St. Lucia

Guadeloupe
Barbados

GAMBIA
PORT
GUINEA

SIERRA LEONE

Caracas

Tobago
Trinidad

SENEGAL

Malden I., 1866

UNITED STATES
OF COLOMBIA
1861–86

VENEZUELA
Bogota

Zone, 1850–85
British GUIANA
French

LIBERIA

IVORY COAST
GOLD C

180 West from 160° Greenwich 140

120

Equator 100

80

Quito

60

Mandus

40

Amazon

20

Galapagos Is.
1832 to Ecuador

ECUADOR

Disputed

Ascension

Starbuck I., 1866

Caroline I.
1868

Marquesas Is.
1842

PERU

Lima

EMPIRE OF

BRAZIL

Bahia
(Salvador)

St. Hele

Wallis Is., 1842/66

Tahiti
1842

BOLIVIA
La Paz

Rio de Janeiro

Tropic of Capricorn

PARAGUAY

Pitcairn I.
1808/93

Asuncion

ARGENTINA

URUGUAY

Tristan da Cunha

CHILE

Santiago

Montevideo
Buenos Aires

Gough

Chatham Is.
1842 to N.Z.

Patagonia

Falkland Is.
1833

Antarctic Circle

SOUTHERN

Spanish Possessions
Portuguese Possessions
British Possessions
French Possessions

1842 *Date of acquisition or period of possession*   B. Belgium, BH. Bhutan, C. Costa Ric

MOLLWEIDE'S EQUAL AREA PROJECTION

AND STATES OF EUROPEAN ORIGIN, 1878

(2080 miles = 1 inch)

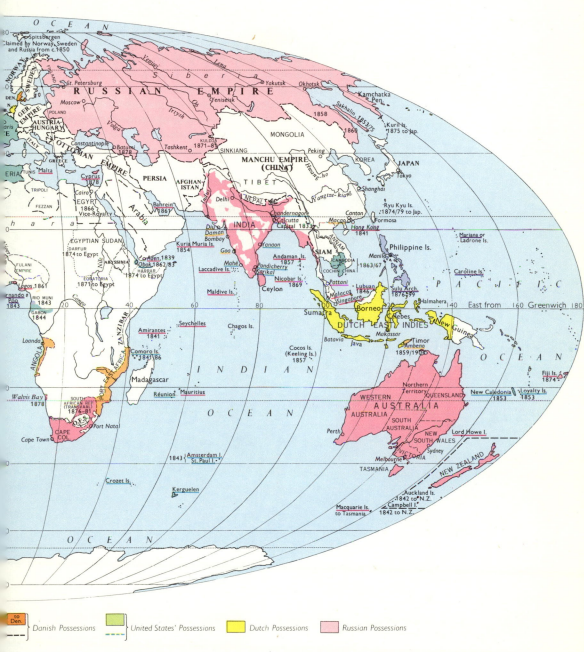

O C E A N

Spitsbergen
Claimed by Norway, Sweden
and Russia from c.1850

NORWAY
SWEDEN
DEN.
GER. EMPIRE
POLAND
AUSTRIA-HUNGARY
ITALY
GREECE
OTTOMAN EMPIRE
Constantinople
Malta
Cyprus 1878
TRIPOLI
TUNIS
FEZZAN

S a h a r a

EGYPT
Cairo
1866
Vice-Royalty

EGYPTIAN SUDAN
DARFUR
1874 to Egypt
ABYSSINIA
EQUATORIA
1871 to Egypt

FULANI EMPIRE
Lagos 1861
Fernando Poo 1843
RIO MUNI 1843
GABON 1844
Loanda

ANGOLA

PORTUGUESE EAST AFRICA

ZANZIBAR

Madagascar

Walvis Bay 1878

SOUTH AFRICAN REP. (TRANSVAAL) 1876-81
O.F.S.
CAPE COL.
Cape Town
Port Natal

RUSSIAN   EMPIRE

St. Petersburg
Moscow
Volga
Irtysh
Yenisei
S i b e r i a
Lena
Yakutsk
Okhotsk
Kamchatka Pen.
Sakhalin 1853/75
Kuril Is. 1875 to Jap.
1858
1860

Yeniseisk
Tashkent
Batumi 1878
KULDJA 1871-81
MONGOLIA
SINKIANG
Peking
Heran-ho
KOREA
JAPAN
Tokyo
Shanghai

PERSIA
AFGHANISTAN
TIBET
MANCHU EMPIRE (CHINA)
Yangtze-kiang
Ryu Kyu Is. 1874/79 to Jap.
Formosa

Arabia
Bahrein 1861
Delhi
NEPAL
Chandernagore
Calcutta
Capital 1833
Macao 1841
Canton
Hong Kong 1841

Aden 1839
Obok 1862/83
1874 to Egypt
HARRAR

Diu
Daman
Bombay
Kuria Muria Is. 1854
Goa
Mahé
Laccadive Is.
Pondicherry
Karikal
INDIA
Rangoon
Andaman Is. 1857
SIAM
ANAM
CAMBODIA
COCHIN CHINA 1863/67
Manila
Philippine Is.
Mariana or Ladrone Is.

Maldive Is.
Nicobar Is. 1869
Ceylon
Pattani
Caroline Is.

P A C I F I C

Seychelles
Amirantes 1841
Chagos Is.
Malacca 1846
Singapore
Sumatra
Borneo
Labuan 1846
Sulu Arch. 1876/99
Halmahera
Celebes
New Guinea

Comoro Is. 1841/86
Cocos (Keeling Is.) 1857
Batavia
Java
DUTCH EAST INDIES
Makassar
Timor
Ambeno 1859/1906

Réunion
Mauritius

I N D I A N

East from   160   Greenwich   180

O C E A N

WESTERN AUSTRALIA
A U S T R A L I A
Perth
SOUTH AUSTRALIA
Northern Territory
QUEENSLAND
New Caledonia 1853
Loyalty Is. 1853
Fiji Is. A 1874

O C E A N

NEW SOUTH WALES
Sydney
VICTORIA
Melbourne
TASMANIA
Lord Howe I.

Amsterdam I. St. Paul I. 1843
Crozet Is.
Kerguelen

NEW ZEALAND
Auckland Is. 1842 to N.Z.
Campbell I. 1842 to N.Z.
Macquarie Is. to Tasmania 1842 to N.Z.

O C E A N

▮ to Den.	Danish Possessions	▮ United States' Possessions	▮ Dutch Possessions	▮ Russian Possessions

G. Guatemala , H. Honduras , N. Netherlands , NIC. Nicaragua , O.F.S. Orange Free State , S. Salvador

COPYRIGHT. GEORGE PHILIP & SON. LTD.

THE WORLD,

Equatorial Scale 1:130,000,000

ARCTIC

Greenland
to Den.

ALASKA
Arctic Circle

Godthaab
Julianehaab

CANADA
Dominion

Vancouver

Montreal
Ottawa
St. Pierre and
Miquelon

Chicago

UNITED STATES
Washington
New York
Azores

San Francisco

Los Angeles
San Diego
Colorado

Bermuda Is.

MADRID
PORTUGAL SPAIN
Gibraltar SPAN.
Madeira
Canary Is.
SPAN.
SAHARA 1912
ALGER

New Orleans
Florida

Tropic of Cancer

Bahama Is.

MEXICO

CUBA

HAITI

Mexico

BR. HONDURAS

Jamaica

Puerto Rico, 1898
St. Thomas
Guadeloupe
St. Lucia
Barbados

RIO DE ORO

Sah
FRENCH WEST AFR

St. Louis
GAMBIA
PORT.
GUINEA
Freetown
SIERRA LEONE
Niger

Hawaiian Is.
1898
Hawaii

Johnston I.

G. H.
NIC.
Canal Zone
1903 to U.S.

St. Croix
Curaçao
Tobago
Trinidad

PACIFIC

Palmyra Is.
1912
Washington I., 1889
Fanning I., 1888

Caracas
VENEZUELA
COLOMBIA
Bogota

British Guiana
Dutch Guiana

C. Verde Is.

LIBERIA

GOLD COAST
Fernando
POO
RIO MUNI
NIG
191
Lagos

West from 140 Greenwich 120
Equator
100

Galapagos Is.
to Ecuador

Quito

ECUADOR

Mandus

Amazon

Jarvis I., 1889

Malden I.
Starbuck I.

Marquesas Is.

OCEAN

Lima
PERU

BRAZIL
From 1889 United States of Brazil

Ascension

Manihiki, 1888 to Br.
1901 to N.Z. Caroline I.

La Paz
BOLIVIA

St. Helena

Society Is.
1880 Tahiti
Tuamotu Arch.

Tacna

Rio de Janeiro

Trinidad
to Brazil

Cook Is.
1888 to Br.
1901 to N.Z.

Tubuai Is.
1881
Rapa I.

Pitcairn I.

Tropic of Capricorn

Antofagasta

PARAGUAY
Asunción

URUGUAY
Montevideo
Buenos Aires

Tristan da Cunha

Easter Is.
1888 to Chile

CHILE

Santiago

Gough I.

ARGENTINA

SO

Falkland Is.

S. Georgia, 1908
S. Sandwich
Group
1908

Antarctic Circle

S. Shetland Is.
1908

Graham Land
Br. claim from 1908

S. Orkney Is.
1908

ATLANTIC OCEAN

| | British Empire | | French Possessions | | Spanish Possessions | | Portuguese Possessions | | United States' Possession |

1914 Date of acquisition   A. Albania, B. Belgium, BH. Bhutan, C. Costa Rica, D.R. Dominican Rep.(from 1905 U.S. special rights), G. Guatemala

P. Panama (1903 indep. Rep.

1914

(2080 miles = 1 inch)

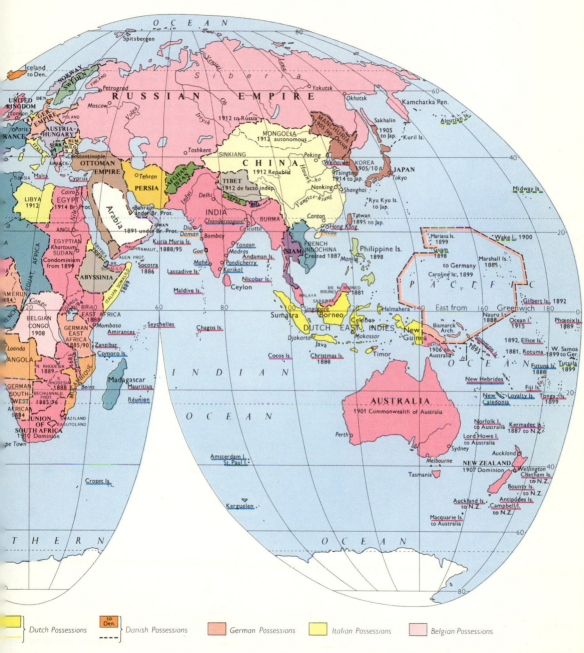

OCEAN
Spitsbergen
Iceland to Den.
UNITED KINGDOM
NORWAY
SWEDEN
FINLAND
Petrograd
Moscow
RUSSIAN EMPIRE
Siberia
Yakutsk
Okhotsk
Kamchatka Pen.
Aleutian Is.
Kuril Is.
1905 to Jap.
Sakhalin
MANCHURIA 1905 Jap. Occup.
MONGOLIA 1912 autonomous
SINKIANG
Peking
CHINA 1912 Republic
Weihaiwei
KOREA 1905/10
JAPAN
Tsingtao 1914 to Jap.
Tokyo
Midway Is.
Tashkent
AFGHAN-ISTAN
PERSIA
Tehran
Bahrain under Br. Prot.
TIBET 1912 de facto indep.
Delhi
NEPAL
Nanking
Shanghai
Ryu Kyu Is. to Jap.
Taiwan 1895 to Jap.
Hong Kong
Macao
INDIA
BURMA
Canton
Mariana Is. 1899
Wake I. 1900
Guam 1898
Marshall Is. 1885
to Germany
Chandernagore
Calcutta
Bombay
Madras
Yangon
FRENCH INDOCHINA Created 1887
Manila
Philippine Is. 1898
Caroline Is. 1899
Andaman Is.
SIAM
Pondicherry
Karikal
Mahé
Goa
Diu
Daman
Gilbert Is. 1892
Laccadive Is.
Nicobar Is.
BR. N. BORNEO BRUNEI 1881
Halmahera
East from Greenwich
Nauru Is. 1888
Ocean I. 1915
Phoenix Is. 1889
Maldive Is.
Ceylon
MALAYA
SARAWAK
Sumatra
Singapore
Borneo
Celebes
DUTCH EAST INDIES
New Guinea
Bismarck Arch.
Solomon Is. 1893
1892, Ellice Is.
1881, Rotuma
W. Samoa 1899 to Ger.
Chagos Is.
Seychelles
Djakarta
Makassar
PAPUA 1906 to Australia
Futuna Is. 1888
Tutuila 1899
Amirantes
Java
Timor
Cocos Is.
Christmas Is. 1888
New Hebrides
Fiji Is.
Zanzibar
Comoro Is.
Madagascar
Mauritius
Réunion
Amsterdam I. St. Paul I.
AUSTRALIA 1901 Commonwealth of Australia
New Caledonia
Loyalty Is.
Tonga Is. 1899
Norfolk I. to Australia
Kermadec Is. 1887 to N.Z.
Crozet Is.
Perth
Lord Howe I. to Australia
Sydney
Auckland
Kerguelen
Melbourne
Tasmania
NEW ZEALAND 1907 Dominion
Wellington
Chatham Is. to N.Z.
Bounty I. to N.Z.
Antipodes Is. to N.Z.
Auckland Is. to N.Z.
Campbell I. to N.Z.
Macquarie Is. to Australia
SOUTHERN OCEAN

	Dutch Possessions		Danish Possessions		German Possessions		Italian Possessions		Belgian Possessions

Honduras, Haiti (from 1915 U.S. special rights), N. Netherlands, NIC. Nicaragua (1909/12 U.S. special rights, 1912 milit. occup.),
der U.S. Protection), S. Salvador

COPYRIGHT. GEORGE PHILIP & SON. LTD.

THE WORLD.

Equatorial Scale 1:130,000,000

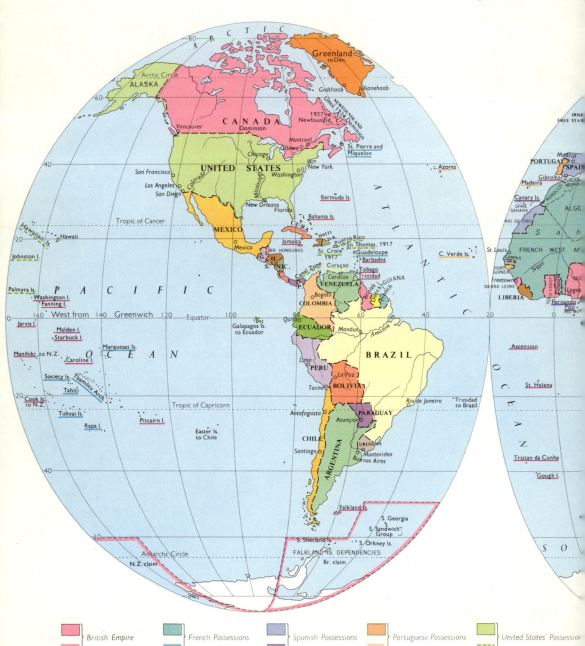

ARCTIC

Greenland
to Den.

Arctic Circle
ALASKA
Godthaab
Julianehaab

60

CANADA
Dominion
Vancouver
1927 ?
Newfoundld.

Montreal
Ottawa
St. Pierre and
Miquelon

40
Chicago

UNITED STATES
San Francisco
Washington
New York

Colorado
Azores

Los Angeles
San Diego

New Orleans
Florida
Bermuda Is.

Tropic of Cancer
MEXICO
Bahama Is.

Hawaiian Is.
Hawaii
CUBA
HAITI

20
Mexico
Jamaica
Puerto Rico
St. Thomas, 1917

Johnston I.
BR. HONDURAS
St. Croix
1917
Guadeloupe
C. Verde Is.

Palmyra Is.
Washington I.
Fanning I.

G. H.
C.
NIC.
Canal Zone
Barbados
Curaçao

West from 140 Greenwich 120
160
Equator
100
Caracas
Tobago
Trinidad

P.
VENEZUELA
British GUIANA
Dutch GUIANA

Jarvis I.
Bogotá
COLOMBIA

Malden I.
Starbuck I.
Galapagos Is.
to Ecuador
Quito
ECUADOR
Manáos
Amazon

Ascension

Manihiki to N.Z.
Marquesas Is.
Lima

Caroline I.
PERU
BRAZIL

Society Is.
Tuamotu Arch.
La Paz
BOLIVIA

St. Helena

Tahiti
Tacna
Rio de Janeiro
Trinidad
to Brazil

Cook Is.
to N.Z.
Tropic of Capricorn

Tubuai Is.
Pitcairn I.
Antofagasta
PARAGUAY
Asunción

Rapa I.
Easter Is.
to Chile
URUGUAY
Tristan da Cunha

CHILE
Santiago
Montevideo
Buenos Aires
Gough I.

40
ARGENTINA

PACIFIC OCEAN

ATLANTIC

60
Falkland Is.
S. Georgia
S. Sandwich
Group

Antarctic Circle
S. Shetland Is.
S. Orkney Is.

N.Z. claim
FALKLAND IS. DEPENDENCIES
Br. claim

MOLLWEIDE'S INTERRUPTED EQUAL AREA PROJECTION

PORTUGAL
SPAIN
Madrid
Gibraltar
Madeira

Canary Is.
Sah

RIO DE ORO
FRENCH WEST AF.

St. Louis
GAMBIA
PORT.
GUINEA

Freetown
SIERRA LEONE
NIC.
Lagos
LIBERIA
Fernando
POO

IRISH
FREE STAT

British Empire
French Possessions
Spanish Possessions
Portuguese Possessions
United States' Possession

A. Albania, B. Belgium, BH. Bhutan, C. Costa Rica, CZ. Czechoslovakia, D.R. Dominican Rep., E. Estonia, G. Guatemala, H. Honduras

1926

(2080 miles = 1 inch)

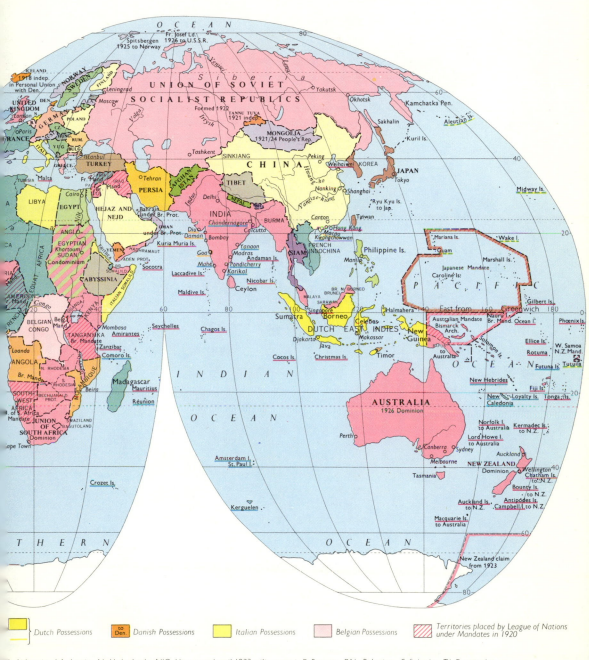

Dutch Possessions   Danish Possessions   Italian Possessions   Belgian Possessions   Territories placed by League of Nations under Mandates in 1920

L. Lithuania, LA. Latvia, N. Netherlands, NIC. Nicaragua (until 1933 milit. occup.), P. Panama, PAL. Palestine, S. Salvador, T.J. Transjordan

COPYRIGHT. GEORGE PHILIP & SON. LTD.

THE WORLD,

Equatorial Scale 1:130,000,000

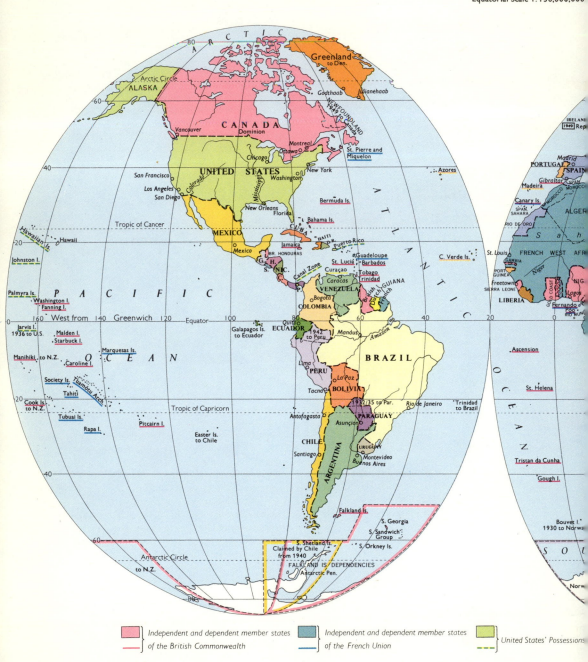

ARCTIC

Greenland
to Den.

Arctic Circle
ALASKA

Godthaab
Julianehaab

NEWFOUNDLAND
1949 Rep.
Canada

CANADA
Dominion

Vancouver

Montreal

Chicago
Ottawa
St. Pierre and
Miquelon

UNITED STATES

San Francisco
Washington
New York

Azores

IRELAND
1949 Rep.

Los Angeles
San Diego

Colorado

Madrid
PORTUGAL SPAIN
Gibraltar

Mississippi

Bermuda Is.

Madeira

SPAN.
MOROCCO

Tropic of Cancer

New Orleans
Florida
Canary Is.
SPAN.
SAHARA

Hawaiian Is.

Hawaii

MEXICO
Bahama Is.

CUBA

RIO DE ORO

Sahara

Johnston I.

Mexico

HAITI

Jamaica
Puerto Rico

St. Louis
GAMBIA
FRENCH WEST AFR

G. H.
S. NIC.

St. Lucia
Guadeloupe
Barbados

PORT.
GUINEA
SIERRA LEONE

Niger

Palmyra Is.
Washington I.
Fanning I.

PACIFIC

Canal Zone

Curaçao
Caracas
Tobago
Trinidad

VENEZUELA

British GUIANA
Dutch French

Freetown

C. Verde Is.

LIBERIA

GOLD COAST

Jarvis I.
1936 to U.S.

West from 140 Greenwich 120

Bogotá
COLOMBIA

Fernando Po

Equator 100

80

60

40

Fernando
RIO MUNI

Jarvis I.
1936 to U.S.

Galapagos Is.
to Ecuador

Quito
ECUADOR

1942
to Peru

Mandus
Amazon

20

Manihiki
to N.Z.

Marquesas Is.

Caroline I.

Lima
PERU

La Paz
BOLIVIA

BRAZIL

Ascension

St. Helena

Society Is.
to N.Z.

Tuamotu Arch.
Tahiti

Tacna

1932/35 to Par.

Rio de Janeiro

Trinidad
to Brazil

Cook Is.
to N.Z.

OCEAN

Tropic of Capricorn

Antofagasta

PARAGUAY
Asunción

Tristan da Cunha

Tubuai Is.

Pitcairn I.

Easter Is.
to Chile

CHILE
Santiago

URUGUAY
Montevideo
Buenos Aires

Gough I.

Rapa I.

ARGENTINA

Antarctic Circle
to N.Z.

Falkland Is.

S. Georgia

Bouvet I.
1930 to Norwa

S. Sandwich
Group

S. Shetland Is.
Claimed by Chile
from 1940

FALKLAND IS DEPENDENCIES
Antarctic Pen.

S. Orkney Is.

SOU

Norw

MOLLWEIDE'S INTERRUPTED EQUAL AREA PROJECTION

Independent and dependent member states
of the British Commonwealth

Independent and dependent member states
of the French Union

United States' Possessions

1949 Date of independence

A. Albania, B. Belgium, BH. Bhutan, C. Costa Rica, CAM. Cambodia, C.Z. Czechoslovakia, D.R. Dominican Rep., G. Guatemala

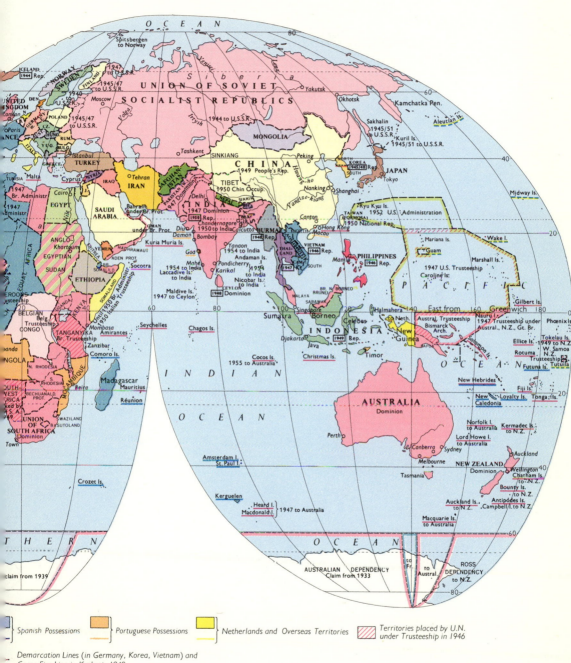

1950

(2080 miles=1 inch)

Spanish Possessions   Portuguese Possessions   Netherlands and Overseas Territories   Territories placed by U.N. under Trusteeship in 1946

Demarcation Lines (in Germany, Korea, Vietnam) and
Cease Fire Line in Kashmir 1949

Honduras, I. Israel, J. Jordan, L. Lebanon, N. Netherlands, NIC. Nicaragua, P. Panama, S. Salvador, Sikkim (1947 independent,1950 Indian Prot.)

COPYRIGHT. GEORGE PHILIP & SON. LTD.

THE WORLD: ACHIEVEMEN

Equatorial Scale 1:130,000,0

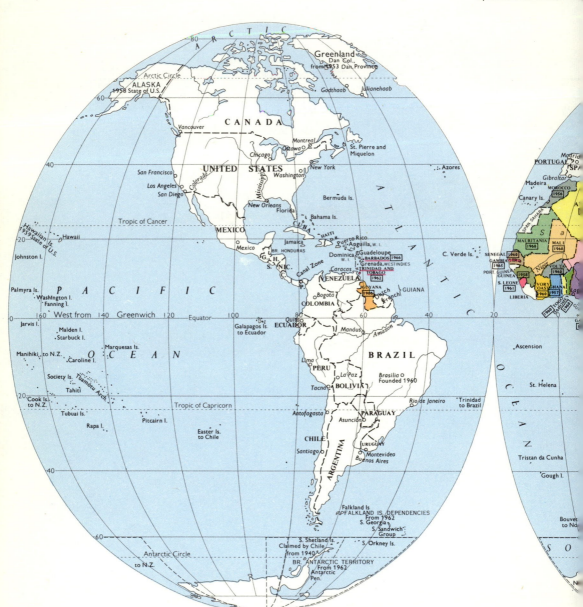

All states which attained independence after 1945 are colou

[1946] *Date of independence after 1*

A. *Albania*, B. *Belgium*, BH. *Bhutan*, BU. *Burundi*, C. *Costa Rica*, CAM. *Cambodia*, CZ. *Czechoslovakia*, D.R. *Dominican Rep.*, G. *Guatem*

W.I. *West Indies, Associated St*

MOLLWEIDE'S INTERRUPTED EQUAL AREA PROJECTION

OF INDEPENDENCE, 1945–68

(2080 miles=1 inch)

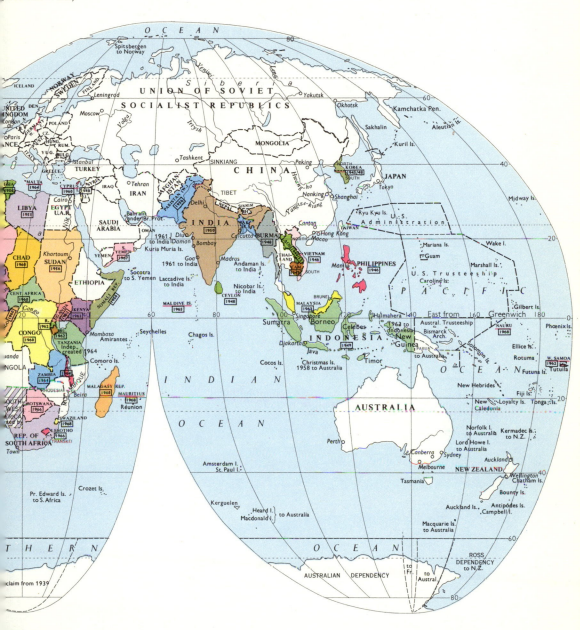

nes of small islands which became independent are underlined in red

- Demarcation Lines (in Germany, Korea, Vietnam) and Cease Fire Line in Kashmir 1949

Honduras, I. Israel, J. Jordan, L. Lebanon, M. Malawi, N. Netherlands, NIC. Nicaragua, P. Panama, R. Rwanda, S. Salvador, Sikkim (Indian Prot.),

United Kingdom from 1967

COPYRIGHT. GEORGE PHILIP & SON. LTD.

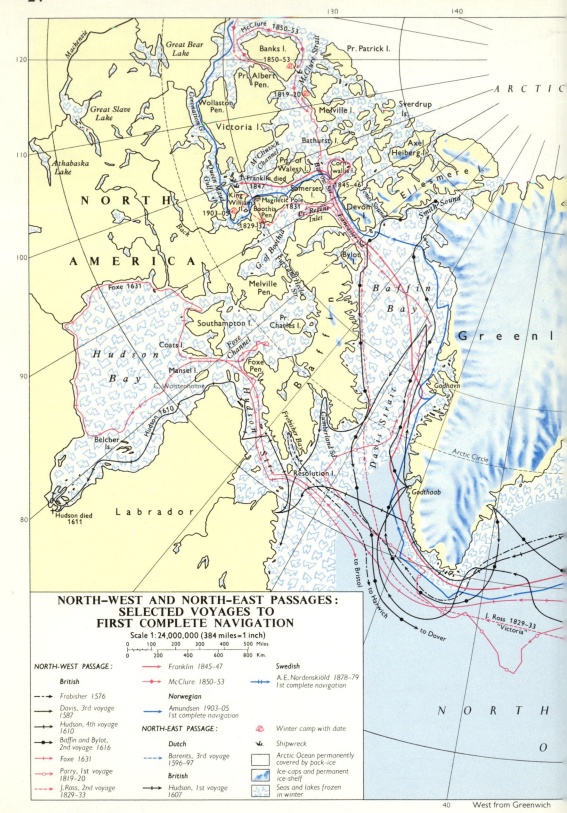

NORTH–WEST AND NORTH–EAST PASSAGES: SELECTED VOYAGES TO FIRST COMPLETE NAVIGATION

Scale 1:24,000,000 (384 miles=1 inch)

0 100 200 300 400 500 Miles
0 200 400 600 800 Km.

NORTH-WEST PASSAGE:

British

–·–·–→ Frobisher 1576

———→ Davis, 3rd voyage 1587

———→ Hudson, 4th voyage 1610

●———→ Baffin and Bylot, 2nd voyage 1616

———→ Foxe 1631

———→ Parry, 1st voyage 1819–20

–·–·–→ J. Ross, 2nd voyage 1829–33

———→ Franklin 1845–47

———→ McClure 1850–53

Norwegian

———→ Amundsen 1903–05 1st complete navigation

NORTH-EAST PASSAGE:

Dutch

–·–·–→ Barents, 3rd voyage 1596–97

British

———→ Hudson, 1st voyage 1607

Swedish

———→ A. E. Nordenskiöld 1878–79 1st complete navigation

🛑 Winter camp with date

⚓ Shipwreck

Arctic Ocean permanently covered by pack-ice

Ice-caps and permanent ice-shelf

Seas and lakes frozen in winter

40   West from Greenwich

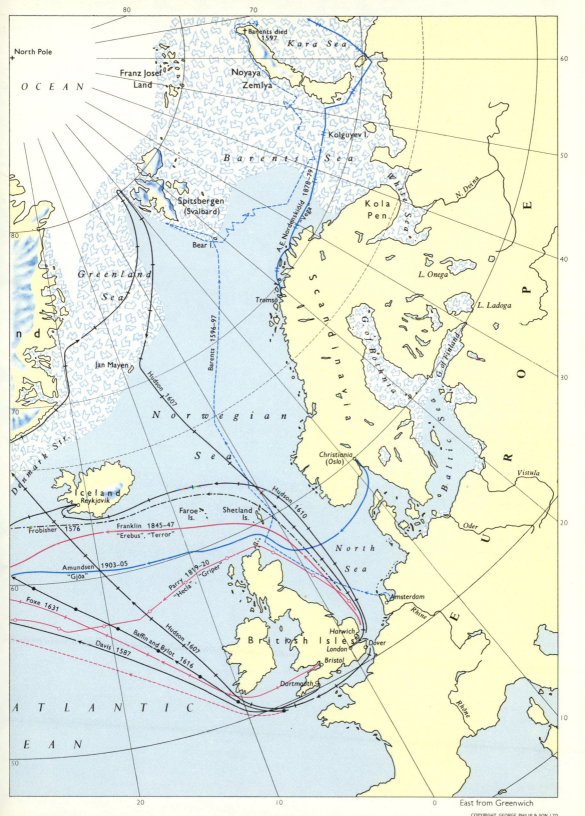

North Pole

OCEAN

Franz Josef Land

† Barents died 1597

Kara Sea

Noyaya Zemlya

Kolguyev I.

B a r e n t s   S e a

White Sea

Kola Pen.

N. Dvina

L. Onega

L. Ladoga

Spitsbergen (Svalbard)

A.E. Nordenskiöld 1878-79

Vega

Bear I.

80

Trömsö

G r e e n l a n d   S e a

Barents 1596-97

Jan Mayen

Hudson 1607

n d

70

S c a n d i n a v i a

Gol. Bothnia

E   U   R   O   P   E

N o r w e g i a n

S e a

Christiania (Oslo)

Vistula

Denmark Str.

Iceland
Reykjavik

Hudson 1610

Baltic Sea

Faroe Is.

Shetland Is.

Oder

Frobisher 1576

Franklin 1845-47
"Erebus", "Terror"

N o r t h

S e a

Amundsen 1903-05
"Gjöa"

Parry 1819-20
"Hecla" "Griper"

Amsterdam

60

Foxe 1631

Rhine

Hudson 1607

Davis 1587

Baffin and Bylot 1616

B r i t i s h   I s l e s

Harwich

London

Dover

Bristol

Dartmouth

Rhine

A T L A N T I C

Rhone

10

E A N

50

20

10

0

East from Greenwich

COPYRIGHT. GEORGE PHILIP & SON. LTD.

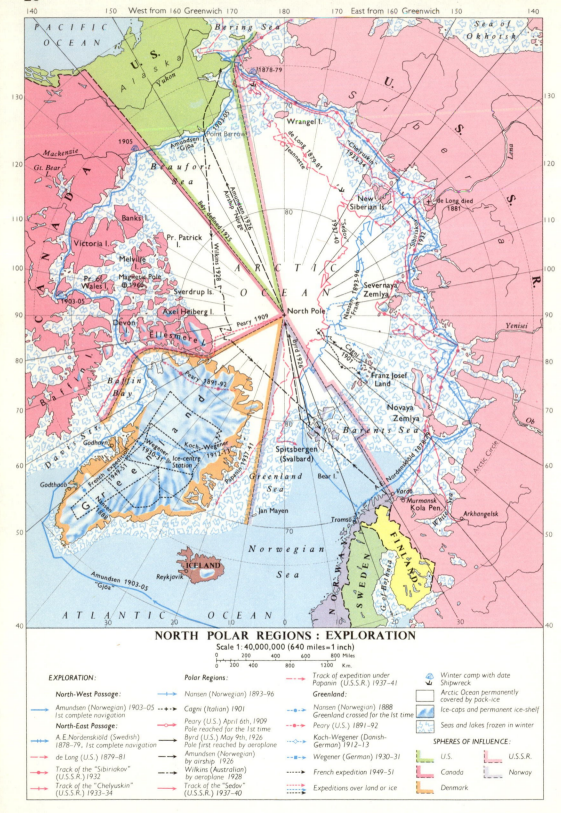

26

West from Greenwich · East from Greenwich

NORTH POLAR REGIONS : EXPLORATION

Scale 1 : 40,000,000 (640 miles=1 inch)

0 200 400 600 800 Miles
0 200 400 800 1200 Km.

EXPLORATION:

North-West Passage:

→ Amundsen (Norwegian) 1903-05
1st complete navigation

North-East Passage:

→ A.E. Nordenskiöld (Swedish)
1878-79. 1st complete navigation

→ de Long (U.S.) 1879-81

→ Track of the "Sibiriakov"
(U.S.S.R.) 1932

→ Track of the "Chelyuskin"
(U.S.S.R.) 1933-34

Polar Regions:

→ Nansen (Norwegian) 1893-96

→ Cagni (Italian) 1901

→ Peary (U.S.) April 6th, 1909
Pole reached for the 1st time

→ Byrd (U.S.) May 9th, 1926
Pole first reached by aeroplane

→ Amundsen (Norwegian)
by airship 1926

→ Wilkins (Australian)
by aeroplane 1928

→ Track of the "Sedov"
(U.S.S.R.) 1937-40

→ Track of expedition under
Papanin (U.S.S.R.) 1937-41

Greenland:

→ Nansen (Norwegian) 1888
Greenland crossed for the 1st time

→ Peary (U.S.) 1891-92

→ Koch-Wegener (Danish-
German) 1912-13

→ Wegener (German) 1930-31

→ French expedition 1949-51

→ Expeditions over land or ice

⚓ Winter camp with date
Shipwreck

☐ Arctic Ocean permanently
covered by pack-ice

☐ Ice-caps and permanent ice-shelf

☐ Seas and lakes frozen in winter

SPHERES OF INFLUENCE:

☐ U.S.   ☐ U.S.S.R.

☐ Canada   ☐ Norway

☐ Denmark

COPYRIGHT. GEORGE PHILIP & SON. LTD.

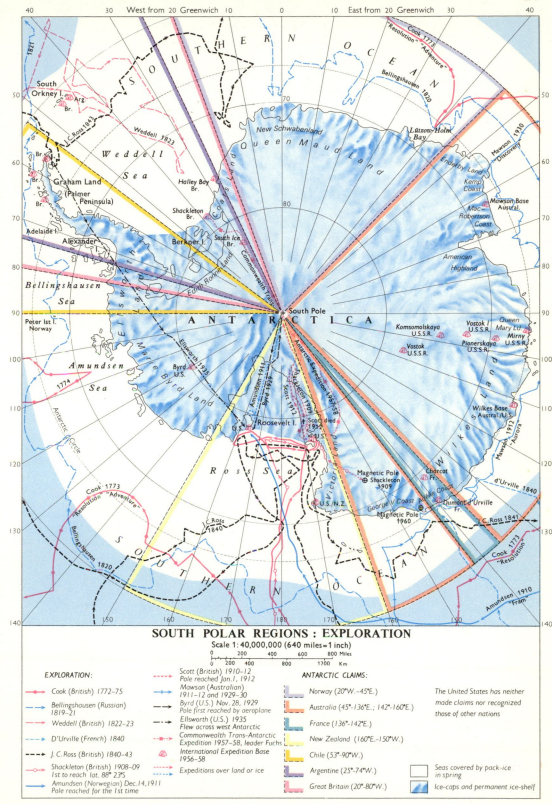

West from Greenwich · East from Greenwich

SOUTHERN OCEAN

"Resolution" Cook 1773 "Adventure"

Bellingshausen 1820

New Schwabenland

Queen Maud Land

Lützow-Holm Bay

Enderby Land

Mawson 1930 "Discovery"

Kemp Coast

Mawson Base Austral.

Mac-Robertson Coast

American Highland

South Orkney I. Arg. Br.

J.C. Ross 1843

Weddell 1823

Weddell Sea

Halley Bay Br.

Shackleton Br.

South Ice Br.

Berkner I.

Graham Land (Palmer Peninsula) Br.

Adelaide I.

Alexander

Bellingshausen Sea

Peter Ist I. Norway

Amundsen Sea

1774

Antarctic Circle

Ellsworth Land

Marie Byrd Land

Byrd U.S.

Amundsen 1911
Byrd 1929
Scott 1912

ANTARCTICA

South Pole

Komsomolskaya U.S.S.R.

Vostok I U.S.S.R.

Vostok U.S.S.R.

Queen Mary Ld.

Mirny U.S.S.R.

Pionerskaya U.S.S.R.

Wilkes Land

Wilkes Base Austral./U.S.

Mawson 1912 "Aurora"

Antarctic Expedition 1957–58

Roosevelt I.

Scott died 1912 U.S.

U.S.

Ross Sea

Ross 1840

U.S./N.Z.

Magnetic Pole Shackleton 1909

Magnetic Pole 1960

Victoria Land

George V Coast

Adélie Coast

Charcot Fr.

Dumont d'Urville Fr.

d'Urville 1840

J.C. Ross 1841

Cook 1773 "Resolution"

Bellingshausen 1820

Amundsen 1910 "Fram"

SOUTHERN OCEAN

SOUTH POLAR REGIONS : EXPLORATION

Scale 1:40,000,000 (640 miles=1 inch)

0 200 400 600 800 Miles

0 200 400 800 1200 Km

EXPLORATION:

- ●—● Cook (British) 1772–75
- ●—● Bellingshausen (Russian) 1819–21
- ●—● Weddell (British) 1822–23
- ●—● D'Urville (French) 1840
- ●—● J.C. Ross (British) 1840–43
- ●—○ Shackleton (British) 1908–09 1st to reach lat. 88° 23′S
- ●—● Amundsen (Norwegian) Dec.14,1911 Pole reached for the 1st time

- ●—● Scott (British) 1910–12 Pole reached Jan.1, 1912
- →—→ Mawson (Australian) 1911–12 and 1929–30
- ←—← Byrd (U.S.) Nov. 28, 1929 Pole first reached by aeroplane
- ●—● Ellsworth (U.S.) 1935 Flew across west Antarctic
- ■—■ Commonwealth Trans-Antarctic Expedition 1957–58, leader Fuchs
- 🛖 International Expedition Base 1956–58
- ·—· Expeditions over land or ice

ANTARCTIC CLAIMS:

- Norway (20°W.–45°E.)
- Australia (45°–136°E.; 142°–160°E.)
- France (136°–142°E.)
- New Zealand (160°E.–150°W.)
- Chile (53°–90°W.)
- Argentine (25°–74°W.)
- Great Britain (20°–80°W.)

The United States has neither made claims nor recognized those of other nations

- Seas covered by pack-ice in spring
- Ice-caps and permanent ice-shelf

COPYRIGHT. GEORGE PHILIP & SON, LTD.

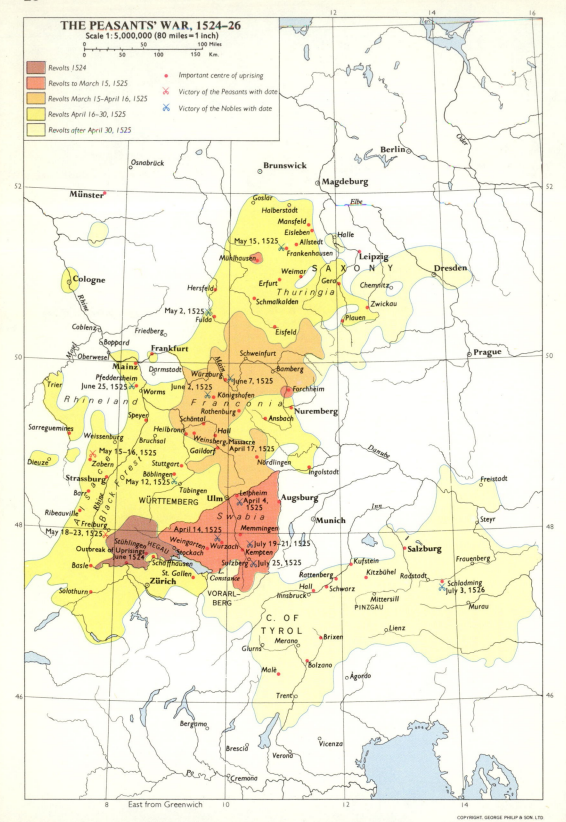

THE PEASANTS' WAR, 1524–26

Scale 1:5,000,000 (80 miles = 1 inch)

0	50	100 Miles
0	50	100 150 Km.

Revolts 1524
Revolts to March 15, 1525
Revolts March 15–April 16, 1525
Revolts April 16–30, 1525
Revolts after April 30, 1525

• Important centre of uprising
✗ Victory of the Peasants with date
✗ Victory of the Nobles with date

Berlin
Brunswick
Magdeburg
Münster
Osnabrück
Goslar
Halberstadt
Mansfeld
Eisleben
Halle
May 15, 1525 Allstedt
Frankenhausen
Mühlhausen Leipzig
Weimar SAXONY Dresden
Hersfeld Erfurt Gera Chemnitz
Thuringia
Schmalkalden Zwickau
May 2, 1525 Plauen
Fulda
Coblenz Eisfeld
Friedberg
Oberwesel Boppard
Frankfurt Schweinfurt Prague
Mainz Darmstadt Würzburg Bamberg
Pfeddersheim Main June 7, 1525
June 25, 1525 Worms June 2, 1525 Forchheim
Trier Rhineland Franconia Nuremberg
Speyer Königshofen
Rothenburg Ansbach
Sarreguemines Heilbronn Hall
Weissenburg Bruchsal Weinsberg, Massacre
May 15–16, 1525 Gaildorf April 17, 1525
Dieuze Zabern Schöntal
Stuttgart Nördlingen Danube
Strassburg Böblingen Ingolstadt
Bars May 12, 1525
Ribeauville Tübingen Leipheim Augsburg Freistadt
May 18–23, 1525 WÜRTTEMBERG Ulm April 4, Steyr
Freiburg 1525
Swabia Munich Inn
Stühlingen April 14, 1525 Memmingen
Outbreak of Weingarten Wurzach July 19–21, 1525 Salzburg
Uprisings Stockach Kempten Kufstein Frauenberg
June 1524 Sulzberg July 25, 1525 Rattenberg Kitzbühel Radstadt
Basle Schaffhausen Kitzbühel Schladming
St. Gallen L. Hall Schwarz July 3, 1526
Zürich Constance Innsbruck Mittersill
VORARL- PINZGAU Murau
BERG Lienz
Solothurn C. OF
TYROL Brixen
Merano
Glurns Bolzano
Malè Ågordo
Trent
Bergamo
Brescia Vicenza
Verona
Po
Cremona

East from Greenwich

COPYRIGHT. GEORGE PHILIP & SON. LTD.

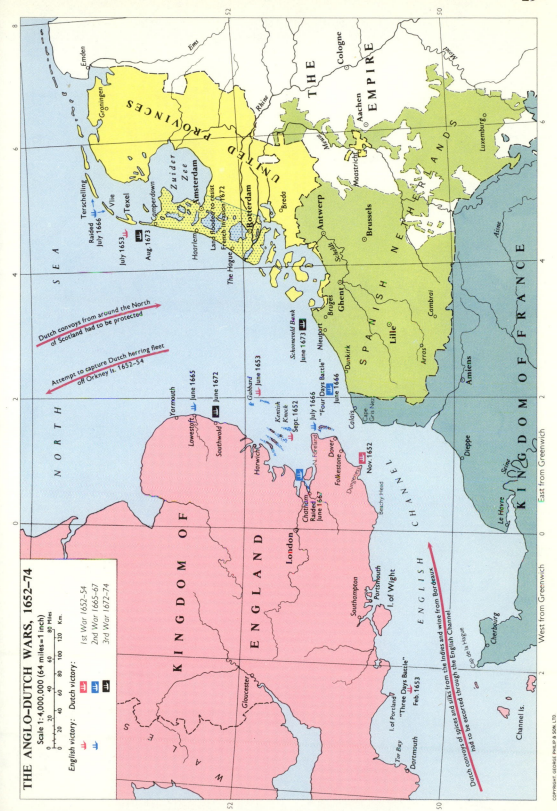

THE ANGLO-DUTCH WARS, 1652–74

Scale 1:4,000,000 (64 miles=1 inch)

```
0   20   40   60   80 Miles
0  20  40  60  80  100  120 Km.
```

1st War 1652–54
2nd War 1665–67
3rd War 1672–74

English victory: Dutch victory:

THE EMPIRE

Cologne
Aachen
Luxemburg
Maastricht

UNITED PROVINCES

Emden
Groningen
Ems
Rhine
Zuider Zee
Amsterdam
Camperdown
Terschelling
Raided July 1666
Vlie
Texel
July 1653
Aug. 1673
Haarlem
Land flooded to resist French invasion 1672
The Hague
Rotterdam
Breda
Antwerp
Brussels

SPANISH NETHERLANDS

Schelde
Ghent
Bruges
Lille
Cambrai
Arras
Nieuport
Dunkirk
Schooneveld Bank June 1673
Cape Gris Nez
Amiens
Aisne
Moel

KINGDOM OF FRANCE

Dieppe
Le Havre
Seine
Cherbourg
Cap de la Hague
Channel Is.

NORTH SEA

Dutch convoys from around the North of Scotland had to be protected

Attempt to capture Dutch herring fleet off Orkney Is. 1652–54

Yarmouth
June 1665
June 1672
Lowestoft
Southwold
Harwich
Gabbard June 1653
Kentish Knock Sept. 1652
July 1666 "Four Days Battle"
June 1666
N. Foreland
Calais
Dover
Folkestone
Dungeness Nov. 1652
Beachy Head

KINGDOM OF ENGLAND

London
Chatham Raided June 1667
Gloucester
Southampton
Portsmouth
I. of Wight
I. of Portland "Three Days Battle" Feb. 1653
Tor Bay
Dartmouth

ENGLISH CHANNEL

Dutch convoys of spices and silks from the Indies and wine from Bordeaux had to be escorted through the English Channel

East from Greenwich
West from Greenwich

COPYRIGHT GEORGE PHILIP & SON LTD.

30

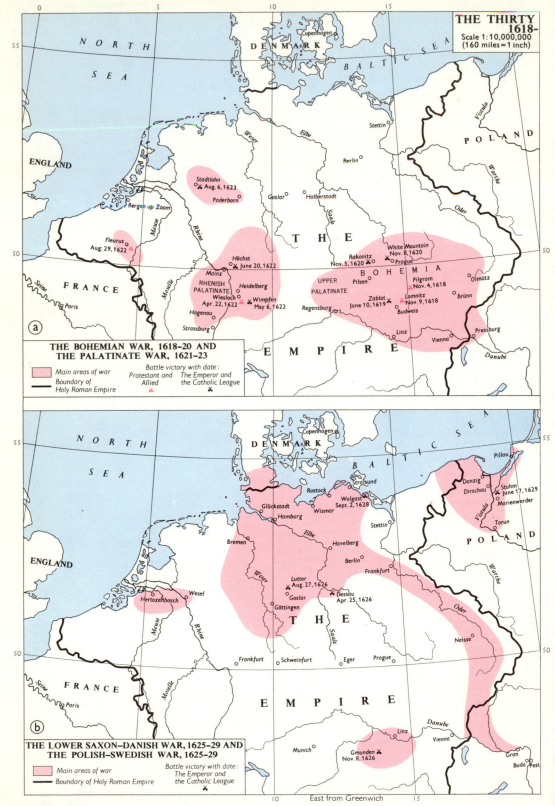

THE THIRTY
1618-
Scale 1:10,000,000
(160 miles = 1 inch)

**THE BOHEMIAN WAR, 1618-20 AND
THE PALATINATE WAR, 1621-23**

Main areas of war
Boundary of
Holy Roman Empire

Battle victory with date:
Protestant and   The Emperor and
Allied   the Catholic League

**THE LOWER SAXON-DANISH WAR, 1625-29 AND
THE POLISH-SWEDISH WAR, 1625-29**

Main areas of war
Boundary of Holy Roman Empire

Battle victory with date:
The Emperor and
the Catholic League

East from Greenwich

COPYRIGHT. GEORGE PHILIP & SON. LTD.

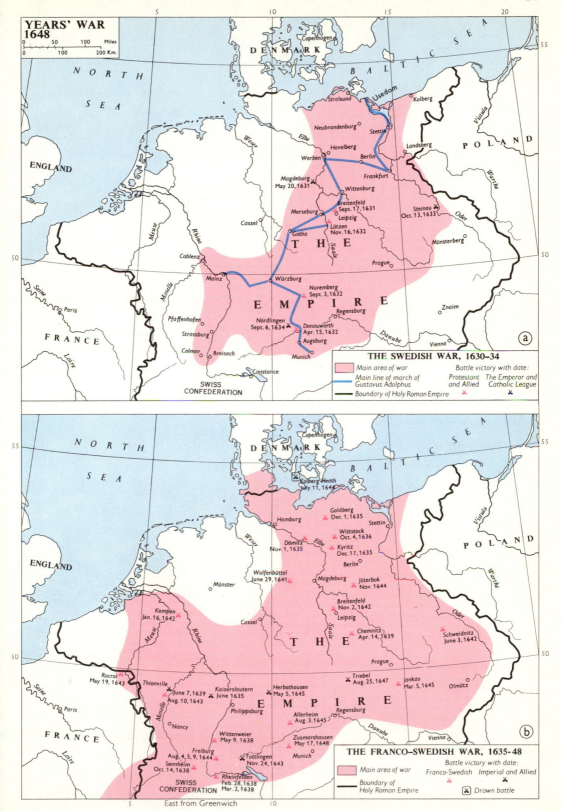

THIRTY YEARS' WAR 1648

YEARS' WAR
1648

Miles
0   50   100
0   100   200 Km.

THE SWEDISH WAR, 1630–34

- Main area of war
- Main line of march of Gustavus Adolphus
- Boundary of Holy Roman Empire

Battle victory with date:
Protestant and Allied ✕   The Emperor and Catholic League ✕

(a)

Magdeburg May 20, 1631
Breitenfeld Sept. 17, 1631
Lützen Nov. 16, 1632
Steinau Oct. 13, 1633
Nuremberg Sept. 3, 1632
Nördlingen Sept. 6, 1634
Donauworth Apr. 15, 1632

THE FRANCO–SWEDISH WAR, 1635–48

- Main area of war
- Boundary of Holy Roman Empire

Battle victory with date:
Franco-Swedish ✕   Imperial and Allied ✕
✕ Drawn battle

(b)

Kolberg Heath July 11, 1644
Goldberg Dec. 1, 1635
Wittstock Oct. 4, 1636
Kyritz Dec. 17, 1635
Dömitz Nov. 1, 1635
Wolfenbüttel June 29, 1641
Jüterbok Nov. 1644
Kempen Jan. 16, 1642
Breitenfeld Nov. 2, 1642
Chemnitz Apr. 14, 1639
Schweidnitz June 3, 1642
Rocroi May 19, 1643
Triebel Aug. 25, 1647
Jankau Mar. 5, 1645
Thionville June 7, 1639 Aug. 10, 1643
Kaiserslautern June 1635
Herbsthausen May 5, 1645
Allerheim Aug. 3, 1645
Zusmarshausen May 17, 1648
Wittenweier May 9, 1638
Freiburg Aug. 4, 5, 9, 1644
Tuttlingen Nov. 24, 1643
Sennheim Oct. 14, 1638
Rheinfelden Feb. 28, 1638 Mar. 2, 1638

East from Greenwich

COPYRIGHT. GEORGE PHILIP & SON. LTD.

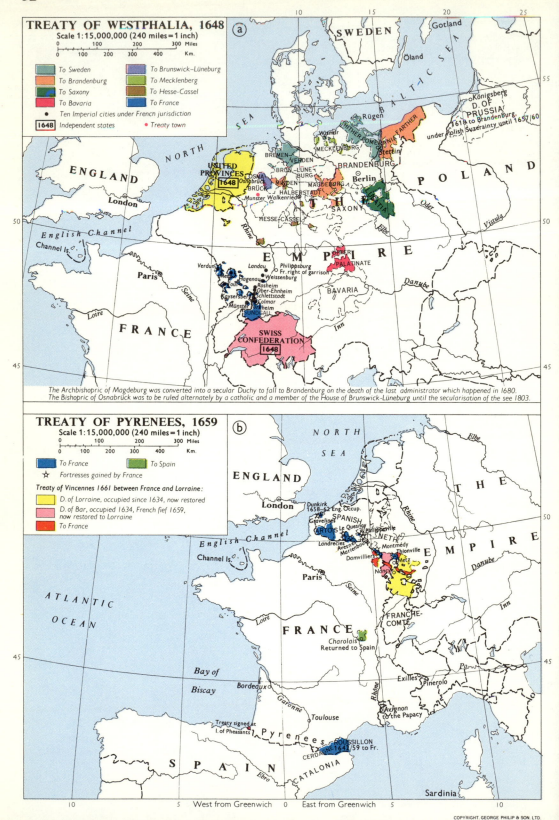

TREATY OF WESTPHALIA, 1648
Scale 1:15,000,000 (240 miles=1 inch)

0   100   200   300 Miles
0   100   200   300   400 Km.

To Sweden
To Brandenburg
To Saxony
To Bavaria
To Brunswick-Lüneburg
To Mecklenberg
To Hesse-Cassel
To France

● Ten Imperial cities under French jurisdiction
1648 Independent states   ● Treaty town

The Archbishopric of Magdeburg was converted into a secular Duchy to fall to Brandenburg on the death of the last administrator which happened in 1680.
The Bishopric of Osnabrück was to be ruled alternately by a catholic and a member of the House of Brunswick-Lüneburg until the secularisation of the see 1803.

TREATY OF PYRENEES, 1659
Scale 1:15,000,000 (240 miles=1 inch)

0   100   200   300 Miles
0   100   200   300   400 Km.

To France   To Spain
☆ Fortresses gained by France

Treaty of Vincennes 1661 between France and Lorraine:
D. of Lorraine, occupied since 1634, now restored
D. of Bar, occupied 1634, French fief 1659, now restored to Lorraine
To France

COPYRIGHT. GEORGE PHILIP & SON, LTD.

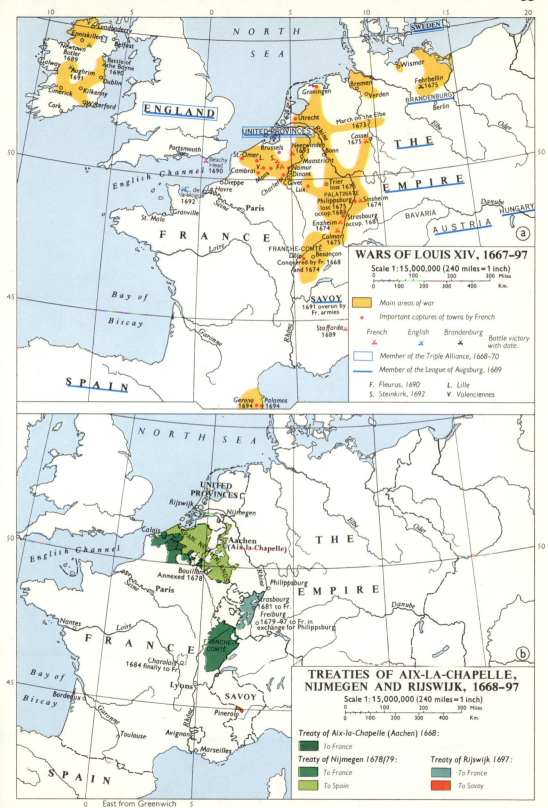

WARS OF LOUIS XIV, 1667–97

Scale 1:15,000,000 (240 miles = 1 inch)

| 0 | 100 | 200 | 300 Miles |

| 0 | 100 | 200 | 300 | 400 Km. |

🟧 Main areas of war

• Important captures of towns by French

French   English   Brandenburg

✕   ✕   ✕   Battle victory with date.

▭ Member of the Triple Alliance, 1668–70

— Member of the League of Augsburg, 1689

F. Fleurus, 1690   L. Lille
S. Steinkirk, 1692   V. Valenciennes

TREATIES OF AIX-LA-CHAPELLE, NIJMEGEN AND RIJSWIJK, 1668–97

Scale 1:15,000,000 (240 miles = 1 inch)

| 0 | 100 | 200 | 300 Miles |

| 0 | 100 | 200 | 300 | 400 Km. |

Treaty of Aix-la-Chapelle (Aachen) 1668:

▨ To France

Treaty of Nijmegen 1678/79:

🟩 To France

🟩 To Spain

Treaty of Rijswijk 1697:

🟦 To France

🟥 To Savoy

East from Greenwich

COPYRIGHT. GEORGE PHILIP & SON. LTD.

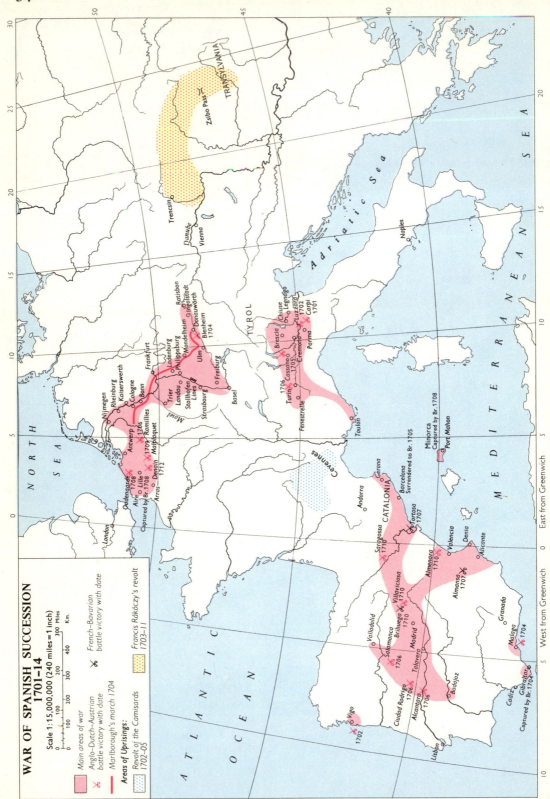

34

WAR OF SPANISH SUCCESSION 1701–14

Scale 1:15,000,000 (240 miles=1 inch)

0   100   200   300   Miles

0   100   200   300   400   Km.

Main areas of war

✗ Anglo–Dutch–Austrian battle victory with date

✗ French–Bavarian battle victory with date

Marlborough's march 1704

Areas of Uprisings:

Revolt of the Camisards 1702–05

Francis Rákóczy's revolt 1703–11

TRANSYLVANIA

Zsibo Pass

Trencsin

Danube

Vienna

NORTH SEA

Nijmegen

Rheinberg

Kaiserswerth

Cologne

Bonn

Antwerp

Oudenarde 1708

Aire 1708

Captured by Br. 1708

Lille 1708

Malplaquet 1709

Arras

Denain 1712

Ramillies 1706

Trier

Landau

Stollhofen Lines

Strasbourg

Frankfurt

Ladenburg

Philippsburg

Freiburg

Basel

Ulm

Blenheim 1704

Mondelheim

Donauwörth

Ingolstadt

Ratisbon

Moel

TYROL

Brescia

Cassano 1705

Turin 1706

Cremona

Parma

Chiuse

Legnago

Luzzara 1702

Carpi 1701

Finestrelle

Toulon

ADRIATIC Sea

Naples

MEDITERRANEAN SEA

Cévennes

Andorra

CATALONIA

Gerona

Barcelona Surrendered to Br. 1705

Tortosa 1707

Minorca Captured by Br. 1708

Port Mahon

Saragossa 1710

Valencia

Denia

Alicante

Almenara 1710

Almansa 1707

Valladolid

Salamanca 1706

Ciudad Rodrigo 1706

Alcantara 1706

Madrid

Talavera

Villaviciosa 1710

Brihuega 1710

Badajoz

Granada

Malaga 1704

Cadiz

Gibraltar Captured by Br. 1704

Lisbon

Vigo 1702

ATLANTIC OCEAN

NORTH SEA

London

East from Greenwich

West from Greenwich

COPYRIGHT GEORGE PHILIP & SON LTD.

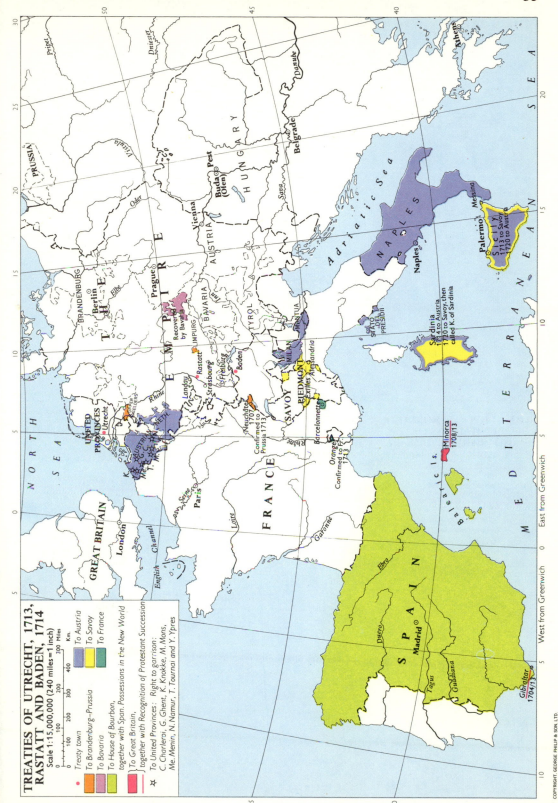

TREATIES OF UTRECHT, 1713, RASTATT AND BADEN, 1714

Scale 1:15,000,000 (240 miles=1 inch)

0 100 200 300 Miles

0 100 200 300 400 Km.

- Treaty town
  To Austria
  To Savoy
  To France
  To Brandenburg–Prussia
  To Bavaria
  To House of Bourbon, together with Span. Possessions in the New World
  To Great Britain, together with Recognition of Protestant Succession
☆ To United Provinces: Right to garrison:
  C. Charleroi, G. Ghent, K. Knokke, M. Mons, Me. Menin, N. Namur, T. Tournai and Y. Ypres

COPYRIGHT. GEORGE PHILIP & SON, LTD

Place labels on map:

PRUSSIA, Priet, Dniester, Vistula, Narew, Warthe, Oder, BRANDENBURG, Berlin, Elbe, T H E, Prague, E M P I R E, RECOVERED by Bavaria, LIMPURG, BAVARIA, Rastatt, Freiburg, Baden, TYROL, Vienna, AUSTRIA, HUNGARY, Buda (Ofen), Pest, Save, Belgrade, Danube, Athens

NORTH SEA, UNITED PROVINCES, Utrecht, AUSTRIAN NETH., K., Rhine, Landau, Strasbourg, Neuchâtel Confirmed to Prussia 1713, Orange Confirmed to France 1713, Barcelonnette, SAVOY, PIEDMONT, Exilles, Susa, Alessandria, MILAN, MANTUA, Adriatic Sea, NAPLES, Naples, STATO DEI PRESIDII, Palermo, Messina, Sardinia 1713 to Savoy, then 1720 to Austria, called K. of Sardinia, Sardinia 1713 to Savoy 1720 to Austria

GREAT BRITAIN, London, English Channel, Seine, Paris, Loire, F R A N C E, Rhône, Garonne, Minorca 1708/13, Balearic Is., MEDITERRANEAN SEA, East from Greenwich, West from Greenwich

S P A I N, Madrid, Ebro, Duero, Tagus, Guadiana, Gibraltar 1704/13

East from Greenwich

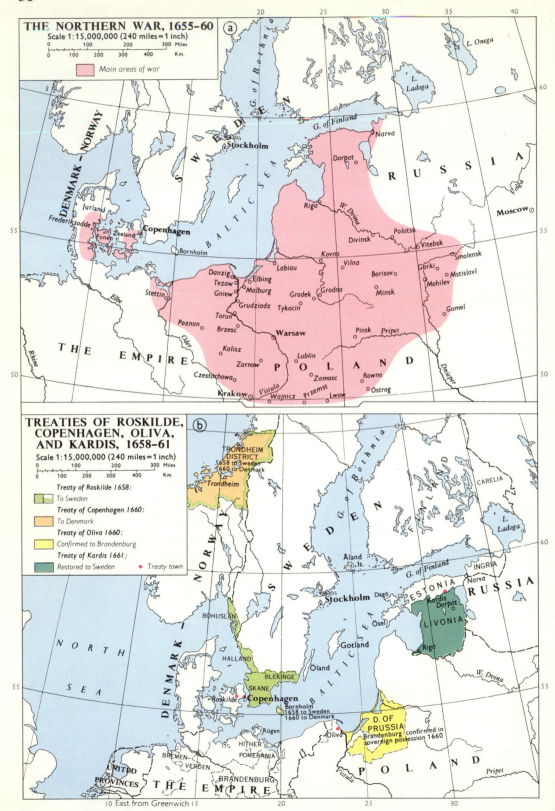

THE NORTHERN WAR, 1655–60 (a)

Scale 1:15,000,000 (240 miles=1 inch)

0 100 200 300 Miles
0 100 200 300 400 Km.

Main areas of war

DENMARK – NORWAY
SWEDEN
RUSSIA
THE EMPIRE
POLAND

L. Onega
L. Ladoga
G. of Bothnia
Narva
Dorpat
Stockholm
Riga
W. Dvina
Divinsk
Polotsk
Vitebsk
Smolensk
Moscow
Volga
Jutland
Frederiksodde
Zeeland
Funen
Copenhagen
Bornholm
BALTIC SEA
Kovno
Vilna
Borisov
Gorki
Mstislavl
Mohilev
Minsk
Gomel
Danzig
Labiau
Elbing
Tezaw
Malburg
Gniew
Grodek
Grodno
Stettin
Grudziadz
Tykocin
Torun
Poznan
Brzesc
Warsaw
Pinsk
Pripet
Kalisz
Lublin
Zarnow
Zamosc
Rowno
Czestochowa
Krakow
Wajnicz
Przemst
Lwow
Ostrog
Dniepr
Vistula
Elbe
Oder
Rhine

20 25 30 35 40
60
55 55
50 50

TREATIES OF ROSKILDE, COPENHAGEN, OLIVA, AND KARDIS, 1658–61 (b)

Scale 1:15,000,000 (240 miles=1 inch)

0 100 200 300 Miles
0 100 200 300 400 Km.

Treaty of Roskilde 1658:
To Sweden

Treaty of Copenhagen 1660:
To Denmark

Treaty of Oliva 1660:
Confirmed to Brandenburg

Treaty of Kardis 1661:
Restored to Sweden   • Treaty town

TRONDHEIM DISTRICT
1658 to Sweden
1660 to Denmark
Trondheim
NORWAY
SWEDEN
DENMARK
BOHUSLAN
HALLAND
BLEKINGE
SKANE
Roskilde
Copenhagen
Bornholm
1658 to Sweden
1660 to Denmark
Rügen
HITHER POMERANIA
BREMEN
VERDEN
BRANDENBURG
UNITED PROVINCES
THE EMPIRE
NORTH SEA
BALTIC SEA
Gotland
Öland
Stockholm
Dago
Ösel
CARELIA
L. Ladoga
G. of Bothnia
FINLAND
G. of Finland
INGRIA
Narva
ESTONIA
Kardis
Dorpat
LIVONIA
Riga
RUSSIA
W. Dvina
Åland Is.
Oliva
D. OF PRUSSIA
Brandenburg confirmed in sovereign possession 1660
POLAND
Vistula
Pripet

10 East from Greenwich 15   20   25   30
60
55 55

COPYRIGHT. GEORGE PHILIP & SON. LTD.

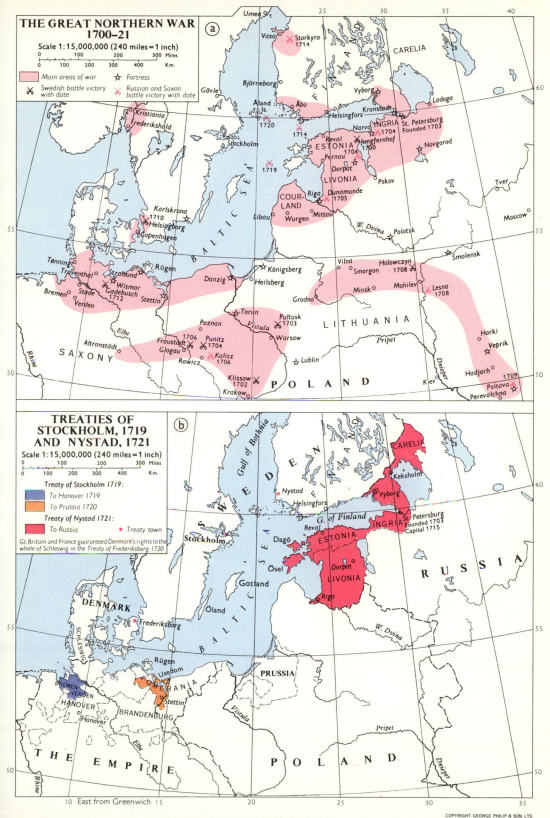

THE GREAT NORTHERN WAR 1700–21

Scale 1:15,000,000 (240 miles=1 inch)

Main areas of war — Fortress

Swedish battle victory with date — Russian and Saxon battle victory with date

TREATIES OF STOCKHOLM, 1719 AND NYSTAD, 1721

Scale 1:15,000,000 (240 miles=1 inch)

Treaty of Stockholm 1719:
To Hanover 1719
To Prussia 1720
Treaty of Nystad 1721:
To Russia — Treaty town

Gt. Britain and France guaranteed Denmark's rights to the whole of Schleswig in the Treaty of Frederiksborg 1720

COPYRIGHT. GEORGE PHILIP & SON. LTD.

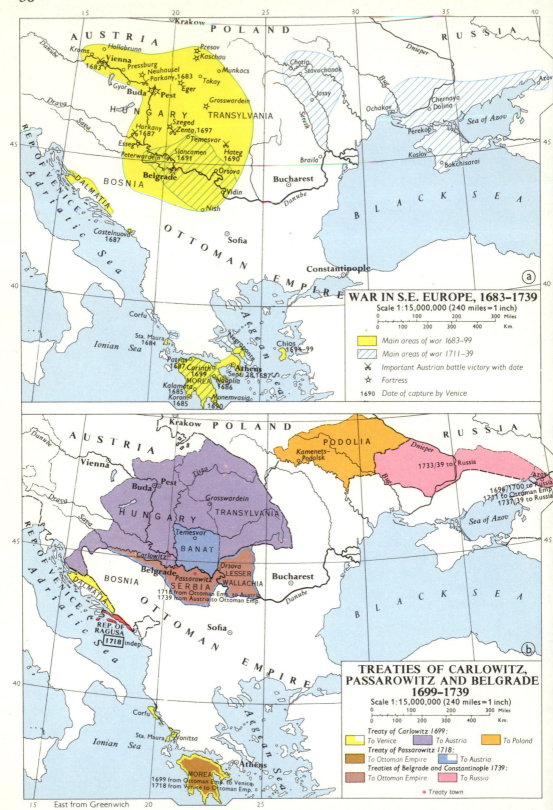

WAR IN S.E. EUROPE, 1683–1739

Scale 1:15,000,000 (240 miles=1 inch)

0	100	200	300 Miles
0 100	200	300	400 Km.

Main areas of war 1683–99

Main areas of war 1711–39

✗ Important Austrian battle victory with date

☆ Fortress

1690 Date of capture by Venice

TREATIES OF CARLOWITZ, PASSAROWITZ AND BELGRADE 1699–1739

Scale 1:15,000,000 (240 miles=1 inch)

0	100	200	300 Miles
0 100	200	300	400 Km.

Treaty of Carlowitz 1699:
To Venice   To Austria   To Poland

Treaty of Passarowitz 1718:
To Ottoman Empire   To Austria

Treaties of Belgrade and Constantinople 1739:
To Ottoman Empire   To Russia

● Treaty town

COPYRIGHT. GEORGE PHILIP & SON, LTD.

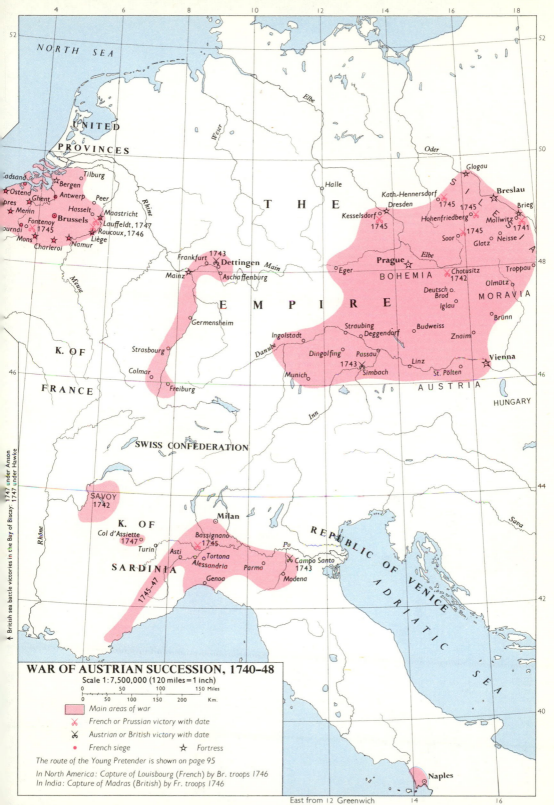

NORTH SEA

UNITED
PROVINCES

THE

Cadsand
Tilburg
Bergen
Antwerp
Peer
Ghent
Hasselt
Maastricht
Menin
Lauffeldt, 1747
pres
Fontenoy
Brussels
Roucoux, 1746
Journal
1745
Liège
Mons
Namur
Charleroi

Rhine

Frankfurt 1743
Dettingen Main
Mainz
Aschaffenburg

Germensheim

K. OF
FRANCE

Meuse

Strasbourg

Colmar

Freiburg

SWISS CONFEDERATION

E   M   P   I   R   E

Halle

Elbe

Oder

Glogau
Breslau
Kath-Hennersdorf
Dresden
1745
1745
Brieg
Kesselsdorf
Hohenfriedberg
Mollwitz
1741
1745
1745
Soor
Glatz
Neisse
Prague
Eger
Chotusitz
Troppau
1742
BOHEMIA
Olmütz
Deutsch
MORAVIA
Brod
Iglau
Brünn
Straubing
Budweiss
Ingolstadt
Deggendorf
Znaim
Danube
Dingolfing Passau
Vienna
1743
Linz
Munich
Simbach
St. Pölten
AUSTRIA
Inn
HUNGARY

Rhine

Sava

SAVOY
1742

K. OF

Milan

Col d'Assiette
1747
Turin
Asti
Bassignano
1745
Tortona
Parma
Po
Campo Santo
1743
Alessandria
SARDINIA
1745-47
Genoa
Modena

REPUBLIC OF VENICE

ADRIATIC

SEA

Naples

East from 12 Greenwich

British sea battle victories in the Bay of Biscay: 1747 under Anson
1747 under Hawke

WAR OF AUSTRIAN SUCCESSION, 1740-48

Scale 1:7,500,000 (120 miles = 1 inch)

0   50   100   150 Miles
0   50   100   150   200   Km.

Main areas of war

✗   French or Prussian victory with date

✗   Austrian or British victory with date

•   French siege   ☆   Fortress

The route of the Young Pretender is shown on page 95

In North America: Capture of Louisbourg (French) by Br. troops 1746
In India: Capture of Madras (British) by Fr. troops 1746

COPYRIGHT. GEORGE PHILIP & SON. LTD.

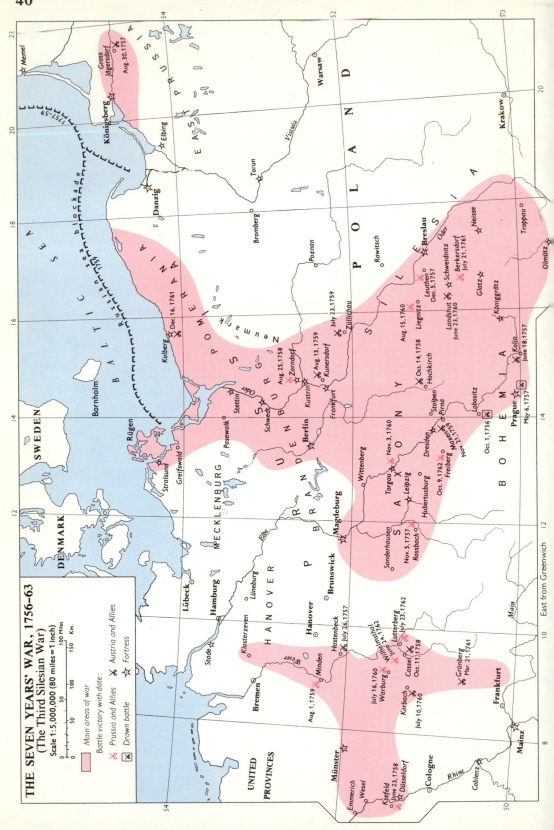

THE SEVEN YEARS' WAR, 1756–63
(The Third Silesian War)
Scale 1:5,000,000 (80 miles=1 inch)

Main areas of war

Battle victory with date::

✕ Prussia and Allies   ✕ Austria and Allies

✕ Drawn battle

☆ Fortress

0   50   100   Miles
0   50   100   150   Km.

SWEDEN

DENMARK

UNITED
PROVINCES

SEA

BALTIC

Bornholm

Rügen

Stralsund

Greifswald

Memel

Königsberg

Gross
Jägersdorf
Aug. 30, 1757

1757-59

Russian seablockade 1758

E A S T   P R U S S I A

Elbing

Danzig

Torun

Bromberg

Warsaw

Krakow

P O L A N D

Poznan

Rawitsch

Pasewalk

Stettin

Schwedt

Frankfurt

Kustrin

Aug. 25, 1758
Zorndorf

Aug. 13, 1759
Kunersdorf

July 23, 1759
Züllichau

S I L E S I A

Breslau

Schweidnitz
July 21, 1761
Berkersdorf

Leuthen
Dec. 5, 1757

Landshut
June 23, 1760

Aug. 15, 1760
Liegnitz

Neisse

Glatz

Königgrätz

Troppau

Olmütz

P O M E R A N I A

Kolberg
Dec. 16, 1761

Neumark

Oder

Bornholm

MECKLENBURG

Lübeck

Hamburg

Bremen

Stade

Lüneburg

Elbe

Magdeburg

Brunswick

B R A N D E N B U R G

Berlin
Nov. 3, 1760

Wittenberg

Leipzig

Torgau

S A X O N Y

Sonderhausen
Nov. 5, 1757
Rossbach

Hubertusburg

Dresden
Freiberg Maxen
Nov. 21, 1759
Nov. 3, 1759
Oct. 9, 1762

Pirna

Stolpen

Lobositz
Oct. 1, 1756

Hochkirch
Oct. 14, 1758

B O H E M I A

Prague
May 6, 1757

Kolin
June 18, 1757

H A N O V E R

Hanover

Hastenbeck
July 26, 1757

Minden
Aug. 1, 1759

Klosterzeven

Wilhelmsthal
June 24, 1762
Lutterberg
July 23, 1762

Cassel
Oct. 11, 1758

July 16, 1760
Warburg

Korbach
July 10, 1760

Grünberg
Mar. 21, 1761

Weser

W E S T P H A L I A

Münster

Emmerich

Wesel

Krefeld
June 23, 1758

Düsseldorf

Cologne

Coblenz

Rhine

Frankfurt

Main

Mainz

East from Greenwich

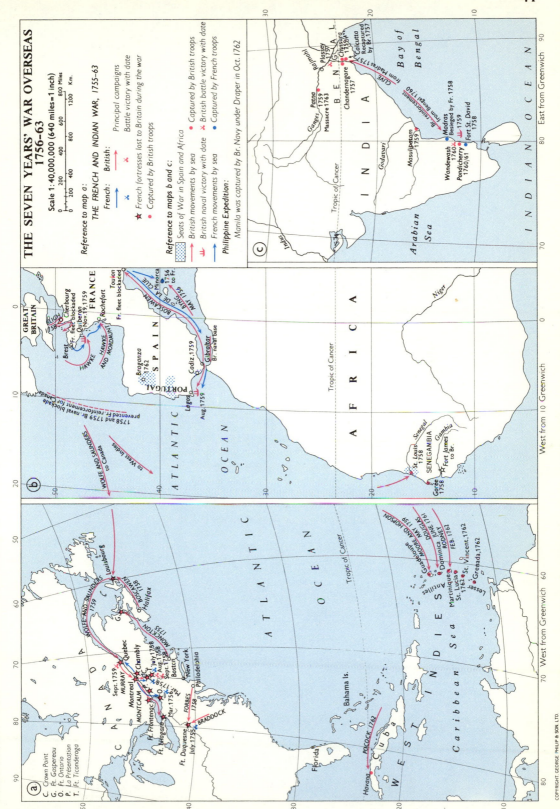

THE SEVEN YEARS' WAR OVERSEAS
1756-63

Scale 1:40,000,000 (640 miles=1 inch)

0 200 400 600 800 1000 1200 Km.

0 200 400 600 800 Miles

Reference to map a:
THE FRENCH AND INDIAN WAR, 1755-63

French: British:
Principal campaigns
Battle victory with date
★ French fortresses lost to Britain during the war
● Captured by British troops

Reference to maps b and c:
▨ Seats of War in Spain and Africa
→ British movements by sea
✗ British naval victory with date
→ French movements by sea

● Captured by British troops
✗ British battle victory with date
● Captured by French troops

Philippine Expedition:
Manila was captured by Br. Navy under Draper in Oct. 1762

C. Crown Point
G. Ft. Gaspereau
O. Ft. Ontario
P. La Présentation
T. Ft. Ticonderoga

COPYRIGHT GEORGE PHILIP & SON, LTD.

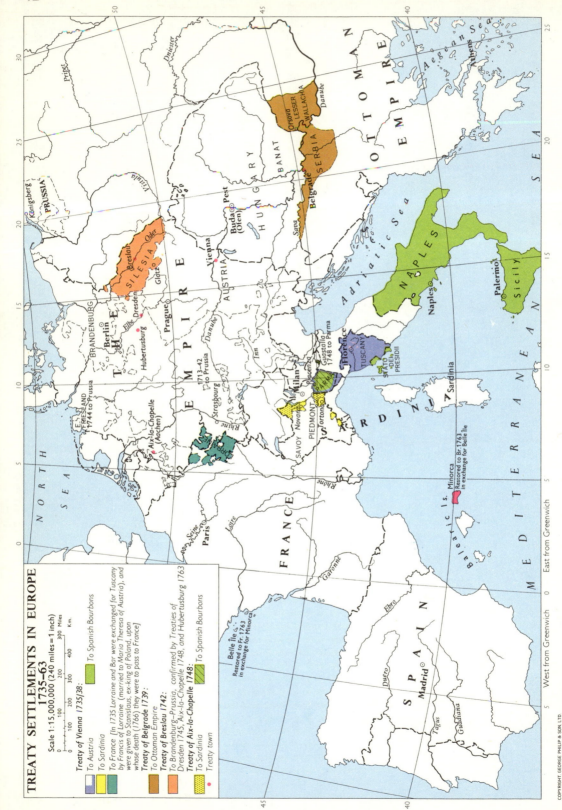

42

TREATY SETTLEMENTS IN EUROPE 1735-63

Scale 1:15,000,000 (240 miles=1 inch)

Km.
0   100   200   300   400
0   100   200   300 Miles

Treaty of Vienna 1735/38:
- To Austria
- To Sardinia
- To France [In 1735 Lorraine and Bar were exchanged for Tuscany by Francis of Lorraine (married to Maria Theresa of Austria), and were given to Stanislaus, ex-king of Poland, upon whose death (1766) they were to pass to France]
- To Spanish Bourbons

Treaty of Belgrade 1739:
- To Ottoman Empire

Treaty of Breslau 1742:
- To Brandenburg–Prussia, confirmed by Treaties of Dresden 1745, Aix-la-Chapelle 1748, and Hubertusburg 1763

Treaty of Aix-la-Chapelle 1748:
- To Sardinia
- To Spanish Bourbons
- Treaty town

COPYRIGHT GEORGE PHILIP & SON LTD.

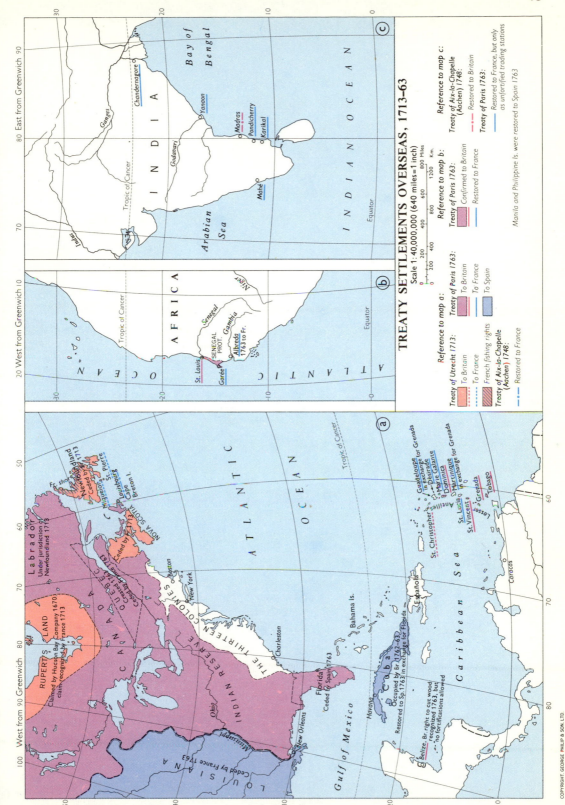

TREATY SETTLEMENTS OVERSEAS, 1713–63

Scale 1:40,000,000 (640 miles=1 inch)

0 200 400 600 800 1200 Km.
0   200   400   600   800 Miles

Reference to map a:

Treaty of Utrecht 1713:
To Britain
To France
French fishing rights

Treaty of Aix-la-Chapelle (Aachen) 1748:
Restored to France

Reference to map b:

Treaty of Paris 1763:
To Britain
To France
To Spain

Reference to map c:

Treaty of Aix-la-Chapelle (Aachen) 1748:
Restored to Britain

Treaty of Paris 1763:
Confirmed to Britain
Restored to France
Restored to France, but only as unfortified trading stations

Manila and Philippine Is. were restored to Spain 1763

COPYRIGHT GEORGE PHILIP & SON. LTD.

WAR IN EUROPE, 1789–1815
(a)
Scale 1:15,000,000 (240 miles = 1 inch)
0 100 200 300 Miles
0 100 200 300 400 Km.
Centres of Uprisings and Revolutionary Wars 1789–95
Centres of the Russo–Turkish War:
1788–95
1806–12
Principal French Campaigns:
Italian Campaign 1796–97
Egyptian Campaign 1798–99
Italian Campaign 1799
Italian Campaign 1800
Campaign against the Third Coalition 1805
Campaign against Prussia and Russia 1806–07
Austrian War 1809
Campaigns of the Peninsular War 1808–13
Russian Campaign 1812–13
Campaign in the War of Liberation 1813
Campaign 1814
Campaign 1815
Battle with date
Sea battle with date
Fortress
10
5
0
5
10
15
50
45
40
35
NORTH
SEA
ATLANTIC
OCEAN
MEDITERRANEAN
Copenhagen
Apr. 2,1801
Sept. 2–5,1807
Heligoland
1807 to Br.
Lübeck
Nov. 6, 1806
Hamburg
Stettin
Oct. 29,1806
Prenzlau
Elbe
Bremen
Camperdown
Oct. 11,1797
Amsterdam
London
Magdeburg
Nov. 8, 1806
Küstrin
Berlin
Oct. 25, 1806
Rhine
Antwerp
Brussels
Waterloo
June 16–18, 1815
Boulogne
Fleurus
June 26, 1794
Jemeppes
Aix-la-Chapelle
Oct. 17, 1806, Halle
Leipzig
Oct. 16–19, 1813
Dresden
Oct. 13,1806, Auerstedt
Apr. 25,1813
Erfurt
Jena, Oct.14, 1806
Bautzen
May 20, 1813
Koblenz
Saalfeld
Oct. 10,1806
Frankfurt
Prague
Le Havre
Seine
Valmy
Sept. 20,1792
Longwy
Mainz
Worms
Main
Würzburg
Bamberg
Brest
Paris
Verdun
Montmirail
Feb. 11, 1814
Châlons-s-M.
Speyer
Mannheim
Oct. 2,1806
Regensburg
Apr. 19–22,1809
Quiberon
Le Mans
Troyes
Strasbourg
July 29,1796
Cannstadt
Ulm
Oct. 17, 1805
Donauwörth
Apr. 17, 1809
Passau
Loire
Stockach
Mar. 25,1799
Munich
Hohenlinden
Dec. 3,1800
Vendée
Memmingen
May 10,1800
Salzburg
Chalon-s-S.
1800
Innsbruck
Aug. 13,1809
La Rochelle
Lyons
Milan
Lodi, May 10,1796
Castiglione, Aug. 5, 1796
Rivoli, Nov. 21, 1796
Bassano, Sept. 8, 1796
Pordenone, Mar. 15,1797
Laibach
Bordeaux
Garonne
Turin
Arcole, Nov. 17, 1796
Marengo
June 14,1800
Mantua, June 5, 1796
Rhône
Gap
Mondovi
Apr. 22, 1796
Piacenza
July 19, 1799
Novi
Aug. 15, 1799
Po
Bologna
Toulouse
Apr. 10, 1814
Avignon
Digne
La Mure
Genoa
Savona
Apr. 11,1796
Arles
Aix
Nice
Marseilles
Cannes
Toulon
Florence
Leghorn
Ancona
Feb. 9, 1797
Tolentino
Adr
La Coruña
Jan. 16, 1809
C. Finisterre
Ferrol
1809
Santander
Nov. 10–11, 1808
Bilbao
Bayonne
Nov. 3, 1808
Astorga
Vitoria
Nov. 5, 1808
June 21, 1813
Pamplona
Sept. 9, 1813
Oporto
July 14, 1808
Burgos
Douro
Valladolid
Tudela, Nov. 23, 1808
Salamanca
Somosierra Pass
Nov. 30, 1808
Sarragossa
Feb. 20, 1809
Ebro
Busacco
Sept. 27, 1810
Madrid
Vimiero
Aug. 21, 1808
Torres Vedras
Talavera
Tagus
Lisbon
July 27–28, 1809
Tortosa
Jan. 2, 1811
Barcelona
Tarragona, June 29, 1811
Gerona, Dec. 10, 1809
Badajoz
Medellin
La Albuera
May 16, 1811
Ciudad Real
Valencia
June 28, 1808
Murviedro
Oct. 25, 1811
Guadiana
Cordoba
Bailen
July 16–19, 1808
Feb. 14, 1797
C. St. Vincent
Seville
Cadiz
Malaga, Aug. 15, 1810
C. Trafalgar
Oct. 21, 1805
Gibraltar
July 22, 1805
Minorca
1798–1802 to Br.
Corsica
Ajaccio
Elba
Civitavecchia
S. Bonifacio
Sardinia
Otricoli
Dec. 9, 1798
Rome
Sept. 12, 1799
Gaeta
Capua
July 18, 1806
Dec. 25,1800, Pozzuoli
Jan. 21,1799, Naples
Malta
Surrendered to Fr., June 12, 1798
Fr. surrendered to Br., Sept. 1800
5
West from Greenwich
0
East from Greenwich
5
10
15

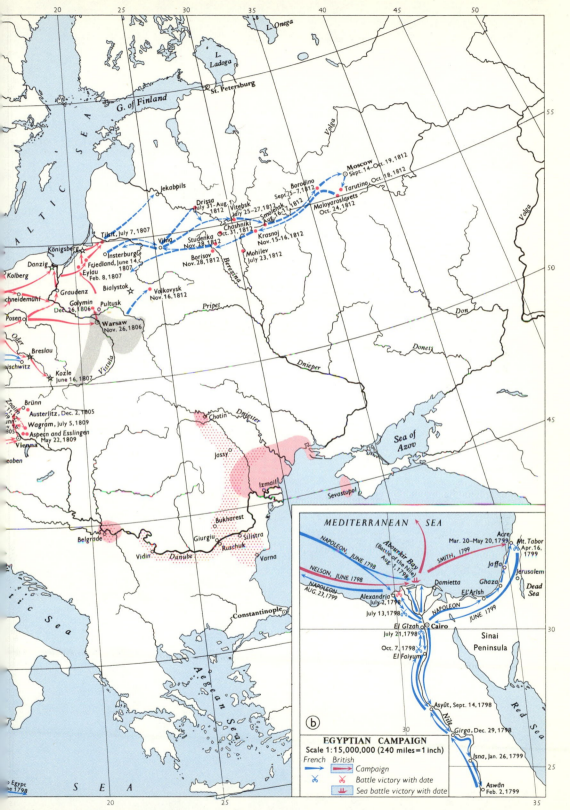

L. Onega

L. Ladoga

St. Petersburg

G. of Finland

BALTIC SEA

Jekabpils

Moscow
Sept. 14–Oct. 19, 1812

Borodino
Sept. 5–7, 1812

Tarutino, Oct. 18, 1812

Drissa
July 31–Aug., 1812

Vitebsk
July 25–27, 1812

Maloyaroslavets
Oct. 24, 1812

Smolensk
Aug. 16–17, 1812

Volga

Tilsit, July 7, 1807

Chashniki
Oct. 31, 1812

Vilna

Königsberg

Insterburg

Krasnoj
Nov. 15–16, 1812

Danzig

Friedland, June 14, 1807

Studenka
Nov. 28, 1812

Eylau
Feb. 8, 1807

Kolberg

Borisov
Nov. 28, 1812

Mohilev
July 23, 1812

Graudenz

Bialystok

Volkovysk
Nov. 16, 1812

Beresina

chneidemühl

Golymin
Dec. 26, 1806

Pultusk

Pripet

Don

Posen

Donets

Oder

Warsaw
Nov. 26, 1806

Breslau

Dnieper

ischwitz

Kozle
June 16, 1807

Vistula

Dniester

Brünn

Chotin

Dniester

Austerlitz, Dec. 2, 1805

Sea of
Azov

Wagram, July 5, 1809

Jassy

Aspern and Esslingen
May 22, 1809

Vienna

eoben

Izmail

Sevastopol

Bukharest

Belgrade

Giurgiu

Silistra

tic Sea

Vidin

Ruschuk

Danube

Varna

Constantinople

Aegean Sea

Egypt
1798

S E A

COPYRIGHT. GEORGE PHILIP & SON. LTD.

MEDITERRANEAN SEA

NAPOLEON, JUNE 1798

Aboukir Bay
(Battle of the Nile)
Aug. 1, 1798

Mar. 20–May 20, 1799

Acre

Mt. Tabor
Apr. 16, 1799

SMITH, 1799

NELSON, JUNE 1798

Jaffa

NAPOLEON
AUG. 23, 1799

Damietta

Jerusalem

Alexandria
July 13, 1798

El'Arish

Ghaza

Dead
Sea

NAPOLEON
JUNE 1799

El Gizah
July 21, 1798

Cairo

Sinai
Peninsula

Oct. 7, 1798
El Faiyum

Asyût, Sept. 14, 1798

Nile

Red Sea

Girga, Dec. 29, 1798

(b)

Isna, Jan. 26, 1799

EGYPTIAN CAMPAIGN
Scale 1:15,000,000 (240 miles=1 inch)
French   *British*

Campaign

Battle victory with date

Sea battle victory with date

Aswân
Feb. 2, 1799

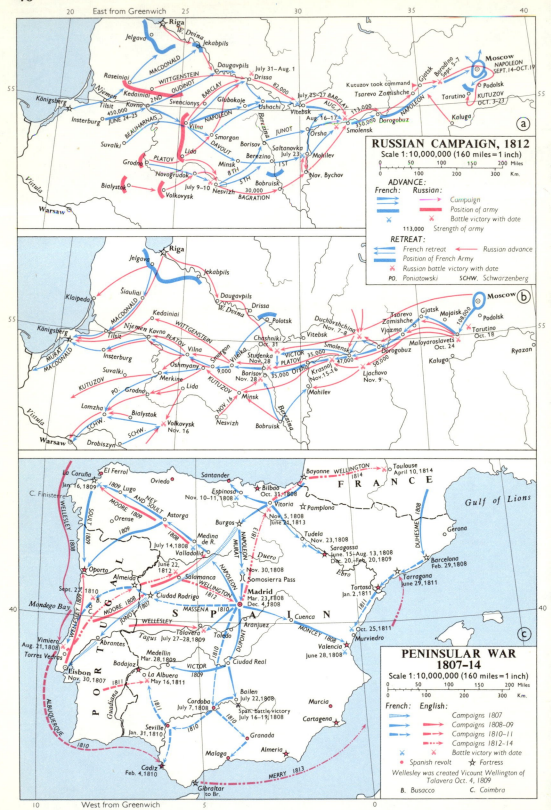

RUSSIAN CAMPAIGN, 1812
Scale 1:10,000,000 (160 miles = 1 inch)

ADVANCE:
French: Russian:
Campaign
Position of army
Battle victory with date
113,000   Strength of army

RETREAT:
French retreat   Russian advance
Position of French Army
Russian battle victory with date
PO. Poniatowski   SCHW. Schwarzenberg

PENINSULAR WAR 1807–14
Scale 1:10,000,000 (160 miles = 1 inch)

French: English:
Campaigns 1807
Campaigns 1808–09
Campaigns 1810–11
Campaigns 1812–14
Battle victory with date
Spanish revolt   Fortress
Wellesley was created Viscount Wellington of Talavera Oct. 4, 1809
B. Busacco   C. Coimbra

COPYRIGHT. GEORGE PHILIP & SON. LTD.

East from Greenwich
4°
4°30′
50°30′
THE WATERLOO CAMPAIGN
JUNE 16–18, 1815
Scale 1: 600,000 (9·6 miles = 1 inch)
0 5 10 Miles
0 5 10 15 Km.
Anglo-Dutch
Prussian
French
Campaigns
Battle victory with date
a
Brussels
Ninove
Dender
Senne
Galmaarden
Hal
PRINCE BERNARD OF ORANGE
JUNE 15–16
WELLINGTON
JUNE 15
Forest of Soignes
Waterloo
Dyle
Wavre
Bierges
Mt. St. Jean
La Haye Sainte
BLÜCHER
JUNE 18
St. Lambert
June 18–19
Dion-le-Mont
BÜLOW
JUNE 17
Hannut
from Liège
June 18
Hougomont
La Belle-Alliance
Plancenoit
Marcq
Corbais
JUNE 17
JUNE 16
NAPOLEON
JUNE 17
Genappe
Mont-St. Guibert
GROUCHY
Mehaigne
Braine-le-Comte
Sennette
Nivelles
Eghezée
Soignies
Arquennes
Quatre Bras
Tilly
Gembloux
June 16
Gemioncourt
Frasnes
Bry
Sombreffe
St.-Amand-la-Haye
Ligny
June 16
Rœulx
Old Roman Road
Fleurus
Meuse
Andenne
Mons
Haine
Gosselies
JUNE 15–16
NEY
NAPOLEON
JUNE 16
Sambre
Namur
Charleroi
Binche
Assesse
Sambre
Thuin
from Beaumont
from Philippeville

BRITISH AND FRENCH NAVAL MOVEMENTS
MARCH–OCTOBER, 1805
b
Equatorial Scale 1: 60,000,000 (960 miles = 1 inch)
British Possessions
French Possessions
Spanish Possessions
Nelson's track
Villeneuve's track
Prevailing winds
Sea battle victory with date
Sea battle victory with date
Boundaries of 1805
UNITED KINGDOM
Land's End
Portsmouth
to Trafalgar Sept. 16, 1805
to Portsmouth Aug. 19, 1805
Bay of Biscay
FRANCE
Rochefort
Toulon
Mar. 29, 1805
July 22, 1805
C. Finesterre
July 26, 1805
Ferrol
Vigo
PORTUGAL
SPAIN
Lisbon
Balearic Is.
Westerly Winds
Flores
Azores
to Port.
NELSON
Lagos
Cadiz
C. St. Vincent
Gibraltar
Trafalgar
Oct. 21, 1805
C. Spartel
VILLENEUVE
NORTH ATLANTIC
OCEAN
Maderia
to Port.
Funchal
Bermuda I.
Santa Cruz
Canary Is.
Teneriffe
NELSON
VILLENEUVE
Tropic of Cancer
AFRICA
North-East Trade Winds
C. Blanco
Puerto Rico
Antigua
WEST INDIES
Guadeloupe
Dominica
St. Lucia
Martinique, Arrival May 14, 1805
St. Vincent
Barbados
Arrival June 4, 1805
Trinidad
Cape Verde Is.
to Port.
Porto Praya
St. Louis
C. Verde
Gorée
Albreda
Ft. James
Freetown
Grain Coast
Ivory Coast
Assinie
Gold Coast
Accra
C. Coast Castle
VICE-ROYALTY OF NEW GRANADA
British
SURINAM
1804–16
GUIANA
French
West from Greenwich
60
50
40
30
20
10
0

COPYRIGHT, GEORGE PHILIP & SON, LTD.

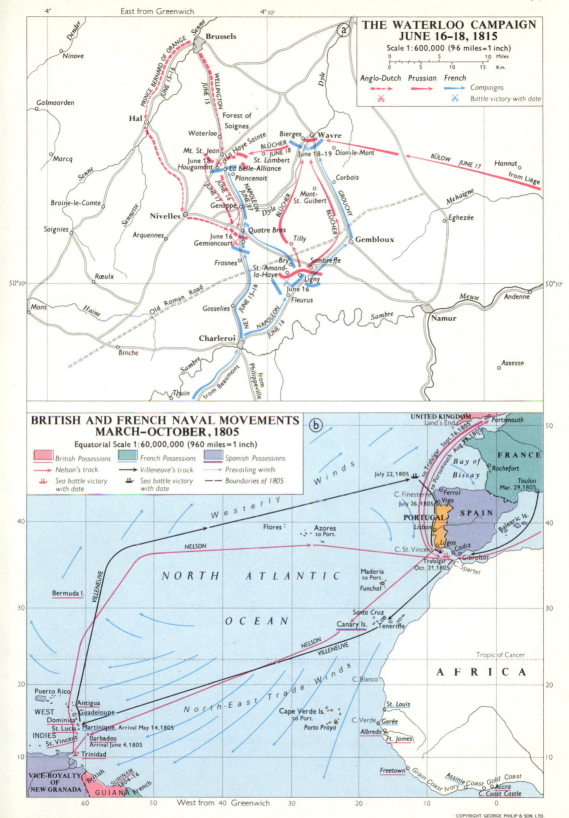

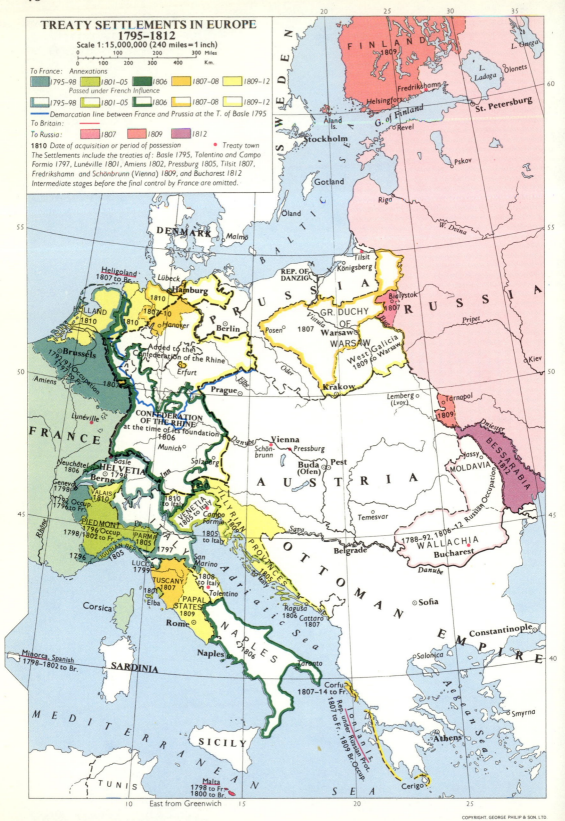

TREATY SETTLEMENTS IN EUROPE
1795–1812
Scale 1:15,000,000 (240 miles = 1 inch)

0   100   200   300 Miles

0   100   200   300   400 Km.

To France: *Annexations*

1795-98   1801-05   1806   1807-08   1809-12

Passed under French Influence

1795-98   1801-05   1806   1807-08   1809-12

Demarcation line between France and Prussia at the T. of Basle 1795

To Britain:

To Russia: 1807   1809   1812

1810 Date of acquisition or period of possession   • Treaty town

The Settlements include the treaties of: Basle 1795, Tolentino and Campo Formio 1797, Lunéville 1801, Amiens 1802, Pressburg 1805, Tilsit 1807, Fredrikshamn and Schönbrunn (Vienna) 1809, and Bucharest 1812. Intermediate stages before the final control by France are omitted.

COPYRIGHT. GEORGE PHILIP & SON. LTD.

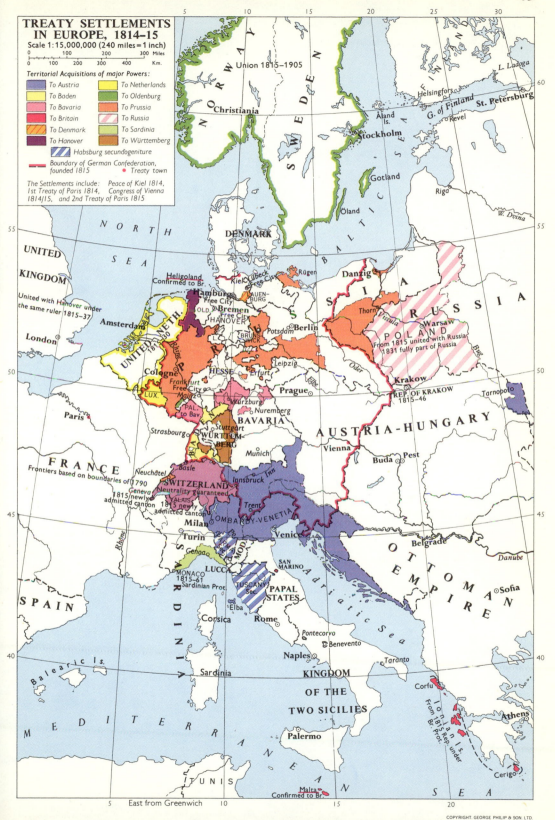

TREATY SETTLEMENTS
IN EUROPE, 1814–15
Scale 1:15,000,000 (240 miles = 1 inch)

Territorial Acquisitions of major Powers:

To Austria
To Baden
To Bavaria
To Britain
To Denmark
To Hanover
To Netherlands
To Oldenburg
To Prussia
To Russia
To Sardinia
To Württemberg
Habsburg secundogeniture
Boundary of German Confederation, founded 1815
Treaty town

The Settlements include: Peace of Kiel 1814,
1st Treaty of Paris 1814, Congress of Vienna
1814/15, and 2nd Treaty of Paris 1815

NORWAY
Union 1815–1905
Christiania
SWEDEN
FINLAND
L. Ladoga
Helsingfors
Åland Is.
G. of Finland
Revel
St. Petersburg
Stockholm
BALTIC SEA
Gotland
Öland
Riga
W. Dvina

NORTH SEA
DENMARK

UNITED KINGDOM
United with Hanover under the same ruler 1815–37
Amsterdam
London

Heligoland
Confirmed to Br.
Kiel
Lübeck
Free City
Rügen
Danzig
Hamburg
Free City
LAUEN-BURG
Thorn
Vistula
RUSSIA
POLAND
From 1815 united with Russia
1831 fully part of Russia
Warsaw
Bug

OLD.
Bremen
Free City
HANOVER
Potsdam
Berlin
BRUNS-WICK
P R U S S I A
Oder
Elbe
Leipzig
Erfurt

UNITED NETH.
Cologne
LUX.
PAL. to Bav.
HESSE
Frankfurt
Free City
Mainz
Würzburg
Nuremberg
Prague
Krakow
REP. OF KRAKOW
1815–46
Tarnopol

Paris
Strasbourg
B A D E N
Stuttgart
WÜRTTEM-BERG
BAVARIA
Munich
Vienna
Buda
Pest
AUSTRIA-HUNGARY

FRANCE
Frontiers based on boundaries of 1790
Neuchâtel
Basle
SWITZERLAND
Neutrality guaranteed.
Geneva
1815 newly admitted canton
VALAIS
1815 newly admitted canton
Innsbruck
Inn
Trent
LOMBARDY-VENETIA
Milan
Venice
Belgrade
Danube
OTTOMAN EMPIRE
Sofia

Rhône
Turin
Genoa
MOD.
LUCCA
MONACO
1815–61
Sardinian Prot.
S A R D I N I A
TUSCANY
Sec.
Elba
PAPAL STATES
Rome
SAN MARINO
Adriatic Sea

SPAIN
Balearic Is.
Corsica
Sardinia
KINGDOM
OF THE
TWO SICILIES
Pontecorvo
Benevento
Naples
Taranto
Corfu
From 1815 Rep. under Br. Prot.
Ionian Is.
Athens
Cerigo

M E D I T E R R A N E A N   S E A

Palermo

TUNIS
Malta
Confirmed to Br.

East from Greenwich

COPYRIGHT. GEORGE PHILIP & SON. LTD.

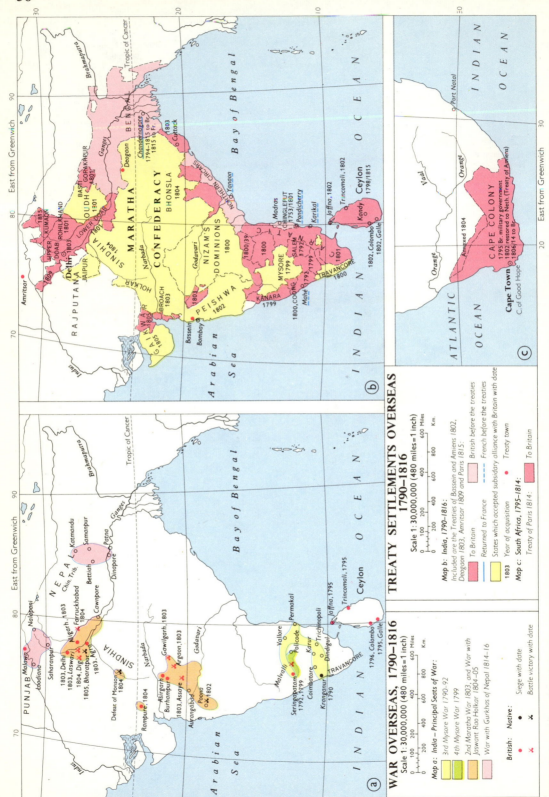

WAR OVERSEAS, 1790–1816

Scale 1 : 30,000,000 (480 miles=1 inch)

0 100 200 300 400 500 600 Miles
0 200 400 600 800 Km.

Map a: India – Principal Seats of War:

3rd Mysore War 1790–92

4th Mysore War 1799

2nd Maratha War 1803, and War with Jaswant Rao Holkar 1804–05

War with Gurkhas of Nepal 1814–16

British: Native:

Siege with date

Battle victory with date

Map b: India, 1790–1816:

Included are the Treaties of Bassein and Amiens 1802, Deogaon 1803, Amritsar 1809 and Paris 1815:

To Britain

Returned to France

States which accepted subsidary alliance with Britain with date

British before the treaties

French before the treaties

1803 Year of acquisition

Treaty town

Map c: South Africa, 1795–1814:

Treaty of Paris 1814:   To Britain

TREATY SETTLEMENTS OVERSEAS 1790–1816

Scale 1 : 30,000,000 (480 miles=1 inch)

0 100 200 300 400 500 600 Miles
0 200 400 600 800 Km.

THE CRIMEAN WAR, 1853–55

Scale 1:8,000,000 (128 miles=1 inch)

Km.
150   200   150   100
Miles
150   100   50   0

British–French:
(Declaration of war: March 27, 1854)
- Naval patrol
- Naval operations
- Campaign 1853–54
- Campaign 1855
- Fortress
- British–Turkish victory with date

Turkish:
(Declaration of war: October 4, 1853)
- Base
- Fortress
- Campaign 1853–54
- Campaign 1855
- British–Turkish victory with date

Russian:
- Naval patrol 1853–54
- Fortification line
- Naval base
- Base
- Fortress
- Campaign 1853–54
- Campaign 1855
- Victory with date

(a)

(b)

THE SEVASTOPOL CAMPAIGN
Scale 1:2,000,000 (32 miles=1 inch)

Km.
40   30   20   10   0
40 Miles
30   20   10   0

Inset (b) labels:
Crimea, Simferopol, Bakhchisarai, Yalta, Alma, Sept. 20, 1854, Kacha, Inkerman, Nov. 5, 1854, Chorgun, Sept. 30, 1854, Oct. 25, 1854, Balaklava, British Headquarters, Sevastopol, Sept. 8, 1855, Kamish, French Headquarters, SEPT. 19, 1854, Eupatoria, Feb. 17, 1855, FEB. 1855, JAN. 1855, MAY 1855 to Sea of Azov, BLACK SEA

R U S S I A N   E M P I R E, O T T O M A N   E M P I R E, B L A C K   S E A, Sea of Azov, Crimea, BESSARABIA, WALLACHIA, BULGARIA

Don, Taganrog, Azov, Yeisk, Mariupol, Berdyansk, Melitopol, Yekaterinoslav, Dnieper, Aleksandrovsk, Kherson, Perekop, Eupatoria, Sevastopol, Sept. 8, 1855, Simferopol, Yalta, Feodosiya, Kerch, Yekaterinodar, Novorossiysk, Sukhumi, Poti, Kutais, Batumi, Trebizond, Amasya, Erzurum, Hasankale, Kars, Akhaltsikhe, Aug. 16, 1855, Nov. 26, 1853, Dec. 1, 1853, Aug. 28–Nov. 28, 1855, JUNE 13, Sinope, Nov. 30, 1853, Ereğli, Bosporus, Üsküdar Skelesi, Scutari, Constantinople, Sea of Marmara, Bursa, Adrianople, Gallipoli, Dardanelles, Besika Bay, Ploydiv, Danube, Silistria, Pruth, Akkerman, Odessa, Ochakov, Varna, Allied base for Crimean Campaign 1854

Dates on routes: NOV. 30, 1853, NOV. 8, 1853, SEPT. 1853, SEPT. 1855, OCT. 1853, OCT. 1855, NOV. 1853, JAN. 1855, MAY 1855, SEPT. 1854, FEB. 1855

East from 30 Greenwich

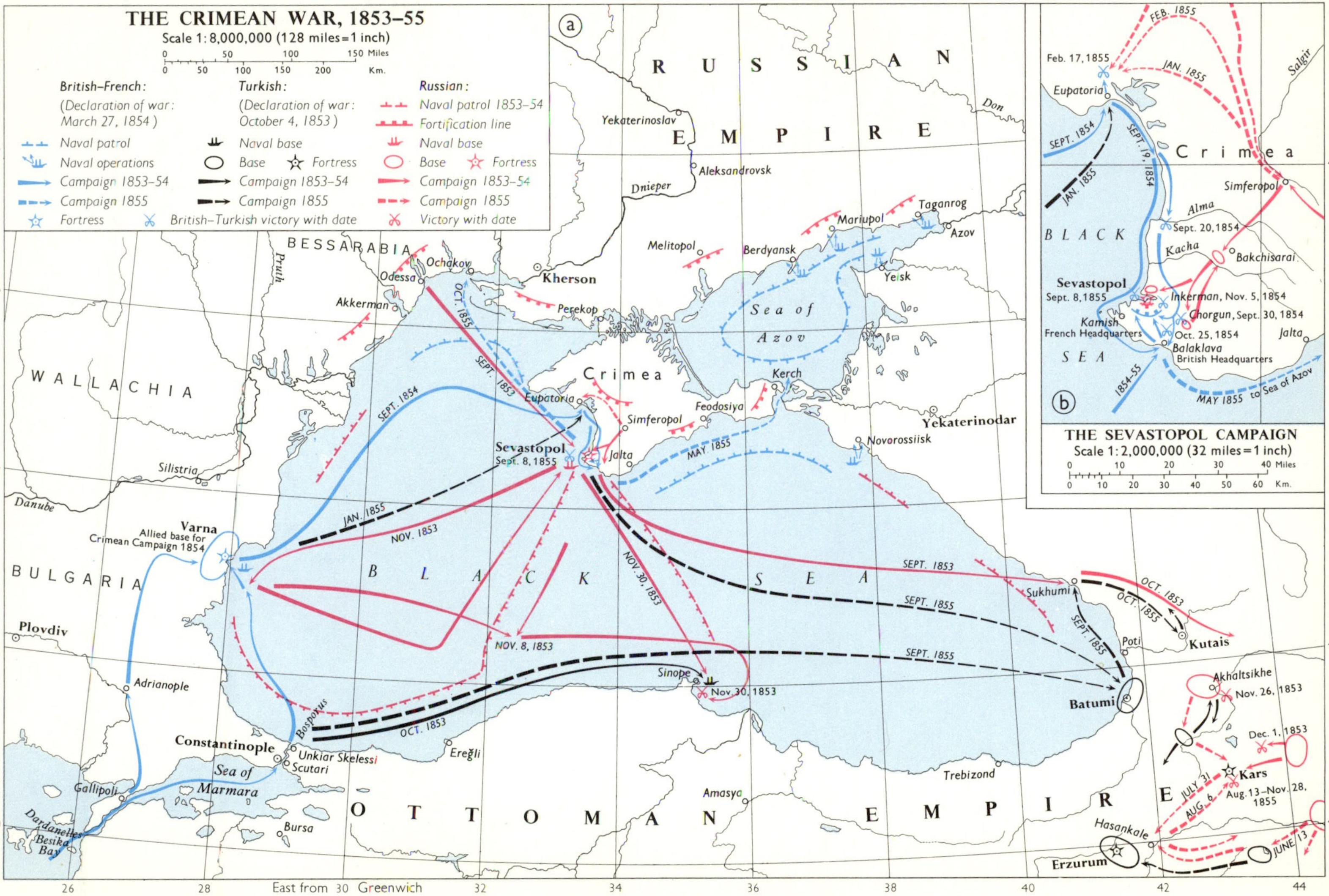

COPYRIGHT GEORGE PHILIP & SON LTD.

THE FIRST WORLD WAR, 1914–18
Scale 1:20,000,000 (320 miles=1 inch)

0   100   200   300   400 Miles
0   200   400   600 Km.

- ·—·—· Frontlines in August 1914
- – – – Russo-German frontier at the beginning of 1915
- ——— Frontlines in November 1918
- Central Powers at the outbreak of war
- States subsequently allied to Central Powers
- States neutral throughout the war
- ——— Max. extent of advance of Central Powers
- ⚓ Sea battle with date
- → Campaigns of the Entente 1918
- Entente Powers at the outbreak of war
- States neutral at the outbreak of war, later joining the Entente

10   East from Greenwich   15

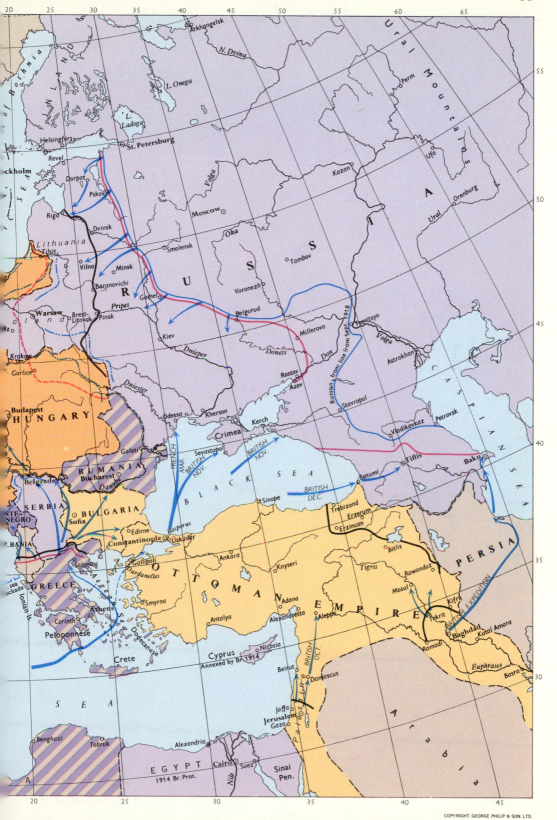

Arkhangelsk
N. Dvina
L. Onega
L. Ladoga
FINLAND
Helsingfors
St. Petersburg
Revel
Dorpat
Pskov
Riga
Dvinsk
Lithuania
Tilsit
Vilna
Minsk
Baranovichi
Smolensk
Gomel
Pripet
Warsaw
Brest-Litovsk
Pinsk
Kiev
Dnieper
Krakow
Gorlice
Dniester
Odessa
Kherson
Crimea
Kerch
Sevastopol
Moscow
Oka
Volga
Tambov
Voronezh
Belgorod
Donets
Millerovo
Don
Rostov
Azov
Kazan
Perm
Ufa
Orenburg
Ural
Ural Mountains
Tsaritsyn
Russian front line from Sept. 1918
Astrakhan
Stavropol
Vladikavkaz
Petrovsk
Tiflis
Baku
Batumi
CASPIAN SEA
R U S S I A
Budapest
HUNGARY
Galati
RUMANIA
Bucharest
Danube
Belgrade
SERBIA
BULGARIA
Sofia
MONTENEGRO
ALBANIA
Edirne
Constantinople
Üsküdar
Bosporus
Gallipoli
Dardanelles
Salonica
GREECE
Ionian Is.
Aegean Sea
Athens
Corinth
Peloponnese
Crete
Dodecanese
Smyrna
BLACK SEA
FRENCH MAR.
BRITISH NOV.
BRITISH DEC.
BRITISH OCT.
Sinope
Trebizond
Erzerum
Erzincan
Bitlis
Ankara
Kayseri
Adana
Alexandretta
Aleppo
Antalya
OTTOMAN EMPIRE
Tigris
Rawanduz
Mosul
Tekrit
Kifri
Baghdad
Kutal Amara
Ramadi
Euphrates
Basra
BRITISH EXPEDITION
PERSIA
Cyprus
Annexed by Br. 1914
Nicosia
Beirut
Damascus
Jaffa
Jerusalem
Gaza
Palestine
Arabia
SEA
Benghazi
Tobruk
Alexandria
Cairo
Suez
Nile
Sinai Pen.
EGYPT
1914 Br. Prot.

COPYRIGHT. GEORGE PHILIP & SON. LTD.

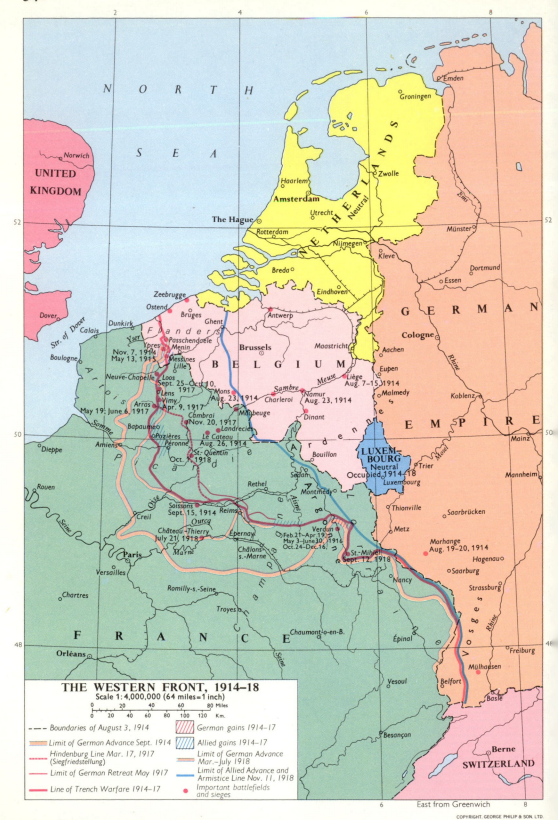

THE WESTERN FRONT, 1914–18
Scale 1 : 4,000,000 (64 miles = 1 inch)

0   20   40   60   80 Miles
0   20   40   60   80 100 120 Km.

- - - Boundaries of August 3, 1914

░░ German gains 1914–17

▬▬ Limit of German Advance Sept. 1914

░░ Allied gains 1914–17

▬▬ Hindenburg Line Mar. 17, 1917
    (Siegfriedstellung)

▬ Limit of German Advance
  Mar.–July 1918

▬ Limit of German Retreat May 1917

▬ Limit of Allied Advance and
  Armistice Line Nov. 11, 1918

▬ Line of Trench Warfare 1914–17

● Important battlefields
  and sieges

East from Greenwich

COPYRIGHT. GEORGE PHILIP & SON, LTD.

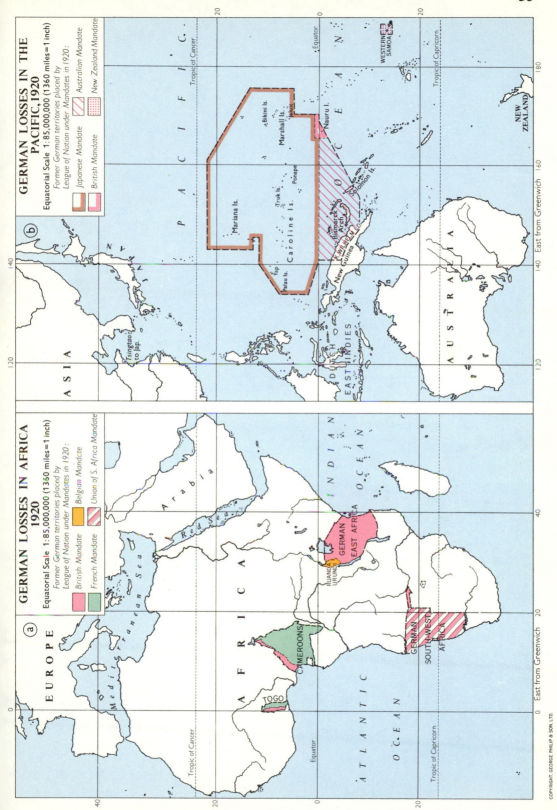

(a) GERMAN LOSSES IN AFRICA 1920

Equatorial Scale 1:85,000,000 (1350 miles=1 inch)

Former German territories placed by League of Nation under Mandates in 1920:

British Mandate   Belgian Mandate

French Mandate   Union of S. Africa Mandate

EUROPE

Mediterranean Sea

Arabia

Red Sea

A F R I C A

RUANDA URUNDI

GERMAN EAST AFRICA

INDIAN OCEAN

CAMEROONS

TOGO

GERMAN SOUTH-WEST AFRICA

ATLANTIC OCEAN

Tropic of Cancer

Equator

Tropic of Capricorn

East from Greenwich

(b) GERMAN LOSSES IN THE PACIFIC, 1920

Equatorial Scale 1:85,000,000 (1350 miles=1 inch)

Former German territories placed by League of Nation under Mandates in 1920:

Japanese Mandate   Australian Mandate

British Mandate   New Zealand Mandate

A S I A

Tsingtao to Jap.

J A P A N

P A C I F I C   O C E A N

Tropic of Cancer

Equator

WESTERN SAMOA

Nauru I.

Bikini Is.

Marshall Is.

Jaluit

Mariana Is.

Truk Is.

Caroline Is.

Ponape

Yap

Palau Is.

Solomon Is.

Bismarck Arch.

K. WILHELM

New Guinea

DUTCH EAST INDIES

A U S T R A L I A

NEW ZEALAND

Tropic of Capricorn

East from Greenwich

COPYRIGHT. GEORGE PHILIP & SON, LTD.

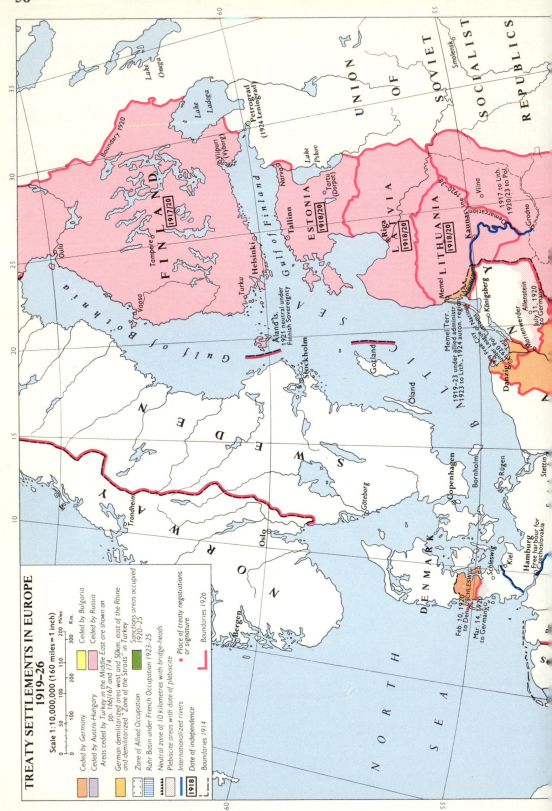

TREATY SETTLEMENTS IN EUROPE
1919–26

Scale 1:10,000,000 (160 miles = 1 inch)

200 Miles
300 Km.

Ceded by Germany
Ceded by Austro-Hungary
Areas ceded by Turkey in the Middle East are shown on pp. 166/167 and 174.
German demilitarized area west and 50km. east of the Rhine and demilitarized "Zone of the Straits" in Turkey

Ceded by Bulgaria
Ceded by Russia

Zone of Allied Occupation
Ruhr Basin under French Occupation 1923–25
Neutral zone of 10 kilometres with bridge-heads
Plebiscite areas with date of plebiscite
Internationalized rivers
Date of independence
Boundaries 1914

Sanctions areas occupied 1920–25

Place of treaty negotiations or signature

Boundaries 1926

1918

UNION   OF   SOVIET   SOCIALIST   REPUBLICS

Smolensk

Lake Onega

Lake Ladoga

Petrograd
(1924 Leningrad)

Boundary 1920

FINLAND
1917/20

Viipuri (Vyborg)

Oulu

Tampere

Vaasa

Turku

Helsinki

Gulf of Finland

Narva

Lake Pskov

Tartu (Dorpat)

ESTONIA
1918/20

Tallinn

Riga

LATVIA
1918/20

Demarcation Line 1920–28

Vilna

1917 to Lith.
1920/23 to Pol.

Grodno

LITHUANIA
1918/20

Kaunas

Memel

Königsberg

Morienwerder

Allenstein
July 11, 1920
to Germany

Memel Terr.
1919–23 under allied administ.
1923 to Lith. 1924 auton. region

Gulf of Bothnia

Åland Is.
1921 neutral under
Finnish Sovereignty

BALTIC   SEA

Stockholm

Gotland

Öland

Danzig

Free City

Treaty of Versailles

SWEDEN

Göteborg

Oslo

Trondheim

NORWAY

Bergen

Rügen

Bornholm

Stettin

Copenhagen

Kiel

Schleswig

Feb. 10, 1920
to Den.

SCHLESWIG

Mar. 14, 1920
to Germany

DENMARK

Hamburg
Free harbour for
Czechoslovakia

NORTH   SEA

POLAND

P O L A N D

1916/18

Warsaw

Kiev

Pripet

Pinsk

Brest-Litovsk

Kowel

1921 to Pol.

Lublin

Lodz

Kielce

Bug

Vistula

Krakow

Czestochowa

Katowice

TESCHEN 1920 to Pol.

Lvov

Czernowitz

1919/20 to Rum.

BESSARABIA
1918/20 to Rum.

Dniester

Pruth

Galati

Bucharest

Danube

1919/20 to Rum.

R U M A N I A

Debreczin

Temesvar

Tisza

1919/20 to Rum.

Koschau

Bratislava

C Z E C H O S L O V A K I A

1918/19

Hultschin 1919/20 to Cz.

Oppeln

Breslau

Olomouc

Brno

Prague

Elbe

Vltava

Dresden

Berlin

Leipzig

Erfurt

Hanover

Magdeburg

Cassel

Münster

Dortmund

Frankfurt

Münich

Ulm

Danube

Vienna

BURGENLAND
Dec.14, 1921 to Aust.

Sopron 1921 to Hung.

1920 to Hung.

Graz

Klagenfurt 1920 to Aust.

Oct.10,1920

A U S T R I A

1918/19

Budapest

H U N G A R Y

Zagreb

Sava

Drava

1920 to Yug.

1919 to Yug.

Y U G O S L A V I A

1918 1918-29 K. of the Croats, Slovenes and Serbs

Belgrade

Sarajevo

Craiova

Sofia

B U L G A R I A

1919 to Yug.

Tsaribrod 1919 to Yug.

Bosilegrad 1919 to Yug.

1919 to Yug.

Strumitsa

1919 to Greece

Adrianople

Constantinople

T U R K E Y

Sea of Marmara

Mudania 1922

1920-22 to Greece

Salonica

G R E E C E

MONTE-NEGRO 1921 to Yug.

Tirana Capital 1920

Durrës (Durazzo)

A L B A N I A

Scutari

Kotor (Cattaro)

Dubrovnik (Ragusa)

Lagosta 1920 to Italy

Pola 1920 to Italy

A D R I A T I C   S E A

Fiume Free City 1920-1924

Trieste

1919/20 to Italy

1919/20 to Italy

Venice

Trent

1919/20 to Italy

I T A L Y

Milan

Turin

Po

Genua

Rapallo

Florence

Rome

Corsica

Sardinia

Ligurian Sea

San Remo

Cannes

Marseilles

Nice

Genf

Locarno

Stresa

Lausanne

Berne

SWITZERLAND

Basle

Rhine

ALSACE LORRAINE 1919/20 to Fr.

SAAR 1919/20-35 League of N. Plebiscite 1935

Occup. until 1930

Occup. until 1926

Occup. until 1929

Strasbourg

Colmar

Colmar

Colmar

Malmédy Sept.20,1920, to Belg.

Eupen

Spa

LUX.

B E L G I U M

Brussels

Compiègne

Boulogne

F R A N C E

Seine

St. Germain

Neuilly

Sèvres

Trianon

Versailles

Paris

Lyons

Rhône

Saône

Amsterdam

The Hague

N E T H E R L A N D S

G E R M A N Y

Odor

M

BLACK SEA

Danube confirmed 1919

East from Greenwich

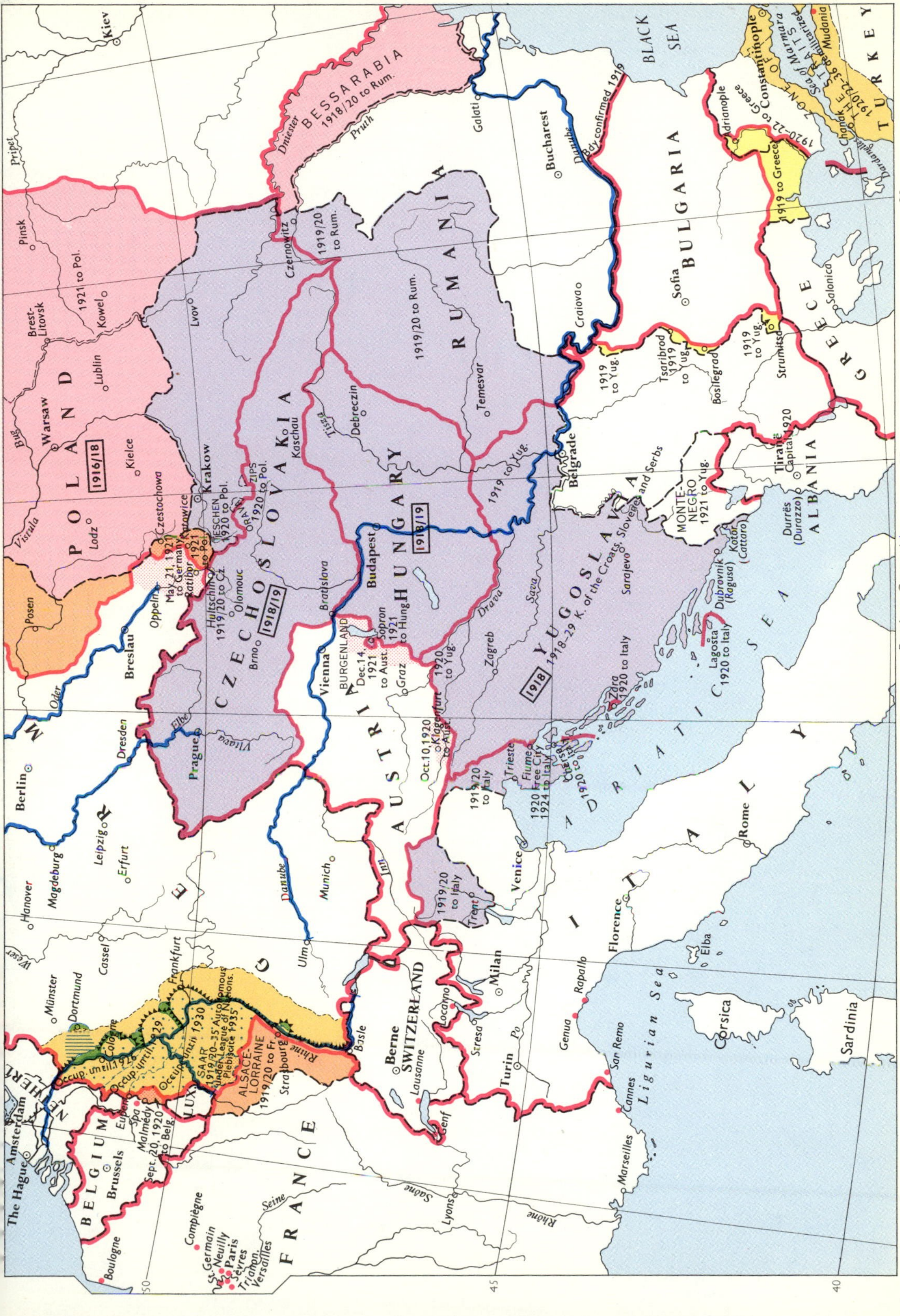

COPYRIGHT GEORGE PHILIP & SON, LTD.

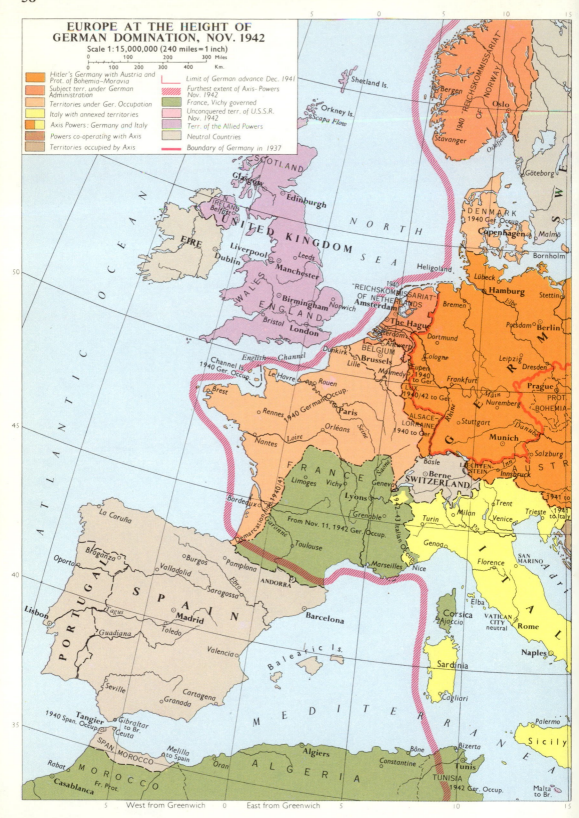

EUROPE AT THE HEIGHT OF GERMAN DOMINATION, NOV. 1942

Scale 1:15,000,000 (240 miles = 1 inch)

Hitler's Germany with Austria and Prot. of Bohemia–Moravia	Limit of German advance Dec. 1941
Subject terr. under German Administration	Furthest extent of Axis-Powers Nov. 1942
Territories under Ger. Occupation	France, Vichy governed
Italy with annexed territories	Unconquered terr. of U.S.S.R. Nov. 1942
Axis Powers: Germany and Italy	Terr. of the Allied Powers
Powers co-operating with Axis	Neutral Countries
Territories occupied by Axis	Boundary of Germany in 1937

West from Greenwich   East from Greenwich

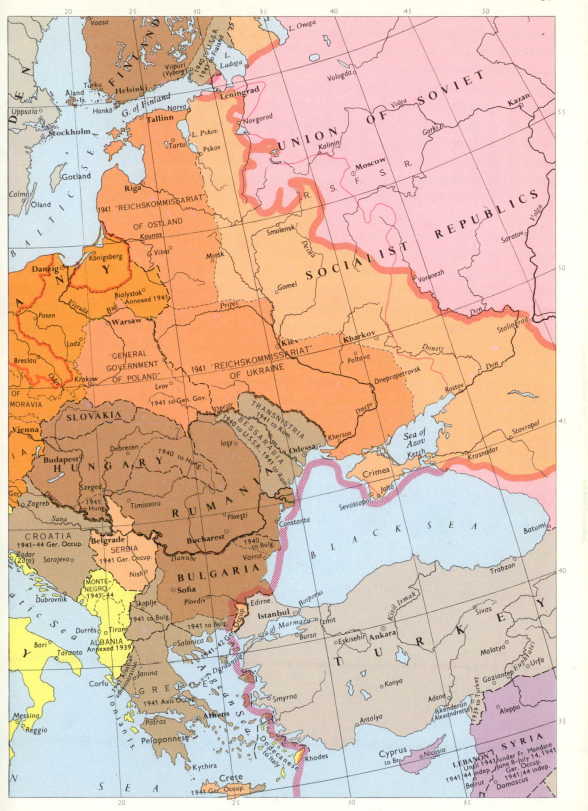
UNION OF SOVIET SOCIALIST REPUBLICS
R. S. F. S. R.
FINLAND
Vaasa
Turku
Helsinki
Aland Is.
Hankö
Viipuri (Vyborg)
1940 to U.S.S.R. 1941 to Finland
L. Onega
L. Ladoga
Vologda
Leningrad
G. of Finland
Narva
Tallinn
Novgorod
Volga
Kazan
Gorki
L. Pskov
Tartu
Pskov
Kalinin
Moscow
Uppsala
Stockholm
Gotland
Calmar
Öland
BALTIC SEA
Riga
1941 "REICHSKOMMISSARIAT" OF OSTLAND
Kaunas
Vilna
Minsk
Smolensk
Desna
Saratov
Königsberg
Danzig
Bialystok Annexed 1941
Vistula
Bug
Posen
Warsaw
Gomel
Voronezh
Pripet
Don
Stalingrad
Lodz
Kiev
Kharkov
Poltava
Donets
Breslau
Oder
"GENERAL GOVERNMENT OF POLAND"
Krakow
Lvov
1941 "REICHSKOMMISSARIAT" OF UKRAINE
Dnepropetrovsk
Rostov
OF MORAVIA
1941 to Gen. Gov.
Dnestr
TRANSNISTRIA 1941 to Rum.
BESSARABIA 1940 to U.S.S.R. 1941 to Rum.
Dnepr
Kherson
Odessa
Sea of Azov
Kerch
Stavropol
Krasnodar
SLOVAKIA
Vienna
Budapest
HUNGARY
Debrecen
1940 to Hung.
Iaşy
RUMANIA
Crimea
Jalta
Sevastopol
Szeged
Timisoara
1941 Hung.
Zagreb
Drava
Sava
Ploeşti
Bucharest
Constanta
BLACK SEA
Batumi
CROATIA 1941–44 Ger. Occup.
Belgrade
SERBIA 1941 Ger. Occup.
Danube
1940 to Bulg.
Varna
Zadar (Zara)
Sarajevo
Nish
BULGARIA
Sofia
Plovdiv
Trabzon
MONTE-NEGRO 1941–44
Dubrovnik
Skoplje
1941 to Bulg.
Edirne
Ger. Occup.
Istanbul
Bosporus
Kizil Irmak
Sivas
TURKEY
Durrës
Tirane
1941 to Bulg.
Sea of Marmara
Izmit
Bursa
Eskisehir
Ankara
Bari
Taranto
ALBANIA Annexed 1939
Salonica
1941–42 Ger.
Dardanelles
Malatya
Euphrates
Urfa
Janina
1941 Albanian administration
Corfu
GREECE
Aegean Sea
Konya
Gaziantep
Smyrna
1941 Axis Occup.
Athens
Adana
Iskenderun (Alexandretta)
1939 to Turkey
Aleppo
Messina
Reggio
Patras
Ionian Is.
Peloponnese
Antalya
Dodecanese to Italy
Rhodes
Cyprus to Br.
Nicosia
SYRIA
LEBANON
Until 1941 under Fr. Mandate
June 8–July 14, 1941 Ger. Occup.
1941/44 indep.
Beirut
Damascus
Kythira
Crete
1941 Ger. Occup.
SEA
20
25
30
35
40
45
50
55

COPYRIGHT GEORGE PHILIP & SON LTD

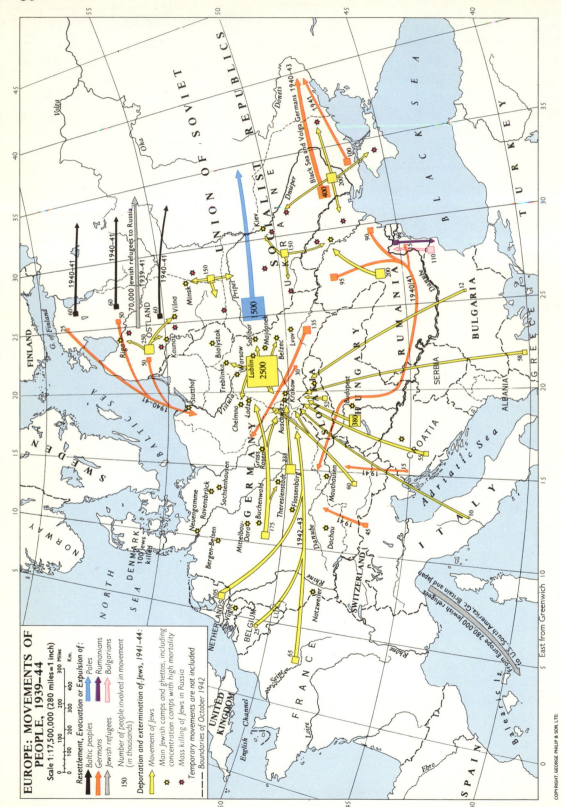

EUROPE: MOVEMENTS OF PEOPLE, 1939–44

Scale 1:17,500,000 (280 miles=1 inch)

Km.
300 Miles

Resettlement, Evacuation or Expulsion of:
Baltic peoples
Germans
Rumanians
Jewish refugees
Bulgarians

150 Number of people involved in movement (in thousands)

Deportation and extermination of Jews, 1941–44:

Movement of Jews

Main Jewish camps and ghettos, including concentration camps with high mortality

Mass killing of Jews in Russia

Temporary movements are not included

Boundaries of October 1942

COPYRIGHT. GEORGE PHILIP & SON, LTD.

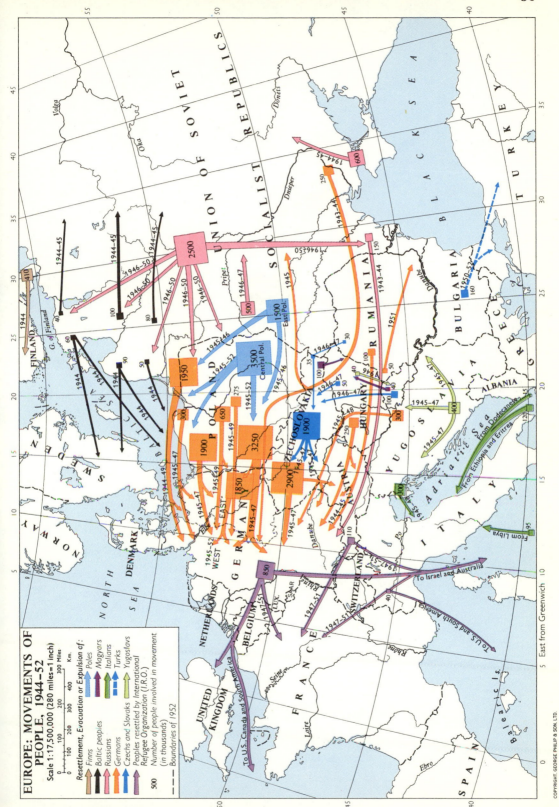

EUROPE: MOVEMENTS OF
PEOPLE, 1944-52

Scale 1:17,500,000 (280 miles=1 inch)

Resettlement, Evacuation or Expulsion of:

Finns Poles
Baltic peoples Magyars
Russians Italians
Germans Turks
Czechs and Slovaks Yugoslavs

Peoples resettled by International
Refugee Organization (I.R.O.)

500 Number of people involved in movement
(in thousands)

- - - Boundaries of 1952

COPYRIGHT. GEORGE PHILIP & SON, LTD.

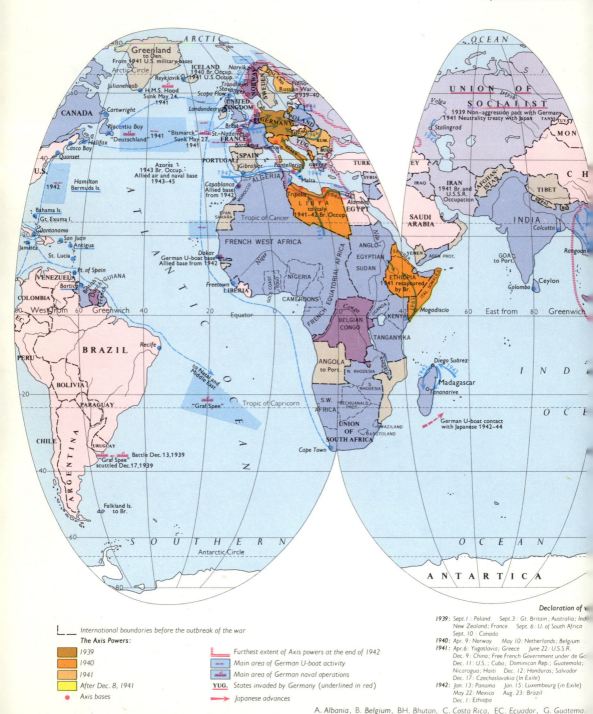

THE SECOND WORLD

Equatorial Scale 1:130,000,00

Map labels (selected, as shown):

ARCTIC OCEAN

Greenland to Den.
From 1941 U.S. military bases
Arctic Circle
ICELAND
1940 Br. Occup.
1941 U.S.Occup.
Narvik
Reykjavik
Trondheim
Stavanger
Scapa Flow
H.M.S. Hood Sunk May 24, 1941
Julianehaab
Cartwright
CANADA
Placentia Bay
"Deutschland" 1941
"Bismarck" Sunk May 27, 1941
Halifax
Casco Bay
Quonset
Hamilton Bermuda Is.
1942
U.S.
Bahama Is.
Gt. Exuma I.
Guantanamo
San Juan
Jamaica
Antigua
St. Lucia
Pt. of Spain
Barticia
Dutch GUIANA
VENEZUELA
COLOMBIA
West from Greenwich
PERU
BRAZIL
Recife
BOLIVIA
PARAGUAY
to Natal and Middle East
"Graf Spee"
Tropic of Capricorn
CHILE
URUGUAY
"Graf Spee" Battle Dec. 13, 1939
scuttled Dec.17, 1939
ARGENTINA
Falkland Is. to Br.
SOUTHERN OCEAN
Antarctic Circle

UNITED KINGDOM
Londonderry
Brest
St-Nazaire
FRANCE
Bordeaux
Genoa
SPAIN
PORTUGAL
Gibraltar
Azores
1943 Br. Occup.
Allied air and naval base 1943-45
Casablanca
Allied base from 1942
MOROCCO
ALGERIA
SPAN. SAHARA
Tropic of Cancer
Dakar
German U-boat base
Allied base from 1942
Freetown
LIBERIA
FRENCH WEST AFRICA
GOLD COAST
TOGO
NIGERIA
CAMEROONS
FRENCH EQUATORIAL AFRICA
Equator
ANGOLA to Port.
N. RHODESIA
S. RHODESIA
S.W. AFRICA
BECHUANALAND PROT.
SWAZILAND
BASUTOLAND
UNION OF SOUTH AFRICA
Cape Town

NORWAY
SWEDEN
FINLAND
Russian War 1939-40
GERMANY
POLAND
YUG.
RUM.
BULG.
GREECE
Pantelleria
Malta
LIBYA to Italy 1941-42 Br. Occup.
EGYPT
Alamein
TURKEY
SYRIA
IRAQ
IRAN
1941 Br. and U.S.S.R. Occupation
AFGHANISTAN
SAUDI ARABIA
YEMEN
ADEN PROT.
ANGLO-EGYPTIAN SUDAN
ETHIOPIA 1941 recaptured by Br.
Mogadiscio
KENYA
UGANDA
BELGIAN CONGO
Congo
TANGANYIKA
Diego Suarez
Madagascar
Tananarive
German U-boat contact with Japanese 1942-44

UNION OF SOCIALIST
Volga
1939 Non-aggression pact with Germany
1941 Neutrality treaty with Japan
Stalingrad
TIBET
NEPAL
BHUTAN
INDIA
Calcutta
Rangoon
GOA to Port.
Colombo
Ceylon
INDIAN OCEAN

Declaration of w

1939: Sept.1 : Poland   Sept.3 : Gt. Britain ; Australia; Ind
New Zealand; France   Sept. 6 : U. of South Africa
Sept. 10 : Canada
1940: Apr. 9 : Norway   May 10: Netherlands; Belgium
1941: Apr.6: Yugoslavia; Greece   June 22: U.S.S.R.
Dec. 9 : China; Free French Government under de Ga
Dec. 11 : U.S. ; Cuba; Dominican Rep.; Guatemala;
Nicaragua; Haiti   Dec. 12: Honduras; Salvador
Dec. 17: Czechoslovakia (In Exile)
1942: Jan. 13: Panama   Jan. 15: Luxembourg (in Exile)
May 22: Mexico   Aug. 23: Brazil
Dec. 1: Ethiopia

A. Albania, B. Belgium, BH. Bhutan, C. Costa Rica, EC. Ecuador, G. Guatema

Legend:

International boundaries before the outbreak of the war

The Axis Powers:

1939
1940
1941
After Dec. 8, 1941

• Axis bases

Furthest extent of Axis powers at the end of 1942
Main area of German U-boat activity
Main area of German naval operations
YUG. States invaded by Germany (underlined in red)
→ Japanese advances

MOLLWEIDE'S INTERRUPTED EQUAL AREA PROJECTION

WAR, 1939–45

(2080 miles = 1 inch)

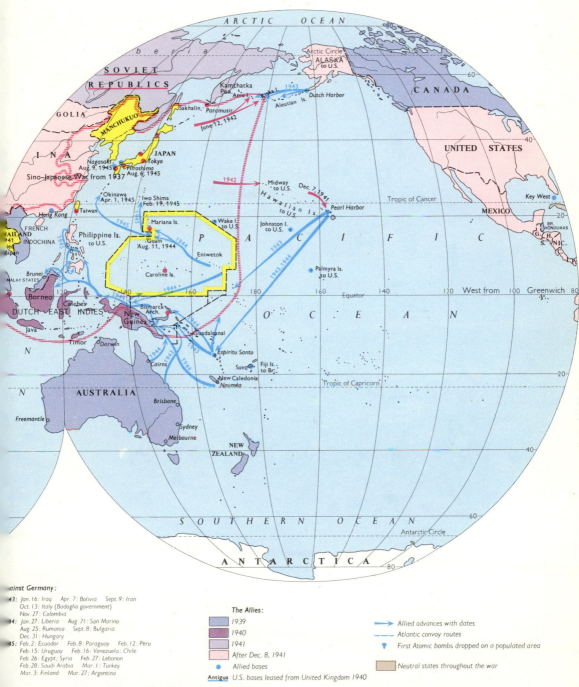

ARCTIC OCEAN

Arctic Circle

ALASKA
to U.S.

SOVIET
REPUBLICS

CANADA

Siberia

GOLIA

MANCHUKUO

Kamchatka
Pen.

Attu I.

Kiska I. 1943

Dutch Harbor

Sakhalin Paramusir

Aleutian Is.

June 12, 1942

UNITED STATES

INA

JAPAN

Nagasaki
Aug. 9, 1945

Tokyo

Hiroshima
Aug. 6, 1945

Sino-Japanese War from 1937

1942

Midway
to U.S.

Dec. 7, 1941

Hawarian Is.
to U.S.

Tropic of Cancer

Key West

MEXICO

Hong Kong

Taiwan

Okinawa
Apr. 1, 1945

Iwo Shima
Feb. 19, 1945

Pearl Harbor

Wake I.
to U.S.

BR.
HONDURAS
G. H.

1945

FRENCH

THAILAND
41
 led
Japan

INDOCHINA

Philippine Is.
to U.S.

Mariana Is.

Johnston I.
to U.S.

S. NIC.

Guam
Aug. 11, 1944

1944

P A C I F I C

1943

Eniwetok

1943 1944

Palmyra Is.
to U.S.

Caroline Is.

1944

Brunei
MALAY STATES

Borneo

Celebes

160

180

Equator

140

120

West from 100 Greenwich 80

DUTCH EAST INDIES

New
Guinea

Bismarck
Arch.

O   C   E   A   N

Java

Timor

Darwin

Guadalcanal

1944

Espiritu Santo

20

Cairns

1944

Suva

Fiji Is.
to Br.

New Caledonia
Nouméa

Tropic of Capricorn

AUSTRALIA

Brisbane

Freemantle

Sydney

Melbourne

NEW
ZEALAND

40

SOUTHERN OCEAN

Antarctic Circle

60

ANTARCTICA

80

COPYRIGHT. GEORGE PHILIP & SON. LTD.

ainst Germany:

43: Jan.16: Iraq   Apr. 7: Bolivia   Sept. 9: Iran
Oct.13: Italy (Badoglio government)
Nov. 27: Colombia

44: Jan.27: Liberia   Aug. 21: San Marino
Aug. 25: Rumania   Sept. 8: Bulgaria
Dec. 31: Hungary

45: Feb. 2: Ecuador   Feb. 8: Paraguay   Feb. 12: Peru
Feb.15: Uruguay   Feb.16: Venezuela; Chile
Feb. 26: Egypt; Syria   Feb. 27: Lebanon
Feb. 28: Saudi Arabia   Mar. 1: Turkey
Mar. 3: Finland   Mar. 27: Argentina

, Honduras, N. Netherlands, NIC. Nicaragua. P. Panama, S. Salvador,

The Allies:

1939

1940

1941

After Dec. 8, 1941

• Allied bases

Antigua U.S. bases leased from United Kingdom 1940

→ Allied advances with dates

---- Atlantic convoy routes

▼ First Atomic bombs dropped on a populated area

Neutral states throughout the war

January: 0°C (32°F)

NORWEGIAN SEA

Reykjavík
Iceland
Lofoten Is.

Faroe Is.

Shetland Is.

ATLANTIC OCEAN

Hebrides
Orkney Is.
Scotland
Edinburgh
Beech
Oslo
Vänern
Stockholm
Vättern
Gotland
BALTIC
Skagerrak
Kattegat
Beech
Zealand
Fünen

Ireland
C. Clear

NORTH SEA

Wales
England
London
Thames
Land's End

English Channel

Elbe
Berlin
Magdeburg
Oder
Sudeten
Harz
Cologne
Frankfurt
Er. Geb.
Prague
Vistula

Bay of Biscay
Bordeaux

C. Finisterre

Seine
Paris
Loire

Central Massif
Vosges
Black Forest
Munich
Danube
Vienna
Drava
Budap
Sava

Cantabrian Mts.
Duero
Pyrenees
Beech
Lyons
Rhône
Milan
Venice
Po
Apennines
Adriatic Alps
Dinaric Alps
Adriatic Sea

Lisbon
Madrid
Castle Aragon
Tagus
Sierra Morena
Valencia
Ebro
Barcelona
Corsica
Florence
Rome

Seville
Balearic Is.
Marseilles
Sardinia
Naples
Tyrrhenian Sea

C. St. Vincent
Sierra Nevada
Str. of Gibraltar

Rif
Great Atlas
Maritime Atlas
Saharan Atlas

MEDITERRANEAN

Sicily
C. Bon
Malta

Ionian Sea

10   5   West from Greenwich 0 East from Greenwich   5   10   15

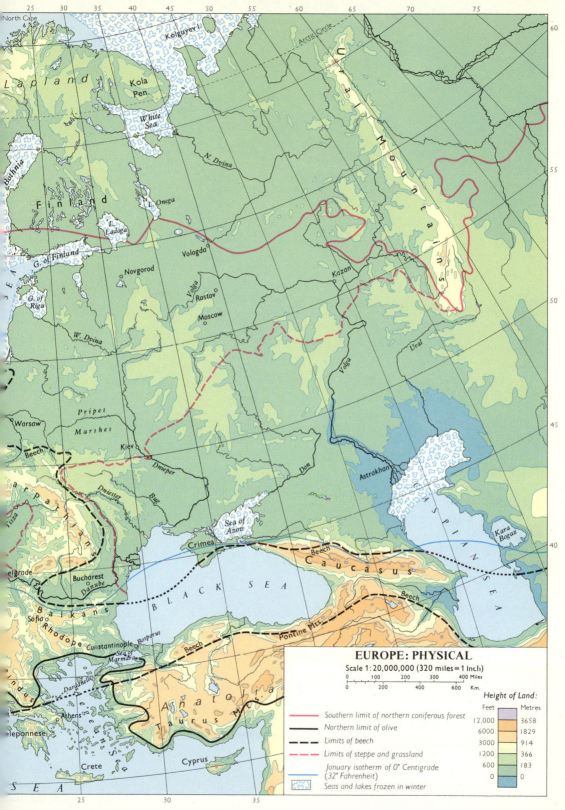

EUROPE: PHYSICAL

Scale 1:20,000,000 (320 miles = 1 inch)

| 0 | 100 | 200 | 300 | 400 Miles |

| 0 | 200 | 400 | 600 Km. |

Height of Land:

	Feet	Metres
	12,000	3658
	6000	1829
	3000	914
	1200	366
	600	183
	0	0

Southern limit of northern coniferous forest
Northern limit of olive
Limits of beech
Limits of steppe and grassland
January isotherm of 0° Centigrade (32° Fahrenheit)
Seas and lakes frozen in winter

COPYRIGHT. GEORGE PHILIP & SON. LTD.

NORTH SEA

Dornoch 1222
Elgin 1224
Aberdeen 12 Cent.
c.1450 to Glasgow
St. Andrews 1472
Glasgow 1492

Viborg c.1060
Ribe 948

Carlisle 1133
Durham 995
York 7 Cent.
Reorganisation 11/12 Cent.

Reorganisation 1152
Tuam 1152
Armagh 445
Dublin 1040 1152
Cashel 1152
St. Davids

Hereford 680
Coventry 1102
Norwich 1094
Bath 1088
Salisbury 1072
Exeter 1050
Thames
London 604
Canterbury 597

Bremen 845
Osnabrück 772
Münster 804
Cologne 795
Liège
Tournai 1146
Mainz 782
Worms
Trier c.800
Metz
Toul
Strassburg 4 Cent.

ATLANTIC OCEAN

St. Malo
Dol 848
Bayeux
Rouen 260
Arras
Amiens
Paris
Seine
Reims 774
Chalons

Nantes
Tours
Orléans
Sens 245
Loire
Bourges 3 Cent.
Autun
Constance 6
Besançon 2 Cent.
Lausanne

Bay of Biscay

Maillezais 1317
Limoges
Tulle 1317
Lyons 178
Vienne 1 Cent.
Tarantaise 794
Milan 324
Turin 1518
1471 exempt
Embrun 794
Genoa 1133

Bordeaux 314
Sarlat
Garonne
Before 1120 to Arles
Avignon 1475
Aix c.800
Arles 417

Santiago de Compostela 1120
Oviedo 1105 exempt
Leon 792
Astorga
Auch 879
Toulouse 1317
Montauban
Narbonne 4 Cent.
to Genoa

714–1091 to Auch, before 1318 to Tarragona
714–1091 to Narbonne
Ampurias
Reorganisation 1077/1133

Braga 1104 renewed
1026–1120 to Toledo
Palencia
Burgos 1574
Salamanca
Segovia 1110
Siguenza
1121
1118
Saragossa 1318
Lerida 1149
Vich
Tarragona 517
Tortosa 1148
1091 renewed
Sassari 1050

Coimbra 1064
Duero
Reorganisation after the Reconquest
Tagus

Lisbon 1393
Badajoz 1255
Evora 1166 1544
S. Marco de Leon, Priorate of Knighthood 13 Cent.
Toledo 681 1088 renewed
Guadiana
Segorbe
Valencia 1458

Majorca
Palma
1237–1775 to Majorca
1237 exempt 1492 to Valencia
to Tarragona

Oristano 11 Cent.
Cagli 11 Ce

Silves 1253
Cordoba 1238
Seville 1248
Cadiz 1267
Granada 1492
Malaga 1487
Almeria 1492
Cartagena—Murcia

MEDITERRAN

West from Greenwich
East from Greenwich

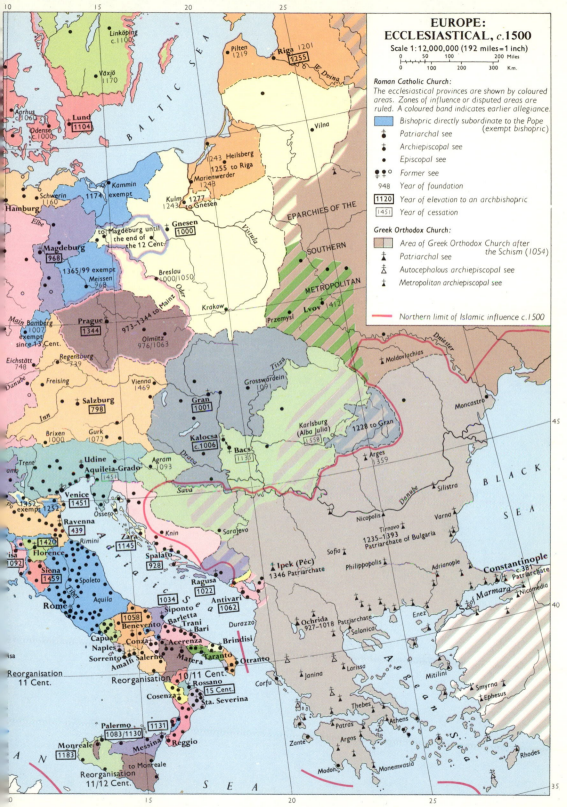

EUROPE: ECCLESIASTICAL, c.1500

Scale 1:12,000,000 (192 miles = 1 inch)

0 — 50 — 100 — 200 Miles
0 — 100 — 200 — 300 Km.

Roman Catholic Church:
The ecclesiastical provinces are shown by coloured areas. Zones of influence or disputed areas are ruled. A coloured band indicates earlier allegiance.

✠ Bishopric directly subordinate to the Pope (exempt bishopric)

✝ Patriarchal see

✠ Archiepiscopal see

• Episcopal see

✠ ✝ ○ Former see

948 Year of foundation

☐1120 Year of elevation to an archbishopric

▢1451 Year of cessation

Greek Orthodox Church:

▨ Area of Greek Orthodox Church after the Schism (1054)

✝ Patriarchal see

△ Autocephalous archiepiscopal see

✝ Metropolitan archiepiscopal see

━━ Northern limit of Islamic influence c.1500

Linköping c.1100
Växjö 1170
Agrhus c.1060
Odense c.1000
Lund 1104
Pilten 1219
Riga 1201 1255
W. Dvina
BALTIC SEA
Vilna
Schwerin 1160
Kammin 1174 exempt
1243 Heilsberg 1255 to Riga
Marienwerder 1243
Hamburg
Elbe
Kulm 1277 1243 to Gnesen
to Magdeburg until the end of the 12 Cent.
Gnesen 1000
EPARCHIES OF THE
Magdeburg 968
1365/99 exempt Meissen 968
Breslau 1000/1050
Oder
Krakow
Przemysl
SOUTHERN
Vistula
Main Bamberg 1007 exempt since 13 Cent.
Prague 1344
973–1344 to Mainz
Olmütz 976/1063
METROPOLITAN
Lvov 1412
Eichstätt 748
Danube
Regensburg 739
Freising
Vienna 1469
Grosswardein 1091
Moldovlachias
Dniester
Salzburg 798
Inn
Gran 1001
Karlsburg (Alba Julia) 1558
1228 to Gran
Moncastro
Brixen 1000
Gurk 1072
Kalocsa c.1006
Bacs 1135
Arges 1359
BLACK SEA
Trent amb
Udine Aquileia-Grado 1451
Agram 1093
Drava
Venice 1451
Po exempt 1252
Osson
Sava
Danube
Silistra
Ravenna 439
Rimini
Knin
Sarajevo
Sofia
Nicopolis
Tirnovo 1235–1393 Patriarchate of Bulgaria
Varna
Zara 1145
Spalato 928
Ragusa 1022
Ipek (Péc) 1346 Patriarchate
Philippopolis
Adrianople
Constantinople c.381 Patriarchate
isa 1092
Florence
Siena 1459
Spoleto
Antivari 1062
Durazzo
Ochrida 927–1018 Patriarchate
Salonica
Enez
S. of Marmara
Nicomedia
Rome
Aquila
1034
Siponto
Barletta Trani Bari
Brindisi
Capua 1058 Benevento Conza Acerenza
Naples Salerno Matera Taranto
Sorrento Amalfi
Otranto
Reorganisation 11 Cent.
Reorganisation 10/11 Cent.
Rossano 15 Cent.
Cosenza Sta. Severina
Corfu
Janina
Larissa
Mitilini
Smyrna
Ephesus
Palermo 1083/1130 1131
Monreale 1183
Messina Reggio
to Monreale
Reorganisation 11/12 Cent.
Zante
Argos
Thebes
Athens
Patras
Monemvasia
Modon
Rhodes
AEGEAN SEA
ADRIATIC Sea
N SEA

COPYRIGHT. GEORGE PHILIP & SON. LTD.

Christiania 1811 · Uppsala 1477 ▲ 1710

NORTH SEA

Aberdeen 1494
St. Andrews 1411
Glasgow 1451 · Edinburgh 1582

Dublin 1591

ATLANTIC OCEAN

Cambridge 1209
Oxford 1190 · London 1828 1663

Groningen 1614
Amsterdam 1631 · Harderwijk 1648 1814
Leiden 1575 · Osnabrück 1630 1633
Utrecht 1636 · Münster 1780 1818 · Paderborn 1614 1819
Louvain 1426 1793 1816 · Cologne 1388 1798
Bonn 1777 1797 · Marburg 1527
Giessen 1607 · 1734

Caen 1432
Paris c.1150 1701
Trier 1473 1797 · Mainz 1476 1798
Pont-à-Mousson 1572 · Heidelberg 1385
Rennes 1735
Angers 1337 · Orléans 1235
Nancy 1572 · Strasbourg 1567 · Tübingen 1477
Nantes 1460 · Bourges 1464
Poitiers 1431
Dijon 1722 · Besançon 1485 · Freiburg 1455
Basle 1460 · Zürich 1523,183
Dôle 1422 1481 · Berne 1528
Lausanne 1537
Geneva 1559

1792 Abolition of all French Universities and Academies. Reorganisation 1795/1806

Lyons 1808
Vercelli 1228
Grenoble 1339 · Turin 1404 1757 · Pavia 139
Bordeaux 1441 · Valence 1452/59 · Piacenza 1248
Cahors 1321 1751 · Orange 1365 1793
Santiago de Compostela 1506 · Oviedo 1604 · Genoa 1243
Orthez 1561 1722 · Avignon 1303 · Aix 1409
Pau 1722 · Toulouse 1233 · Montpellier 1289
Valladolid 1346 · Palencia 1208 · Huesca 1359 · Perpignan 1349
Salamanca 1243 · Saragossa 1474 · Lerida 1300
Siguenza 1489 1835 · Cervera 1717
Coimbra 1290 · Madrid 1736 1713 · Alcalá 1508 1836 · Barcelona 1430

Bay of Biscay

Lisbon 1290
Evora 1550
Valencia 1500 · Palma 1483 · Cagliari 1626
Seville 1502
Granada 1540

MEDITERRANE

West from Greenwich · East from Greenwich

Stockholm · Åbo (Turku) moved to Helsingfors · Dorpat. △ St. Petersburg · Moscow · Kazan
39 1753 · 1640 · 1827 1632 1656 1801 · 1724 · 1755 · 1804

EUROPE:
UNIVERSITIES TO 1830
Scale 1:12,000,000 (192 miles = 1 inch)
0   50   100   200 Miles
0   100   200   300 Km.

University · Academy of Sciences
● ▲ Foundation before 1400
● ▲ Foundation 1400–1600
● ▲ Foundation after 1600

1367   Year of foundation
1793   Year of cessation

BALTIC SEA

W. Dvina

Copenhagen
1478 1743

Lund
1668

Königsberg
1544

Vilna
1578 1831

Kiel
65

Greifswald 1456

Bützow
1760 1789

Rostock
1419

Elbe

Berlin
1701/1812

Frankfurt
506 1811

Oder

Breslau
1702

Vistula

Krakow
1364

Lvov
1784

Dniester

nstedt 1576
809

Wittenberg
1502 1806

tingen
1734

Halle

379 1816

Leipzig
1409

rt

Jena
1558

rzburg

Prague
1348 1759

Bamberg
1648 1803

Olmütz
1573 1778

Erlangen
1743

olstadt
9 1800

Danube

Tyrnau
1635 1770

Tissa

Dillingen
549 1804

Landshut
1800 1826

Linz
1669

Pressburg
1467

549 1804

Munich
1759

Vienna
1365

Buda (Ofen)
1777

Salzburg
1623 1810

1389 1526

Inn

Innsbruck
1763,1792 1810

Graz
1585

Drava

Danube

Sava

Fünfkirchen
1367 1526

BLACK SEA

Vicenza
1204

Treviso
1318

Padua
1222 1779

rma
502

Ferrara 1391

Bologna
1200 1712

lo

3 1200 1712

1349 Florence
1582

1215

Arezzo

Urbino
1564

Siena
1300

Perugia
1276

Camerino
1727

S. of Marmara

Rome
1603

1303

Aegean Sea

Naples
1224

Salerno
1173

N

Palermo
1621 1637

Messina
1549

Catania
1434

SEA

15   20   25

COPYRIGHT. GEORGE PHILIP & SON. LTD.

EUROPE, c.1500

Scale 1:15,000,000 (240 miles=1 inch)

0   100   200   300 Miles

0   100   200   300   400 Km.

━━━ *Boundary of the Holy Roman Empire*
■ *Church Lands*
■ *Lands of the Union of Calmar*
■ *Electorate of Brandenburg*
■ *Saxony (Electorate and Duchy)*
■ *Lands of the House of Habsburg*
■ *Bohemia and Hungary, united under the same crown from 1490*
■ *Venetian Lands*

Faroe Is.
1380 to Den.

Shetland Is.
1468 to Scot.

Orkney Is.
1468 to Scot.

Sărna

Union of C
1397–152

Bergen

Oslo

Göteborg

SCOTLAND

DENMARK – NORWAY

Aalborg

Copenhagen

Malm

Bornholm

Edinburgh

I. OF MAN

York

SCHLESWIG

HOLSTEIN

NORTH SEA

ATLANTIC OCEAN

Hebrides

IRELAND

Dublin

WALES
Incorporated
into England
1535

ENGLAND

Oxford   Cambridge

London

Amsterdam
HOLLAND

Utrecht

ZEELAND

Bremen

Hamburg

BRANDENBURG

Ber

THE

Magdeburg

Berlin

E

English Channel

Channel Is.

FLANDERS   Brussels
Calais   BRABANT
ARTOIS
HAINAUT

LUX.

Cologne

Aachen

Rhine

Trier

Frankfurt

Nuremberg

M

P

I

SAXONY

Dresden

BOH
Prague

BRITTANY

NORMANDY

Paris

Seine

LORRAINE

Strassburg

Danube

BAVARIA

Munich

Nantes

FRANCE

Loire

BURGUNDY

Basle

Berne

SWISS
CONFEDERATION

TYROL

CARINTHI

Bordeaux

Charolais

Lyons

Geneva

SAVOY
Turin
1499–1512,
1515–21 to Fr.

Milan
1499–1512,
1515–28 to Fr.

Venice

Ferrara

CARN

Garonne

Toulouse

Rhône

NAVARRE
1512 to Spain

Pamplona

Avignon
to the Papacy

Marseilles

Genoa
1499–1512,
1515–28 to Fr.

Pisa

San
Marino

Florence

PAPAL
STATES

Siena

PORTUGAL

Lisbon

La Coruña

Valladolid

Duero

SPAIN

Madrid

CASTILE

Toledo

Tagus

Guadiana

Seville

ARAGON

Saragossa

Ebro

United 1479

Valencia

Barcelona

ANDORRA

ROUSSILLON

Balearic Is.

Corsica
to Genoa

Sardinia
to Spain

Cagliari

Rome

Beneven

Naples

GRANADA
1492 to Spain

Granada

MEDITERRANEAN

Tangier
1471–1580
to Port.

Ceuta
1415–1580
to Port.

Gibraltar

Melilla
1496 to Spain

Algiers
1510–29 to Spain

Oran
1509–1706
to Spain

Bugia
1510–55 to Spain

ALGIERS

Bona

Biserta
1535–74
to Spain

Tunis

Paler

Sici
to Sp

MOROCCO

FEZ

TUNIS

Malta
1530 to Knights of St

50

45

40

35

10   5   0   5   10

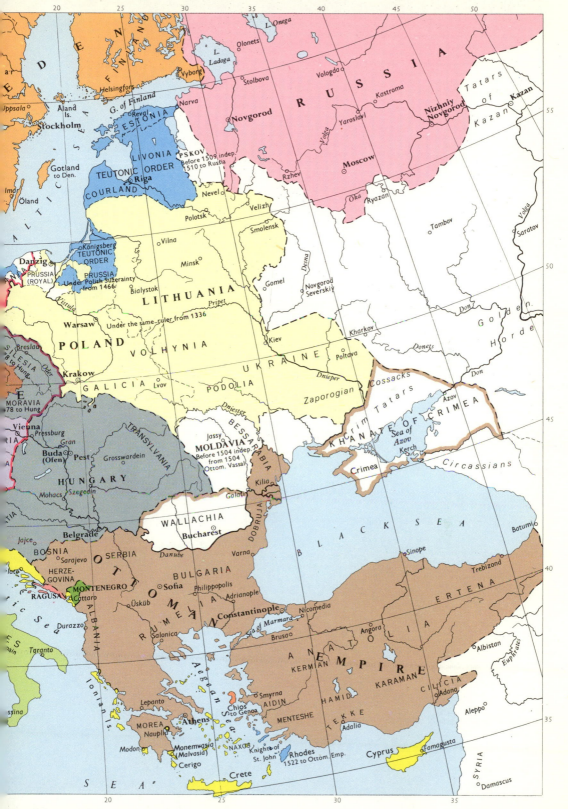

SEDEN

FINLAND

L. Onega

Olonets

L. Ladoga

Vyborg

Helsingfors

Uppsala

Åland Is.

G. of Finland

Stolbova

Vologda

RUSSIA

Stockholm

Reval

ESTONIA

Narva

Novgorod

Kastroma

Gotland to Den.

Imar

Öland

LIVONIA

TEUTONIC ORDER

Riga

COURLAND

PSKOV
Before 1509 indep.
1510 to Russia

Nevel

Polotsk

Velizh

Rzhev

Yaroslavl

Moscow

Nizhniy
Novgorod

Tatars
of
Kazan

Kazan

55

Oka

Ryazan

Tambov

Saratov

Königsberg
TEUTONIC
ORDER

Vilna

Smolensk

Danzig

PRUSSIA
(ROYAL)

PRUSSIA
Under Polish Suzerainty
from 1466

Minsk

Gomel

Novgorod
Severskiy

Desna

Golden

50

Bialystok

LITHUANIA

Pripet

Volga

Don

Warsaw

Under the same ruler from 1386

Kiev

Kharkov

Poltava

Donets

Don

Horde

Krakow

POLAND

VOLHYNIA

Lvov

UKRAINE

Dnieper

SILESIA
to Hung.

Breslau

GALICIA

PODOLIA

Dniester

Zaporogian

Cossacks

Khrim Tatars

Azov

45

MORAVIA
78 to Hung.

Vienna

Pressburg

TRANSYLVANIA

BESSARABIA

Jassy

MOLDAVIA
Before 1504 indep.
from 1504
Ottom. Vassal

KHANATE OF CRIMEA

Sea of
Azov

Kerch

Gran

Buda
(Ofen)

Pest

Grosswardein

Kilia

Crimea

Circassians

Mohacs

Szegedin

Galati

HUNGARY

DOBRUJA

WALLACHIA

Bucharest

BLACK   SEA

Batumi

Belgrade

Danube

Varna

Sinope

Trebizond

40

BOSNIA

Sarajevo

SERBIA

BULGARIA

HERZE-
GOVINA

Jajce

MONTENEGRO

Sofia

Philippopolis

ERTENA

RAGUSA

Cattaro

Üsküb

Adrianople

Nicomedia

Angora

Albistan

Durazzo

ALBANIA

RUMELIA

Constantinople

Sea of Marmara

Brusa

ANATOLIA

Euphrates

Taranto

Salonica

KERMIAN

EMPIRE

Aleppo

Ionians

OTTOMAN

KARAMANE

CILICIA

Adana

Lepanto

Smyrna

AIDIN

HAMID

TEKKE

MENTESHE

35

Chios
to Genoa

MOREA

Athens

Adalia

Nauplia

Messina

Modon

Monemvasia
(Malvasia)

NAXOS

Knights of
St. John

Rhodes
1522 to Ottom. Emp.

Cyprus

Famagusta

SYRIA

Cerigo

Crete

Damascus

S   E   A

COPYRIGHT GEORGE PHILIP & SON. LTD.

72

EUROPE, c.1648

Scale 1:15,000,000 (240 miles=1 inch)

0   100   200   300 Miles
0   100 200 300 400 Km.

Boundary of the Holy Roman Empire
Church Lands
Electorate of Brandenburg
Electorate of Saxony
Lands of the House of Habsburg
(Austrian Branch)
Spanish Lands
Venetian Lands
1648   Date of independence

Paroe Is.
to Den.

Shetland Is.

Orkney Is.

Hebrides

SCOTLAND

Edinburgh

Under the same
ruler
from 1603

I. OF
MAN

Durham
York

ENGLAND

WALES

Oxford Cambridge

Bristol   London

ATLANTIC OCEAN

IRELAND

Dublin

English   Channel

Channel Is.

BRITTANY

NORMANDY

Paris

Nantes

Loire
Tours

Orléans

Seine

FRANCE

Bordeaux

Garonne

Toulouse

Lyons

NAVARRE

Pamplona

Saragossa

Ebro

Andorra

ROUSSILLON
1642/59 to Fr.

Marseilles

Valladolid

Madrid

Toledo

Duero

CASTILE

SPAIN

ARAGON

Barcelona

Balearic Is.

Corsica
to Genoa

1557/59
to Spain

Sardinia
to Spain

Cagliari

La Coruña

Oporto

PORTUGAL
1580-1640 to Spain

Lisbon

Tagus

Guadiana

Seville

GRANADA

Granada

Valencia

MEDITERRANEAN

Tangier
1580-1640 to Sp.
1640-62 to Port.

Gibraltar
1580 to Spain

Ceuta

Melilla

Oran

MOROCCO

Algiers

Bugia

ALGIERS

Bona

Biserta

Tunis

TUNIS

NORTH SEA

NORWAY
united 1380-1814

DENMARK

Bergen

Christiania

Göteborg

SWEDEN

Särna

Copenhagen

Aalborg

Malmö

Bornholm

Heligoland

1648
to Swede

Lübeck Hamburg

Bremen

Stettin

BRANDENBUR

Berl

Brunswick Magdeburg

THE

SAXONY

Dresden

BOH
Prague

EMPI

Amsterdam

UNITED PROVINCES
1648

SPANISH
NETHER

Calais Brussels

Aachen

Cologne

Mainz

Frankfurt

Trier

Nuremberg

Danu

BAVARIA

Munich

Salzburg

A

TYROL

CARINTHIA

CARNI

Verdun

Strassburg

FRANCHE
COMTE

Basle

SWISS
CONFEDERATION
1648

Geneva

Berne

Charolais

Rhône

SAVOY

Turin

Milan

Venice

Ferrara

San
Marino

Genoa

1557/59
to Spain

Florence

PAPAL
STATES

Rome

Benevent

Naples

Saler

Avignon
to the Papacy

Palerm

Sicil
to Sp

Malta
to Knights of
St. John

10   5   0   5   10

5   West from Greenwich   0   East from Greenwich   5   10

50

45

40

35

L. Onega

Olonets

EDEN

FINLAND

Helsingfors

Uppsala

Åland Is.

Stockholm

Gotland

Calmar

Oland

Vyborg

L. Ladoga

G. of Finland

Reval

ESTONIA

Narva

INGRIA

LIVONIA

Riga

COURLAND

BALTIC SEA

Königsberg

D. OF PRUSSIA

1637-57/58 to Pol.

Under Polish Suzerainty until 1657/60.

Danzig

Vistula

Bialystok

Warsaw

Krakow

POLAND

LITHUANIA

Vilna

Minsk

Pripet

VOLHYNIA

GALICIA

Lvov

PODOLIA

Dniester

Stolbova

Novgorod

L. Ladoga

Nevel

Polotsk

Velizh

Smolensk

Gomel

Desna

Kiev

UKRAINE

Dnieper

Zaporogian Cossacks

Vologda

Rzhev

Volga

Rostov

Moscow

Oka

Tambov

RUSSIA

Nizhniy Novgorod

Kazan

Saratov

Volga

Don

Kharkov

Donets

Poltava

Don

Breslau

SILESIA

A

E

MORAVIA

Vienna

RIA

IA

Pressburg

HUNGARY

Buda (Ofen)

Pest

Grosswardein

1664 to Ottoman Emp.

HUNGARY

Mohacs

Temesvar

Erlau

TRANSYLVANIA

Jassy

MOLDAVIA

BESSARABIA

JEDISAN

KHANATE OF CRIMEA

Azov

Sea of Azov

Kerch

Crimea

Circassians

Crim Tatars

WALLACHIA

Bucharest

Danube

DOBRUJA

Kilia

Galati

Belgrade

Nish

SERBIA

BOSNIA

Sarajevo

HERZE-GOVINA

RAGUSA

Cattaro

MONTENEGRO

ALBANIA

Durazzo

Jajce

alata

atic Sea

ES

Taranto

Messina

OTTOMAN

RUMELIA

BULGARIA

Sofia

Üsküb

Salonica

Varna

Adrianople

Constantinople

Sea of Marmara

Brusa

Nicomedia

BLACK SEA

Sinope

Trebizond

Batumi

Angora

ANATOLIA

EMPIRE

KARAMAN

Konia

Kayseri

Albistan

Adana

Aleppo

Euphrates

Smyrna

Aegean Sea

MOREA

Nauplia

Athens

Modon

Monemvasia (Malvasia)

Cerigo

Crete

Rhodes

Cyprus

Famagusta

SYRIA

Damascus

SEA

COPYRIGHT. GEORGE PHILIP & SON. LTD.

EUROPE, *c.*1721

Scale 1:15,000,000 (240 miles=1 inch)

| | | | |

Boundary of the Holy Roman Empire

Church Lands

Venetian Lands

Brandenburg-Prussia

Lands of the House of Habsburg (Austrian Branch)

Gt. Britain and Hanover, united under the same ruler since 1714

Poland and El. of Saxony, united under the same ruler 1697–1763

1710 Date of independence

SWEDEN
FINLAND
Helsingfors
Uppsala
Aland Is.
Stockholm
G. of Finland
Gotland
Calmar
Öland
BALTIC SEA
Vyborg
L. Ladoga
L. Onega
Olonets
St. Petersburg
INGRIA
Narva
Reval
ESTONIA
1721 to Russia
LIVONIA
Riga
Novgorod
Vologda
Volga
Nizhniy Novgorod
Kazan
Rostov
Moscow
Rzhev
RUSSIA
Oka
Tambov
Saratov
Smolensk
Desna
Don
Donets
Kharkov
Poltava
Kiev
COURLAND
Nevel
Velizh
Polotsk
Tauroggen
1688/90 to Prussia
Vilna
Minsk
Königsberg
K. OF PRUSSIA
From 1701
C. OF SERREY
1688/90 to Prussia
Danzig
Grodno
Bialystok
Gomel
LITHUANIA
Pripet
Vistula
Poznan
Warsaw
POLAND
Lublin
VOLHYNIA
UKRAINE
Breslau
SILESIA
Oder
Krakow
GALICIA
Lvov
PODOLIA
1672–99 to Ottoman Emp.
Dnieper
Zaporogian
Under Russian Sovereignty
Cossacks
from 1654/67
Azov
1696–1711 to Russia
KHANATE OF CRIMEA
Sea of Azov
Crimea
Kerch
Circassians
MORAVIA
Kaschau
Dniester
BESSARABIA
JEDISAN
Jassy
MOLDAVIA
Vienna
Pressburg
Erlau
Buda (Ofen)
Pest
Grosswardein
1699 to Austria
HUNGARY
TRANSYLVANIA
Mohacs
Temesvar
BANAT
1718 to Aust.
Kilia
Galati
WALLACHIA
Bucharest
DOBRUJA
BLACK SEA
Batumi
Belgrade
Passarowitz
1718–39 to Aust.
SERBIA
1718–39 to Aust.
Jajce
BOSNIA
Sarajevo
Zara
HERZE-GOVINA
Danube
Varna
Sinope
Trebizond
Nish
BULGARIA
Sofia
Philippopolis
Adrianople
MONTENEGRO
RAGUSA
Cattaro
1718
Amasia
OTTOMAN EMPIRE
RUMELIA
Constantinople
Scutari
Nicomedia
Sea of Marmara
Sivas
Üsküb
ALBANIA
Durazzo
Salonica
Brusa
Angora
ANATOLIA
Kayseri
Albistan
Taranto
Euphrates
Janina
Ionian Is.
Aegean Sea
Konia
KARAMAN
Smyrna
Adana
Aleppo
Messina
Reggio
MOREA
1685/99–1715/18 to Ven.
Athens
Nauplia
Adalia
Modon
Monemvasia (Malvasia)
Cerigo
Rhodes
Cyprus
Famagusta
SYRIA
Crete
Damascus
SEA

EUROPE, *c.***1812**

Scale 1:15,000,000 (240 miles = 1 inch)

| 0 | 100 | 200 | 300 Miles |

| 0 | 100 | 200 | 300 | 400 | Km. |

- - - *Boundary of Confederation of the Rhine*

French Empire

States ruled by Napoleon's family

Other dependent states

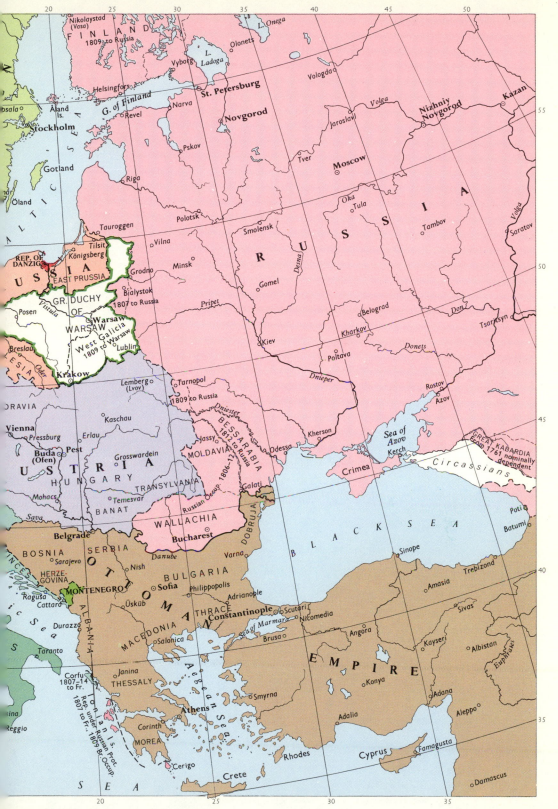

FINLAND 1809 to Russia

Nikolaystad (Vasa)

Uppsala

L. Onega

Olonets

L. Ladoga

Vyborg

Helsingfors

G. of Finland

St. Petersburg

Narva

Novgorod

Vologda

Åland Is.

Revel

Stockholm

Pskov

Tver

Jaroslavl

Nizhniy Novgorod

Kazan

Gotland

Riga

Moscow

Öland

Polotsk

Smolensk

Oka

Tula

Tambov

Saratov

Volga

R U S S I A

Tauroggen

Vilna

Minsk

Gomel

Desna

Belograd

Don

Tsaritsyn

Tilsit

Königsberg

Grodno

REP. OF DANZIG

EAST PRUSSIA

GR. DUCHY OF WARSAW

Bialystok 1807 to Russia

Pripet

Kiev

Kharkov

Donets

Posen

Warsaw

West Galicia 1809 to Warsaw

Lublin

Poltava

Dnieper

Rostov

Breslau

Oder

Krakow

Lemberg (Lvov)

Tarnopol

1809 to Russia

Dniester

Azov

Sea of Azov

Kerch

GREAT KABARDIA from 1761 nominally dependent

MORAVIA

Vienna

Pressburg

Erlau

Kaschau

BESSARABIA 1812 to Russia

Jassy

Kherson

Odessa

Crimea

Circassians

Buda (Ofen)

Pest

Grosswardein

MOLDAVIA

Russian Occup. 1806–12

Galati

A U S T R I A

H U N G A R Y

TRANSYLVANIA

BLACK SEA

Poti

Batumi

Mohacs

Temesvar

BANAT

WALLACHIA

DOBRUJA

Sava

Belgrade

Bucharest

Varna

Sinope

Trebizond

BOSNIA

Sarajevo

SERBIA

Nish

Danube

BULGARIA

Sofia

Philippopolis

Adrianople

Amasia

Sivas

HERZE-GOVINA

MONTENEGRO

Üsküb

O T T O M A N

THRACE

Constantinople

Scutari

Nicomedia

Angora

Kayseri

Albistan

Ragusa

Cattaro

ALBANIA

MACEDONIA

Salonica

Brusa

Sea of Marmara

Euphrates

Durazzo

Aegean Sea

E M P I R E

Konya

Adana

Taranto

Janina

Corfu 1807–14 to Fr.

THESSALY

Smyrna

Aleppo

Reggio

Ion. Is. Rep. under Russian Prot. 1807 to Fr. 1809 Br. Occup.

Athens

Corinth

MOREA

Adalia

Adana

Cerigo

Crete

Rhodes

Cyprus

Famagusta

S E A

Damascus

COPYRIGHT. GEORGE PHILIP & SON. LTD.

EUROPE, *c.***1815**

Scale 1:15,000,000 (240 miles = 1 inch)

0   100   200   300 Miles
0   100   200   300   400 Km.

— — — *Boundary of German Confederation, 1815*

▨ *United Kingdom and Hanover, united under the same ruler 1815-37*

▨ *Austro-Hungarian military boundary zones, with date of duration*

Sec. *Habsburg secundogeniture*

OL. *Oldenburg*

Nikolaystad (Vasa)
L. Onega
FINLAND
Helsingfors
G. of Finland
Kronstadt
St. Petersburg
Vyborg
L. Ladoga
Olonets
Vologda
Volga
Nizhniy Novgorod
Kazan
Aland Is.
Narva
Revel
Novgorod
Jaroslavl
Stockholm
Upsala
Oland
Gotland
Pskov
Tver
Moscow
R U S S I A
Riga
Polotsk
Smolensk
Oka
Tula
Tambov
Saratov
Volga
55
50
Danzig
Königsberg
Tauroggen
Vilna
EAST PRUSSIA
Grodno
Minsk
Desna
Gomel
Belograd
Don
Tsaritsyn
Thorn
Bialystok
P O L A N D
Bug
Pripet
Kharkov
Donets
Pinsk
Warsaw
From 1815 united with Russia
1831 fully part of Russia
Lublin
Kalish
Breslau
Kiev
Poltava
Rostov
Azov
Krakow
Vistula
REP. OF KRAKOW
1815-46
Lemberg (Lvov)
Tarnopol
1815 Austria
Dnieper
SILESIA
MORAVIA
TRO-HUNGARIAN
Dniester
Kherson
Sea of Azov
Kerch
GREAT KABARDIA
From 1825 complete
Russian Control
45
Vienna
Pressburg
Erlau
Jassy
Odessa
Crimea
Circassians
Buda (Ofen)
Pest
Grosswardein
MOLDAVIA
Trib.
Sevastopol
Poti
Batumi
EMPIRE
H U N G A R Y
Temesvar
Galati
B L A C K   S E A
Mohacs
1764-1851
Sava
1702-1878
1742-1872
WALLACHIA
Trib.
Bucharest
DOBRUJA
Sinope
Trebizond
40
Belgrade
Danube
Varna
Amasia
SERBIA
Trib.
Nish
BULGARIA
Sivas
BOSNIA
Sarajevo
Sofia
Philippopolis
Adrianople
DALMATIA
HERZE-GOVINA
MONTENEGRO
Üsküb
O T T O M A N
Scutari
Angora
Kayseri
Albistan
Ragusa
ALBANIA
MACEDONIA
THRACE
Constantinople
Nicomedia
Sea of Marmara
Brusa
Euphrates
Aleppo
Cattaro
Durazzo
Salonica
E M P I R E
Konya
Adana
SICILIES
Taranto
Janina
Smyrna
Adalia
Messina
Reggio
Corfu
Ionian Is.
From 1815 Rep. under
Br. Prot.
Patras
Corinth
MOREA
Athens
Rhodes
Cyprus
Famagusta
Cerigo
Crete
Damascus
S E A

COPYRIGHT GEORGE PHILIP & SON LTD.

EUROPE, c.1914
Scale 1:15,000,000 (240 miles = 1 inch)

0   100   200   300   Miles
0   100   200   300   400   Km.

1830   Date of independence

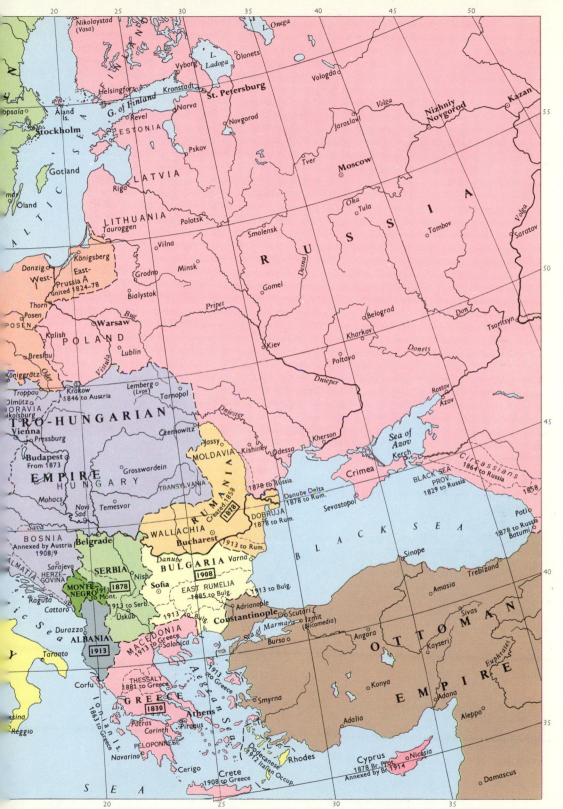
RUSSIA
St. Petersburg
Moscow
FINLAND
ESTONIA
LATVIA
LITHUANIA
POLAND
Warsaw
AUSTRO-HUNGARIAN EMPIRE
HUNGARY
Vienna
Budapest From 1873
RUMANIA Created 1858 1878
MOLDAVIA
WALLACHIA
Bucharest
TRANSYLVANIA
BULGARIA 1908
Sofia
EAST RUMELIA 1885 to Bulg.
SERBIA 1878
Belgrade
MONTE-NEGRO 1878
1913 to Mont.
1913 to Serb.
BOSNIA Annexed by Austria 1908/9
HERZE-GOVINA
ALBANIA 1913
MACEDONIA 1913 to Greece
GREECE 1830
THESSALY 1881 to Greece
Ionian Is. 1863 to Greece
Crete 1908 to Greece
Dodecanese 1912 Italian Occup.
Cyprus 1878 Br. Prot. Annexed by Br. 1914
OTTOMAN EMPIRE
Constantinople
BLACK SEA
Sea of Azov
Crimea
Krakow 1846 to Austria
East-Prussia A united 1824–78
Danube Delta 1878 to Rum.
DOBRUJA 1878 to Rum.
1913 to Rum.
1913 to Bulg.
1878 to Russia
BLACK SEA PROV. 1829 to Russia
Circassians 1864 to Russia
1878 to Russia Batumi
Aegean Sea
Ionian Sea
Baltic Sea
G. of Finland
Kazan
Nizhniy Novgorod
Kiev
Odessa
Sevastopol
Athens
Smyrna
Angora
Damascus
Aleppo
COPYRIGHT. GEORGE PHILIP & SON. LTD.

EUROPE, c. 1926

Scale 1:15,000,000 (240 miles = 1 inch)

0   100   200   300 Miles
0   100 200 300 400 Km.

1916	Date of independence
	Demilitarized areas west and 50km. east of the Rhine and demilitarized "Zone of the Straits" in Turkey
S.A.	Sanjak of Alexandretta, 1920 autonomous within French Mandate of Syria
R.S.F.S.R.	Russian Soviet Federal Socialist Republic
A.S.S.R.	Autonomous Soviet Socialist Republic
S.S.R.	Soviet Socialist Republic
A.R.	Autonomous Region

10   5   0   5   10

Faroe Is.
to Den.

Shetland Is.

Scapa Flow
Orkney Is.

NORWAY

Bergen

Oslo
(Christiania)

Stavanger

Göteborg

A T L A N T I C   O C E A N

Hebrides

SCOTLAND

Glasgow

Edinburgh

N O R T H

S E A

DENMARK

Aalborg

Copenhagen

Malmö

Bornho

1920 to Den.

Heligoland

Lübeck

Hamburg

Rostock

Stettin

Berlin

G E R M

Leipzig

Dresden

Elbe

Prague

Plzeň

UNITED KINGDOM OF
GREAT BRITAIN AND
NORTHERN IRELAND
From 1927

IRELAND
1920
Belfast

IRISH
FREE
STATE
From 1922
1921 Dominion

Limerick

Cork

Dublin

Liverpool

Manchester

Sheffield

Leeds

Birmingham

Norwich

ENGLAND

WALES

Bristol

London

Amsterdam

The Hague

NETHERLANDS

Antwerp

BELGIUM

Brussels

Malmédy

Eupen

Cologne

Dortmund

Bremen

Hanover

50

Channel Is.

English Channel

Le Havre

Rouen

Neuilly

Brest

St. Germain
Versailles

Sèvres

Paris

Lille

Wiesbaden

SAAR

Frankfurt

1919/20-35
Autonomous
under League of Nations

Nuremberg

Rennes

Orléans

Seine

ALSACE-
LORRAINE
1919/20 to Fr.

Mulhouse

Stuttgart

Munich

Danube

Salzbu

45

Nantes

Loire

F R A N C E

Saône

Basle
Zürich

SWITZERLAND

Berne

Lausanne

Locarno

Geneva

LIECHTEN-
STEIN

Innsbruck

A U S T

Inn

Klagen

Rhône

Lyons

Grenoble

Trent

I T A L

Milan

Venice

Trieste

Fiume
1924
to Italy

Bordeaux

Garonne

Toulouse

Turin

Genoa

Rapallo

Bologna

La Coruña

Santander

Bilbao

Braganza

Burgos

Pamplona

Nice

Cannes

MONACO
Fr. Prot.

Florence

SAN
MARINO

40

Oporto

Valladolid

Duero

Ebro

Saragossa

ANDORRA

Marseilles

Elba

Corsica

Ajaccio

VATICAN
CITY
1929

Rome

P O R T U G A L

S P A I N

Madrid

Barcelona

Balearic Is.

Sardinia

Naples

Lisbon

Tagus

Toledo

Guadiana

Valencia

Cagliari

Seville

Granada

Cartagena

35

Algeciras

Tangier
1923-56
International
Zone

Gibraltar
to Br.

Ceuta

ER-RIF

Alhucemas

Melilla

M E D I T E R R A N E

Sic

Paler

Rabat

Casablanca

MOROCCO

ORAN

Oran

Algiers

ALGIERS
to France

Constantine

CONSTANTINE

Bona

TUNISIA
Fr. Prot.

Tunis

Malta
to Br.

Vaasa
Tampere
FINLAND
1917/20
Helsinki (Helsingfors)
Turku
Åland Is.
1921 neutral under Finnish Sovereignty
Uppsala
Stockholm
G. of Finland
Narva
Tallinn
ESTONIA
1918/20
Tartu (Dorpat)
L. Pskov
Gotland
Riga
LATVIA
1918/20
Calmar
Öland
LITHUANIA
1918/20
Memel Terr.
1923 to Lith.
1924 Autonomous
Kaunas
BALTIC SEA
DENMARK
Danzig
1919 Free City under League of Nations
Königsberg
EAST PRUSSIA
Bydgoszcz
Poznan
Breslau
Hultschin
Ostrava
Brno
ECHOSLOVAKIA
1918/19
Vienna
Bratislava
Graz
Sopron
HUNGARY
1918/19
Budapest
Debrecen
Oradea
Drava
Zagreb
Sava
YUGOSLAVIA
1918
1918–29
K. of the Croats, Slovenes and Serbs
Belgrade
Zara
1920 to Italy
Sarajevo
Lagosta
1920 to Italy
Dubrovnik
Kotor
Durrës
Tirane
ALBANIA
Bari
Taranto
Messina
Reggio

Petrozavodsk
L. Onega
Olonets
L. Ladoga
Viipuri
Kronstadt
Leningrad (Petrograd)
Vologda
Novgorod
UNION OF SOVIET
L. Pskov
Pskov
Rzhev
Tver
Moscow
R. S. F. S. R.
Formed 1917
Smolensk
Kaluga
Oka
Vitebsk
1924/26 to White Russian S.S.R.
Minsk
WHITE RUSSIAN S.S.R.
1922 to U.S.S.R.
Grodno
Bialystok
Bug
Warsaw
1916
1918 Republic
Brest-Litovsk
Pripet
Gomel
Desna
POLAND
Lodz
Krakow
Vistula
Lvov
Kiev
Dnieper
UKRAINIAN S.S.R.
1922 to U.S.S.R.
Dniester
Demarcation Line 1918–34
MOLDAVIAN A.S.S.R. 1924
Iaşy
Kishinev
Odessa
RUMANIA
Izmail
Ploeşti
Danube
Bucharest
Timisoara
Constanta
Varna
Plevna
Nish
BULGARIA
Sofia
Plovdiv (Philippopolis)
MACEDONIA
Skopje (Üsküb)
Salonica
Janina
Corfu
GREECE
Patras
Athens
Peloponnese
Kythira
Crete

Turku
Demarcation Line 1920–38
Vilna

SOCIALIST REPUBLICS

MARI A.R. 1920
CHUVASH A.S.S.R. 1925
TATAR A.S.S.R. 1920
Kazan
Volga
Nizhniy Novgorod
VOTIAK A.R. 1920
Saratov
GERMAN REP. OF VOLGA A.S.S.R. 1923
Formed 1922
Voronezh
Don
Stalingrad (Tsaritsyn)
KALMYK A.R. 1920
Kharkov
Poltava
Donets
Dnepropetrovsk (Yekaterinoslav)
Rostov
Kherson
Sea of Azov
Kerch
Krasnodar
Stavropol
CRIMEAN A.S.S.R. 1921
ADYGE-CHERKESS A.R. 1922
KARACHAI-CHERKESS A.R. 1922
ABKHAZIAN S.S.R. 1922
Sevastopol
BLACK SEA
Sinope
Zonguldak
Bosporus
Edirne
Istanbul (Constantinople)
Izmit
Mudania
Gallipoli
Chanak
Dardanelles
Sea of Marmara
Eskisehir
Ankara
Capital 1923
Amasia
Kizil Irmak
TURKEY
From 1923 Republic
Sivas
Kayseri
Malatya
Konya
Smyrna
Antalya
Adana
Alexandretta
S.A. 1920
Gaziantep
Urfa
Aleppo
Euphrates
TERR. OF ALAWITES
1924/42
Cyprus
1925 Br. Col.
Nicosia
SYRIA
1920 Fr. Mandate
LEBANON
1920 Fr. Mandate
Beirut
Damascus
Trabzon
Batumi
Rhodes
Dodecanese to Italy

Aegean Sea
Ionian Is.
Aegean Sea

COPYRIGHT. GEORGE PHILIP & SON. LTD.

EUROPE AFTER 1945

Scale 1:15,000,000 (240 miles=1 inch)

0   100   200   300 Miles
0   100   200   300   400 Km.

1956 Date of independence

International boundaries 1945

Functioning (de facto) boundary

Free State of Trieste, 1947–54:
Zone "A": Anglo-American administration from 1947;
1954 to Italy
Zone "B": Yugoslav military administration from 1947;
1954 to Yugoslavia

The "Iron Curtain" from 1955

UNION OF SOVIET SOCIALIST REPUBLICS
R. S. F. S. R.
FINLAND
Vaasa
Turku
Helsinki
Åland Is.
G. of Finland
Kronstadt
KARELIAN A.S.S.R. 1940–56 S.S.R.
1945/47 to U.S.S.R.
L. Onega
L. Ladoga
Olonets
Leningrad
Vologda
Narva
Tallinn
ESTONIAN S.S.R. From 1940
Tartu
L. Pskov
Pskov
Novgorod
Stockholm
Gotland
Öland
Riga
LATVIAN S.S.R. From 1940
LITHUANIAN S.S.R. From 1940
Kaunas
Vilna
Vitebsk
Kalinin
Moscow
Volga
Gorki
MARI A.S.S.R. From 1936
CHUVASH A.S.S.R.
TATAR A.S.S.R.
UDMURT A.S.S.R. From 1934
MORDOVIAN A.S.S.R. From 1934
Oka
Saratov
Incorporated into U.S.S.R. 1945
Gdansk (Danzig)
Incorporated into Poland 1945
Grodno
Minsk
WHITE RUSSIAN S.S.R.
Desna
Bialystok
Bydgoszcz
Poznan
Bug
Warsaw
POLAND
Lodz
Brest
Pripet
Gomel
1945/47 to U.S.S.R.
Voronezh
Don
Stalingrad
Kiev
Kharkov
Poltava
Donets
Dnepropetrovsk
KALMYK A.R.
UKRAINIAN S.S.R.
Vistula
Krakow
Cesky Tesin 1945 to Cz.
Ostrava
Lvov
Dnestr
Rostov
Dnepr
CZECHOSLOVAKIA
Brno
Bratislava
1945/47 to Cz.
1945/47 to U.S.S.R.
Chernovtsy
MOLDAVIAN S.S.R.
Kishinev
1940-41 1944/47 to U.S.S.R.
Iasy
Kherson
Sea of Azov
Kerch
Krasnodar
Stavropol
Budapest
Debrecen
1945/47 to Rum.
Oradea
HUNGARY
Szeged
RUMANIA From 1947 Rep.
Crimea
ADYGE-CHERKESS A.R.
KARACHAI-CHERKESS A.R.
ABKHAZIAN S.S.R.
Sevastopol
Jalta
Zagreb
Timisoara
Sava
Ploeşti
Constanta
YUGOSLAVIA From 1945 Rep.
Belgrade
Bucharest
BLACK SEA
Batumi
Sarajevo
Danube
Varna
Sinope
Trabzon
Nish
BULGARIA From 1946 Rep.
Sofia
Plovdiv
Dubrovnik
Edirne
Bosporus
Zonguldak
Kizil Irmak
Sivas
Skoplje
Istanbul
Sea of Marmara
Izmit
Bursa
Durrës
Tiranë
ALBANIA From 1946 Rep.
Bari
Taranto
Salonica
Eskisehir
Ankara
TURKEY
Malatya
Euphrates
Urfa
Dardanelles
Janina
Corfu
GREECE
Monarchy restored 1946
Aegean Sea
Smyrna
Konya
Gaziantep
Adana
Iskenderun (Alexandretta)
1939 to Turkey
Aleppo
Ionian Is.
Athens
Patras
Peloponnese
Antalya
Dodecanese 1945/47 to Greece
Rhodes
Cyprus Until 1960 Br. Col.
Nicosia
SYRIA
Kythira
LEBANON
Beirut
Damascus
Crete
SEA
20
25
30
35
40
45
50
55

COPYRIGHT, GEORGE PHILIP & SON, LTD.

EUROPE: RAILWAYS, 1870

Scale 1:15,000,000 (240 miles = 1 inch)

Railways   Height of Land

Feet 3000 / Metres 914
0 / 0

G. of Bothnia
L. Onega
L. Ladoga
Tavastehus
Vyborg
Gävle
Helsingfors
St. Petersburg
G. of Finland
Uppsala
Stockholm
Ivanovo
Nizhniy Novgorod
Vyshniy Volochek
Linköping
Pskov
G. of Riga
BALTIC SEA
Riga
Moscow
Kolomna
Dünaburg
Morshansk
Vitebsk
Smolensk
Orel
Königsberg
Danzig
Voronezh
Borisoglebsk
Grodno
Kursk
Bromberg
Warsaw
Brest
Lódz
Kharkov
Kiev
Breslau
Poltava
Krakow
Vinnitsa
Lemberg
Taganrog
Brünn
Czernowitz
Miskolcz
Vienna
Pressburg
Jassy
Sea of Azov
Debreczin
Kishinev
Odessa
Buda (Ofen)
Graz
Grosswardein
Szegedin
Karlsburg
Fünfkirchen
Galati
Agram
Temesvar
Esseg
Bucharest
BLACK SEA
Weisskirchen
Craiova
Varna
Adriatic Sea
Foggia
Bari
Brindisi
Taranto
Aegean Sea
Smyrna
Aydin
Messina
Ionian Sea
Catania
MEDITERRANEAN SEA
20 25 30 35 40 45 50
55 50 45 40 35
20 25 30 35

COPYRIGHT, GEORGE PHILIP & SON. LTD.

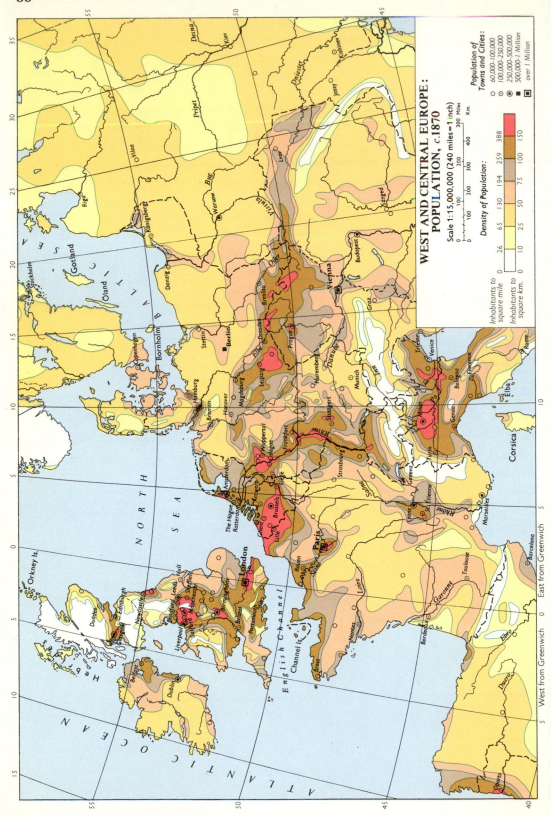

WEST AND CENTRAL EUROPE:
POPULATION, c.1870

Scale 1:15,000,000 (240 miles=1 inch)

Density of Population:

Inhabitants to square mile	Inhabitants to square km.
0	0
26	10
65	25
130	50
194	75
259	100
388	150

Population of
Towns and Cities:

60,000–100,000
100,000–250,000
250,000–500,000
500,000–1 Million
over 1 Million

COPYRIGHT GEORGE PHILIP & SON, LTD.

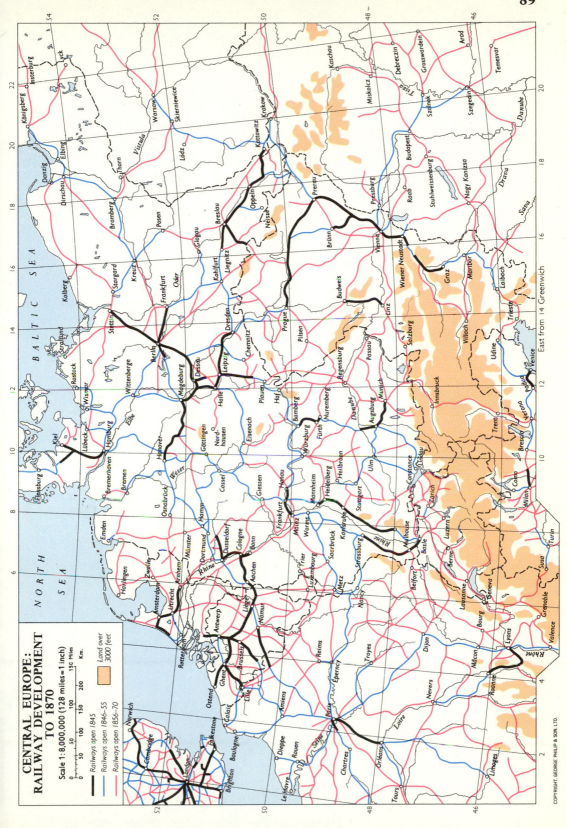

CENTRAL EUROPE:
RAILWAY DEVELOPMENT
TO 1870

Scale 1:8,000,000 (128 miles=1 inch)

Land over
3000 feet

Railways open 1845
Railways open 1846–55
Railways open 1856–70

Miles
0   50   100   150
0   50   100   150   200
Km.

BALTIC SEA

NORTH SEA

East from 14 Greenwich

COPYRIGHT, GEORGE PHILIP & SON, LTD.

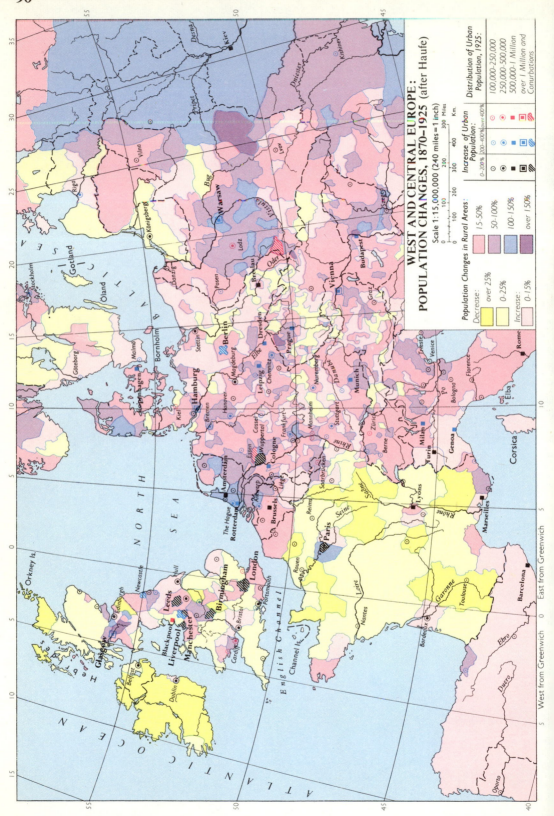

**WEST AND CENTRAL EUROPE:
POPULATION CHANGES, 1870–1925** (after Haufe)

Scale 1:15,000,000 (240 miles = 1 inch)

0 100 200 300 Miles
0 100 200 300 400 Km.

Population Changes in Rural Areas:

Decrease:
over 25%
0–25%

Increase:
0–15%
15–50%
50–100%
100–150%
over 150%

Increase of Urban Population:
0–200% 200–400% over 400%

Distribution of Urban Population, 1925:
100,000–250,000
250,000–500,000
500,000–1 Million
over 1 Million and Conurbations

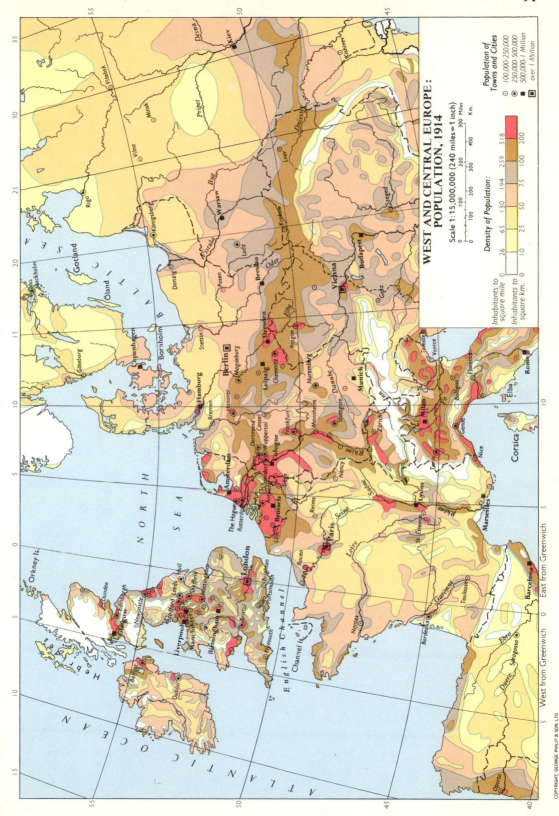

WEST AND CENTRAL EUROPE:
POPULATION, 1914

Scale 1:15,000,000 (240 miles = 1 inch)

Density of Population:

Inhabitants to square mile	26	65	130	194	259	518
Inhabitants to square km.	0	10	25	50	75	100	200

Population of Towns and Cities

- ⊙ 100,000–250,000
- ◉ 250,000–500,000
- ■ 500,000–1 Million
- ▣ over 1 Million

COPYRIGHT. GEORGE PHILIP & SON, LTD

WEST AND CENTRAL EUROPE: INDUSTRIES, 1914

Scale 1:15,000,000 (240 miles=1 inch)

Miles 300 400 200 100 0
Km. 0 100 200 300

Legend:
- ▲ Iron manufactures
- ✿ Machine building and metal manufacture
- ⊥ Ship building
- ● Chemicals
- ● Woollen goods
- ◀ Linen
- ■ Cotton goods
- ◆ Silk
- ⬭ Industrial districts
- ⦀ Coalfields
- ⦙ Lignite
- ◍ Iron ore deposits
- ◕ Potash deposits
- ⌐⌐ Boundaries 1914

COPYRIGHT. GEORGE PHILIP & SON, LTD.

West from Greenwich   East from Greenwich

Map labels: Kiev, Dniester, Pripet, Bucharest, Danube, Sofia, Belgrade, Sarajevo, Warsaw, Vistula, Krakow, Budapest, Brünn, Or'l, Prague, Vienna, Graz, Berlin, Elbe, Chemnitz, Brno, Munich, Danube, Rome, Stuttgart, Frankfurt, Rhine, Berne, Milan, Genoa, Nancy, Lyons, Rhône, Copenhagen, Stockholm, Danzig, Amsterdam, Brussels, Seine-Paris, Loire, Nantes, Bordeaux, Ebro, London, Edinburgh, Dublin

ATLANTIC OCEAN, NORTH SEA, BALTIC SEA, Adriatic Sea, English Channel

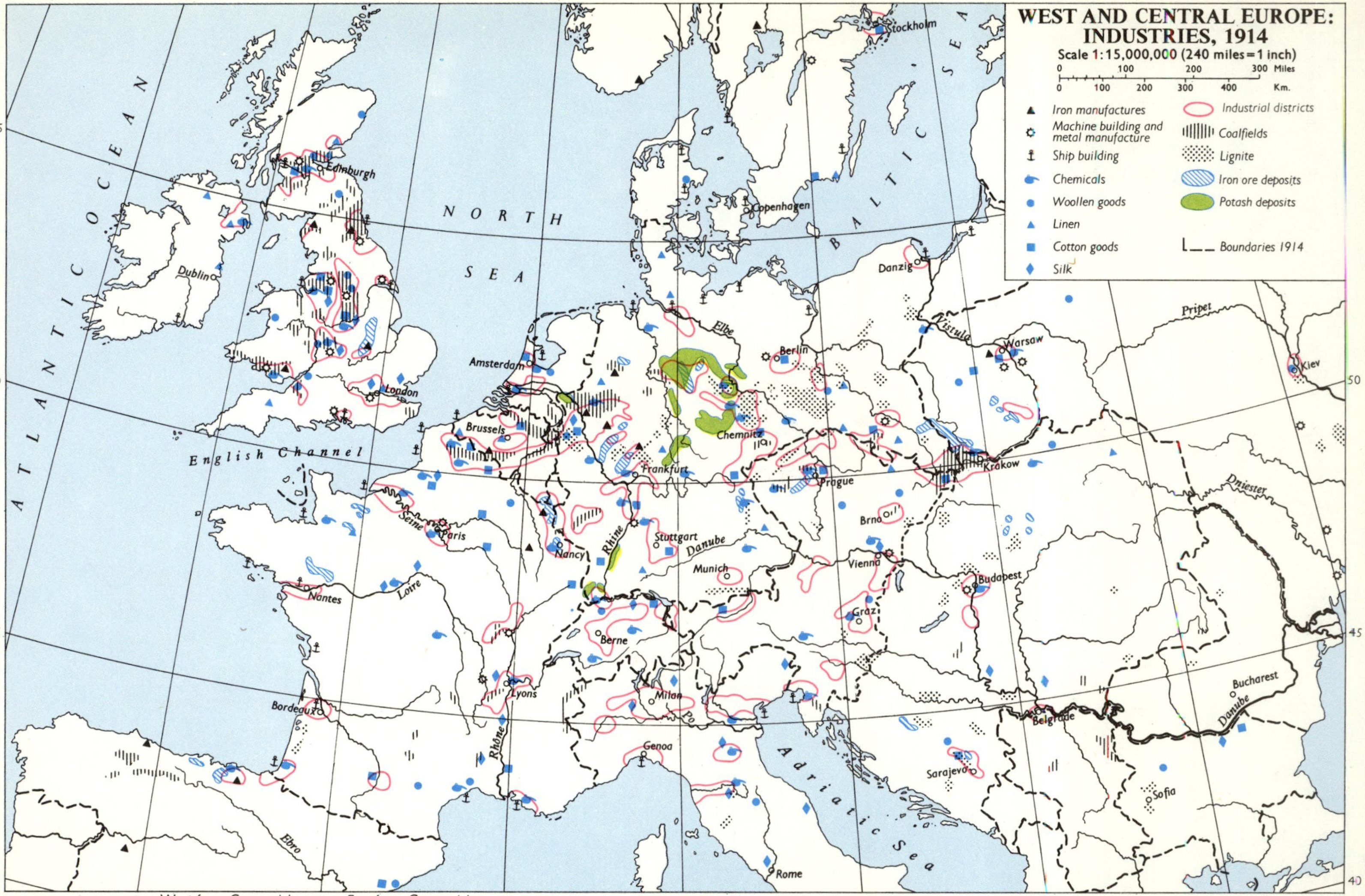

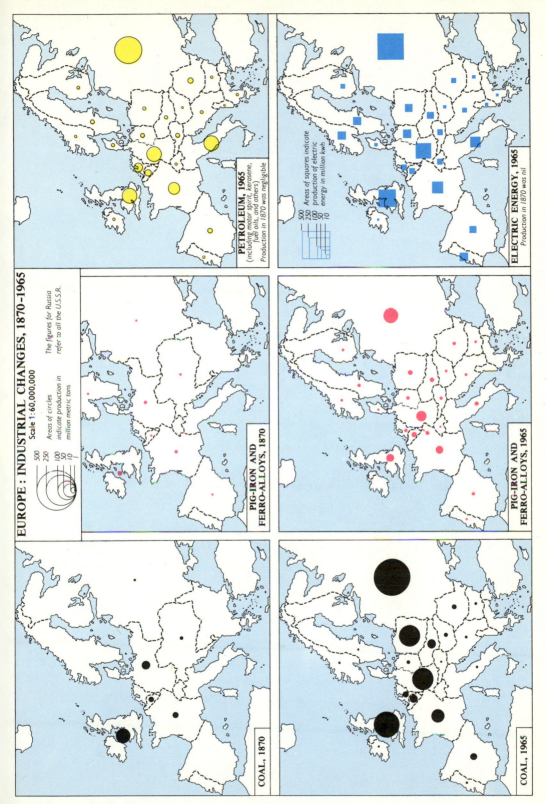

93

EUROPE: INDUSTRIAL CHANGES, 1870-1965

Scale 1: 60,000,000

Areas of circles
indicate production in
million metric tons

500
250
100
50
10

The figures for Russia
refer to all the U.S.S.R.

PETROLEUM, 1965
(including motor spirit, kerosene,
fuel oils, and others)
Production in 1870 was negligible

Areas of squares indicate
production of electric
energy in million kwh

500
250
100
50
10

ELECTRIC ENERGY, 1965
Production in 1870 was nil

PIG-IRON AND
FERRO-ALLOYS, 1870

PIG-IRON AND
FERRO-ALLOYS, 1965

COAL, 1870

COAL, 1965

COPYRIGHT. GEORGE PHILIP & SON, LTD

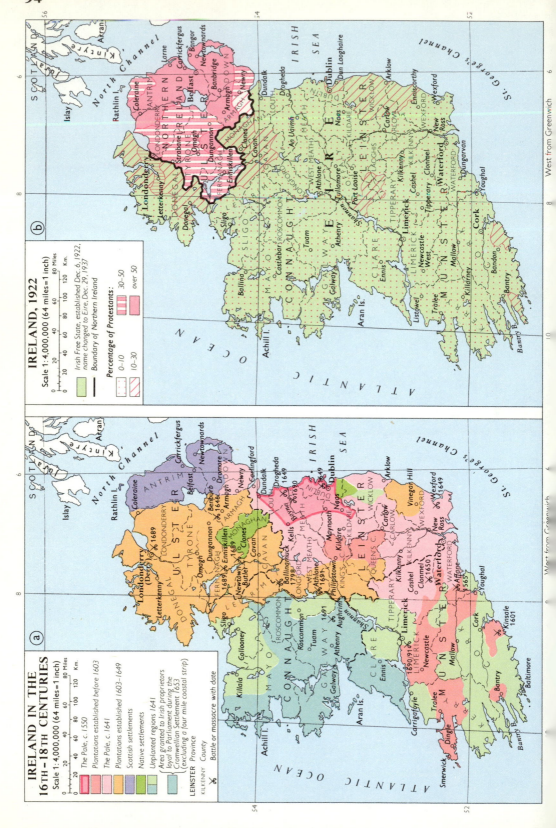

IRELAND IN THE 16TH–18TH CENTURIES

Scale 1:4,000,000 (64 miles=1 inch)

The Pale, c.1550
Plantations established before 1603
The Pale, c.1641
Plantations established 1603–1649
Scottish settlements
Native settlements
Unplanted regions 1641
Area granted to Irish proprietors loyal to Parliament during the Cromwellian Settlement 1653 (excluding a four mile coastal strip)

LEINSTER Province
KILKENNY County
✕ Battle or massacre with date

IRELAND, 1922

Scale 1:4,000,000 (64 miles=1 inch)

Irish Free State, established Dec. 6, 1922, name changed to Eire, Dec. 29, 1937
Boundary of Northern Ireland

Percentage of Protestants:
0–10
10–30
30–50
over 50

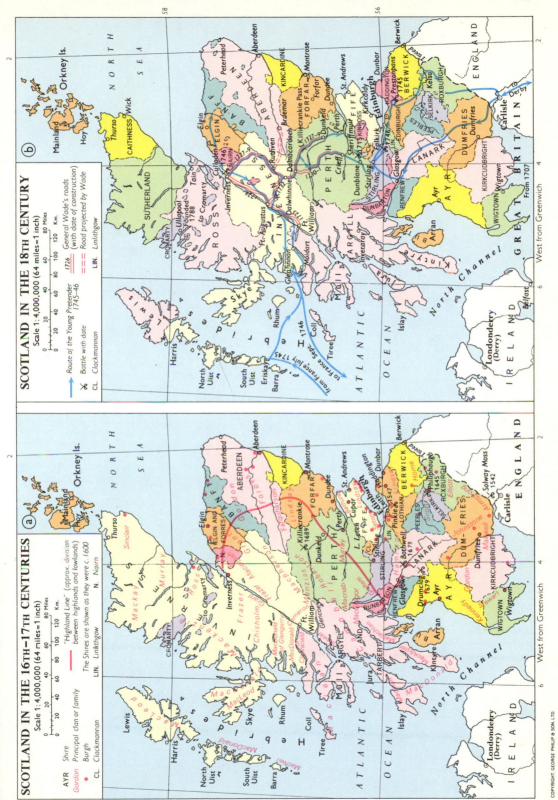

SCOTLAND IN THE 16TH–17TH CENTURIES

Scale 1:4,000,000 (64 miles=1 inch)

| 0 | 20 | 40 | 60 | 80 Miles |
| 0 | 20 | 40 | 60 | 80 | 100 | 120 | Km. |

AYR   Shire
Gordon   Principal clan or family
●   Burgh

"Highland Line" (approx. division between highlands and lowlands)
The Shires are shown as they were c. 1600

LIN. Linlithgow   N. Nairn
CL. Clackmannan

SCOTLAND IN THE 18TH CENTURY

Scale 1:4,000,000 (64 miles=1 inch)

| 0 | 20 | 40 | 60 | 80 Miles |
| 0 | 20 | 40 | 60 | 80 | 100 | 120 | Km. |

Route of the Young Pretender
1745–46
✕ Battle with date
CL. Clackmannan

1726   General Wade's roads (with date of construction)
Road projected by Wade
LIN. Linlithgow

COPYRIGHT GEORGE PHILIP & SON LTD

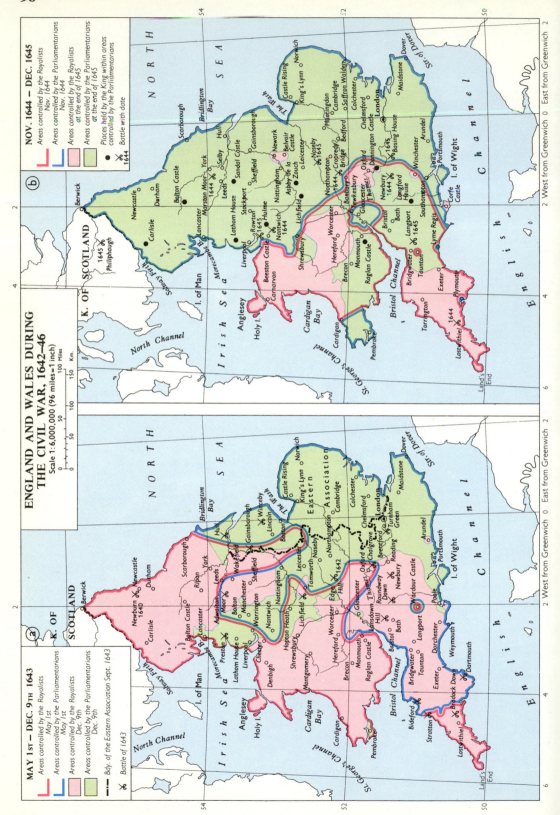

ENGLAND AND WALES DURING
THE CIVIL WAR, 1642–46
Scale 1:6,000,000 (96 miles=1 inch)

MAY 1st – DEC. 9TH 1643
- Areas controlled by the Royalists May 1st
- Areas controlled by the Parliamentarians May 1st
- Areas controlled by the Royalists Dec. 9th
- Areas controlled by the Parliamentarians Dec. 9th
- Bdy. of the Eastern Association Sept. 1643
- ✗ Battle of 1643

NOV. 1644 – DEC. 1645
- Areas controlled by the Royalists Nov. 1644
- Areas controlled by the Parliamentarians Nov. 1644
- Areas controlled by the Royalists at the end of 1645
- Areas controlled by the Parliamentarians at the end of 1645
- ● Places held by the King within areas controlled by the Parliamentarians
- ✗ Battle with date

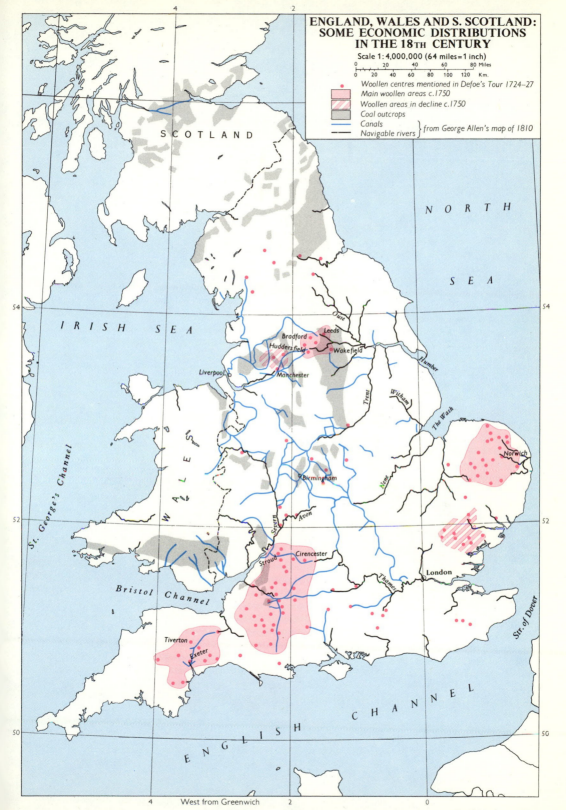

ENGLAND, WALES AND S. SCOTLAND:
SOME ECONOMIC DISTRIBUTIONS
IN THE 18TH CENTURY

Scale 1 : 4,000,000 (64 miles=1 inch)

| | 20 | 40 | 60 | 80 Miles |

0 20 40 60 80 100 120 Km.

- *Woollen centres mentioned in Defoe's Tour 1724–27*
- Main woollen areas c.1750
- Woollen areas in decline c.1750
- *Coal outcrops*
- Canals } from George Allen's map of 1810
- Navigable rivers

SCOTLAND

NORTH SEA

IRISH SEA

54

Ouse
Leeds
Bradford
Huddersfield   Wakefield
Liverpool
Manchester
Trent   Witham   Humber

The Wash

Norwich

Birmingham   Nene

52   Avon

Severn

Stroud   Cirencester

Thames   London

Tiverton

Exeter

Bristol Channel

St. George's Channel

WALES

Str. of Dover

50

ENGLISH CHANNEL

West from Greenwich

COPYRIGHT. GEORGE PHILIP & SON. LTD.

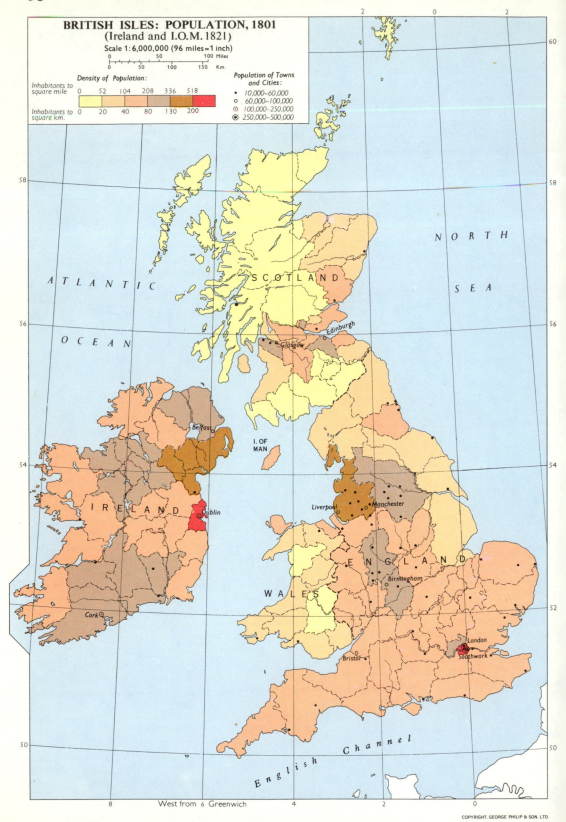

BRITISH ISLES: POPULATION, 1801
(Ireland and I.O.M. 1821)
Scale 1: 6,000,000 (96 miles = 1 inch)

0   50   100 Miles

0   50   100   150 Km.

Density of Population:

Inhabitants to square mile
0   52   104   208   336   518

Inhabitants to square km.
0   20   40   80   130   200

Population of Towns and Cities:
- · 10,000–60,000
- ○ 60,000–100,000
- ⊙ 100,000–250,000
- ◉ 250,000–500,000

NORTH SEA

ATLANTIC

OCEAN

SCOTLAND

Edinburgh

Glasgow

Belfast

I. OF MAN

IRELAND

Dublin

Liverpool   Manchester

ENGLAND

Cork

WALES

Birmingham

London
Southwark

Bristol

ENGLISH Channel

West from 6 Greenwich

COPYRIGHT. GEORGE PHILIP & SON. LTD.

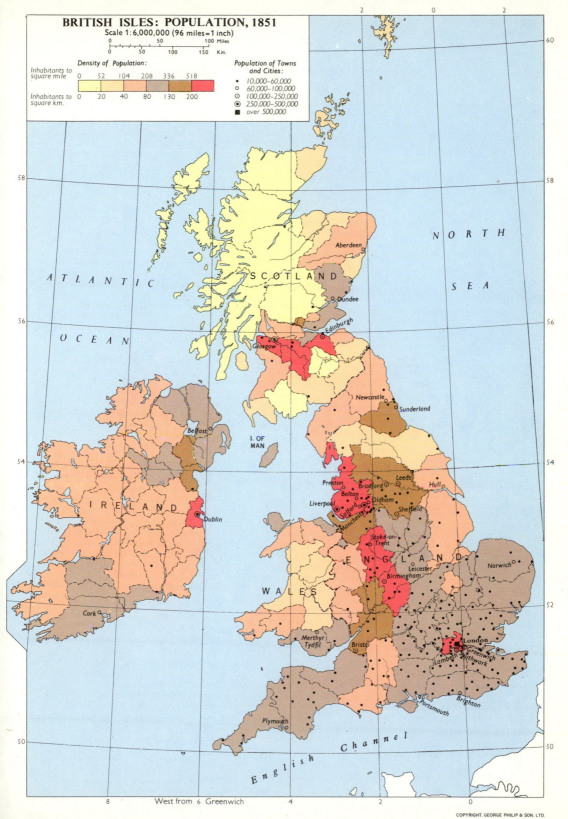

BRITISH ISLES: POPULATION, 1851

Scale 1:6,000,000 (96 miles=1 inch)

Density of Population:

Inhabitants to square mile
0   52   104 208 336 518

Inhabitants to square km.
0   20   40   80   130 200

Population of Towns and Cities:
· 10,000–60,000
○ 60,000–100,000
◉ 100,000–250,000
◉ 250,000–500,000
■ over 500,000

NORTH SEA

ATLANTIC OCEAN

SCOTLAND
Aberdeen
Dundee
Glasgow Edinburgh
Newcastle
Sunderland

IRELAND
Belfast
I. OF MAN
Dublin
Cork

Preston Bradford Leeds
Bolton Hull
Liverpool Oldham
Salford Sheffield
Manchester
Stoke-on-Trent
ENGLAND
Leicester Norwich
Birmingham
WALES
Merthyr Tydfil
Bristol
London
Lambeth Greenwich
Southwark
Portsmouth Brighton
Plymouth

English Channel

West from Greenwich

COPYRIGHT. GEORGE PHILIP & SON. LTD.

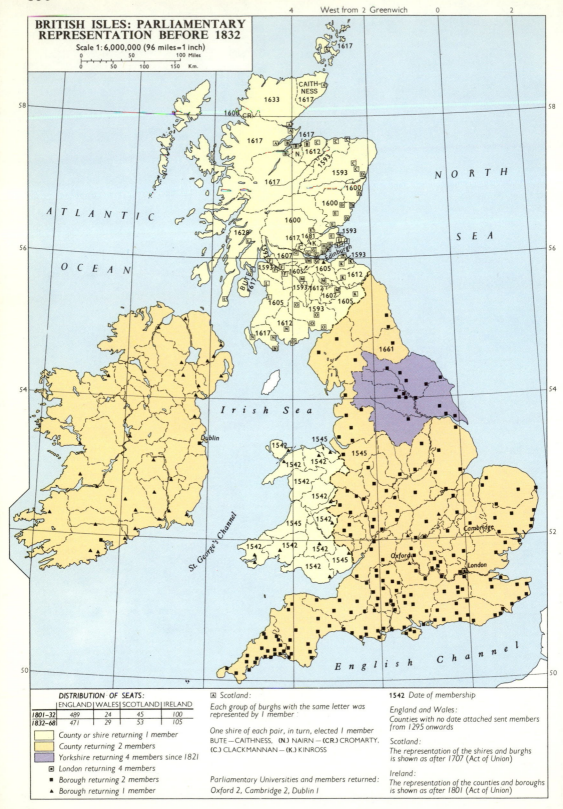

BRITISH ISLES: PARLIAMENTARY REPRESENTATION BEFORE 1832

Scale 1: 6,000,000 (96 miles=1 inch)

0   50   100 Miles

0   50   100   150 Km.

West from 2 Greenwich

4   2   0   2

ATLANTIC OCEAN

NORTH SEA

Irish Sea

St. George's Channel

English Channel

1617
CAITH-NESS 1617
1633
1617
1608 CR.
1617
1617
1612
1593
1593
1600
1600
1600
1629
1617 1681
1593
1607
1607 1593
Edinburgh 1593
1593 1605
1605
1612
1593 1612
1607
1605
1605
1593
1612
1617
N.

1661

Dublin

1542
1545
1542 1542
1545
1542
1542
1542
1545
1542
1545
1542 1542
1542 1545
1542

Cambridge

Oxford

London

DISTRIBUTION OF SEATS:

	ENGLAND	WALES	SCOTLAND	IRELAND
1801–32	489	24	45	100
1832–68	471	29	53	105

☐ County or shire returning 1 member
▨ County returning 2 members
▨ Yorkshire returning 4 members since 1821
⊡ London returning 4 members
■ Borough returning 2 members
▲ Borough returning 1 member

Ⓐ *Scotland:*
Each group of burghs with the same letter was represented by 1 member

One shire of each pair, in turn, elected 1 member
BUTE — CAITHNESS, (N.) NAIRN — (CR.) CROMARTY,
(C.) CLACKMANNAN — (K.) KINROSS

Parliamentary Universities and members returned:
Oxford 2, Cambridge 2, Dublin 1

1542 Date of membership

England and Wales:
Counties with no date attached sent members from 1295 onwards

Scotland:
The representation of the shires and burghs is shown as after 1707 (Act of Union)

Ireland:
The representation of the counties and boroughs is shown as after 1801 (Act of Union)

COPYRIGHT. GEORGE PHILIP & SON. LTD.

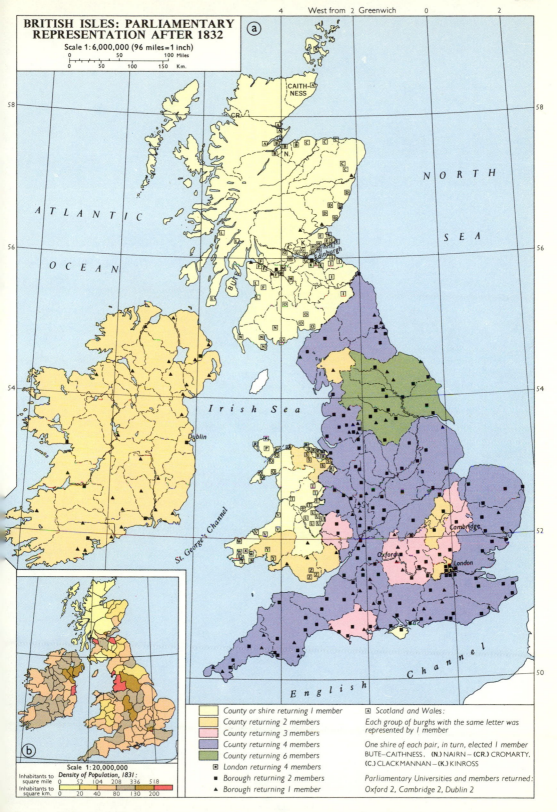

BRITISH ISLES: PARLIAMENTARY REPRESENTATION AFTER 1832

Scale 1:6,000,000 (96 miles=1 inch)

County or shire returning 1 member
County returning 2 members
County returning 3 members
County returning 4 members
County returning 6 members
London returning 4 members
Borough returning 2 members
Borough returning 1 member

Scotland and Wales:
Each group of burghs with the same letter was represented by 1 member

One shire of each pair, in turn, elected 1 member
BUTE–CAITHNESS. (N.) NAIRN – (CR.) CROMARTY, (C.) CLACKMANNAN – (K.) KINROSS

Parliamentary Universities and members returned:
Oxford 2, Cambridge 2, Dublin 2

Scale 1:20,000,000
Density of Population, 1831:
Inhabitants to square mile: 0 52 104 208 336 518
Inhabitants to square km: 0 20 40 80 130 200

COPYRIGHT. GEORGE PHILIP & SON. LTD.

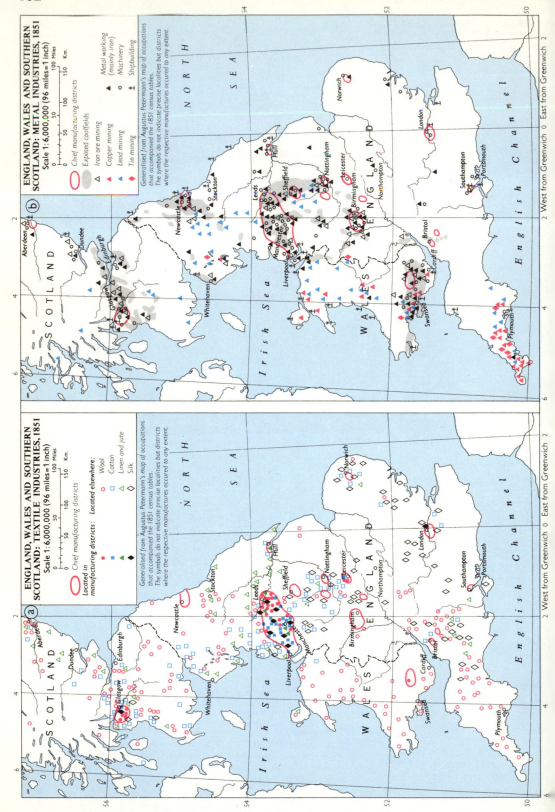

ENGLAND, WALES AND SOUTHERN SCOTLAND: TEXTILE INDUSTRIES, 1851
Scale 1:6,000,000 (96 miles=1 inch)

Chief manufacturing districts:
Located in manufacturing districts:
Located elsewhere:
Wool
Cotton
Linen and jute
Silk

Generalised from Augustus Petermann's map of occupations that accompanied the 1851 census tables.
The symbols do not indicate precise localities but districts where the respective manufactures occurred to any extent.

ENGLAND, WALES AND SOUTHERN SCOTLAND: METAL INDUSTRIES, 1851
Scale 1:6,000,000 (96 miles=1 inch)

Chief manufacturing districts
Exposed coalfields
Iron ore mining
Copper mining
Lead mining
Tin mining
Metal working (mainly iron)
Machinery
Shipbuilding

Generalised from Augustus Petermann's map of occupations that accompanied the 1851 census tables.
The symbols do not indicate precise localities but districts where the respective manufactures occurred to any extent.

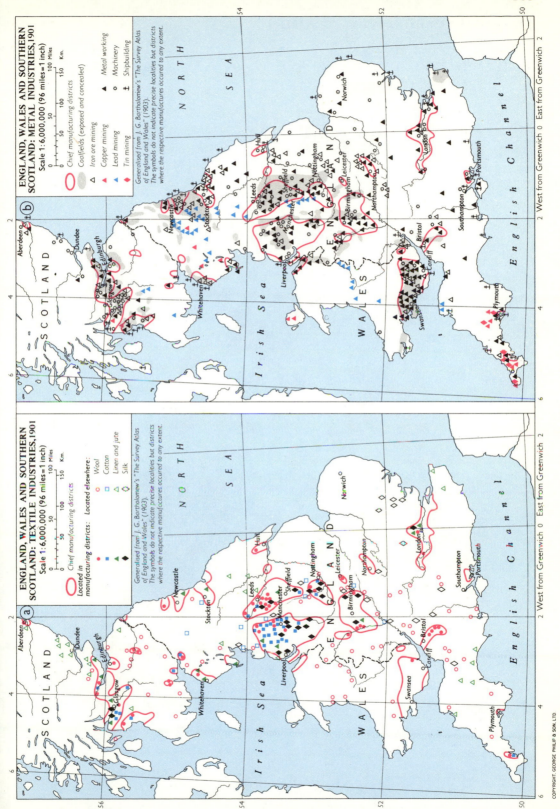

ENGLAND, WALES AND SOUTHERN SCOTLAND: METAL INDUSTRIES, 1901

Scale 1:6,000,000 (96 miles=1 inch)

Chief manufacturing districts
Coalfields (exposed and concealed)
Iron ore mining   Metal working
Copper mining   Machinery
Lead mining   Shipbuilding
Tin mining

Generalised from J. G. Bartholomew's "The Survey Atlas of England and Wales" (1903). The symbols do not indicate precise localities but districts where the respective manufactures occurred to any extent.

ENGLAND, WALES AND SOUTHERN SCOTLAND: TEXTILE INDUSTRIES, 1901

Scale 1:6,000,000 (96 miles=1 inch)

Chief manufacturing districts: Located elsewhere:
Located in manufacturing districts:
Wool
Cotton
Linen and jute
Silk

Generalised from J. G. Bartholomew's "The Survey Atlas of England and Wales" (1903). The symbols do not indicate precise localities but districts where the respective manufactures occurred to any extent.

COPYRIGHT GEORGE PHILIP & SON LTD

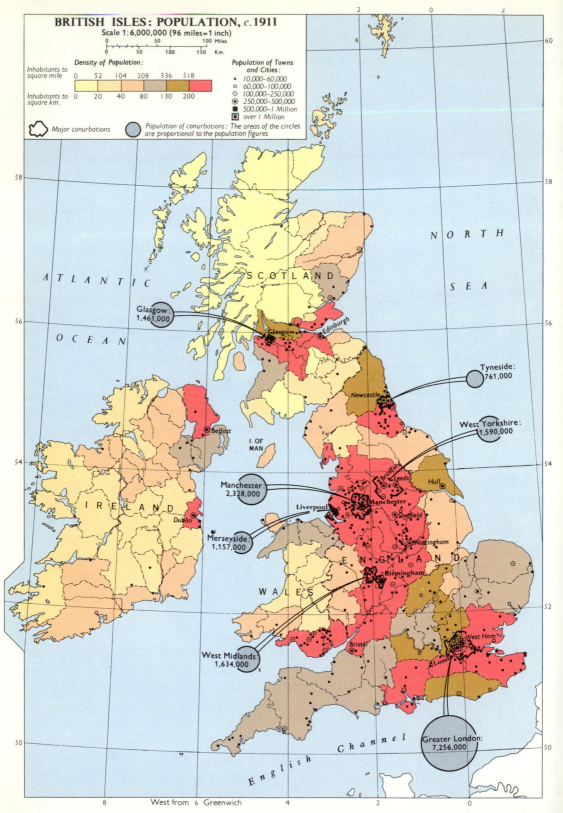

104

BRITISH ISLES: POPULATION, *c.*1911

Scale 1:6,000,000 (96 miles=1 inch)

Density of Population:

Inhabitants to square mile
0   52   104   208   336   518

Inhabitants to square km.
0   20   40   80   130   200

Population of Towns and Cities:
· 10,000–60,000
○ 60,000–100,000
⊙ 100,000–250,000
◉ 250,000–500,000
■ 500,000–1 Million
▣ over 1 Million

Major conurbations

Population of conurbations: The areas of the circles are proportional to the population figures

Glasgow: 1,461,000

Tyneside: 761,000

West Yorkshire: 1,590,000

Manchester: 2,328,000

Merseyside: 1,157,000

West Midlands: 1,634,000

Greater London: 7,256,000

SCOTLAND

Edinburgh
Glasgow
Belfast
I. OF MAN
Newcastle
Bradford   Leeds
Hull
Liverpool
Manchester
Sheffield
Nottingham
Dublin
IRELAND
ENGLAND
Birmingham
WALES
Bristol
West Ham
London

ATLANTIC OCEAN

NORTH SEA

English Channel

West from Greenwich
8   6   4   2   0

COPYRIGHT. GEORGE PHILIP & SON. LTD.

(a)
LONDON, c. 1700
Scale 1:50,000 (0·8 miles = 1 inch)
Built-up areas
Important buildings
Parks
City wall
River access steps, usually with ferry connections
Horse-ferry
St. Street
ISLINGTON
St. Pancras
To Hampstead
New River Pond
Pasture Ground
Tottenham Court
Marylebone Park
MARYLEBONE
South Hampton House
Montague House
Salt Peter House
TIBURN ROAD
Grays Inn
HIGH HOLBORN
Turnmill Brook
ALDERSGATE
Bun Hill Fields
Artillery Ground
SHOREDITCH
MILE END
WHITE CHAPEL
WHITE HORSE LANE
Lincolns Inn Fields
Lincolns Inn
Smithfield
Fleet Prison
Newgate
FLEET ST.
Moore Fields
BISHOPSGATE
Gresham College
Guildhall
CITY OF LONDON
Royal Exchange
Aldgate
Goodmans Field
Pest House Ground
Pasture Ground
Convent Garden
Somerset House
Temple
St. Pauls Cathedral
Trinity House
STRAND
Savoy
PICCADILLY
PALL MALL ST.
The Admiralty
Scotland Yard
White Hall
Hyde Park
St. James's Palace
St. James's Park
The Decoy
Buckingham House
Westminster Abbey
Parliament House
CITY OF WESTMINSTER
London Bridge
Billingsgate
Tower
Garden Grounds
SOUTHWARK
TOOLEY ST.
Savory Dock
Thames
Lambeth Palace
Tuthill Fields
LAMBETH
BLACKMAN ST.
KENT ST.
BARNABY ST.
NEWINGTON
Vauxhall Gardens
To Deptford

(b)
PARIS, c. 1700
Scale 1:50,000 (0·8 miles = 1 inch)
Built-up areas
Important buildings
Parks
City wall
Faub. Faubourg
MONCEAUX
NOUVELLE FRANCE
LES PORCHERONS
LE ROULE
LA VILLE
FAUBOURG MONTMARTRE
FAUBOURG DE RICHELIEU
FAUB. ST. DENIS
FAUBOURG ST. MARTIN
Porte St. Denis
Porte St. Martin
FAUBOURG DU TEMPLE
FAUBOURG ST. HONORÉ
Porte St. Honoré
Porte de Richelieu
Place de Louis le Grand
Place des Victoires
RUE ST. HONORÉ
RUE ST. MARTIN
le Temple
Champs Elysées
Porte de la Conference
Seine
les Tuileries
le Louvre
Pont Royal
Pont Neuf
PINCOUR
Hôtel Royal des Invalides
Place Vauban
FAUBOURG ST. GERMAIN
Collège des Quatre-Nations
Île du Palais
Notre Dame
Île St. Louis
Place Royal
la Bastille
FAUBOURG ST. ANTOINE
Île Louvier
RUE DE SEVE
RUE DE VAUGIRARD
la Sorbonne
les Chartreux
FAUB. ST. MICHEL
Ste. Géneviève
FAUBOURG ST. VICTOR
RAMBOUILLET
FAUBOURG ST. JACQUES
FAUBOURG ST. MARCEAU
Hôpital de la Salpêtrière

COPYRIGHT, GEORGE PHILIP & SON, LTD.

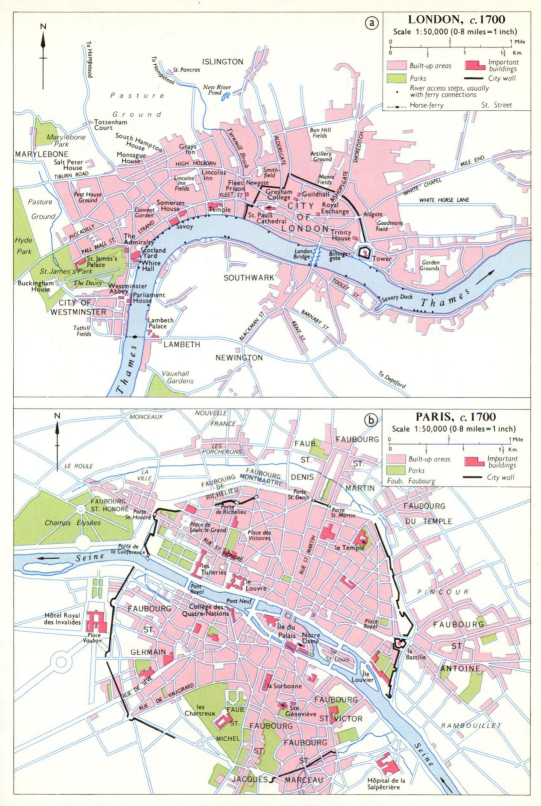

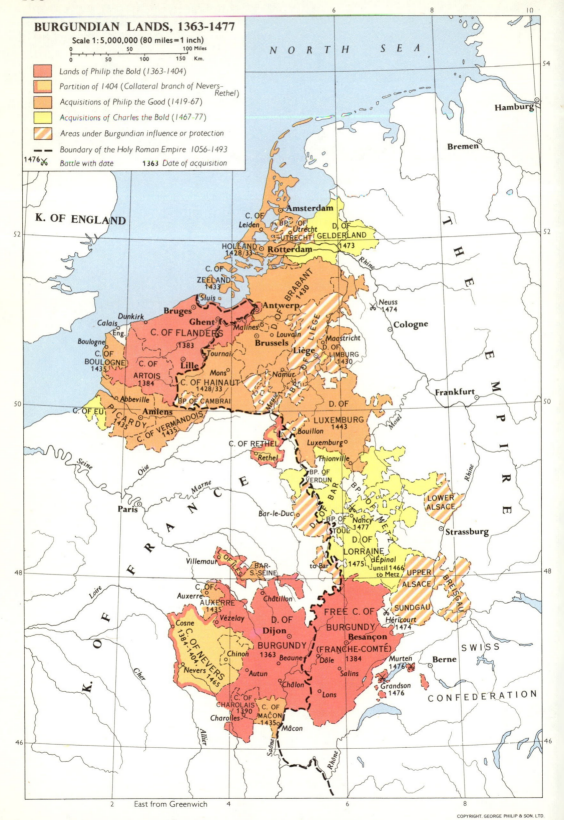

BURGUNDIAN LANDS, 1363-1477

Scale 1:5,000,000 (80 miles=1 inch)

Lands of Philip the Bold (1363-1404)

Partition of 1404 (Collateral branch of Nevers-Rethel)

Acquisitions of Philip the Good (1419-67)

Acquisitions of Charles the Bold (1467-77)

Areas under Burgundian influence or protection

Boundary of the Holy Roman Empire 1056-1493

1476 ✕ Battle with date   1363 Date of acquisition

NORTH SEA

THE

Hamburg

Bremen

K. OF ENGLAND

Amsterdam

C. OF Leiden

BP. OF Utrecht

D. OF GELDERLAND

UTRECHT

HOLLAND 1428/33

Rotterdam

1473

Rhine

C. OF ZEELAND 1433

Sluis

BRABANT 1430

Antwerp

D. OF LIEGE

Neuss 1474

Cologne

Bruges

Ghent

Malines

Louvain

Maastricht

D. OF LIMBURG 1430

Calais

Dunkirk

C. OF FLANDERS 1383

Brussels

Liège

Eng.

Boulogne

Tournai

Mons

C. OF HAINAUT 1428/33

Namur

Frankfurt

C. OF BOULOGNE 1435

C. OF ARTOIS 1384

Lille

BP. OF CAMBRAI

D. OF

Abbeville

Amiens

LUXEMBURG 1443

Mosel

C. OF EU 1435

PICARDY

C. OF VERMANDOIS 1435

Bouillon

Luxemburg

Seine

C. OF RETHEL

Rethel

Thionville

BP. OF VERDUN

Oise

Marne

Bar-le-Duc

BP. OF

Paris

D. OF BAR

BP. OF TOUL

Nancy 1477

Strassburg

F R A N C E

Villemaur

C. OF LE

BAR-S-SEINE

D. OF LORRAINE 1475

Épinal until 1466 to Metz

LOWER ALSACE

to Bar

Loire

C. OF AUXERRE 1435

Auxerre

Châtillon

Cosne

Vézelay

D. OF BURGUNDY

FREE C. OF BURGUNDY

UPPER ALSACE

BREISGAU

SUNDGAU

Chinon

Dijon

1363

Beaune

Besançon (FRANCHE-COMTÉ) 1384

Héricourt 1474

Cher

C. OF NEVERS 1384-1404

Nevers 1465

Autun

Dôle

Salins

Murten 1476

Berne

SWISS

Châlon

Lons

Grandson 1476

K. OF

C. OF CHAROLAIS 1390

C. OF MÂCON 1435

CONFEDERATION

Charolles

Mâcon

Allier

Saône

Rhône

East from Greenwich

COPYRIGHT. GEORGE PHILIP & SON. LTD.

FRANCE, *c.*1500

Scale 1:7,500,000 (120 miles=1 inch)

0   50   100   150 Miles

0 50 100 150 200 Km.

French royal domain 1477 (including appanages)

Fiefs which fell to the French crown 1477-1527

Fiefs of Charles of Bourbon, taken in 1527 by
    the French crown

Other French fiefs

1498   Date of acquisition

NORTH SEA

Amsterdam

London

K. OF ENGLAND

Ghent

Calais 1347-1558
to Eng.

Brussels

Boulogne
Occupied by England
1544-50

C. OF
ARTOIS
1477-93

Arras

Frankfurt

English Channel

Dieppe

Cherbourg

Langueville

Caen

Rouen

Amiens

C. OF
PICARDY
1477/82

St. Quentin

Soissons

C. OF
RETHEL

Reims

Nancy

Strassburg

NORMANDY

Seine

ILE - DE -
FRANCE

Paris

D. OF VALOIS
1515

Vertus

BARROIS
MOUVANT
to Bar

Channel Is.

Brest

Rennes

Vannes

D. OF BRITTANY
1491

C. OF
ALENÇON
1525

C. OF
PERCHE
1474/83

Nemours

Troyes

CHAMPAGNE

Bassigny
to Barrois
mouvant

Le Mans

C. OF MAINE
1481

C. OF
DUNOIS

D. OF
Orléans

Sens

Auxerre

Semur

D. OF
Dijon

Berne

Nantes

ANJOU

Angers

D. OF
VENDOME

Blois

C. OF
BLOIS

ORLÉANS
1498

Tours

TOURAINE

Sancerre

Bourges

C. OF
NEVERS

Nevers

BURGUNDY
1477/82

POITOU

Parthenay

Châtellerault

BERRY

Moulins

D. OF BOURBON

C. OF
CHAROLAIS
1477-93 to Fr.
1493 to Habsburgs

Poitiers

Mâcon

AUNIS

Niort

Rochefort

SAINTONGE

C. OF
Guéret

LA-MARCHE

C. OF
Angoulême
1515

Limoges

Clermont

Thiers

FOREZ

C. OF

Montbrison

Lyons

Vienne

Bay of

Biscay

Angoulême

V.C. OF
LIMOGES

C. OF
Périgueux

D. OF
AUVERGNE

Grenoble

Bordeaux

Garonne

PÉRIGORD

Turenne

Murat

Le Puy

Valence

DAUPHINÉ

GUYENNE

Castillon

Cahors

C. OF

Rodez

C. OF
RODEZ

Orange

C. OF
VENAISSIN
to the Papacy

C. OF
PROVENCE
1481

Santander

Bayonne

S. OF
ALBRET
1520 Duchy

Agen

Montauban

Albi

Avignon

Arles

Aix

Bilbao

C. OF ARMAGNAC
1497

Auch

Toulouse

ASTARAC

Montpellier

LANGUEDOC

Marseilles

V.C. OF
Pau
BÉARN

Tarbes

C. OF

C. OF
BIGORRE

C. OF
COMINGES

FOIX

1507

Narbonne

Gulf of Lions

SOULE

K. OF

NAVARRE

Pamplona

ROUSSILLON

CERDAGNE
1462-93

Saragossa

K. OF SPAIN

Barcelona

MEDITERRANEAN

Tarragona

SEA

THE EMPIRE

Rhine

COPYRIGHT. GEORGE PHILIP & SON. LTD.

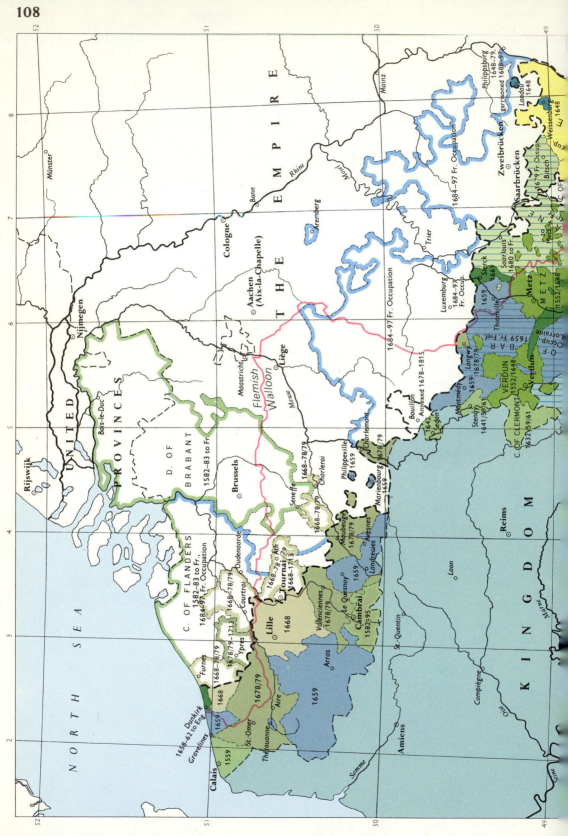

NORTH SEA

UNITED PROVINCES

THE EMPIRE

KINGDOM

Münster

Nijmegen

Rijswijk

Bois-le-Duc 1582–83 to Fr.

D. OF BRABANT 1582–83 to Fr.

Brussels

Maastricht

Flemish

Walloon

Liège

Cologne

Bonn

Aremberg

Rhine

Mosel

Trier

Mainz

Aachen (Aix-la-Chapelle)

Meuse

1684–97 Fr. Occupation

1684–97 Fr. Occupation

Annexed 1678–1815

Bouillon

Sedan 1642

Luxemburg 1684–97 Fr. Occup.

Zweibrücken

Saarbrücken

Sierck

Saarlouis 1680 to Fr.

Thionville 1659

Metz

METZ 1552/1648

Charlemont

Philippeville 1659

Mariembourg 1678/79 1659

Charleroi 1668–78/79

Seneffe 1668–78/79

Oudenaarde

Ath 1668–78/79

Tournai 1668–1713 1668/79

Courtrai

Ypres 1678/79–1713

Furnes 1668–78/79

1668

Dunkirk 1658–62 to Eng.

Gravelines 1659

Calais

St. Omer 1678/79

Thérouanne

Aire

1659

Maubeuge 1678/79

Avesnes 1659

Landrecies

Le Quesnoy 1659

Valenciennes 1678/79

Cambrai 1582–95

Arras 1659

St.-Quentin

Laon

Reims

Amiens

Compiègne

Longwy 1678/79

Montmédy 1659

Stenay 1641/59/61

Verdun

VERDUN 1552/1648

C. OF CLERMONT 1632/59/61

B A R Occup. 1659 Fr. Fief.

OF Occup. Lorraine

Landau 1648

Weissenburg 1648

Philippsburg 1644/97

garrisoned 1688–97

1679 Fr. Occup.

Bitsch

Toul

Thann

C. OF FLANDERS 1582–83 to Fr... 1684–97 Fr. Occupation

Lille 1668

Somme

Marne

Oise

Seine

C. OF. OT

Philippsburg 1648–79

N O R T H   S E A

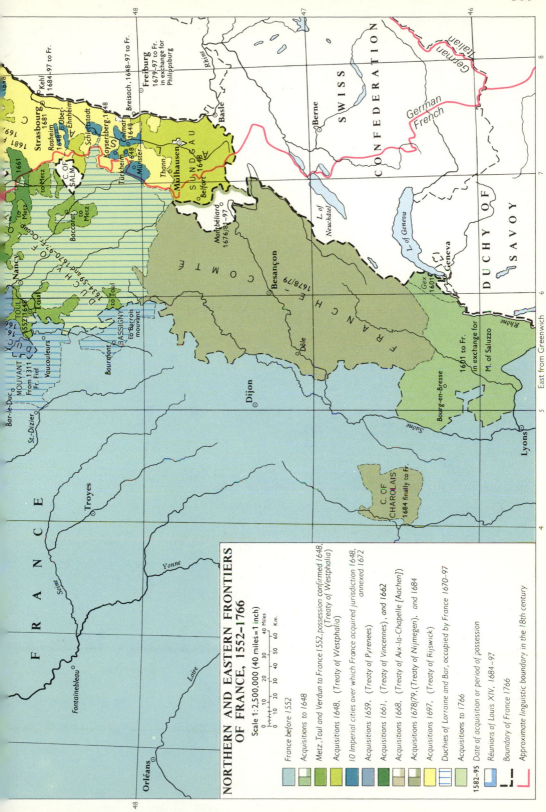

NORTHERN AND EASTERN FRONTIERS OF FRANCE, 1552–1766

Scale 1:2,500,000 (40 miles=1 inch)

```
            10   20   30   40 Miles
0   10  20  30  40  50  60  Km.
```

France before 1552

Acquisitions to 1648

Metz, Toul and Verdun to France 1552, possession confirmed 1648. (Treaty of Westphalia)

Acquisitions 1648. (Treaty of Westphalia)

10 Imperial cities over which France acquired jurisdiction 1648, annexed 1672

Acquisitions 1659. (Treaty of Pyrenees)

Acquisitions 1661, (Treaty of Vincennes), and 1662

Acquisitions 1668. (Treaty of Aix-la-Chapelle [Aachen])

Acquisitions 1678/79. (Treaty of Nijmegen), and 1684

Acquisitions 1697. (Treaty of Rijswick)

Duchies of Lorraine and Bar, occupied by France 1670–97

Acquisitions to 1766

1582–95   Date of acquisition or period of possession

Réunions of Louis XIV, 1684–97

Boundary of France 1766

Approximate linguistic boundary in the 18th century

COPYRIGHT. GEORGE PHILIP & SON LTD.

Map labels: Kehl 1684–97 to Fr.; Strasbourg 1681; Rosheim 1648; Ober-Ehnheim 1648; Schlettstadt; Kaysersberg 1648; Colmar 1648; Türkheim; Münster 1648; Thann; Freiburg 1679–97 to Fr. in exchange for Philippsburg; Breisach, 1648–97 to Fr.; Basle; Rhine; SWISS CONFEDERATION; German; French; Italian; Berne; Mülhausen; SUNDGAU; Belfort 1648; Montbéliard 1676/81–97; L. of Neuchâtel; L. of Geneva; Geneva; Gex 1601; DUCHY OF SAVOY; Besançon; FRANCHE COMTÉ 1678/79; Dole; Rhône; Saône; Bourg-en-Bresse; 1601 to Fr. in exchange for M. of Saluzzo; Lyons; to Metz; Nancy; Baccarat to Metz; DUCHY OF LORRAINE 1634–59 and 1670–97 F. occup.; C. OF SALM; BASSIGNY to Barrois mouvant; Bourmont; Vaucouleurs; TOUL to Metz 1552/1648; Toul; Bar-le-Duc; BAROIS MOUVANT From 1311 Fr. Fief; St.-Dizier; Dijon; Troyes; C. OF CHAROLAIS 1684 finally to Fr.; Seine; Yonne; Loire; Fontainebleau; Orléans; FRANCE; East from Greenwich

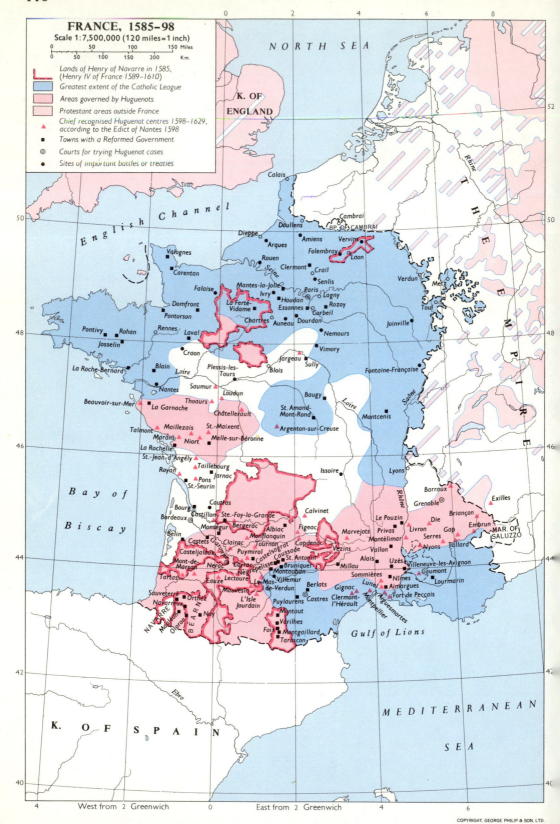

FRANCE, 1585–98

Scale 1:7,500,000 (120 miles=1 inch)

0	50	100 150 Miles
0	50 100	150 200 Km.

Lands of Henry of Navarre in 1585,
(Henry IV of France 1589–1610)

Greatest extent of the Catholic League

Areas governed by Huguenots

Protestant areas outside France

▲ Chief recognised Huguenot centres 1598–1629,
according to the Edict of Nantes 1598

■ Towns with a Reformed Government

◎ Courts for trying Huguenot cases

● Sites of important battles or treaties

NORTH SEA

K. OF ENGLAND

English Channel

THE EMPIRE

Calais

Doullens   Cambrai
   BP. OF CAMBRAI
Dieppe   Arques   Amiens   Vervins
   Folembray   Laon
Rouen   Clermont   Crail   Verdun   Metz
Valognes   Seine   Senlis
Carentan   Mantes-la-Jolie   Paris   Lagny   Toul
Falaise   Ivry   Houdan   Rozoy   Joinville
Domfront   La Ferté-   Essonnes   Carbeil
Pontorson   Vidame   Auneau   Dourdan   Nemours
   Chartres   Vimory
Pontivy   Rohan   Rennes   Laval   Jargeau   Fontaine-Française
Josselin   Craon   Blois   Sully
   Saône
La Roche-Bernard   Blain   Loire   Plessis-les-   Baugy   Montcenis
   Tours
   Nantes   Saumur   Loudun   St. Amand-   Loire
Beauvoir-sur-Mer   Thouars   Mont-Rond
   La Garnache   Châtellerault
   Maillezais   St.-Maixent   Argenton-sur-Creuse
Talmont   Marans   Niort   Melle-sur-Béronne
   La Rochelle
   St.-Jean-d'Angély   Issoire   Lyons
   Royan   Taillebourg
   Pons   Jarnac   Barraux
   St.-Seurin   Grenoble   Exilles
   Cautres   Calvinet   Le Pouzin   Die   Briançon
Bordeaux   Castillon   Ste.-Foy-la-Grande   Figeac   Marvejots   Privas   Livron   Gap   Embrun
   Monsegur   Bergerac   Montélimar   Serres   MAR. OF
Belin   Clairac   Albiac   Tournon   Vallon   Nyons   Tallard   SALUZZO
   Castets   Monflanquin   Castelsagrat   Capdenac   Vezins   Alais   Uzès   Villeneuve-les-Avignon
   Casteljaloux   Puymirol   St. Antonin   Millau   Sommières   Nîmes   Gaumont
Mont-de-   Lavrac   Castelsagrat   Bruniquel   Montauban   Lunel   Aimargues   Lourmarin
Marsan   Néracs   Negrepelisse   Le Mas-   Berlats   Gignac   Fort de Peccais
Tartas   Lectoure   Villemur-   Castres   Clermont-   Aiguesmortes
Sauveterre   Eauze   de-Verdun   Puylaurens   l'Hérault   Montpellier
Navarreux   Mauvesin   Montaut
   Orthez   L'Isle   Varilhes   Gulf of Lions
NAVARRE   Nay   Jourdain   Foix
   Oloron   BÉARN   Montgaillard
   Tarascon

Bay of
Biscay

Ebro

K. OF SPAIN

MEDITERRANEAN
SEA

West from 2 Greenwich   East from 2 Greenwich

COPYRIGHT. GEORGE PHILIP & SON. LTD.

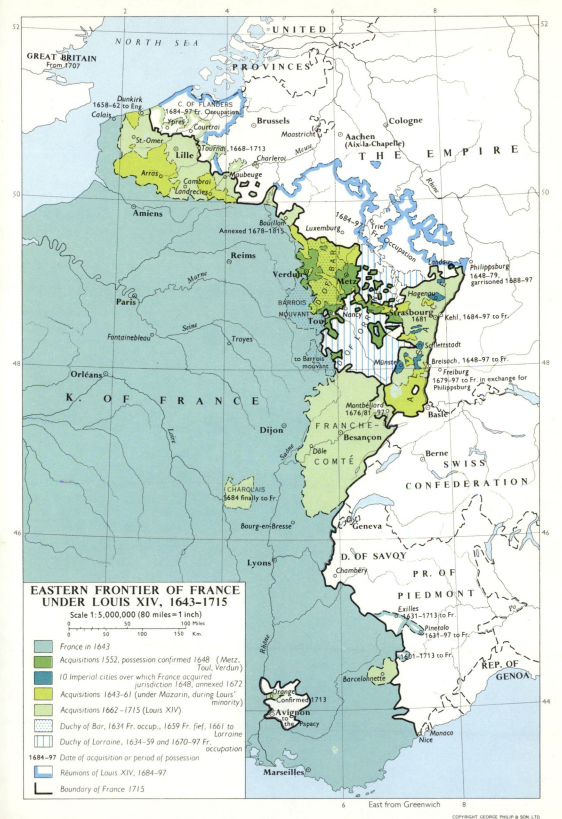

EASTERN FRONTIER OF FRANCE
UNDER LOUIS XIV, 1643–1715

Scale 1:5,000,000 (80 miles = 1 inch)

0   50   100 Miles

0   50   100   150 Km.

France in 1643

Acquisitions 1552, possession confirmed 1648 (Metz, Toul, Verdun)

10 Imperial cities over which France acquired jurisdiction 1648, annexed 1672

Acquisitions 1643–61 (under Mazarin, during Louis' minority)

Acquisitions 1662–1715 (Louis XIV)

Duchy of Bar, 1634 Fr. occup., 1659 Fr. fief, 1661 to Lorraine

Duchy of Lorraine, 1634–59 and 1670–97 Fr. occupation

1684–97   Date of acquisition or period of possession

Réunions of Louis XIV, 1684–97

Boundary of France 1715

COPYRIGHT. GEORGE PHILIP & SON. LTD.

East from Greenwich

West from Greenwich 0 East from Greenwich

FRANCE, 1632: POST ROADS

Scale 1:10,000,000 (160 miles = 1 inch)

0 50 100 150 200 Miles
0 100 200 300 Km.

—— Post roads —— Other important roads

⌐╌╌ Boundary of France

Corsica Until 1768 (to Genoa)

FRANCE, 1789: CUSTOMS AND TAX AREAS

Scale 1:10,000,000 (160 miles = 1 inch)

0 50 100 150 200 Miles
0 100 200 300 Km.

Customs Areas:

—— Boundary of the "cinq grosses fermes"

—— Boundary of the "provinces réputées étrangères"

—— Boundary of the "provinces d'étranger effectif"

Tax Areas:

Region of the great salt tax (grande gabelle)

Region of the little salt tax (petite gabelle)

Region of the Rethel salt tax (gabelle du Rethel)

Region of the salt-works (gabelle du saline)

Region of the "quart-bouillon"

Region of the "redeemed provinces"

Region of the "free provinces"

The figures show the relative prices paid for the same amount of salt in various parts

○ Seat of a tax office

⌐╌╌ Boundaries of tax areas

COPYRIGHT. GEORGE PHILIP & SON. LTD.

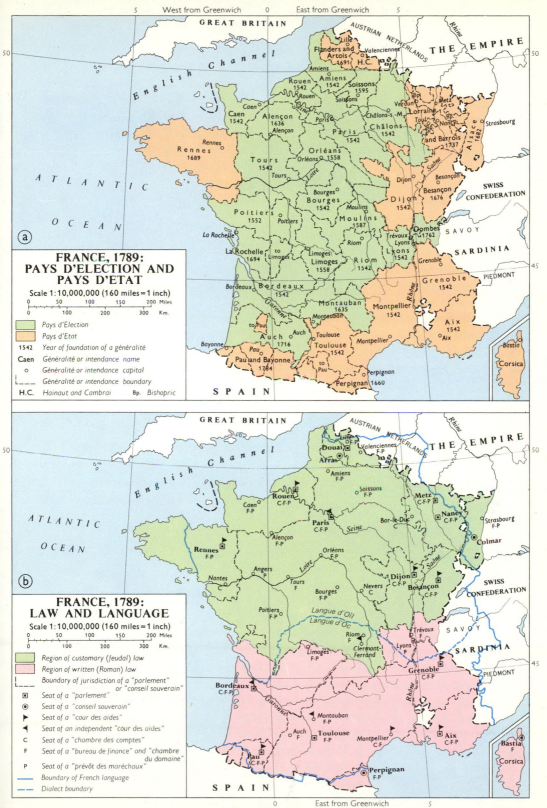

Map (a):

FRANCE, 1789:
PAYS D'ELECTION AND PAYS D'ETAT

Scale 1:10,000,000 (160 miles = 1 inch)

0   50   100   150   200 Miles
0   100   200   300 Km.

☐ Pays d'Election
☐ Pays d'Etat
1542   Year of foundation of a généralité
Caen   Généralité or intendance name
○   Généralité or intendance capital
└┘ --- Généralité or intendance boundary
H.C. Hainaut and Cambrai   **Bp.** Bishopric

Map (b):

FRANCE, 1789:
LAW AND LANGUAGE

Scale 1:10,000,000 (160 miles = 1 inch)

0   50   100   150   200 Miles
0   100   200   300 Km.

☐ Region of customary (feudal) law
☐ Region of written (Roman) law
└┘ --- Boundary of jurisdiction of a "parlement"
            or "conseil souverain"
⊡   Seat of a "parlement"
⊙   Seat of a "conseil souverain"
▶   Seat of a "cour des aides"
◀   Seat of an independent "cour des aides"
C   Seat of a "chambre des comptes"
F   Seat of a "bureau de finance" and "chambre
            du domaine"
P   Seat of a "prévôt des maréchaux"
──── Boundary of French language
── ── Dialect boundary

COPYRIGHT. GEORGE PHILIP & SON. LTD.

West from Greenwich
East from Greenwich
FRANCE, 1789: ECCLESIASTICAL
Scale 1:10,000,000 (160 miles = 1 inch)
0 50 100 150 200 Miles
0 100 200 300 Km.
Monastic Establishments:
Chief Abbey of an order
Grand priory
Noble chapter
Dioceses:
"Foreign clergy"
Boundary of an archbishopric
Archiepiscopal see
Episcopal see
A. Apt, B. Beziers, C. Carcassonne, Cav. Cavaillon, D. Digne, M. Mirepoix, Mo. Montpellier, O. Orange, P. Pamiers, R. Rieux, S. Senez, St.-A. St.-Antoine, St.-P. St.-Papoul
GREAT BRITAIN
AUSTRIAN NETHERLANDS
THE EMPIRE
Rhine
English Channel
ATLANTIC OCEAN
SWISS CONFEDERATION
SAVOY
K. OF SARDINIA
PIEDMONT
SPAIN
Bourbourg
St.-Omer
Boulogne
Arras
Denain
Maubeuge
Cambrai
Avesnes
Amiens
Prémontré
Noyon
Laon
Rouen
Bourgachard
Beauvais
Senlis
Soissons
Reims
Verdun
Metz
Bouxières-aux-Dames
Strasbourg
Nancy
Andlau
Toul
Bayeux
Lisieux
Coutances
Évreux
Châlons-s.-M.
Paris
Meaux
Tréguier
St.-Pol-de-Léon
St.-Malo
Sées
Avranches
Seine
Troyes
Poussay
St.-Dié
Épinal
Remiremont
St.-Brieuc
Dol
Chartres
Clairvaux
Langres
Morimont
Quimper
Rennes
Orléans
Sens
Le Mans
Montigny
Lure
Vannes
Blois
Auxerre
Dijon
Baume-les-Dames
Angers
Loire
Nantes
Tours
Nevers
Cîteaux
Besançon
Fontevrault
Bourges
Autun
Château-Chalon
Lons-le-Saunier
Chalon-s.-S.
Cigny
Luçon
Poitiers
Ainay
Cluny
St.-Claude
Mâcon
La Rochelle
Lyons
Saintes
Limoges
Vienne
St.-Chef
La Grande Chartreuse
Angoulême
Grenoble
Chancelade
Tulle
Brioude
St.-A.
Périgueux
Le Puy
Valence
Sarlat
Bordeaux
Die
Gap
Embrun
Mende
Vivers
St.-Paul
Cahors
Vaison
Sisteron
Rodez
Alais
Uzès
Bazas
Agen
Glandèves
Condom
Montauban
Vabres
Avignon
Nîmes
Grasse
Lectoure
Albi
St.-Gilles
Riez
Dax
Aire
Lavaur
Castres
Lodève
Arles
Aix
Vence
Auch
Toulouse
Fréjus
Bayonne
Lescar
Lombez
St.-Pons
Mo.
Agde
Marseilles
Oloron
Tarbes
St.-P.
Narbonne
Toulon
Comminges
Couserans
Alet
Perpignan
Nebbio
Accia
Corsica
Ajaccio

FRANCE, 1802: ECCLESIASTICAL
Scale 1:10,000,000 (160 miles = 1 inch)
0 50 100 150 200 Miles
0 100 200 300 Km.
Boundary of an archbishopric
Archiepiscopal see
Archiepiscopal see, suppressed in 1802
Archiepiscopal see, erected in 1802
Episcopal see
Episcopal see, suppressed in 1802
Episcopal see, erected in 1802
UNITED KINGDOM
THE EMPIRE
English Channel
ATLANTIC OCEAN
HELVETIC REP.
Rhine
SPAIN
East from Greenwich
Ghent
Malines
Aix-la-Chapelle
Namur
Liège
Arras
Mayence
Trèves
Amiens
Rouen
Soissons
Metz
Bayeux
Coutances
Évreux
Meaux
Paris
Nancy
Strasbourg
Sées
Versailles
Seine
Troyes
St.-Brieuc
Rennes
Quimper
Le Mans
Orléans
Vannes
Angers
Loire
Nantes
Tours
Dijon
Besançon
Bourges
Autun
Poitiers
Mâcon
La Rochelle
Clermont-Ferrand
Lyons
Limoges
Chambéry
Angoulême
Grenoble
Le Puy
St.-Flour
Bordeaux
Valence
Mende
Cahors
Digne
Agen
Nice
Montpellier
Aix
Bayonne
Toulouse
Carcassonne
1802 to Aix
Corsica
Ajaccio

COPYRIGHT. GEORGE PHILIP & SON. LTD.

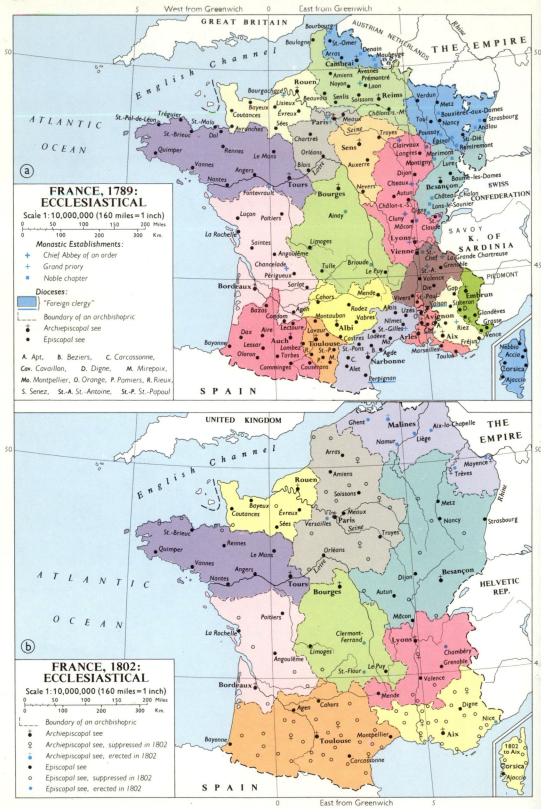

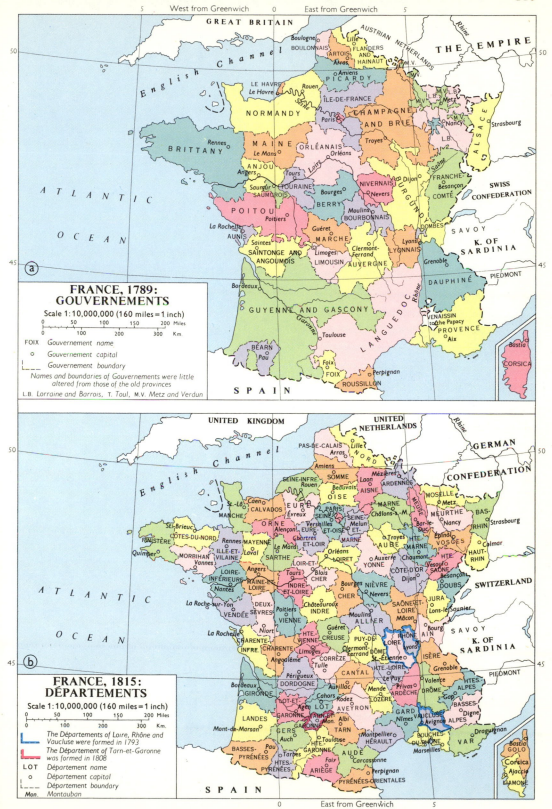

FRANCE, 1789: GOUVERNEMENTS

Scale 1:10,000,000 (160 miles = 1 inch)

| | 50 | 100 | 150 | 200 Miles |
| 0 | 100 | 200 | 300 | Km. |

FOIX   *Gouvernement name*
○   *Gouvernement capital*
   Gouvernement boundary
Names and boundaries of Gouvernements were little altered from those of the old provinces
L.B. *Lorraine and Barrois,* T. *Toul,* M.V. *Metz and Verdun*

GREAT BRITAIN
AUSTRIAN NETHERLANDS
THE EMPIRE
English Channel
West from Greenwich   East from Greenwich
Rhine
Boulogne
BOULONNAIS
Lille
FLANDERS AND HAINAUT
Arras
ARTOIS
Amiens
PICARDY
LE HAVRE
Le Havre
Rouen
ÎLE-DE-FRANCE
M.V.
M.V.
M.V. L.B.
L.B.
Metz
Strasbourg
NORMANDY
CHAMPAGNE AND BRIE
Nancy
ALSACE
Paris
Seine
BRITTANY
Rennes
MAINE
ORLÉANAIS
Troyes
T.
L.B.
Le Mans
Orléans
ANJOU
Loire
Angers
TOURAINE
Tours
Bourges
NIVERNAIS
Dijon
FRANCHE COMTÉ
Besançon
SWISS CONFEDERATION
SAUMUROIS
Saumur
POITOU
BERRY
Nevers
BURGUNDY
Saône
Poitiers
Moulins
BOURBONNAIS
DOMBES
SAVOY
La Rochelle
MARCHE
Guéret
K. OF SARDINIA
AUNIS
Limoges
Lyons
Saintes
LIMOUSIN
Clermont-Ferrand
LYONNAIS
Grenoble
SAINTONGE AND ANGOUMOIS
AUVERGNE
DAUPHINÉ
PIEDMONT
Bordeaux
Rhône
GUYENNE AND GASCONY
VENAISSIN to the Papacy
Toulouse
LANGUEDOC
PROVENCE
Aix
Garonne
BÉARN
Pau
Foix
FOIX
Perpignan
ROUSSILLON
SPAIN
ATLANTIC OCEAN
Bastia
CORSICA

ATLANTIC OCEAN

FRANCE, 1815: DÉPARTEMENTS

Scale 1:10,000,000 (160 miles = 1 inch)

| | 50 | 100 | 150 | 200 Miles |
| 0 | 100 | 200 | 300 | Km. |

   The Départements of Loire, Rhône and Vaucluse were formed in 1793
   The Département of Tarn-et-Garonne was formed in 1808
LOT   *Département name*
○   *Département capital*
   Département boundary
Mon.   *Montauban*

UNITED KINGDOM
UNITED NETHERLANDS
GERMAN CONFEDERATION
English Channel
Rhine
PAS-DE-CALAIS
Lille
Arras
NORD
Amiens
SOMME
Mézières
ARDENNES
SEINE-INFRE.
Rouen
OISE
Laon
AISNE
MOSELLE
Caen
EURE
Beauvais
MARNE
Metz
St-Lô
CALVADOS
Évreux
Châlons-s.-M.
MEURTHE
Nancy
BAS-RHIN
Strasbourg
MANCHE
ORNE
SEINE
PARIS
SEINE-ET-OISE
Bar-le-Duc
MEUSE
St-Brieuc
CÔTES-DU-NORD
Alençon
Versailles
Melun
SEINE-ET-MARNE
Épinal
VOSGES
FINISTÈRE
Rennes
MAYENNE
Chartres
EURE-ET-LOIR
Troyes
AUBE
HTE.-SAÔNE
HAUT-RHIN
Colmar
Quimper
ILLE-ET-VILAINE
Laval
SARTHE
Le Mans
LOIRET
Orléans
Auxerre
YONNE
Chaumont
HTE.-MARNE
Vesoul
Besançon
MORBIHAN
Vannes
LOIRE-ET-CHER
Blois
CÔTE-D'OR
Dijon
DOUBS
Angers
MAINE-ET-LOIRE
Tours
INDRE-ET-LOIRE
Bourges
NIÈVRE
SAÔNE-ET-LOIRE
JURA
SWITZERLAND
LOIRE-INFÉRIEURE
Nantes
CHER
Nevers
Lons-le-Saunier
La Roche-sur-Yon
DEUX-SÈVRES
Poitiers
Châteauroux
INDRE
Moulins
ALLIER
Mâcon
Bourg
AIN
SAVOY
VENDÉE
Niort
VIENNE
Guéret
CREUSE
PUY-DE-DÔME
RHÔNE
Lyons
K. OF SARDINIA
CHARENTE-INFRE.
HTE.-VIENNE
Limoges
Clermont-Ferrand
St-Étienne
LOIRE
ISÈRE
La Rochelle
CHARENTE
Angoulême
CORRÈZE
Tulle
CANTAL
HTE.-LOIRE
Le Puy
Privas
ARDÈCHE
Grenoble
PIEDMONT
Périgueux
DORDOGNE
Valence
DRÔME
HTES.-ALPES
Gap
Bordeaux
GIRONDE
LOT-ET-GARONNE
Cahors
LOT
Rodez
AVEYRON
Mende
LOZÈRE
GARD
Nîmes
VAUCLUSE
Avignon
BASSES-ALPES
Digne
LANDES
Agen
TARN-ET-GARONNE
Mon.
Albi
TARN
Montpellier
HÉRAULT
BOUCHES-DU-RHÔNE
Marseilles
VAR
Draguignan
Mont-de-Marsan
GERS
Auch
HTE.-GARONNE
Toulouse
AUDE
Pau
BASSES-PYRÉNÉES
Tarbes
HTES.-PYRÉNÉES
ARIÈGE
Foix
Carcassonne
Perpignan
PYRÉNÉES-ORIENTALES
SPAIN
East from Greenwich
Bastia
GOLO
Corsica
Ajaccio
LIAMONE
ATLANTIC OCEAN

COPYRIGHT. GEORGE PHILIP & SON. LTD.

PARIS, 1789
Scale 1:25,000 (0.4 miles=1 inch)

Built-up areas:
By 1700
Extensions by 1789
Important buildings
Parks
Churches +

Gal. Galerie   Q. Quai   R. Rue

¼ ½ ¾ Mile
¼ ½ ¾ 1 Km.

N

Seine

FAUBOURG ST. VICTOR

la Bastille
les Célestins
Grand Arsenal
Île Louvier
Île St. Louis
Q. D'ANJOU
Q. DE BOURBON
Q. D'ORLEANS
St. Victor
RUE DU FAUB. ST. VICTOR
les Bernardins
St. Étienne
Ste. Geneviève
RUE ST. VICTOR
RUE DU FAUB. ST. JACQUES
RUE D'ENFER

le Temple
RUE ST. LOUIS
RUE DU TEMPLE
St. Martin des Champs
St. Nicolas des Champs
la Soubise
RUE SAINT MARTIN
RUE ST. LOUIS
RUE ST. AUGUSTIN
RUE ST. ANTOINE
Place Royale
RUE ST. ANTOINE
VIEILLE RUE DU TEMPLE
RUE DE LA VERRERIE
RUE DU ROI DE SICILE
Quai des Ormes
Hôtel de Ville
QUAI DE LA GRÈVE
Porte St. Denis
RUE SAINT DENIS
Notre Dame
GRANDS DEGRÉS
la Sorbonne
RUE ST. JACQUES
RUE DE LA HARPE

RUE MONTMARTRE
R. DU FAUBOURG MONTMARTRE
RUE RICHELIEU
les Halles
Cimetière des Innocents
Bibliothèque Royale
Place des Victoires
Palais Royal
le Louvre
Pont Neuf
Île du Palais
la Conciergerie
Q. DE LA MÉGISSERIE
Q. DES MORFONDUS
Q. DES AUGUSTINS

RUE SAINT HONORÉ
les Capucines
la Madeleine
FAUBOURG ST. HONORÉ
RUE DU FAUBOURG ST. HONORÉ
Place Vendôme
Palais Colisée
Champs Élysées
COURS LA REINE
PORT AUX PIERRES
Seine
Place de Louis XV
Q. DE LA CONFÉRENCE
Pont de la Concorde Built 1787-91
Quai des Tuileries
Jardin des Tuileries
les Tuileries
GAL. DU LOUVRE
Pont Royal
Q. DES THÉATINS
Collège des Quatre-Nations
Q. MALAQUIS
St. Germain des Prés
la Charité
RUE DU FOUR
RUE DE L'UNIVERSITÉ
Q. D'ORSAY
Q. DE BOURBON
Pal. Bourbon
FAUBOURG ST. GERMAIN
RUE DE GRENELLE
RUE SAINT DOMINIQUE
RUE DE VAUGIRARD
RUE DE SÈVRES
Jardin du Luxembourg
les Chartreux
les Incurables
NOUVEAU COURS
Place Vauban
Hôtel Royal des Invalides
École Royal Militaire
CHEMIN DE SÈVE ET DE MEUDON
RUE DE BEROY
RUE DE CHARENTON
RUE DE LA ROCHETTE
RUE DU FAUB. ST. ANTOINE
CHEMIN VERD
DES CHANTIERS
RUE DE LA RAPÉE

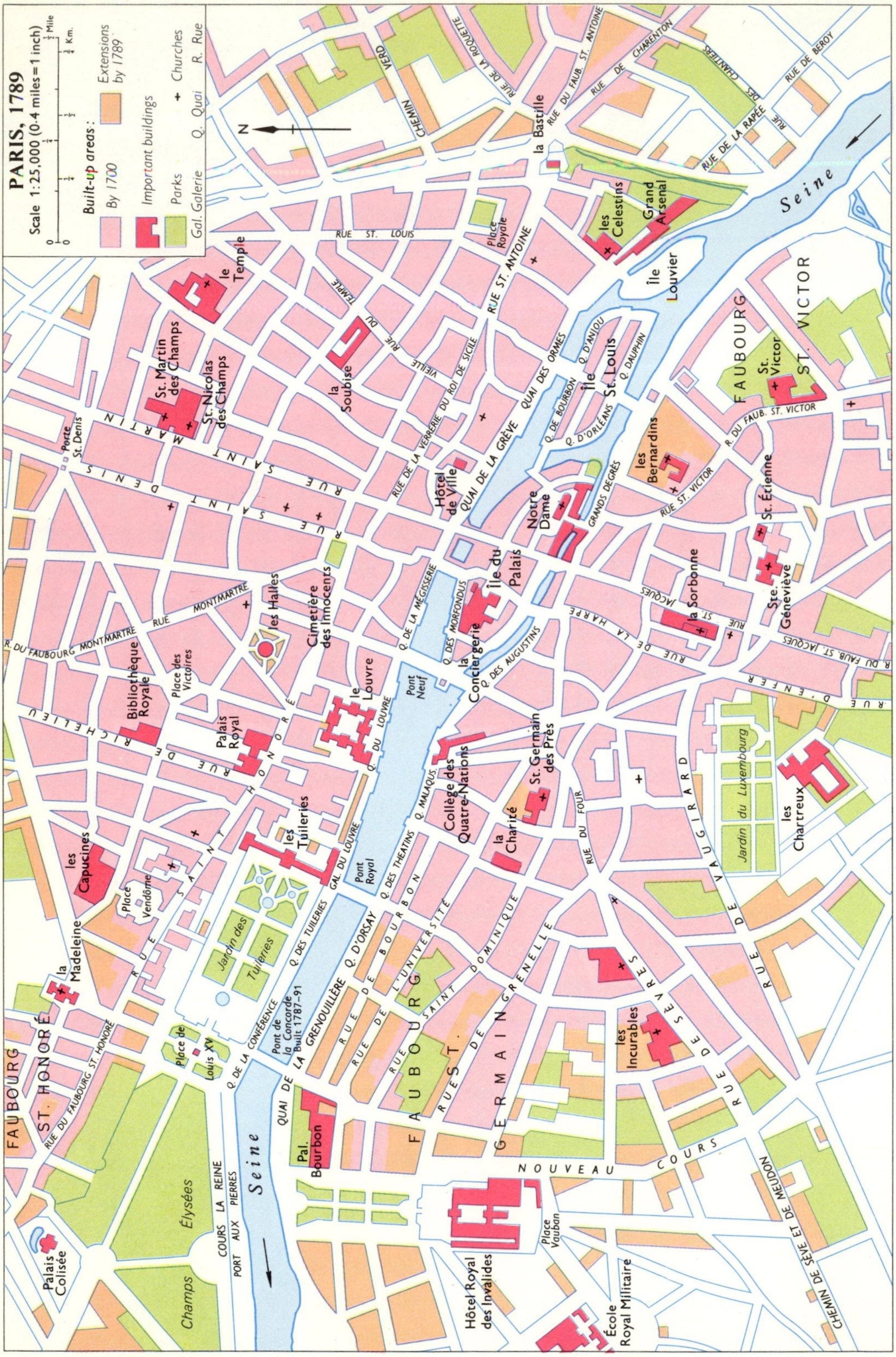

COPYRIGHT GEORGE PHILIP & SON LTD

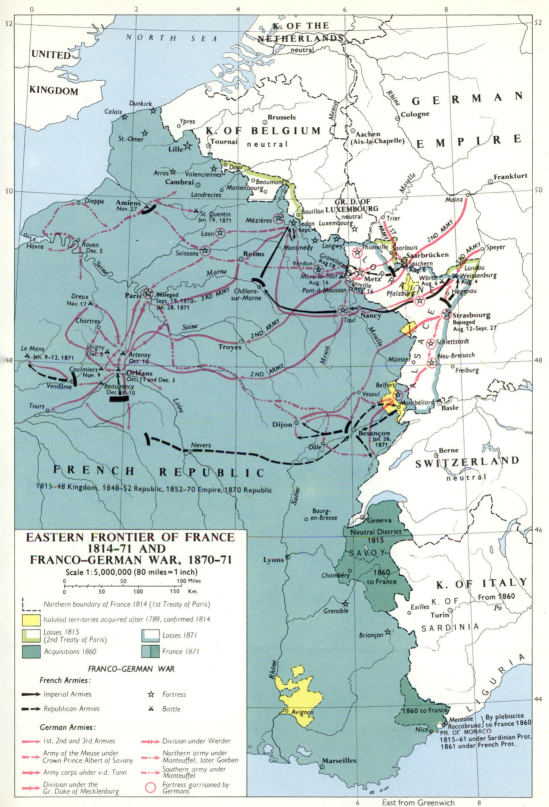

NORTH SEA

UNITED

KINGDOM

K. OF THE
NETHERLANDS
neutral

Dunkirk
Calais
Ypres
St.-Omer
Lille
Brussels
K. OF BELGIUM
neutral
Tournai
Aachen
(Aix-la-Chapelle)

GERMAN

Cologne

EMPIRE

Arras
Valenciennes
Cambrai
Landrecies
Marienbourg
Beaumont
Frankfurt
Mainz

Dieppe
Amiens
Nov. 27
St. Quentin
Jan. 19, 1871
Mézières
Sedan
Sept. 1
Bouillon
GR. D. OF
LUXEMBOURG
neutral
Luxembourg
Trier

Le
Havre
Rouen
Dec. 5
Soissons
Laon
Reims
Montmédy
Verdun
Longwy
Thionville
Saarlouis
Saarbrücken
Spichern
Aug. 6
1ST ARMY
2ND ARMY
Speyer

Dreux
Nov. 17
Paris
Besieged
Sept. 19, 1870–
Jan. 28, 1871
Chartres
Marne
3RD ARMY
Châlons-
sur-Marne
Gravelotte
Aug. 18
Mars-la-Tour
Aug. 16
Pont-à-Mousson
Metz
Ionville
Aug. 16
Pfalzburg
Wörth
Aug. 6
Weisenburg
Aug. 4
Landau
Hagenau

Seine
Loigny
Dec. 2
Artenay
Oct. 10
Troyes
2ND ARMY
Taul
Nancy
Strasbourg
Besieged
Aug. 12–Sept. 27

Le Mans
Jan. 9–12, 1871
Coulmiers
Nov. 9
Vendôme
Orléans
Oct. 11 and Dec. 3
Beaugency
Dec. 8–10
Loire
2ND ARMY
Schlettstadt
Neu-Breisach
Münster
Freiburg

Tours
Nevers
Dijon
Dôle
Belfort
Vesoul
Montbéliard
Besançon
Jan. 26,
1871
Basle
Berne

FRENCH REPUBLIC

1815–48 Kingdom, 1848–52 Republic, 1852–70 Empire, 1870 Republic

Bourg-
en-Bresse
Geneva
Neutral District
1815
SWITZERLAND
neutral

Lyons
Chambéry
SAVOY
1860
to France
K. OF ITALY
From 1860
Po

EASTERN FRONTIER OF FRANCE
1814–71 AND
FRANCO–GERMAN WAR, 1870–71

Scale 1:5,000,000 (80 miles = 1 inch)

0   50   100 Miles
0   50   100   150 Km.

Grenoble
Exilles
K. OF
TURIN
SARDINIA

Briançon

LIGURIA

Northern boundary of France 1814 (1st Treaty of Paris)

Isolated territories acquired after 1789, confirmed 1814

Losses 1815
(2nd Treaty of Paris)   Losses 1871

Acquisitions 1860   France 1871

FRANCO–GERMAN WAR

French Armies:

➡ Imperial Armies   ☆ Fortress

⇢ Republican Armies   ✕ Battle

German Armies:

➡ 1st, 2nd and 3rd Armies   ⇒ Division under Werder

➡ Army of the Meuse under
Crown Prince Albert of Saxony   ⇢ Northern army under
Manteuffel, later Goeben

➡ Army corps under v.d. Tann   ⇢ Southern army under
Manteuffel

➡ Division under the
Gr. Duke of Mecklenburg   ⭕ Fortress garrisoned by
Germans

Rhine
Avignon
Mentone
Roccabruna } to France 1860
Nice
PR. OF MONACO
1815–61 under Sardinian Prot.
1861 under French Prot.
By plebiscite
1860 to France

Marseilles

6   East from Greenwich   8

COPYRIGHT. GEORGE PHILIP & SON. LTD.

HANSEATIC LEAGUE AND THE BALTIC
1370 – c.1500

Scale 1:10,000,000 (160 miles=1 inch)

| 0 | 50 | 100 | 150 | 200 Miles |
| 0 | 100 | 200 | 300 Km. |

- **●** Principal towns *of the Hanseatic League*
- **·** Other towns
- **■** Foreign Counting Houses (Faktoreien)
- **▪** Other Foreign Depots
- **◉ ○** Towns not members of the Hanseatic League
- *Posen* Trade Fair
- Principal Hanseatic trade routes by sea
- Principal competitive English and Dutch trade routes by sea
- Principal trade routes by land
- Seas and lakes frozen in winter

NORWEGIAN SEA

NORWAY

Union 1397

Klar

Shetland Is.

Orkney Is.

Bergen
German Wharf
Closed c.1560

Oslo

Tönsberg

Skagerrak

Vänern

SCOTLAND

Edinburgh Berwick

NORTH SEA

Warberg

Aalborg Kattegat

DENMARK

Sound Helsin

Roskilde Copenhagen
Svendborg

Malm

Falste

Flensburg

Dublin

York Hull

Chester

Boston

Barth

Kiel Rostock Stra

Hamburg Lübeck Wismar Anklam

Pritzwalk

Lynn

Norwich

Yarmouth

Emden Bremen Elbe

WALES ENGLAND

Oxford Ipswich

Bristol

Amsterdam Stavoren

Deventer Hanover Brunswick

Berlin

Osnabrück

Münster

Magdeburg

Fran

Plymouth Southampton

London
Steelyard
Closed 1598

Middelburg Brielle
Utrecht Tiel

Venlo

Göttingen

Halle

Leipzig

Damme
Bruges
Closed 1553

Antwerp
1553–76

Calais

Ypres Ghent

Cologne

Erfurt

English Channel

Dieppe

Dinant

Rhine

Frankfurt

Rouen

Mainz

Pra

Seine

Paris

Metz

Nuremberg

THE EMP

Rennes

FRANCE

Nördlingen

Danu

Nantes

Strassburg

West from Greenwich 0 East from Greenwich

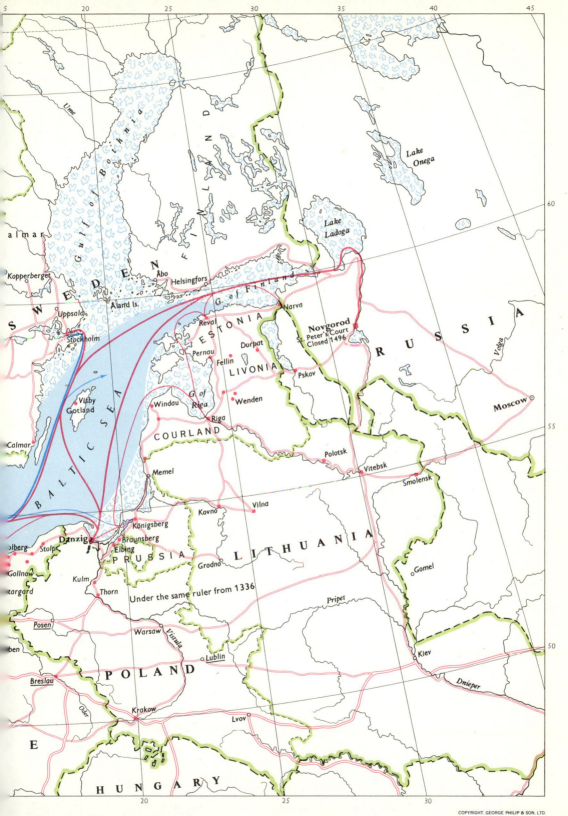

Ume

Kopperberget

almar

S W E D E N

Gulf of Bothnia

F I N L A N D

Åbo

Helsingfors

Aland Is.

G. of Finland

Lake Onega

Lake Ladoga

Uppsala

Stockholm

Reval

ESTONIA

Narva

Novgorod
St. Peter's Court
Closed 1496

R U S S I A

Volga

Dorpat

Pernau

Fellin

L I V O N I A

Pskov

Visby
Gotland

B A L T I C   S E A

Windau

G. of Riga

Wenden

Riga

C O U R L A N D

Polotsk

Vitebsk

Smolensk

Moscow

Calmar

Memel

Kovno

Vilna

L I T H U A N I A

olberg

Stolp

Königsberg

Danzig

Braunsberg

Elbing

P R U S S I A

Grodno

Gomel

Gollnow

Kulm

Thorn

Under the same ruler from 1336

Pripet

targard

Posen

Warsaw

Vistula

Lublin

Kiev

Dnieper

ben

Breslau

P O L A N D

Oder

Krakow

Lvov

60

55

50

E

H U N G A R Y

COPYRIGHT. GEORGE PHILIP & SON, LTD.

SPREAD OF GERMAN SETTLEMENTS EASTWARDS BY THE 15TH CENTURY

Scale 1:10,000,000 (160 miles = 1 inch)

	Boundary between Germans and Slavs, c.800
	Germans
	Scandinavians	Teutonic Group
	Slavonic Group
	Romanic Group
	Letto–Lithuanian Group
	Finnish Group
	Magyars (Ugrian Group)
1240	Date of foundation of German settlement

East from Greenwich

COPYRIGHT. GEORGE PHILIP & SON. LTD.

East from Greenwich

THE IMPERIAL CIRCLES, c.1512

Scale 1:10,000,000 (160 miles = 1 inch)

Boundary of the Holy Roman Empire   Boundaries of the German Circles

- Austrian Circle
- Burgundian Circle
- Rhenish Palatinate Circle
- Franconian Circle
- Bavarian Circle
- Swabian Circle
- Upper Rhine Circle
- Lower Rhine-Westphalian Circle
- Upper Saxon Circle
- Lower Saxon Circle
- Districts not included in the Circles

COPYRIGHT. GEORGE PHILIP & SON. LTD.

K. OF
ENGLAND

NORTH SEA

Heligoland
(to Holstein)   DITHMARSCHEN   D. OF SCHLESWIG

D. OF
HOLSTEIN

Lübeck

Ritzebüttel   Ratzebur

C. OF
EAST
FRIESLAND   Jever   Hamburg   Ladenburg

Leeuwarden   Groningen   ABP. OF   BP. OF
VERDEN

C. OF   OLDEN-   BREMEN
FRIESLAND   BURG   Bremen   Verden   D. OF
BRUNSWICK-
LÜNEBURG

Amsterdam   BP. OF   BP. OF   Wildeshausen   C. OF   Hanover
UTRECHT   HOYA   Br

C. OF
HOLLAND   Utrecht   Bentheim   Lingen   BP. OF   Wolfenbüttel
MINDEN   BP. OF

Ravenstein   D. OF   Tecklenburg   RAVENSBG.   HILDESHM.
GELDERLAND   C. OF   C. OF
LIPPE   Goslar

C. OF   Münster   MÜNSTER
ZEELAND   D. OF   Lippstadt   BP. OF   BERG
KLEVE   Wesel   PADERBORN   Nordhauser

Ghent   Antwerp   Dortmund   C. OF   to Mainz
C. OF FLANDERS   D. OF   MARK   Cassel   Mühlhausen   Eff

Lille   Brussels   ABP. OF   D. OF   WESTPHALIA   Eisena
boundary   BRABANT   JÜLICH   BERG   to   Waldeck   LDG. OF
until 1453   COLOGNE   Cologne   HERSFELD

C. OF   Liège   Aachen   Cologne   HESSE   BP. OF
ARTIS   C. OF   FULDA
HAINAUT   C. OF NASSAU   Wetzlar   HENNEBG.
Cambrai   Coblenz   BP. OF

DUCHY OF   Mainz   Frankfurt   Schweinfurt
LUXEMBURG   ABP. OF TRIER   Darmstadt   ABP.   WÜRZBURG

Sedan   Bouillon   Trier   Worms   OF   Würzburg   Bamber
Luxemburg   Mosel   to Mainz   MAINZ
BP. OF   Heidelberg   Rothenburg   MAR.
VERDUN   ZWEI-   PALATINATE   ANSB
Verdun   D. OF BAR   Saarbrücken   BRÜCKEN   Heilbronn   Hall

BARROIS   Toul   Weissenburg   BADEN   Nördlingen
MOUVANT   BP. OF   Hagenau   D. OF   Stuttgart
TOUL   Metz   Esslingen

Paris   Nancy   Strassburg   WÜRTTEMBERG   Ulm   Augsbu

to Toul   Schlettstadt   Reutlingen   BP
Münster   Rottweil   Zollern   Biberach   Kaufbeuren
to Barrois   Calmar   AUGSBU
mouvant   BP. OF   FÜRSTENBERG   Wangen   Kempt

Mülhausen   BREISGAU   Constance   Alsny
SUNDGAU   Lindau   VORARL-
Montbéliard   Basle   BERG

FREE COUNTY   BP. OF
Besançon   BASLE   Zürich

OF BURGUNDY   Berne

Pontarlier   SWISS CONFEDERATION   C.
1477–93 to Fr.

K. OF FRANCE

Geneva

Rhône   D. OF SAVOY   D. OF   REP.
MILAN

CENTRAL EUROPE, c.1500

Scale 1:5,000,000 (80 miles=1 inch)

0   50   100 Miles
0   50   100   150 Km.

Archbishopric
Boundary of the Holy Roman Empire
Church Lands
House of Hohenzollern
House of Wittelsbach (Palatine Branch)
House of Wittelsbach (Bavarian Branch)
House of Wettin (Albertine Branch)
House of Wettin (Ernestine Branch)
House of Habsburg (Austrian Branch)
House of Habsburg (Lands formerly held by Burgundy)
Free Cantons of Swiss Confederation
Allied Cantons of Swiss Confederation
Imperial Free Cities

STR. Strasburg,   BRUN.–W. Brunswick–Wolfenbüttel
The areas in the Empire left uncoloured were divided into petty states

East from Greenwich

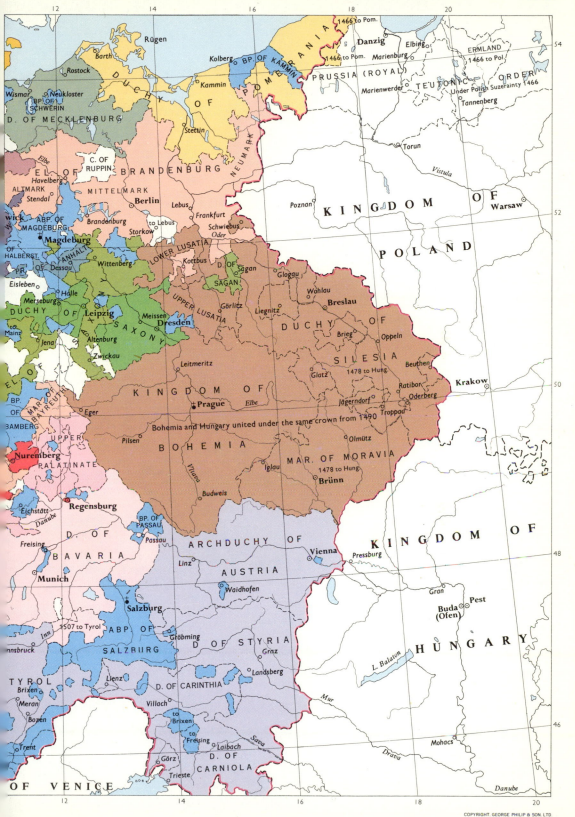

Rügen
Barth
Rostock
Wismar
Neukloster
BP. OF SCHWERIN
D. OF MECKLENBURG
DUCHY OF POMERANIA
1466 to Pom.
Danzig
Elbing
ERMLAND
1466 to Pol.
1466 to Pom.
Marienburg
Kolberg
BP. OF KAMMIN
Kammin
PRUSSIA (ROYAL)
Marienwerder
TEUTONIC ORDER
Under Polish Suzerainty 1466
Tannenberg
Stettin
NEUMARK
Torun
Vistula
Elbe
C. OF RUPPIN
EL. OF BRANDENBURG
Havelberg
ALTMARK
Stendal
MITTELMARK
Berlin
Lebus
Frankfurt
Poznan
KINGDOM OF POLAND
Warsaw
ABP. OF MAGDEBURG
Magdeburg
Brandenburg
Storkow
to Lebus
Schwiebus
Oder
OF HALBERST.
ANHALT
Dessau
Wittenberg
LOWER LUSATIA
Kottbus
D. OF SAGAN
Sagan
Glogau
Eisleben
Halle
Merseburg
DUCHY OF SAXONY
Leipzig
Meissen
Dresden
to Mainz
Jena
Altenburg
Zwickau
UPPER LUSATIA
Görlitz
Liegnitz
Wohlau
Breslau
DUCHY OF SILESIA
Brieg
Oppeln
1478 to Hung.
Beuthen
Glatz
Krakow
Leitmeritz
EL. OF
BP. OF BAMBERG
MAR. OF BAYREUTH
KINGDOM OF BOHEMIA
Prague
Elbe
Eger
Ratibor
Oderberg
Jägerndorf
Troppau
Bohemia and Hungary united under the same crown from 1490
Pilsen
Olmütz
UPPER PALATINATE
Nuremberg
MAR. OF MORAVIA
1478 to Hung.
Iglau
Brünn
Vltava
Budweis
Eichstätt
Regensburg
Danube
BP. OF PASSAU
Passau
D. OF BAVARIA
Freising
Munich
ARCHDUCHY OF AUSTRIA
Vienna
Linz
Pressburg
KINGDOM OF HUNGARY
Waidhofen
Gran
Buda (Ofen)
Pest
Salzburg
ABP. OF SALZBURG
1507 to Tyrol
Inn
Innsbruck
Gröbming
D. OF STYRIA
Graz
L. Balaton
TYROL
Brixen
Meran
Bozen
Trent
Lienz
D. OF CARINTHIA
Landsberg
Villach
Mur
to Brixen
to Freising
Laibach
Sava
Drava
Mohacs
Görz
D. OF CARNIOLA
Trieste
OF VENICE
Danube

COPYRIGHT. GEORGE PHILIP & SON. LTD.

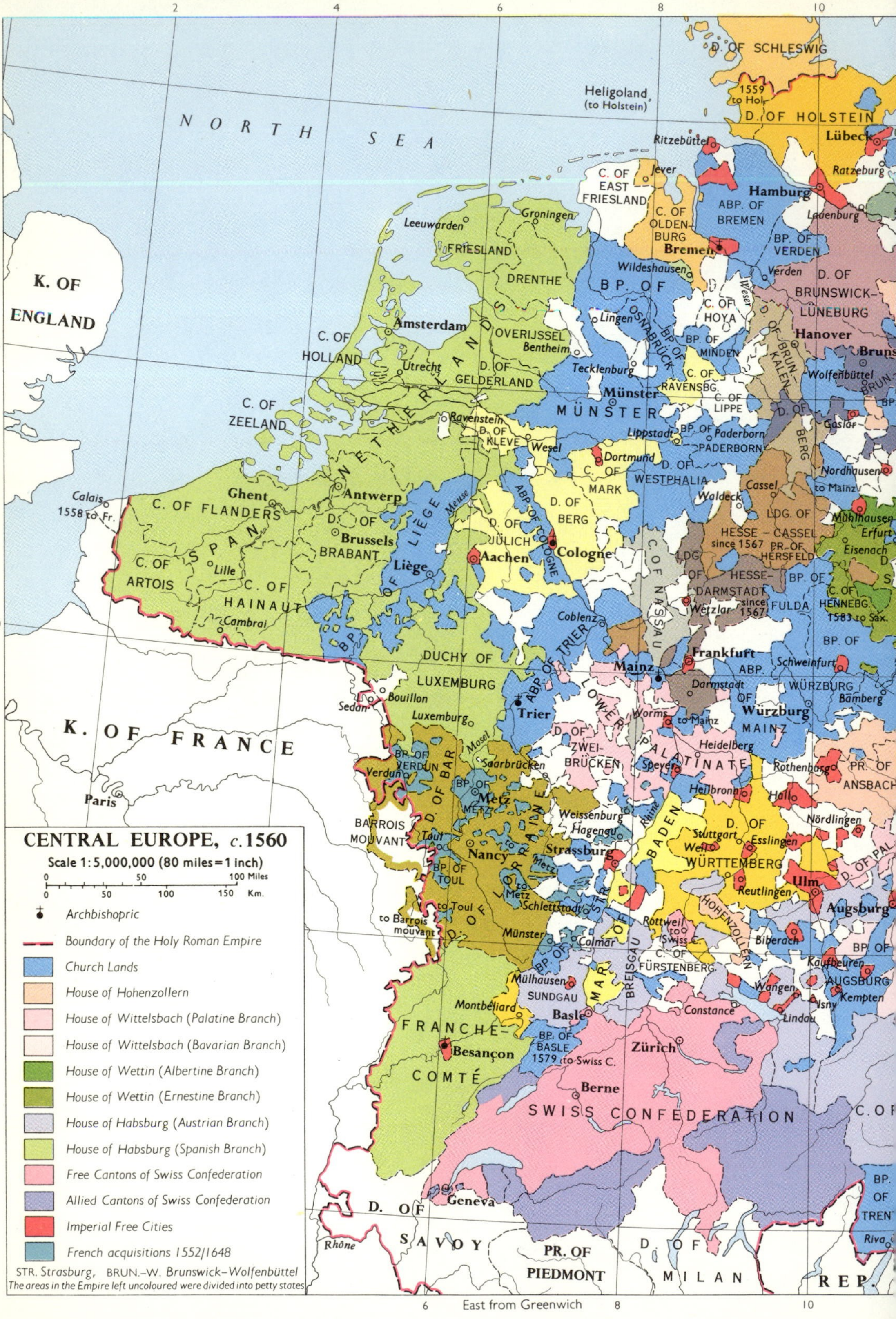
CENTRAL EUROPE, c.1560
Scale 1:5,000,000 (80 miles=1 inch)
0 50 100 Miles
0 50 100 150 Km.
Archbishopric
Boundary of the Holy Roman Empire
Church Lands
House of Hohenzollern
House of Wittelsbach (Palatine Branch)
House of Wittelsbach (Bavarian Branch)
House of Wettin (Albertine Branch)
House of Wettin (Ernestine Branch)
House of Habsburg (Austrian Branch)
House of Habsburg (Spanish Branch)
Free Cantons of Swiss Confederation
Allied Cantons of Swiss Confederation
Imperial Free Cities
French acquisitions 1552/1648
STR. Strasburg, BRUN.-W. Brunswick-Wolfenbüttel
The areas in the Empire left uncoloured were divided into petty states
East from Greenwich
NORTH SEA
K. OF ENGLAND
K. OF FRANCE
D. OF SCHLESWIG
1559 to Hol.
D. OF HOLSTEIN
Heligoland (to Holstein)
Lübeck
Ratzeburg
Ritzebüttel
Hamburg
Lauenburg
C. OF EAST FRIESLAND
Jever
C. OF OLDENBURG
ABP. OF BREMEN
Bremen
BP. OF VERDEN
Verden
D. OF BRUNSWICK-LÜNEBURG
Hanover
Wildeshausen
BP. OF OSNABRÜCK
C. OF HOYA
BP. OF MINDEN
Lingen
Tecklenburg
C. OF RAVENSBG.
C. OF LIPPE
Münster
MÜNSTER
Wolfenbüttel
Goslar
Lippstadt
BP. OF PADERBORN
Paderborn
Dortmund
C. OF MARK
D. OF WESTPHALIA
Nordhausen to Mainz
Cassel
Waldeck
LDG. OF HESSE-CASSEL since 1567
PR. OF HERSFELD
Mühlhausen
Erfurt
Eisenach
LDG. OF HESSE-DARMSTADT since 1567
BP. OF FULDA
C. OF HENNEBG. 1583 to Sax.
Wetzlar
C. OF NASSAU
Leeuwarden
Groningen
FRIESLAND
DRENTHE
Amsterdam
C. OF HOLLAND
OVERIJSSEL
Bentheim
Utrecht
D. OF GELDERLAND
NETHERLANDS
C. OF ZEELAND
Ravenstein
D. OF KLEVE
Wesel
D. OF BERG
D. OF JÜLICH
ABP. OF COLOGNE
Cologne
Aachen
Calais 1558 to Fr.
Ghent
C. OF FLANDERS
Antwerp
D. OF BRABANT
Brussels
SPAN.
C. OF ARTOIS
Lille
C. OF HAINAUT
Cambrai
BP. OF LIÈGE
Liège
Meuse
Coblenz
ABP. OF TRIER
Frankfurt
Mainz
ABP. OF MAINZ
Schweinfurt
BP. OF WÜRZBURG
Würzburg
Bamberg
Darmstadt
DUCHY OF LUXEMBURG
Luxemburg
Bouillon
Sedan
Trier
Worms
to Mainz
LOWER PALATINATE
Heidelberg
Speyer
D. OF ZWEIBRÜCKEN
Saarbrücken
Mosel
BP. OF VERDUN
Verdun
D. OF BAR
BP. OF METZ
Metz
Rothenburg
PR. OF ANSBACH
Heilbronn
Hall
Nördlingen
Weissenburg
Hagenau
BADEN
D. OF WÜRTTEMBERG
Stuttgart
Weil
Esslingen
Ulm
Reutlingen
Augsburg
BARROIS MOUVANT
Toul
Nancy
Strassburg
BP. OF TOUL
D. OF LORRAINE
Schlettstadt
to Toul
to Metz
to Barrois mouvant
Münster
Colmar
Rottweil to Swiss C.
HOHENZOLLERN
Biberach
C. OF FÜRSTENBERG
BREISGAU
STR.
Kaufbeuren
BP. OF AUGSBURG
Kempten
Wangen
Isny
Lindau
Mülhausen
SUNDGAU
Montbéliard
Basle
Constance
BP. OF BASLE 1579 to Swiss C.
Zürich
FRANCHE-COMTÉ
Besançon
Berne
SWISS CONFEDERATION
Geneva
D. OF SAVOY
Rhône
PR. OF PIEDMONT
D. OF MILAN
BP. OF TRENT
Riva
REP.
2 4 6 8 10
54 52 50

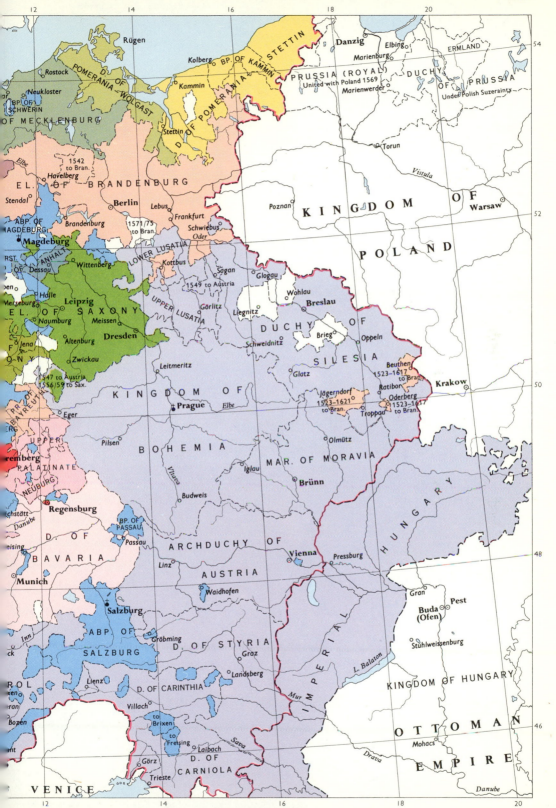

12 14 16 18 20

Rügen

D. OF POMERANIA-WOLGAST

Rostock

Neukloster

BP. OF SCHWERIN

OF MECKLENBURG

Kolberg   BP. OF KAMMIN   STETTIN

Danzig   Elbing   ERMLAND

Marienburg

PRUSSIA (ROYAL)   DUCHY

United with Poland 1569   OF PRUSSIA

Marienwerder   Under Polish Suzerainty

Kammin

D. OF POMERANIA

Stettin

Elbe

1542
to Bran.

Havelberg

EL.   OF   BRANDENBURG

Stendal

Berlin   Lebus

Torun

Vistula

Brandenburg   1571/75
to Bran.

BP. OF
MAGDEBURG   Frankfurt

Schwiebus

Poznan   KINGDOM   OF

Warsaw

54

52

Magdeburg   Oder

ANHALT

RST.
OF   Dessau

Wittenberg   LOWER LUSATIA

Kottbus

Sagan   Glogau

POLAND

Halle

Leipzig

Naumburg   Meissen

Merseburg

1549 to Austria

Görlitz

Liegnitz

Wohlau

Breslau

Brieg   Oppeln

Beuthen
1523-1617
to Bran.

Krakow

50

EL. OF   SAXONY

Dresden

UPPER LUSATIA

Schweidnitz

DUCHY   OF

SILESIA

Jena

Altenburg

SONY   Zwickau

1547 to Austria
1556/59 to Sax.

Leitmeritz

Glatz

Ratibor

Jägerndorf
1523-1621
to Bran.

Oderberg
1523-1617
to Bran.

Troppau

RST. OF
BAYREUTH

Eger

KINGDOM   OF

Prague   Elbe

Olmütz

UPPER
emberg

Pilsen

BOHEMIA

Iglau

MAR. OF MORAVIA

Brünn

PALATINATE

NEUBURG

chstätt

Regensburg

Vltava

Budweis

HUNGARY

Danube

D. OF

BP. OF
PASSAU

Passau

ARCHDUCHY   OF

eising

BAVARIA

Linz

AUSTRIA

Vienna   Pressburg

48

Munich

Waidhofen

Gran

Inn

Salzburg

ABP.   OF

Gröbming

Buda
(Ofen)   Pest

Stuhlweissenburg

ck

SALZBURG

D. OF STYRIA

Graz

ROL

Lienz

Landsberg

L. Balaton

KINGDOM OF HUNGARY

xen
eran

Villach

D. OF CARINTHIA

Mur

Bozen

Brixen

to
Freising   Laibach

Sava

OTTOMAN

46

ent

Görz

D. OF

Mohacs

Trieste   CARNIOLA

Drava

EMPIRE

VENICE

Danube

12 14 16 18 20

COPYRIGHT. GEORGE PHILIP & SON. LTD.

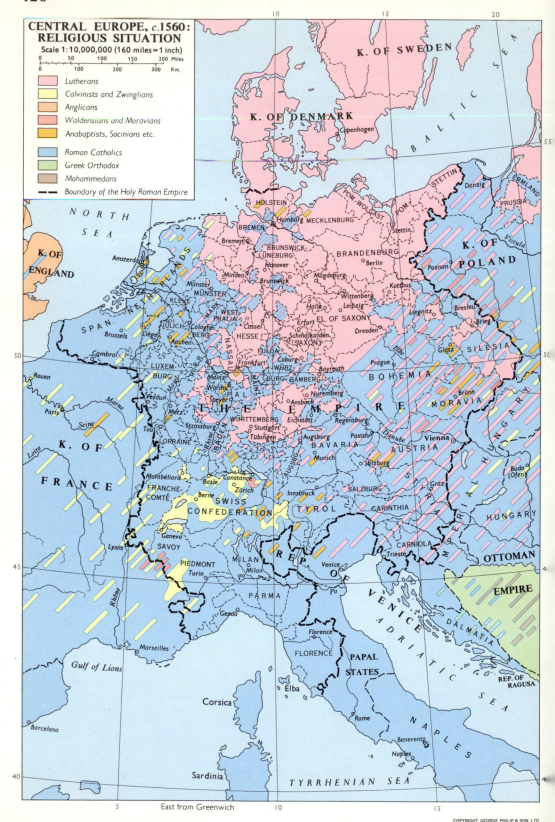

Central Europe, c.1560: RELIGIOUS SITUATION

Scale 1:10,000,000 (160 miles = 1 inch)

Lutherans

Calvinists and Zwinglians

Anglicans

Waldensians and Moravians

Anabaptists, Socinians etc.

Roman Catholics

Greek Orthodox

Mohammedans

Boundary of the Holy Roman Empire

K. OF SWEDEN

BALTIC SEA

K. OF DENMARK

Copenhagen

NORTH SEA

HOLSTEIN

BREMEN

Hamburg MECKLENBURG

POM-WOLGAST

POMERANIA

STETTIN

Danzig

ERMLAND

PRUSSIA

K. OF ENGLAND

Amsterdam

Bremen

BRUNSWICK-LÜNEBURG

Hanover

BRANDENBURG

Berlin

Stettin

Poznan

K. OF POLAND

Vistula

NETHERLANDS

Minden

Brunswick

Magdeburg

SPAN.

Brussels

Münster

MÜNSTER

KLEVE

MARK

WEST-PHALIA

Wittenberg

Leipzig

Kottbus

Liegnitz

Breslau

Brieg

SILESIA

Glatz

JÜLICH

Cologne

BERG

Aachen

Cassel

HESSE

Schmalkalden

SAXONY

Erfurt EL. OF SAXONY

Dresden

Prague

BOHEMIA

Brünn

MORAVIA

Liège

Cambrai

LUXEM-BURG

NASSAU

Fulda

Coburg

Bayreuth

Rouen

Mainz

FRANKFURT

Worms

Speyer

PALATINATE

WÜRZ-BURG BAMBERG

Nuremberg

Ansbach

Paris

Marne

Seine

Verdun

Metz

THE

EMPIRE

Eichstätt

Regensburg

Passau

Vienna

AUSTRIA

IMPERIAL HUNGARY

Toul

LORRAINE

Strassburg

BADEN

WÜRTTEMBERG

Stuttgart

Tübingen

Augsburg

AUGSBURG

Munich

BAVARIA

Salzburg

Graz

Buda (Ofen)

HUNGARY

K. OF FRANCE

Loire

Montbéliard

Basle

Constance

Zürich

Berne

SWISS CONFEDERATION

Innsbruck

TYROL

SALZBURG

CARINTHIA

Geneva

SAVOY

FRANCHE-COMTÉ

Lyons

Rhône

PIEDMONT

Turin

MILAN

Milan

Po

REP. OF VENICE

Venice

Trieste

CARNIOLA

OTTOMAN

EMPIRE

DALMATIA

Marseilles

PARMA

Genoa

Po

ADRIATIC SEA

REP. OF RAGUSA

Gulf of Lions

Barcelona

FLORENCE

Florence

Elba

PAPAL STATES

Rome

NAPLES

Benevento

Naples

Corsica

Sardinia

TYRRHENIAN SEA

East from Greenwich

COPYRIGHT. GEORGE PHILIP & SON. LTD.

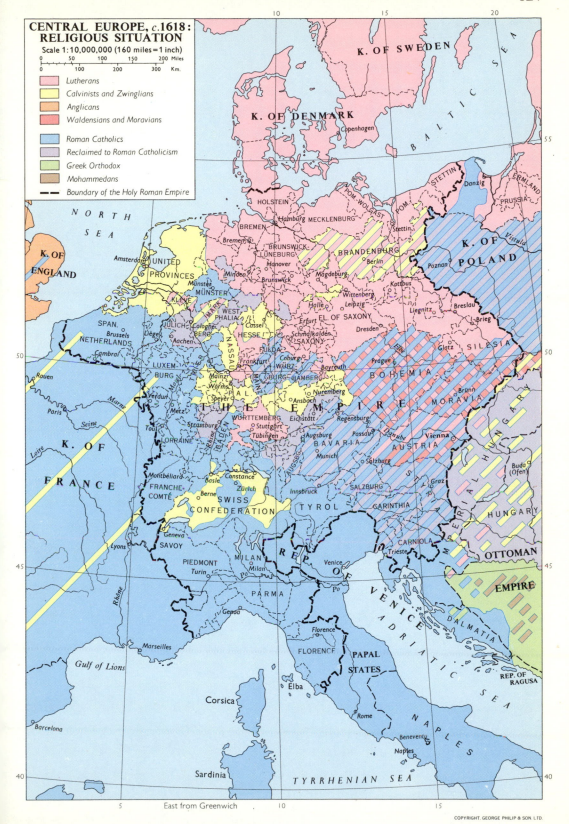

**CENTRAL EUROPE, *c.*1618:
RELIGIOUS SITUATION**

Scale 1:10,000,000 (160 miles = 1 inch)

	Miles
0 50 100 150 200	Miles
100 200 300	Km.

- *Lutherans*
- *Calvinists and Zwinglians*
- *Anglicans*
- *Waldensians and Moravians*

- *Roman Catholics*
- *Reclaimed to Roman Catholicism*
- *Greek Orthodox*
- *Mohammedans*
- – – – *Boundary of the Holy Roman Empire*

K. OF SWEDEN

K. OF DENMARK

Copenhagen

BALTIC SEA

STETTIN

Danzig

ERMLAND

PRUSSIA

NORTH SEA

HOLSTEIN

POM-WOLGAST

POM.

Stettin

K. OF ENGLAND

BREMEN

Hamburg MECKLENBURG

Bremen

Amsterdam UNITED PROVINCES

MÜNSTER

Minden

Hanover

Brunswick

BRUNSWICK-LÜNEBURG

BRANDENBURG

Berlin

Magdeburg

Kottbus

K. OF POLAND

Poznan

Münster

KLEVE

MÜNSTER

MARK

WEST-PHALIA

Cassel

Halle

Wittenberg

Leipzig

EL. OF SAXONY

Erfurt

Breslau

SILESIA

SPAN. NETHERLANDS

Brussels

Cambrai

Liège

Cologne

JULICH

BERG

Aachen

HESSE

NASSAU

Schmalkalden

SAXONY

Dresden

Glatz

Prague

BOHEMIA

Brünn

MORAVIA

Rouen

Paris

Seine

Marne

LUXEM-BURG

Verdun

Metz

Mainz

Worms

Speyer

FRANKFURT

Coburg

BAMBERG

WÜRZ-BURG

Ansbach

Nuremberg

Bayreuth

THE EMPIRE

Toul

LORRAINE

Strassburg

Rhine

BADEN

WÜRTTEMBERG

Stuttgart

Tübingen

Eichstätt

Regensburg

Augsburg

BAVARIA

Munich

Passau

Danube

AUSTRIA

Vienna

IMPERIAL HUNGARY

Buda (Ofen)

HUNGARY

K. OF FRANCE

Loire

Montbéliard

FRANCHE-COMTÉ

Basle

Berne

Constance

Zürich

SWISS CONFEDERATION

Innsbruck

TYROL

SALZBURG

Salzburg

Graz

CARINTHIA

Geneva

SAVOY

Lyons

Rhône

PIEDMONT

Turin

MILAN

Milan

Po

REP. OF VENICE

Venice

Trieste

CARNIOLA

OTTOMAN

EMPIRE

DALMATIA

PARMA

Genoa

Po

ADRIATIC SEA

REP. OF RAGUSA

Marseilles

Gulf of Lions

FLORENCE

Florence

Elba

PAPAL STATES

Rome

Benevento

Naples

NAPLES

Barcelona

Corsica

Sardinia

TYRRHENIAN SEA

East from Greenwich

COPYRIGHT. GEORGE PHILIP & SON LTD.

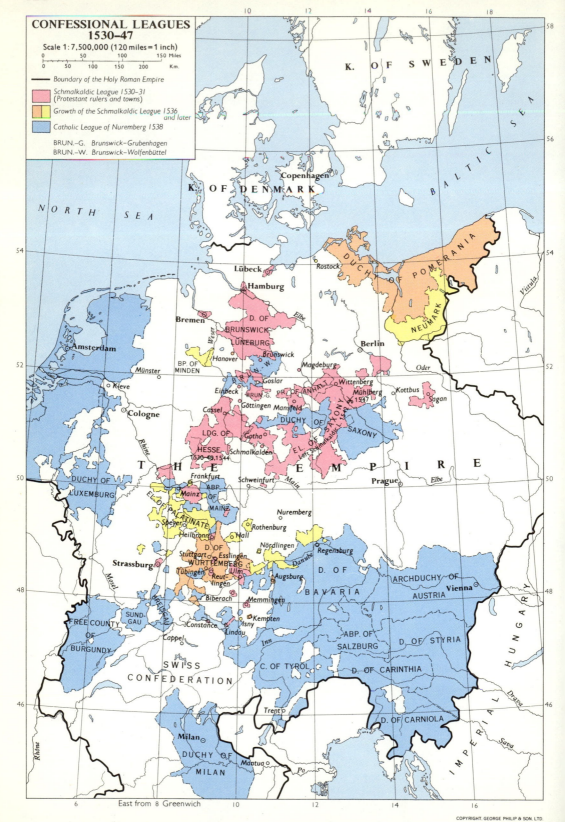

CONFESSIONAL LEAGUES
1530–47

Scale 1 : 7,500,000 (120 miles = 1 inch)

0   50   100   150 Miles
0   50   100   150   200   Km.

—— Boundary of the Holy Roman Empire

Schmalkaldic League 1530–31
(Protestant rulers and towns)

Growth of the Schmalkaldic League 1536
and later

Catholic League of Nuremberg 1538

BRUN.–G. Brunswick–Grubenhagen
BRUN.–W. Brunswick–Wolfenbüttel

K. OF SWEDEN

BALTIC SEA

Copenhagen

K. OF DENMARK

NORTH SEA

Rostock
DUCHY OF
POMERANIA
NEUMARK

Lübeck
Hamburg

Bremen

D. OF
BRUNSWICK-
LÜNEBURG

Hanover
Brunswick
Berlin

Amsterdam
Münster
BP. OF
MINDEN

Kleve

Cologne

Einbeck
BRUN.-G.
Goslar
Magdeburg

PR. OF ANHALT
Wittenberg
Mühlberg
△ 1547
Kottbus
Sagan

Cassel
Göttingen
Mansfeld

LDG. OF
HESSE
1530–49,1544
Gotha
DUCHY OF
SAXONY
EL. OF SAXONY 1547

Schmalkalden
Lge Schmalkaldic 1531

SAXONY

THE

Frankfurt
Schweinfurt
Main
Prague
Elbe

DUCHY OF
LUXEMBURG

EMPIRE

ABP. OF
MAINZ
Mainz

EL. OF
PALATINATE
Speyer
Heilbronn

Nuremberg

Rothenburg

Hall
Nördlingen
Regensburg
Danube

Strassburg

D. OF
WÜRTTEMBERG
Stuttgart
Esslingen
Tübingen
Reut-
lingen
Ulm
Augsburg

D. OF
BAVARIA
ARCHDUCHY OF
AUSTRIA
Vienna

Biberach
Memmingen

FREE COUNTY
OF
BURGUNDY

SUND-
GAU
BREISGAU

Constance
Cappel
Lindau
Kempten
Isny

ABP. OF
SALZBURG
D. OF STYRIA

SWISS
CONFEDERATION

C. OF TYROL
Inn
D. OF CARINTHIA

D. OF CARNIOLA

IMPERIAL HUNGARY

Trent

Milan

DUCHY OF
MILAN
Mantua
Po

East from 8 Greenwich

COPYRIGHT. GEORGE PHILIP & SON. LTD.

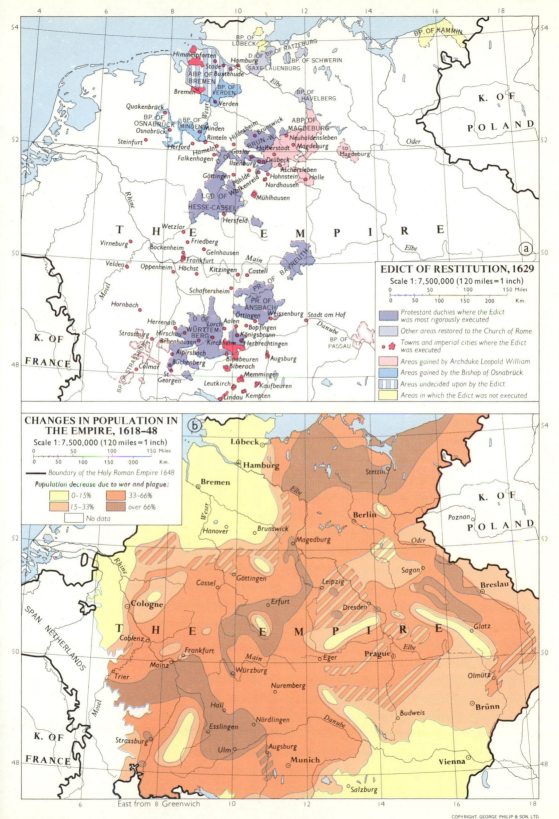

EDICT OF RESTITUTION, 1629

Scale 1:7,500,000 (120 miles = 1 inch)

0 ___ 50 ___ 100 ___ 150 Miles
0 ___ 50 ___ 100 ___ 150 ___ 200 Km.

Protestant duchies where the Edict was most rigorously executed

Other areas restored to the Church of Rome

Towns and imperial cities where the Edict was executed

Areas gained by Archduke Leopold William

Areas gained by the Bishop of Osnabrück

Areas undecided upon by the Edict

Areas in which the Edict was not executed

Place names on map (a):
BP. OF LÜBECK, BP. OF RATZEBURG, BP. OF KAMMIN, Himmelpforten, Stade, Hamburg, D. OF SAXE-LAUENBURG, BP. OF SCHWERIN, ABP. OF BREMEN, BP. OF Buxtehude, Bremen, BP. OF VERDEN, Verden, Elbe, BP. OF HAVELBERG, ABP. OF MAGDEBURG, Quakenbrück, BP. OF OSNABRÜCK, BP. OF MINDEN, Minden, Hildesheim, Brunswick, Neuhaldensleben, Magdeburg, Oder, K. OF POLAND, Osnabrück, Steinfurt, Rinteln, BRUN.-W, Halberstadt, to Magdeburg, Herford, Hameln, Goslar, Drübeck, Aschersleben, Halle, Falkenhagen, Ilsenburg, Pöhlde, Hohnstein, Göttingen, Wolkenried, Nordhausen, LGD. OF HESSE-CASSEL, Mühlhausen, Hersfeld, Wetzlar, THE EMPIRE, Elbe, Virneburg, Friedberg, Gelnhausen, Bockenheim, Frankfurt, Main, Velden, Oppenheim, Höchst, Kitzingen, Castell, BAYREUTH, Moel, Schaftersheim, PR. OF ANSBACH, Hornbach, Herrenalb, Öttingen, Weissenburg, Stadt am Hof, D. OF WÜRTTEMBERG, Lorch, Aalen, Bopfingen, Königsbronn, Strassburg, Hirschau, Kirchheim, Herbrechtingen, Danube, Rebenhausen, Alpirsbach, Blaubeuren, Augsburg, BP. OF PASSAU, Colmar, Büchenberg, Biberach, Memmingen, St. Georgen, BP. OF STRASSBURG, Leutkirch, Kempten, Kaufbeuren, Lindau, K. OF FRANCE, Rhine

CHANGES IN POPULATION IN THE EMPIRE, 1618–48

Scale 1:7,500,000 (120 miles = 1 inch)

0 ___ 50 ___ 100 ___ 150 Miles
0 ___ 50 ___ 100 ___ 150 ___ 200 Km.

Boundary of the Holy Roman Empire 1648

Population decrease due to war and plague:

0-15%

15-33%

33-66%

over 66%

No data

Place names on map (b):
Lübeck, Hamburg, Stettin, Bremen, Berlin, K. OF POLAND, Poznan, Hanover, Brunswick, Magdeburg, Oder, Weser, Elbe, Rhine, THE EMPIRE, Cassel, Göttingen, Leipzig, Sagan, Breslau, SPAN. NETHERLANDS, Cologne, Erfurt, Dresden, Glatz, Coblenz, Frankfurt, Eger, Prague, Elbe, Olmütz, Mainz, Main, Würzburg, Trier, Nuremberg, Brünn, Hall, Moel, Nördlingen, Danube, Budweis, Strassburg, Esslingen, Ulm, Augsburg, K. OF FRANCE, Munich, Vienna, Salzburg

East from 8 Greenwich

COPYRIGHT. GEORGE PHILIP & SON. LTD.

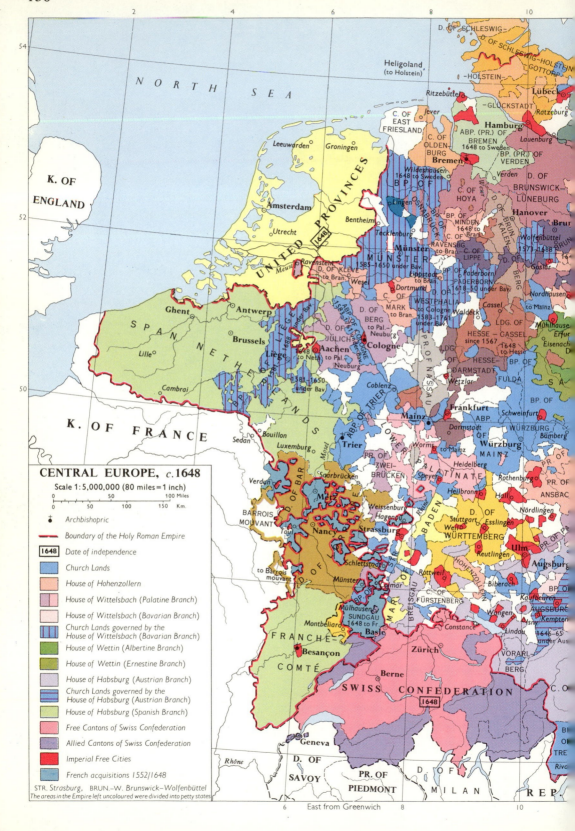

NORTH SEA

Heligoland
(to Holstein)

K. OF
ENGLAND

D. OF SCHLESWIG-
D. OF SCHLESWIG-HOLSTEIN
HOLSTEIN-GOTTORP
-HOLSTEIN

Ritzebüttel
-GLÜCKSTADT
Lübeck
Ratzeburg

C. OF
EAST
FRIESLAND
Jever
C. OF
OLDEN-
BURG
Hamburg
ABP. (PR.) OF
BREMEN
1648 to Sweden
BP. (PR.) OF
VERDEN
Lauenburg

Leeuwarden
Groningen
Bremen
Verden
D. OF
BRUNSWICK-
LÜNEBURG

Wildeshausen
1648 to Sweden
BP. OF
OSNABRÜCK
C. OF
HOYA

Amsterdam
Bentheim
BP. OF
MINDEN
1648 to
C. OF Bran
Hanover
Brun

Utrecht
Tecklenburg
Wolfenbüttel
1573-1688
BRUN

Lingen to Bran
MÜNSTER
1585-1650 under Bav
Goslar

Münster
LIPPE
C. OF
RAVENSBG.
to Bran
Nordhausen
to Mainz

Ravenstein
D. OF KLEVE
to Bran
Wesel
BP. OF
PADERBORN
1618-50 under Bav
Cassel
LDG. OF
Mühlhause
Erfu

Ghent
Antwerp
Dortmund
PADERBORN
WESTPHALIA
to Cologne
1583-176
under Bav
Waldeck
HESSE-CASSEL
since 1567
Eisenach
D

Brussels
C. OF
MARK
to Bran.
LDG
to Mainz
HESSE-
LDG. OF
to Hesse

Lille
Liège
D. OF
BERG
1583 to Pal.-
Neuburg
Cologne
HESSE-
DARMSTADT
BP. OF
FULDA
SA

SPANISH NETHERLANDS

Aachen
JÜLICH
to Pal.-
Neuburg
Wetzlar

Cambrai
1581-1650
under Bav
Coblenz
BP. OF
Darmstadt
ABP. OF
Schweinfurt

K. OF FRANCE

Bouillon
Sedan
Luxemburg
Trier
ABP. OF TRIER
Mainz
Frankfurt
ABP.
WÜRZBURG
Bamberg

Verdun
Mosel
Worms
Würzburg
PR. OF
ANSBAC

BARROIS
MOUVANT
Saarbrücken
ZWEI-
BRÜCKEN
Speyer
Heidelberg
Rothenburg
PR. OF
PR. OF PA

Metz
Weissenburg
Hagenau
Heilbronn
Hall
Nördlingen

Toul
Nancy
Strasburg
D. OF
WÜRTTEMBERG
Stuttgart
Esslingen
Reutlingen
Ulm
Augsburg

Schlettstadt
Rottweil
BADEN
HOHENZOLLERN
Biberach

Münster
Colmar
C. OF
FÜRSTENBERG
Wangen
Kaufbeuren
AUGSBURG
Kempten

Mülhausen
SUNDGAU
1648 to Fr.
BREISGAU
Constance
Lindau
1646-65
under Aus

Montbéliard
Basle
VORARL
BERG
C. O

FRANCHE-
Besançon
Zürich

COMTÉ
Berne
SWISS CONFEDERATION

Geneva
1648

Rhône
D. OF
SAVOY
PR. OF
PIEDMONT
D. OF
MILAN
REP

East from Greenwich

CENTRAL EUROPE, c.1648

Scale 1:5,000,000 (80 miles=1 inch)

0   50   100 Miles
0   50   100   150 Km.

- Archbishopric
- Boundary of the Holy Roman Empire
- 1648   Date of independence
- Church Lands
- House of Hohenzollern
- House of Wittelsbach (Palatine Branch)
- House of Wittelsbach (Bavarian Branch)
- Church Lands governed by the House of Wittelsbach (Bavarian Branch)
- House of Wettin (Albertine Branch)
- House of Wettin (Ernestine Branch)
- House of Habsburg (Austrian Branch)
- Church Lands governed by the House of Habsburg (Austrian Branch)
- House of Habsburg (Spanish Branch)
- Free Cantons of Swiss Confederation
- Allied Cantons of Swiss Confederation
- Imperial Free Cities
- French acquisitions 1552/1648

STR. Strasburg,   BRUN.-W. Brunswick-Wolfenbüttel
The areas in the Empire left uncoloured were divided into petty states

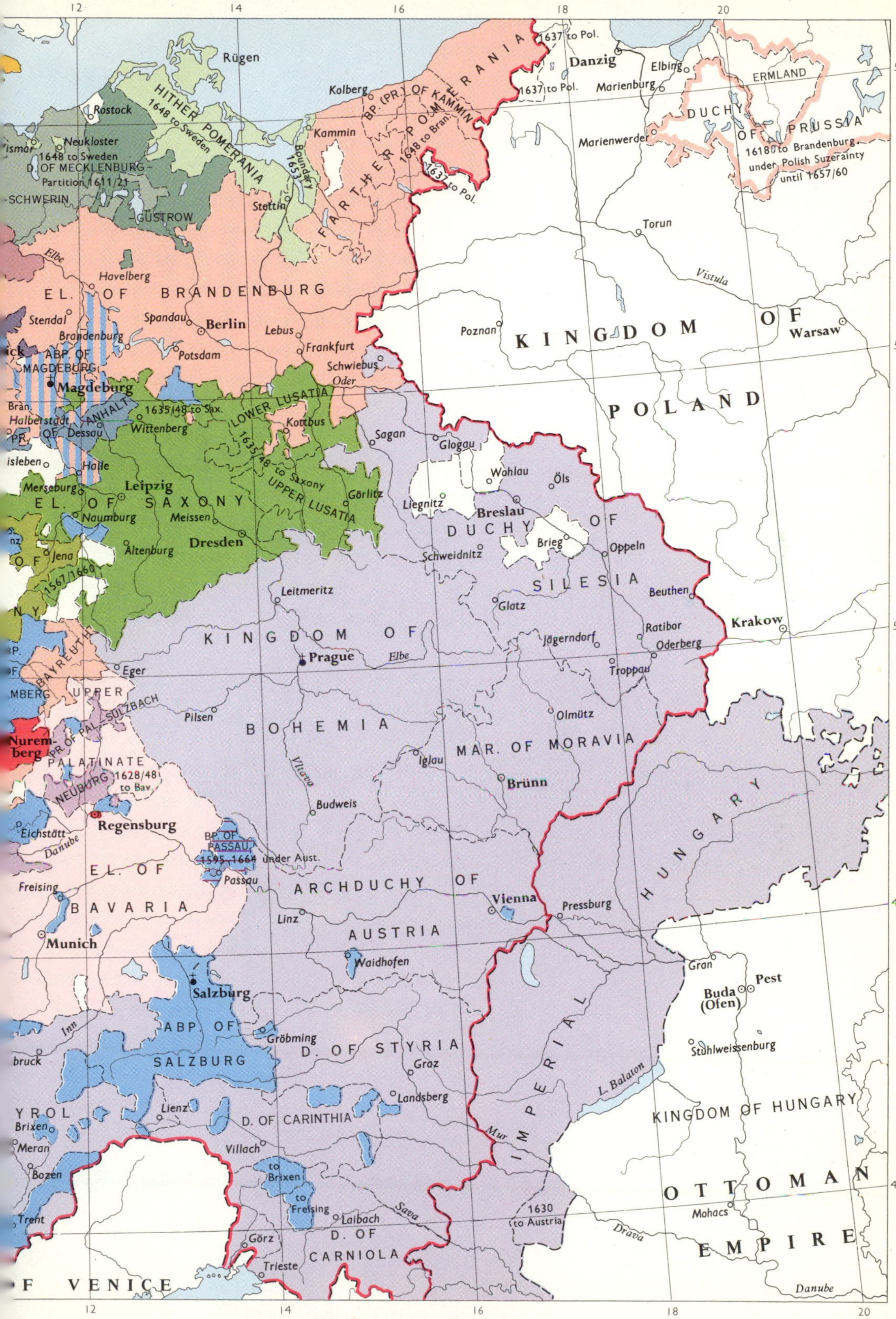
Rügen
Rostock
HITHER POMERANIA 1648 to Sweden
Neukloster
1648 to Sweden
D. OF MECKLENBURG
Partition 1611/21
SCHWERIN
GÜSTROW
Kolberg
Kammin
BP. (PR.) OF KAMMIN
1648 to Bran.
FARTHER POMERANIA
Boundary 1653
Stettin
1637 to Pol.
1637 to Pol.
1637 to Pol.
Danzig
Elbing
Marienburg
ERMLAND
Marienwerder
DUCHY OF PRUSSIA
1618 to Brandenburg under Polish Suzerainty until 1657/60
Torun
Vistula
Havelberg
EL. OF BRANDENBURG
Stendal
Spandau
Berlin
Lebus
Brandenburg
Potsdam
Frankfurt
ABP. OF MAGDEBURG
Magdeburg
Schwiebus
Oder
Poznan
KINGDOM OF POLAND
Warsaw
ANHALT
1635/48 to Sax.
LOWER LUSATIA
Kottbus
Halberstadt
PR. OF Dessau
Wittenberg
1635/48 to Saxony
UPPER LUSATIA
Sagan
Glogau
Halle
Merseburg
Leipzig
EL. OF SAXONY
Görlitz
Wohlau
Öls
Naumburg
Meissen
Liegnitz
Breslau
DUCHY OF SILESIA
Jena
1567/1660
Altenburg
Dresden
Brieg
Oppeln
Schweidnitz
Leitmeritz
Glatz
Beuthen
Ratibor
Krakow
KINGDOM OF BOHEMIA
Prague
Elbe
Jägerndorf
Oderberg
Troppau
BAYREUTH
Eger
UPPER PALATINATE
PR. OF PAL.-SULZBACH
Pilsen
Olmütz
Nurem-berg
MAR. OF MORAVIA
Iglau
Brünn
Vltava
NEUBURG 1628/48 to Bav.
Budweis
Regensburg
Eichstätt
Danube
BP. OF PASSAU 1595-1664 under Aust.
Passau
EL. OF BAVARIA
Freising
ARCHDUCHY OF AUSTRIA
Vienna
Pressburg
Linz
Munich
Waidhofen
IMPERIAL HUNGARY
Gran
Buda (Ofen)
Pest
Salzburg
ABP. OF SALZBURG
Inn
Gröbming
D. OF STYRIA
Stuhlweissenburg
Graz
L. Balaton
Lienz
Landsberg
D. OF CARINTHIA
TYROL
Brixen
KINGDOM OF HUNGARY
Meran
Villach
Mur
Bozen
to Brixen
to Freising
OTTOMAN EMPIRE
Sava
1630 to Austria
Trent
Laibach
Mohacs
Drava
Görz
D. OF CARNIOLA
Trieste
VENICE
Danube
12
14
16
18
20
54
52
50
48
46
COPYRIGHT. GEORGE PHILIP & SON, LTD.

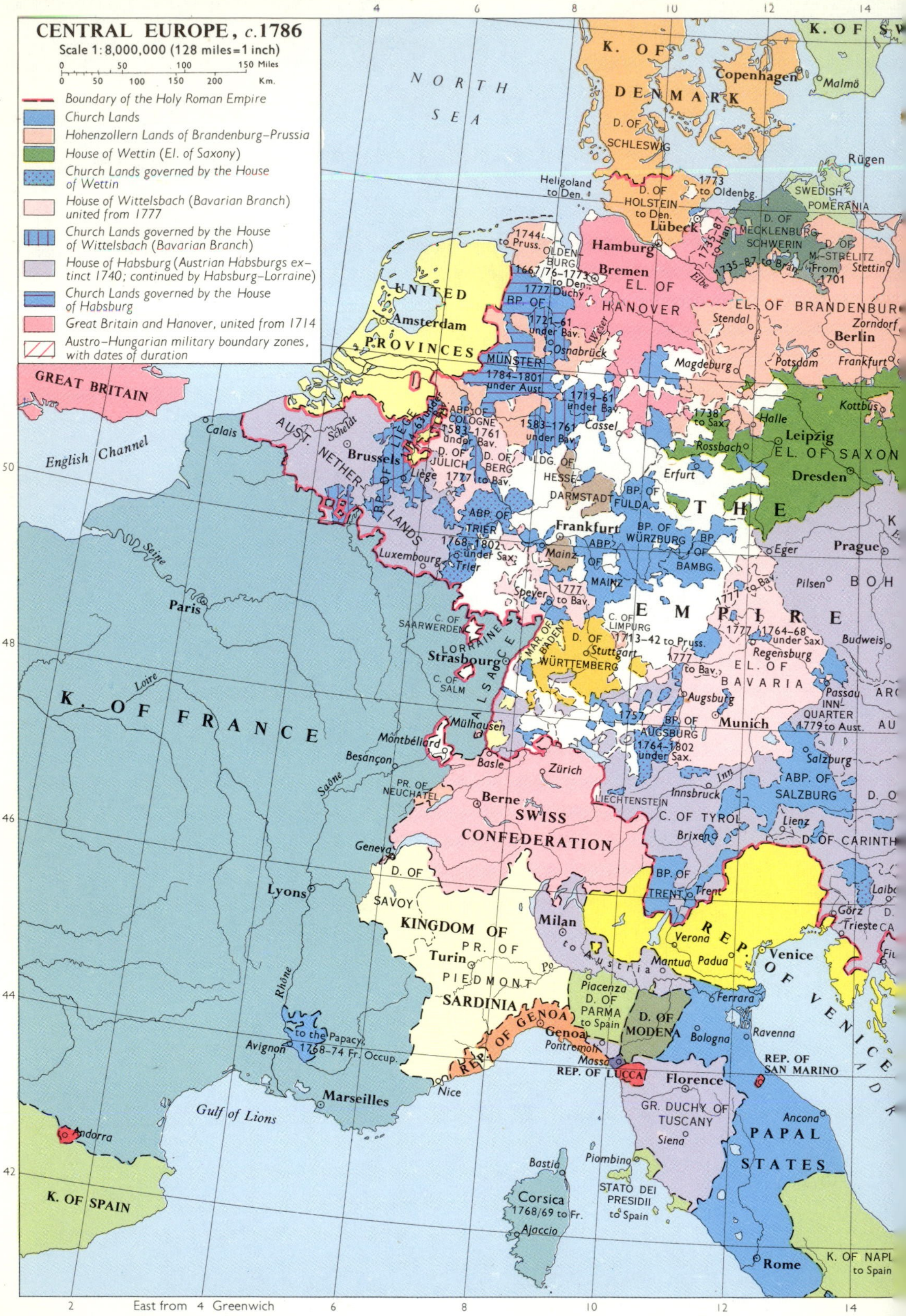
CENTRAL EUROPE, c.1786
Scale 1:8,000,000 (128 miles=1 inch)
Boundary of the Holy Roman Empire
Church Lands
Hohenzollern Lands of Brandenburg-Prussia
House of Wettin (El. of Saxony)
Church Lands governed by the House of Wettin
House of Wittelsbach (Bavarian Branch) united from 1777
Church Lands governed by the House of Wittelsbach (Bavarian Branch)
House of Habsburg (Austrian Habsburgs extinct 1740; continued by Habsburg-Lorraine)
Church Lands governed by the House of Habsburg
Great Britain and Hanover, united from 1714
Austro-Hungarian military boundary zones, with dates of duration
NORTH SEA
K. OF DENMARK
Copenhagen
Malmö
D. OF SCHLESWIG
Rügen
Heligoland to Den.
D. OF HOLSTEIN to Den.
1773 to Oldenbg.
SWEDISH POMERANIA
Lübeck
D. OF MECKLENBURG-SCHWERIN
D. OF M.-STRELITZ
Hamburg
Bremen
EL. OF HANOVER
UNITED PROVINCES
Amsterdam
MÜNSTER 1784–1801 under Aust.
Osnabrück
EL. OF BRANDENBURG
Stendal
Berlin
Zorndorf
Magdeburg
Potsdam
Frankfurt
GREAT BRITAIN
Calais
English Channel
AUST. NETHERLANDS
Brussels
Liège
ABP. OF COLOGNE 1583–1761 under Bav.
D. OF JÜLICH 1777
D. OF BERG 1777 to Bav.
Cassel
Halle
Leipzig
EL. OF SAXONY
Rossbach
Dresden
Kottbus
Erfurt
HESSE-DARMSTADT
BP. OF FULDA
ABP. OF TRIER 1768–1802 under Sax.
Trier
Luxembourg
Frankfurt
BP. OF WÜRZBURG
BP. OF BAMBG.
ABP. OF MAINZ
Mainz
Speyer
THE EMPIRE
Prague
Eger
Pilsen
BOHEMIA
Paris
Seine
C. OF SAARWERDEN
LORRAINE
ALSACE
Strasbourg
C. OF SALM
MAR. OF BADEN
D. OF WÜRTTEMBERG
Stuttgart
C. OF LIMPURG 1713–42 to Pruss.
EL. OF BAVARIA
Regensburg
Budweis
Augsburg
BP. OF AUGSBURG 1764–1802 under Sax.
Munich
Passau
INN-QUARTER 1779 to Aust.
K. OF FRANCE
Loire
Mülhausen
Montbéliard
Besançon
Basle
Zürich
Saône
PR. OF NEUCHATEL
Berne
SWISS CONFEDERATION
LIECHTENSTEIN
Innsbruck
C. OF TYROL
Brixen
Lienz
ABP. OF SALZBURG
Salzburg
D. OF CARINTHIA
Geneva
D. OF SAVOY
Lyons
KINGDOM OF SARDINIA
PR. OF PIEDMONT
Turin
Po
Milan
BP. OF TRENT
Trent
Verona
Mantua
Padua
REP. OF VENICE
Venice
Görz
Trieste
Rhône
Piacenza
D. OF PARMA to Spain
D. OF MODENA
Ferrara
Bologna
Ravenna
REP. OF GENOA
Genoa
Pontremoli
Massa
REP. OF LUCCA
to the Papacy, 1768–74 Fr. Occup.
Avignon
Marseilles
Nice
Gulf of Lions
Florence
REP. OF SAN MARINO
GR. DUCHY OF TUSCANY
Siena
Ancona
PAPAL STATES
Andorra
K. OF SPAIN
Bastia
Corsica 1768/69 to Fr.
Ajaccio
Piombino
STATO DEI PRESIDII to Spain
Rome
K. OF NAPLES to Spain
East from Greenwich

SAMOGITIA

Tauroggen
1688/90–1795 to Prussia

Polotsk

Smolensk

BALTIC SEA

Königsberg

EAST PRUSSIA

ERMLAND

Danzig   Elbing

WEST PRUSSIA
1772 to Pruss.

K. OF PRUSSIA

NETZE DISTRICT

Torun

Poznan

GREAT POLAND

Vistula

Liegnitz

Breslau

Leuthen

Landshut

DUCHY OF
SILESIA
1742 to Pruss.

Neustadt

AUSTRIAN SILESIA

Olmütz

Iglau

MAR. OF MORAVIA

Brünn

Neisse   Ratibor

Teschen

Krakow

LITTLE
POLAND

Piotrków

Lublin

Vilna

C. OF
SERREY
1688/90–1793 to Prussia

Minsk

LITHUANIA

BLACK RUSSIA

Bialystok

MAZOVIA

Warsaw

K. OF POLAND

PODLESIA

VOLHYNIA

Pripet

RUSSIAN

WHITE RUTHENIA

EMPIRE

Gomel

LITTLE RUSSIA

Kiev

UKRAINE

K. OF GALICIA   AND   LODOMERIA
1772 to Austria

RED RUSSIA

Lemberg
(Lvov)

Z I P S
1770/72 to Hung.

Kolomea

Czernowitz

PODOLIA

Bar

Pressburg

HY OF

Vienna

Gran

Erlau

Debreczin

D. OF
BUKOVINA
1775 to Aus.

BESSARABIA

Jassy

Kishinev

RIA

St.Gotthard

Buda
(Ofen)

Pest

L. Balaton

K. OF HUNGARY
Hereditary Monarchy from 1684.
1699 to Austria

Grosswardein

GR. PR. OF
TRANSYLVANIA
1699 to Austria,
1765 Gr. Pr.

MOLDAVIA

va

Mures

Szegedin

Debreczin

1764–1851

Galati

Ismail

CIVIL-
CROATIA
1701

K. OF
SLAVONIA

CIVIL-SLAVONIA 1743

1701–1878

Mohacs

Temesvar

B A N A T
1718 to Austria

1742–1851

Kronstadt

1538/1737–1878

Peterwardein

Belgrade

WALLACHIA

Bucharest

Constanta

Sava

Sabac

Passarowitz

Craiova

Danube

O T T O M A N

SERBIA

B U L G A R I A

Varna

BLACK
SEA

DALMATIA

Spalato

Sarajevo

HERZEGOVINA

Nish

Sofia

Burgas

REP. OF
RAGUSA

Ragusa

Cattaro

MONTENEGRO

Scutari

Üsküb
(Skoplje)

E M P I R E

Philippopolis

Adrianople

R U M E L I A

Constantinople

COPYRIGHT. GEORGE PHILIP & SON, LTD.

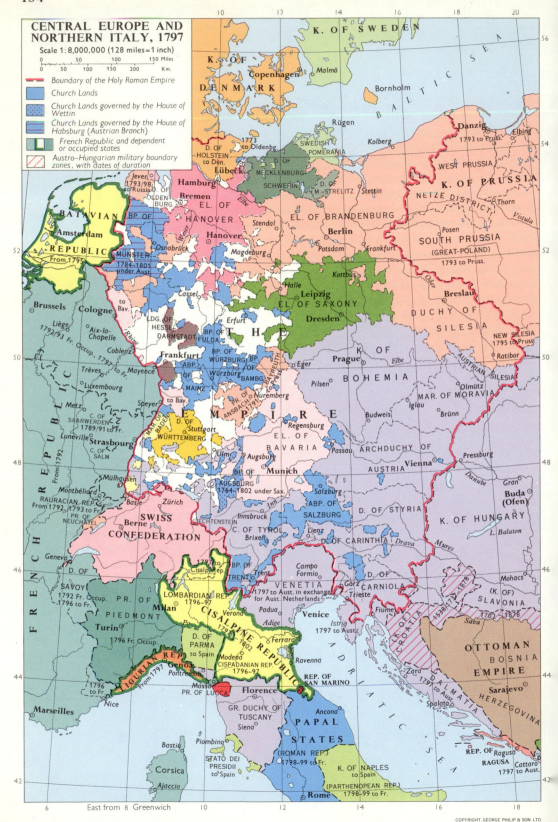

134

CENTRAL EUROPE AND NORTHERN ITALY, 1797

Scale 1:8,000,000 (128 miles=1 inch)

0   50   100   150 Miles
0   50 100 150   200   Km.

- Boundary of the Holy Roman Empire
- Church Lands
- Church Lands governed by the House of Wettin
- Church Lands governed by the House of Habsburg (Austrian Branch)
- French Republic and dependent or occupied states
- Austro–Hungarian military boundary zones, with dates of duration

K. OF SWEDEN

BALTIC SEA

K. OF DENMARK

Copenhagen
Malmö
Bornholm
Rügen
Kolberg
Danzig 1793 to Pruss.
Elbing

D. OF HOLSTEIN 1773 to Oldenbg.
to Den.

Lübeck
D. OF MECKLENBURG-SCHWERIN
Stettin
WEST PRUSSIA
Thorn
NETZE DISTRICT
Vistula

SWEDISH POMERANIA
D. OF M.-STRELITZ

K. OF PRUSSIA

Jever, 1793/98, to Russia.
D. OF OLDENBURG
Hamburg
Bremen
BP. OF

Amsterdam
BATAVIAN REPUBLIC From 1795

EL. OF HANOVER
Hanover
Osnabrück
MÜNSTER 1784–1801 under Aust.

Stendal
Magdeburg
Potsdam
EL. OF BRANDENBURG
Berlin
Frankfurt
Kottbus

Posen
SOUTH PRUSSIA (GREAT POLAND) 1793 to Pruss.

Breslau
DUCHY OF SILESIA
NEW SILESIA 1795 to Pruss.

Brussels
Cologne
to Bav.
Liège
Aix-la-Chapelle
1792/93 Fr. Occup. 1797 to Fr.
Coblenz

Cassel
LDG. OF HESSE-DARMSTADT
BP. OF FULDA
Erfurt

Halle
Leipzig
EL. OF SAXONY
Dresden

Olmütz
MAR. OF MORAVIA
AUSTRIAN SILESIA
Ratibor

T   H   E

Trèves
Luxembourg
Metz
C. OF SAARWERDEN 1789/91 to Fr.
Speyer
to Bav.

Frankfurt
BP. OF WÜRZBURG
Mayence
MAR. OF BADEN
BP. OF MAINZ

Würzburg
BP. OF BAMBG.
PR. OF ANSBACH 1791
BAYREUTH
Nuremberg

Eger
Pilsen
Prague
K. OF BOHEMIA
Elbe

Iglau
Brünn
Budweis

Strasbourg
C. OF SALM
Luneville 1792
PR. OF NEUCHÂTEL

D. OF WÜRTTEMBERG
Stuttgart
Ulm
Augsburg

E   M   P   I   R   E

BP. OF AUGSBURG 1764–1802 under Sax.
Munich
EL. OF BAVARIA
Regensburg
Passau

ARCHDUCHY OF AUSTRIA
Vienna
Danube
Gran
Pressburg
Buda (Ofen)

Mülhusen
Montbéliard
RAURACIAN REP. From 1792, 1793 to Fr.
Basle
Zürich

SWISS CONFEDERATION
Berne
LIECHTENSTEIN
Innsbruck
C. OF TYROL
Brixen

Salzburg
ABP. OF SALZBURG
D. OF STYRIA
Lienz
D. OF CARINTHIA

K. OF HUNGARY
L. Balaton
Mohacs

Geneva
D. OF
SAVOY 1792 Fr. Occup. 1796 to Fr.

1797 to Cisalp. Rep.
BP. OF TRENTO
Trent
Campo Formio

VENETIA
1797 to Aust. in exchange for Aust. Netherlands
Görz
Trieste
D. OF CARNIOLA

(K. OF) SLAVONIA
1538/1718–1876

PR. OF PIEDMONT
Milan
LOMBARDIAN REP. 1796–97
Verona
Padua
Adige

Venice
1797 to Aust.
Istria
Fiume
CROATIA
1797 to Aust.

Turin
1796 Fr. Occup.
D. OF PARMA to Spain
Po
Modena
CISPADANIAN REP. 1796–97
Ferrara
Ravenna

C   I   S   A   L   P   I   N   E   R   E   P   U   B   L   I   C
1797–1802

REP. OF SAN MARINO

Sava
Zara
1797 to Aust.
DALMATIA
Spalato

OTTOMAN
BOSNIA
EMPIRE

LIGURIAN REP. From 1797
Genoa
Pontremoli
1796 to Fr.
Nice
Massa
PR. OF LUCCA
Florence

Sarajevo
HERZEGOVINA

Marseilles

Bastia
Corsica
Ajaccio

Piombino
STATO DEI PRESIDI to Spain
GR. DUCHY OF TUSCANY
Siena

Ancona
PAPAL STATES
(ROMAN REP.) 1798–99 to Fr.

ADRIATIC SEA

REP. OF Ragusa
RAGUSA
Cattaro 1797

Rome

K. OF NAPLES to Spain
(PARTHENOPEAN REP.) 1798–99 to Fr.

East from Greenwich

COPYRIGHT. GEORGE PHILIP & SON, LTD.

CENTRAL EUROPE AND NORTHERN ITALY, 1803

Scale 1: 8,000,000 (128 miles=1 inch)

0 50 100 150 Miles
0 50 100 150 200 Km.

▬▬▬ *Boundary of the Holy Roman Empire*
⬜ *Brandenburg–Prussia*
⬜ *House of Wittelsbach (Bavarian Branch)*
⬜ *House of Habsburg (Austrian Branch) and Secundogeniture*
⬜ *French Republic and dependent states*
⬜ *Austro–Hungarian military boundary zones, with dates of duration*

K. OF SWEDEN

BALTIC SEA

K. OF DENMARK

Copenhagen
Malmö
Bornholm
Rügen
Kolberg
Danzig
Elbing
WEST PRUSSIA
K. OF PRUSSIA
Thorn
Posen
SOUTH PRUSSIA

D. OF HOLSTEIN to Den.
to Oldenbg.
SWEDISH POMERANIA
D. OF MECKLENBURG
SCHWERIN
D. OF M.-STRELITZ
Stettin
NETZE DISTRICT
Jever to Russia
Hamburg
Lübeck
Bremen
D. OF OLDEN-BURG
EL. OF HANOVER
Osnabrück
Münster
Hanover
Stendal
Magdeburg
EL. OF BRANDENBURG
Berlin
Potsdam
Frankfurt
Kottbus
Oder
Breslau
DUCHY OF SILESIA
Glatz
NEW SILESIA
Ratibor
Vistula

BATAVIAN REPUBLIC
Amsterdam
Brussels
Liège
Cologne
Aix-la-Chapelle
1803 to Pruss.
1803 to Pruss.
1803 to Pruss.
BERG to Bav.
LDG. OF Cassel
HESSE
DARMSTADT
1803 to Pruss.
1803 From 1803
Halle
Erfurt
1803 to Pruss.
Leipzig
EL. OF SAXONY
Dresden
THURINGIAN STATES
T   H   E
Eger
Prague
K. OF
BOHEMIA
Pilsen
Budweis
MAR. OF MORAVIA
Olmütz
Brünn
AUSTRIAN SILESIA

Coblenz
to Hesse
Frankfurt
Mayence
Trèves
Luxembourg
Moselle
Speyer
Strasbourg
PR. OF ANSBACH
Nuremberg
to Bavaria
PR. OF BAYREUTH to Pruss.
E   M   P   I   R   E
Salzburg to Salzburg
Regensburg
EL. OF BAVARIA
Passau
ARCHDUCHY OF
Pressburg
EL. OF BADEN From 1803
Stuttgart
EL. OF WÜRTTEMBERG From 1803
Ulm
Augsburg
Munich
Hohenlinden
AUSTRIA
Vienna
Danube
Gran
Buda (Ofen)

FRENCH REPUBLIC
1792-1804
Mülhouse 1798 to Fr.
Montbéliard
PR. OF NEUCHÂTEL
Geneva 1798 to Fr.
D. OF SAVOY
Basle
Zürich
BREIS-GAU
Helv.
LIECHTENSTEIN
HELVETIC REPUBLIC
1798-1803
Berne
REP. OF VALAIS 1802-10
Innsbruck
C. OF TYROL
Brixen
Lienz
EL. OF SALZBURG
Salzburg
D. OF STYRIA
D. OF CARINTHIA
Drava
L. Balaton
Mures
K. OF HUNGARY
Mohács

Marengo 1798/1802 to Fr.
PR. OF PIEDMONT
Turin
Nice
Milan
1802 to Ital. Rep.
ITALIAN REPUBLIC
1802-05
Verona
Padua
Adige
Trent
Campo Formio
D. OF LAIBACH
Görz
Trieste
CARNIOLA
VENETIA
Venice
Fiume
CROATIA
1538/1717 1878
SLAVONIA
1702 1878
Sava
OTTOMAN
BOSNIA
EMPIRE
HERZEGOVINA
Sarajevo

REP. OF VALAIS
REP. OF GENOA
IGURIAN REP.
1797-1805
Pontremoli
Genoa
Massa
REP. OF LUCCA
1799-1805
Florence
PARMA to Spain
Guastalla
Modena
Bologna
Ravenna
Ferrara
Po
REP. OF SAN MARINO
Ancona 1803 to Fr.
A   D   R   I   A   T   I   C
Zara
DALMATIA
Spalato
REP. OF RAGUSA
RAGUSA
Cattaro

Marseilles
Corsica
Bastia
Ajaccio
Piombino 1801 to Fr.
Elba
Orbetello 1801 to Etruria
K. OF ETRURIA
Siena
Kingdom 1801 to Spain
PAPAL
STATES
Rome
K. OF NAPLES
to Spain
S   E   A

6 East from 8 Greenwich 10 12 14 16 18

COPYRIGHT. GEORGE PHILIP & SON. LTD.

CENTRAL EUROPE AND NORTHERN ITALY, 1806

Scale 1: 8,000,000 (128 miles=1 inch)

- - - Boundary of the Confederation of the Rhine at its foundation, 12th July 1806
French Empire
States ruled by Napoleon's family
Other dependent states
Austro-Hungarian military boundary zones, with dates of duration

K. OF SWEDEN

K. OF DENMARK

Copenhagen

Malmö

Bornholm

Rügen

Kolberg

Danzig

WEST PRUSSIA

BALTIC SEA

Lübeck

Hamburg

D. OF MECKLENBURG-SCHWERIN

D. OF M. STRELITZ

Stettin

Thorn

Heligoland to Den.

Jever to Russia until 1807

D. OF OLDEN-BURG

Bremen

HANOVER 1805/06 to Prussia

Hanover

Stendal

BRANDENBURG

Berlin

Frankfurt

Posen

Vistula

SOUTH PRUSSIA

K. OF HOLLAND 1806-10

Amsterdam

Osnabrück

Brunswick

Magdeburg

Potsdam

Glogau

Breslau

SILESIA

NEW SILESIA

Brussels

Cologne

Liège

Münster

GR. D. OF BERG From 1806

Cassel EL. OF HESSE

Halle

Auerstedt

Kottbus

K. OF SAXONY

Leipzig

Dresden From 1806

Ratibor

AUSTRIAN SILESIA

Aix-la-Chapelle

Erfurt

Jena

THURINGIAN STATES

Fulda

Treves

Mayence

Frankfurt

GR. D. OF WÜRZBURG 1805-1

BAYREUTH 1806 to Bav.

Eger

Prague

BOHEMIA

Olmütz

MORAVIA

Luxembourg

Speyer

PR. OF 1806 to Bav.

1806 to Bav.

Pilsen

Iglau

Brünn

Austerlitz

Strasbourg

GR. D. OF BADEN From 1805

CONFEDERATION

1806 to Bav.

1805 to Bav.

Regensburg

1805 to Bav.

Budweis

AUSTRIAN

Pressburg

K. OF WÜRTTEMBERG From 1805

1806 to Württ.

Ulm

Augsburg

Passau

AUSTRIA Vienna

Gran

Buda (Ofen)

Basle

PR. OF NEUCHÂTEL 1806 to Fr.

1805 to Baden

OF THE RHINE

K. OF Munich

BAVARIA From 1805

Salzburg Berchtesgaden

Schönbrunn

EMPIRE From 1804

STYRIA

K. OF HUNGARY

Zürich

Constance 1805 to Baden

1805 to Bav.

LIECHTENSTEIN

Innsbruck

SALZBURG 1805 to Aust.

L. Balaton

Geneva

BERNE

HELVETIA From 1803

TYROL

1805 to Bav.

CARINTHIA

Drava

Mures

Mohacs

REP. OF VALAIS 1802-10

Brixen

Lienz

Laibach

CARNIOLA

Trieste

SLAVONIA

1538 1737-1878

(K. OF) SLAVONIA

OTTOMAN

Milan

Trent

VENETIA 1805 to Italy

Fiume

1702-1878

(K. OF) CROATIA

BOSNIA

EMPIRE

Turin

KINGDOM

Verona

Padua

Venice

1805 to Italy

Sava

HERZEGOVINA

Marseilles

Nice

LIGURIAN REP. 1805 to Fr.

Genoa

OF

ITALY From 1805

Guastalla 1806 to Fr. Italy

PARMA 1805 to Fr.

Modena

Bologna

Ferrara

Ravenna

Zara

DALMATIA 1805 to Italy

Spalato

Sarajevo

Pontremoli

Massa

1806 to Lucca

PR. OF LUCCA From 1805

Florence

REP. OF SAN MARINO

ADRIATIC

Spalato

Ragusa 1806-08 to Russia

Corsica

Ajaccio

Bastia

Piombino 1805 Pr.

Elba

K. OF ETRURIA to Spain

Siena

Ancona

PAPAL STATES

SEA

Cattaro 1805 to Italy 1806-07 to Russia

K. OF NAPLES 1806

Rome

East from Greenwich

COPYRIGHT GEORGE PHILIP & SON LTD.

CENTRAL EUROPE AND
NORTHERN ITALY, 1810

Scale 1:8,000,000 (128 miles=1 inch)

0   50   100   150 Miles
0 50 100 150   200 Km.

- - - Boundary of the Confederation of the Rhine
  French Empire
  States ruled by Napoleon's family
  Other dependent states

K. OF SWEDEN

BALTIC SEA

K. OF DENMARK

Copenhagen   Malmö

Bornholm

Rügen

SWEDISH POMERANIA

Kolberg

REP. OF DANZIG
1807-14
Danzig

Heligoland
1807/14 to Br.

Lübeck

Jever
1807
to Holland

Hamburg
1810 to Fr.

Bremen

HANOVER
1807 to Fr.
1810 to Westphalia

D. OF
MECKLENBURG-
SCHWERIN

D. OF
M.-STRELITZ

Stettin

Graudenz

Thorn

1807
to Berg
Osnabrück

1807
to Westphalia

Hanover

Stendal

K. OF
BRANDENBURG

Magdeburg

Berlin

Potsdam

Frankfurt

GR. D. OF
WARSAW
From 1807 to Sax.,
1809 Gr. Duchy

Posen

Vistula

K. OF
HOLLAND

Amsterdam

1810 to Fr.

Münster

Brunswick

WESTPHALIA
From 1807

Cassel

Halle

Kottbus

K. OF
SAXONY

Leipzig

Dresden

Breslau

SILESIA

1809
to
Warsaw

Ratibor

Brussels

Liège

Cologne

Aix-la-
Chapelle

GR. D. OF
BERG

GR. D.
OF
HESSE

1810
to Hesse

Erfurt
1807-14
to Fr.

THURINGIAN
STATES

GR. D. OF
FRANKFURT
From 1810

GR. D. OF
WÜRZBURG

Würzburg

Eger

Prague

BOHEMIA

Elbe

Pilsen

Budweis

Iglau

Brünn

Olmütz

MORAVIA

AUSTRIAN SILESIA

Trèves

Mayence

Luxembourg

Moselle

Rhine

1807 to Fr.

Frankfurt

1810
to Hesse

PR. OF
BAYREUTH
1807 to Fr.

Nuremberg

K. OF

A U S T R I A N

Strasbourg

GR. D. OF BADEN

K. OF
BADEN

Stuttgart
WÜRTTEMBG.

Ulm

K. OF
WÜRTT.

1810
to Würt.

1810
to Bav.

Regensburg

B A V A R I A

Augsburg

Passau

Danube

Wagram

Schönbrunn
Aspern

Pressburg

Munich

1810
to Bav.

AUSTRIA   Vienna

E M P I R E

Buda
(Ofen)

1810
to Baden

1810
to Würt.

Basle

Zürich

Salzburg

Inn

SALZBURG
1810 to Bav.

STYRIA

K. OF HUNGARY

L. Balaton

Neuchâtel

Berne

HELVETIA

LIECHTENSTEIN

Innsbruck

TYROL

Brixen

1810
to Fr.

Lienz

CARINTHIA

Drava

Mures

Geneva

REP. OF
VALAIS
1810 to Fr.

1810 to Italy
Trent

Laibach

I L L Y R I A N   P R O V I N C E S

1809 to Fr.

Fiume

Trieste

VENETIA

Zara

Mohacs

(K. OF)
SLAVONIA

F R E N C H

E M P I R E

Milan

K I N G D O M

Verona

Padua

Venice

OTTOMAN

BOSNIA

EMPIRE

Turin

Po

Parma

O F

Ferrara

A D R I A T I C

HERZEGOVINA

Sarajevo

Genoa

Modena

Bologna

Ravenna

I T A L Y

S E A

Pontremoli

Massa
PR. OF LUCCA

REP. OF SAN MARINO

Marseilles

Nice

Florence

GR. DUCHY OF
TUSCANY
1807 to Fr.

Ancona
1808
to Italy

Ragusa
1808 to Fr.

Cattaro
1807 to Fr.

Bastia

Elba

PR. OF
PIOMBINO

PAPAL

Corsica

Ajaccio

S T A T E S
1809 to Fr.

K. OF NAPLES

Rome

East from   Greenwich

COPYRIGHT. GEORGE PHILIP & SON. LTD.

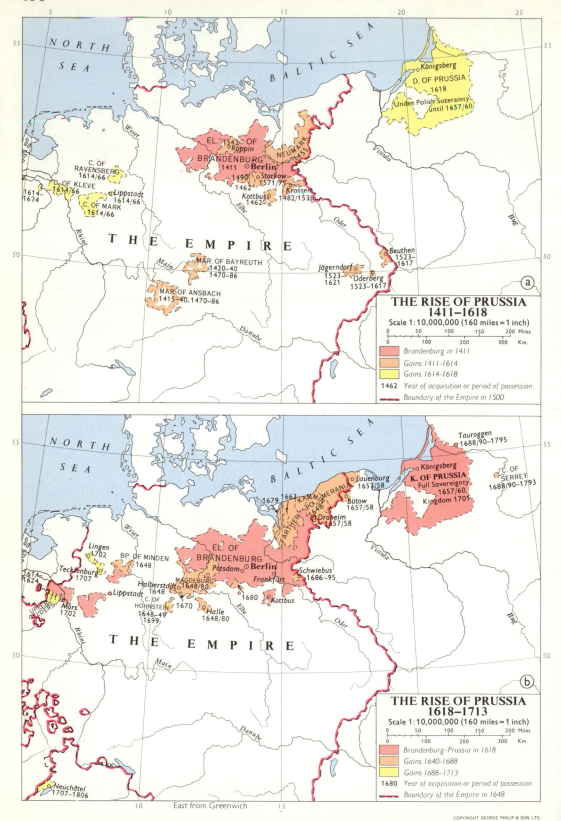

THE RISE OF PRUSSIA
1411–1618
Scale 1:10,000,000 (160 miles = 1 inch)

| 0 | 50 | 100 | 150 | 200 Miles |

0   100   200   300 Km.

Brandenburg in 1411
Gains 1411–1614
Gains 1614–1618

1462 Year of acquisition or period of possession
Boundary of the Empire in 1500

THE RISE OF PRUSSIA
1618–1713
Scale 1:10,000,000 (160 miles = 1 inch)

| 0 | 50 | 100 | 150 | 200 Miles |

0   100   200   300 Km.

Brandenburg-Prussia in 1618
Gains 1640–1688
Gains 1688–1713

1680 Year of acquisition or period of possession
Boundary of the Empire in 1648

East from Greenwich

COPYRIGHT. GEORGE PHILIP & SON. LTD.

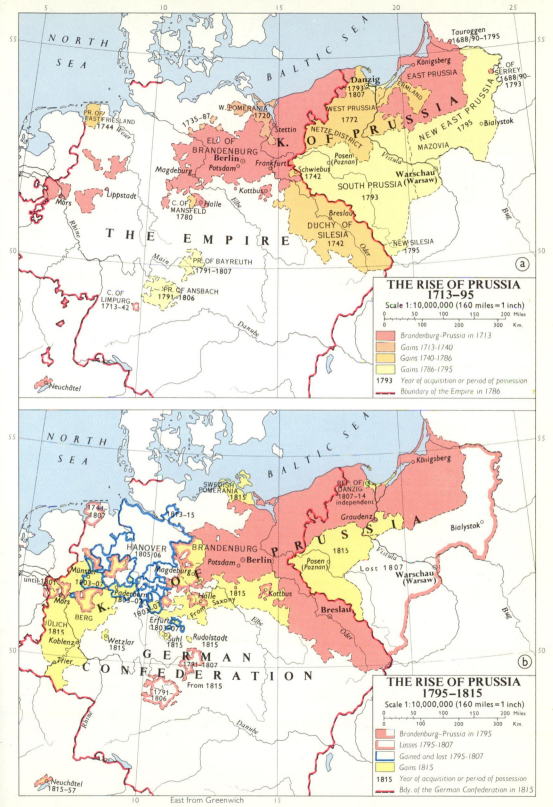

**THE RISE OF PRUSSIA
1713–95**

Scale 1:10,000,000 (160 miles = 1 inch)

	Brandenburg-Prussia in 1713
	Gains 1713-1740
	Gains 1740-1786
	Gains 1786-1795

1793 Year of acquisition or period of possession

Boundary of the Empire in 1786

**THE RISE OF PRUSSIA
1795–1815**

Scale 1:10,000,000 (160 miles = 1 inch)

	Brandenburg-Prussia in 1795
	Losses 1795-1807
	Gained and lost 1795-1807
	Gains 1815

1815 Year of acquisition or period of possession

Bdy. of the German Confederation in 1815

East from Greenwich

COPYRIGHT. GEORGE PHILIP & SON, LTD.

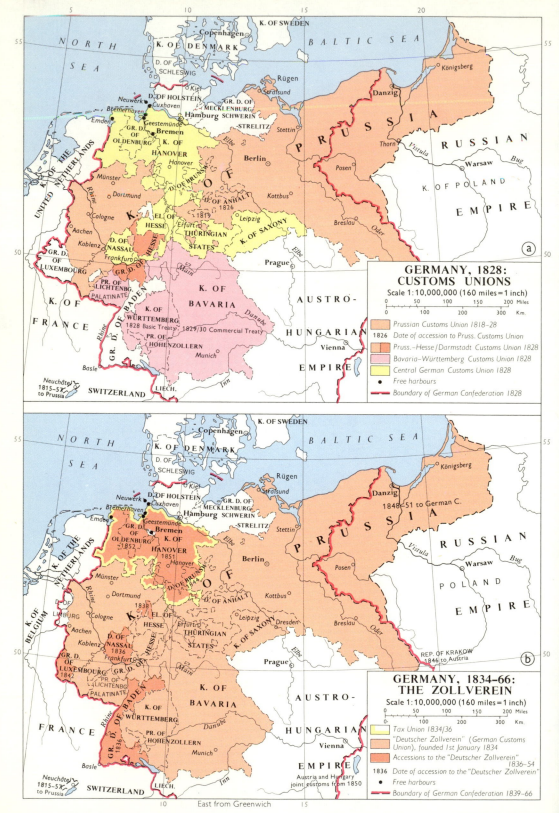

GERMANY, 1828: CUSTOMS UNIONS

Scale 1:10,000,000 (160 miles=1 inch)

0   50   100   150   200 Miles
0   100   200   300 Km.

Prussian Customs Union 1818–28
1826 Date of accession to Pruss. Customs Union
Pruss.-Hesse/Darmstadt Customs Union 1828
Bavaria-Württemberg Customs Union 1828
Central German Customs Union 1828
• Free harbours
Boundary of German Confederation 1828

GERMANY, 1834–66: THE ZOLLVEREIN

Scale 1:10,000,000 (160 miles=1 inch)

0   50   100   150   200 Miles
0   100   200   300 Km.

Tax Union 1834/36
"Deutscher Zollverein" (German Customs Union), founded 1st January 1834
Accessions to the "Deutscher Zollverein" 1836–54
1836 Date of accession to the "Deutscher Zollverein"
• Free harbours
Austria and Hungary joint customs from 1850
Boundary of German Confederation 1839–66

East from Greenwich

COPYRIGHT. GEORGE PHILIP & SON. LTD.

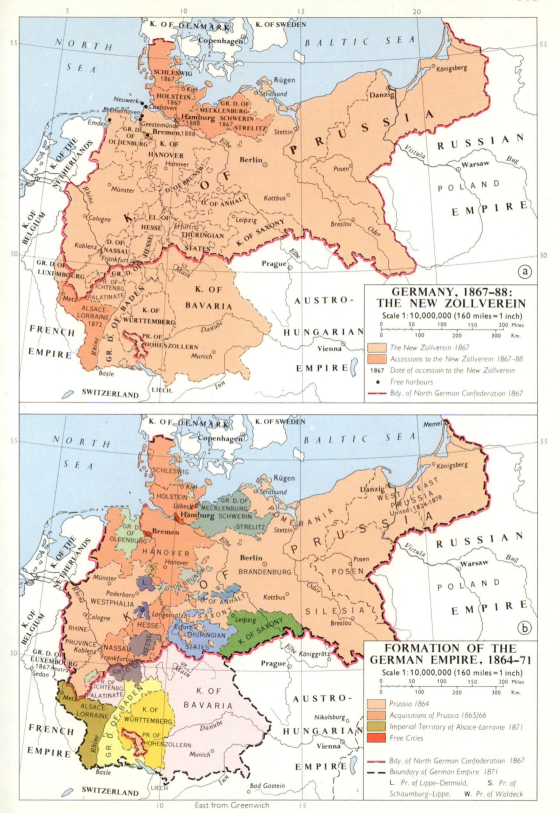

GERMANY, 1867–88:
THE NEW ZOLLVEREIN

Scale 1:10,000,000 (160 miles = 1 inch)

	0	50	100	150	200	Miles
0	100	200	300	Km.

The New Zollverein 1867

Accessions to the New Zollverein 1867–88

1867   Date of accession to the New Zollverein

•   Free harbours

——   Bdy. of North German Confederation 1867

FORMATION OF THE
GERMAN EMPIRE, 1864–71

Scale 1:10,000,000 (160 miles = 1 inch)

	0	50	100	150	200	Miles
0	100	200	300	Km.

Prussia 1864

Acquisitions of Prussia 1865/66

Imperial Territory of Alsace-Lorraine 1871

Free Cities

——   Bdy. of North German Confederation 1867

----   Boundary of German Empire 1871

L. Pr. of Lippe-Detmold,   S. Pr. of
Schaumburg-Lippe,   W. Pr. of Waldeck

COPYRIGHT. GEORGE PHILIP & SON. LTD.

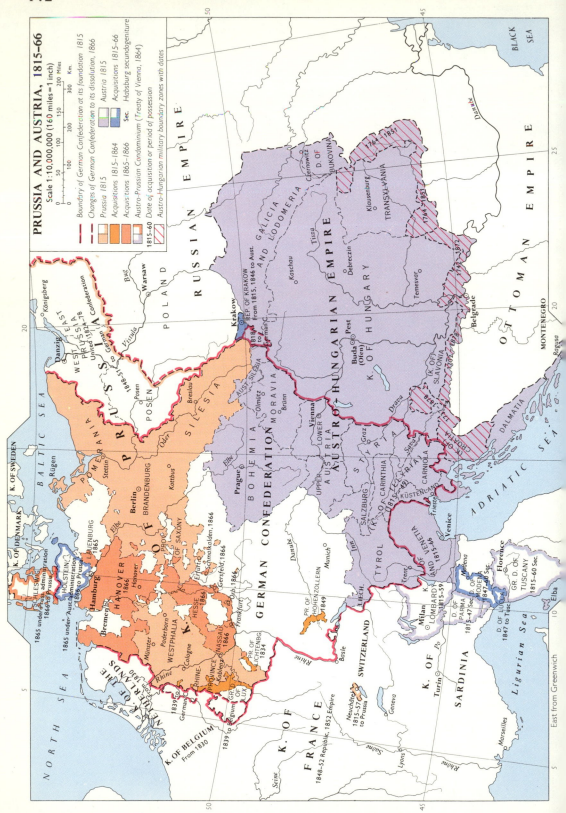

PRUSSIA AND AUSTRIA, 1815–66

Scale 1:10,000,000 (160 miles=1 inch)

0   100   200   300 Km.
0   50   100   150   200 Miles

Boundary of German Confederation at its foundation, 1815
Changes of German Confederation to its dissolution, 1866
Prussia 1815
Acquisitions 1815–1864
Acquisitions 1865–1866
Austria 1815
Acquisitions 1815–66
Sec. Hapsburg secundogeniture
Austro-Prussian Condominium (Treaty of Vienna, 1864)
Date of acquisition or period of possession
Austro-Hungarian military boundary zones with dates

1815–60

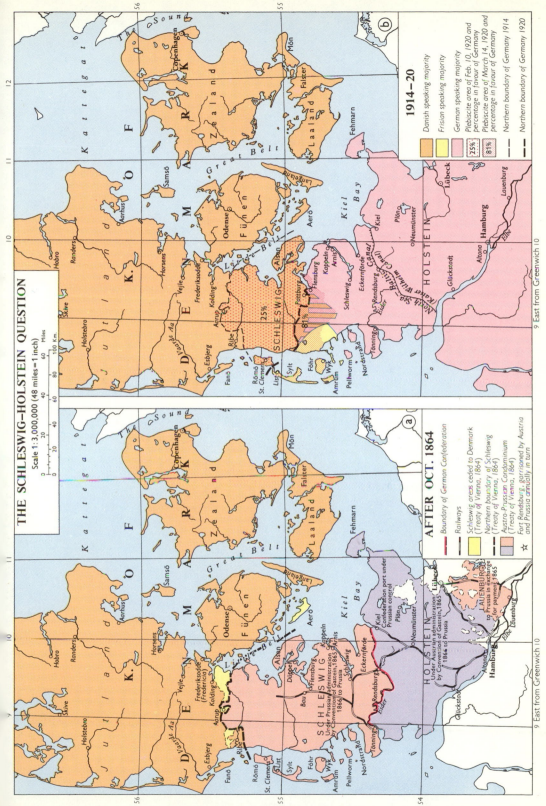

THE SCHLESWIG-HOLSTEIN QUESTION

Scale 1 : 3,000,000 (48 miles = 1 inch)

1914–20

Danish speaking majority

Frisian speaking majority

German speaking majority

25%   Plebiscite area of Feb. 10, 1920 and percentage in favour of Germany

81%   Plebiscite area of March 14, 1920 and percentage in favour of Germany

Northern boundary of Germany 1914

Northern boundary of Germany 1920

AFTER OCT. 1864

Boundary of German Confederation

Railways

Schleswig areas ceded to Denmark (Treaty of Vienna, 1864)

Northern boundary of Schleswig (Treaty of Vienna, 1864)

Austro-Prussian Condominium (Treaty of Vienna, 1864)

Fort Rendsburg, garrisoned by Austria and Prussia annually in turn

COPYRIGHT. GEORGE PHILIP & SON, LTD.

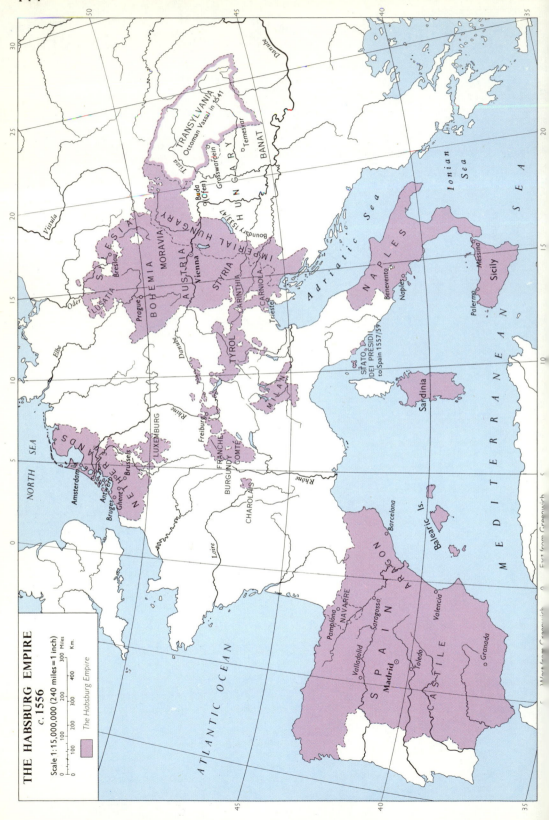

144

THE HABSBURG EMPIRE
c. 1556

Scale 1:15,000,000 (240 miles=1 inch)

0 100 200 300 400 Km.

0 100 200 300 Miles

The Habsburg Empire

NORTH SEA

Amsterdam
Antwerp
Bruges
Ghent
Brussels
NETHERLANDS
LUXEMBURG

ATLANTIC OCEAN

Loire

Rhine

FRANCHE
COMTÉ
BURGUNDY
CHAROLAIS

Rhône

Freiburg

TYROL
MILAN

Danube

Elbe
Oder

Prague
BOHEMIA
LUSATIA
SILESIA
Breslau

MORAVIA
AUSTRIA
Vienna
STYRIA
CARINTHIA
CARNIOLA
Trieste

Vistula

Danzig

TRANSYLVANIA
Ottoman Vassal in 1541
Tisza
Grosswardein
Buda
(Ofen)
Boundary 1541
IMPERIAL HUNGARY
HUNGARY
BANAT
Temesvár

Adriatic Sea

Ionian Sea

NAPLES
Benevento
Naples
STATO DEI PRESIDI
to Spain 1557/59

Sardinia

Palermo
Messina
Sicily

MEDITERRANEAN SEA

Barcelona
ARAGON
Balearic Is.
Valencia
NAVARRE
Pamplona
Saragossa
Valladolid
SPAIN
Madrid
CASTILE
Toledo
Granada

East from Greenwich

West from Greenwich

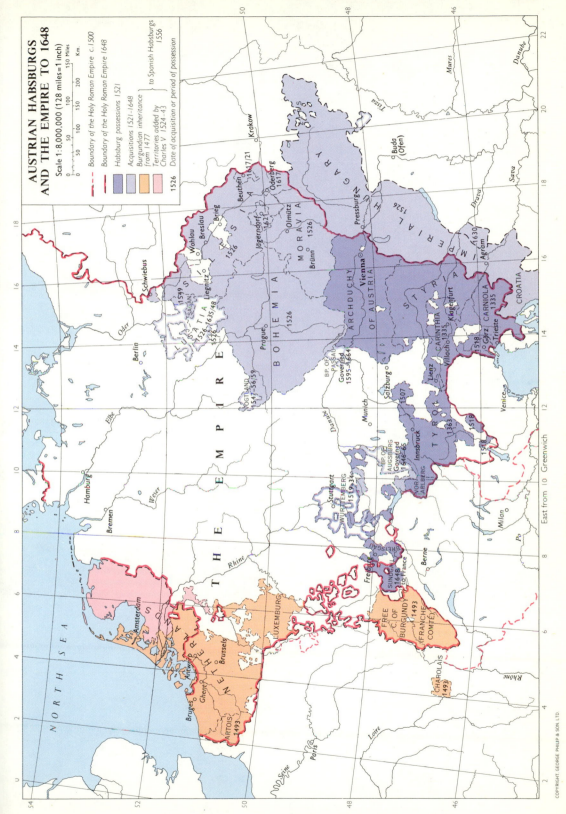

AUSTRIAN HABSBURGS
AND THE EMPIRE TO 1648

Scale 1:8,000,000 (128 miles=1 inch)

0   50   100   120   150   Miles
0   50   100   150   200   Km.

Boundary of the Holy Roman Empire c.1500
Boundary of the Holy Roman Empire 1648
Habsburg possessions 1521
Acquisitions 1521-1648
Burgundian inheritance from 1477
Territories added by Charles V 1524-43   to Spanish Habsburgs 1556
1526   Date of acquisition or period of possession

NORTH SEA

East from 10 Greenwich

COPYRIGHT GEORGE PHILIP & SON LTD

THE   EMPIRE

Hamburg
Bremen
Berlin
Elbe
Weser
Rhine
Amsterdam
Bruges
Ghent
Brussels
Antwerp
ARTOIS 1493
LUXEMBURG
Paris
Seine
Loire

Schwiebus
Wohlau
Breslau
Brieg
Liegnitz
SILESIA
LUSATIA
Oder
Krakow
Beuthen 1617/21
Jägerndorf 1621
Oderberg 1617
Olmutz
Brünn
MORAVIA 1526
Prague
BOHEMIA 1526
VOGTLAND 1547-56/59
Munich
Danube
BP. OF PASSAU Governed 1595-1664
Salzburg
BP. OF AUGSBURG Governed 1646-65
Stuttgart
WÜRTEMBERG 1519-34
VOR ARLBERG
BREISGAU
Freiburg
Berne
Milan
Po
Rhône

Pressburg
Vienna
ARCHDUCHY OF AUSTRIA
HUNGARY
Budd (Ofen)
Tisza
Mures
Danube
Sava
Drava
STYRIA
CARINTHIA 1335
Villach 1335
Klagenfurt
Lienz
TYROL
Innsbruck 1507
1363
1518
Venice
CARNIOLA 1335
Görz
Trieste 1518
CROATIA
Agram 1630
Danube

NETHERLANDS

FREE C. OF BURGUNDY 1493 (FRANCHE COMTÉ)
CHAROLAIS 1493
SUNDGAU 1648 to France

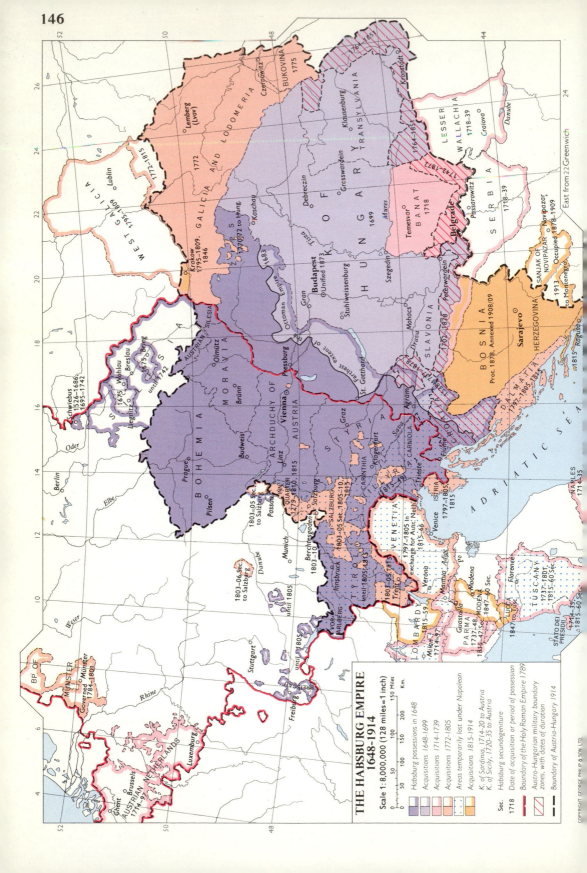
THE HABSBURG EMPIRE
1648-1914
Scale 1:8,000,000 (128 miles=1 inch)
Habsburg possessions in 1648
Acquisitions 1648-1699
Acquisitions 1714-1739
Acquisitions 1772-1805
Areas temporarily lost under Napoleon
Acquisitions 1815-1914
K. of Sardinia, 1714-20 to Austria
K. of Sicily, 1720-35 to Austria
Sec. Habsburg secundogeniture
1718 Date of acquisition or period of possession
Boundary of the Holy Roman Empire 1789
Austro-Hungarian military boundary zones, with dates of duration
Boundary of Austria-Hungary 1914
BOHEMIA
MORAVIA
ARCHDUCHY OF AUSTRIA
HUNGARY
TRANSYLVANIA
GALICIA AND LODOMERIA
WEST GALICIA 1795-1809
BUKOVINA 1775
BANAT 1718
SLAVONIA
CROATIA
BOSNIA
Prot. 1878, Annexed 1908/09
HERZEGOVINA
DALMATIA 1797-1805, 1815
VENETIA
1797-1805 In exchange for Aust. Neth.
1815-66
LOMBARDY 1815-59
TYROL
SALZBURG
CARINTHIA
CARNIOLA
STYRIA
ISTRIA 1797-1805, 1815
SERBIA 1718-39
LESSER WALLACHIA 1718-39
SANJAK OF NOVIPAZAR
Occupied 1878-1909
1913 to Montenegro
TUSCANY 1737-1801, 1815-60 Sec.
PARMA 1737-48, 1815-47 Sec.
MODENA 1847-60 Sec.
LUCCA 1847 to Tusc.
STATO DEI PRESIDII 1714-35, 1815-60 Sec.
NAPLES 1714-35
AUSTRIAN NETHERLANDS 1714-97
MÜNSTER
BP OF
Governed 1784-1801
ADRIATIC SEA
Ottoman Empire 1683
Farthest extent of the
Budapest
Unified 1873
Vienna
Sarajevo
Belgrade
Prague
Pilsen
Budweis
Brünn
Olmütz
Linz
Pressburg
Graz
Klagenfurt
Trieste
Fiume
Agram
Venice
Verona
Mantua
Milan 1714-97
Trent
Innsbruck
Salzburg
Passau
Munich
Stuttgart
Freiburg
Berlin
Breslau
Brieg
Wohlau
Liegnitz
Krakow 1795-1809, 1846
Lemberg (Lvov)
Lublin
Czernowitz
Kaschau
Debreczin
Grosswardein
Klausenburg
Kronstadt
Szegedin
Temesvar
Peterwardein
Passarowitz
Craiova
Mohacs
Gran
Stuhlweissenburg
St. Gotthard
Novipazar
Ragusa
Florence
Modena
Guastalla
Ghent
Brussels
Luxemburg
Münster
Schwiebus 1526-1686, 1695-1742
SILESIA until 1742
AUSTRIAN SILESIA
ZIPS 1770/72 to Hung.
1675
1772
1772-1815
1699
1764-1851
1742-1872
1702-1878
1538-1878
1878
1815
INN QUARTER 1779-1810, 1815
1803-05 Sec., 1805-10, 1815
1803-05, 1815
ILLYRIA 1815-49
until 1805, 1815
VORARLBERG
BREISGAU
until 1805
1803-06 Sec. to Salzburg
1803-05 Sec. to Salzburg
Berchtesgaden 1803-10
Danube
Rhine
Elbe
Oder
Weser
Tisza
Mures
Drava
Sava
Adige
Po
East from 22 Greenwich

COPYRIGHT GEORGE PHILIP & SON LTD

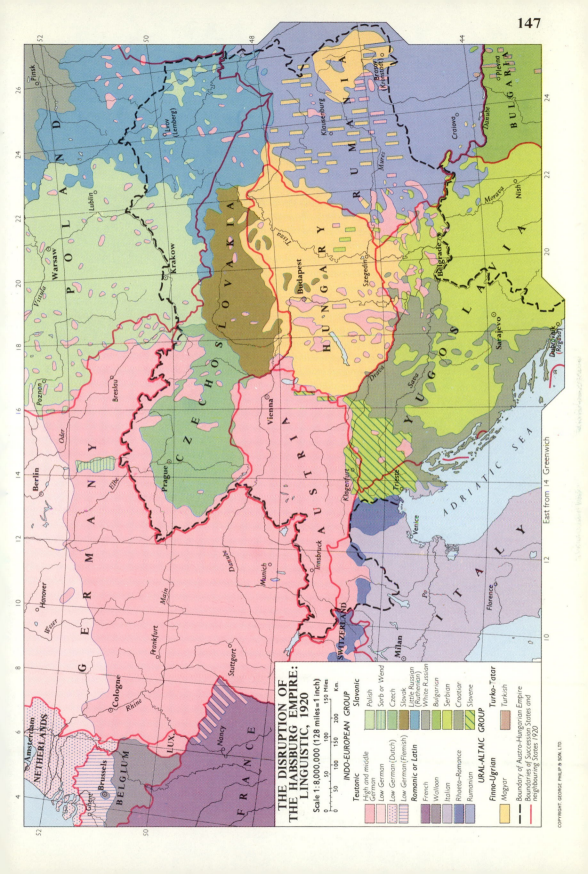

THE DISRUPTION OF
THE HABSBURG EMPIRE:
LINGUISTIC, 1920

Scale 1:8,000,000 (128 miles=1 inch)

Miles	Km.
0 50 100 150 200 Miles	0 50 100 150 200 Km.

INDO-EUROPEAN GROUP

Teutonic
High and middle German
Low German
Low German (Dutch)
Low German (Flemish)

Slavonic
Polish
Sorb or Wend
Czech
Slovak
Little Russian (Ruthenian)
White Russian
Bulgarian
Serbian
Croatian
Slovene

Romanic or Latin
French
Walloon
Italian
Rhaeto-Romance
Rumanian

URAL-ALTAIC GROUP

Finno-Ugrian
Magyar

Turko-Tatar
Turkish

Boundary of Austro-Hungarian Empire
Boundaries of Succession States and neighbouring States 1920

COPYRIGHT: GEORGE PHILIP & SON, LTD.

East from 14 Greenwich

CENTRAL EUROPE TO 1939

Scale 1:12,000,000 (192 miles=1 inch)

0 50 100 200 Miles
0 100 200 300 Km.

Bdy. of Czechoslovakia 1937
Annexed by Germany 1938
Annexed by Germany by Sept. 1, 1939
Annexed by Germany by Dec. 31, 1939
Russian occupation by Dec. 31, 1939
Mar. 16, 1939 Date of annexation or occupation
Polish territory to Slovakia 1939

CENTRAL EUROPE 1945

Scale 1:12,000,000 (192 miles=1 inch)

0 50 100 200 Miles
0 100 200 300 Km.

International boundary 1945
Functioning (de facto) boundary
Allied Control Zones of Germany and Austria:
British   American
French   Russian
City divided into 4 Occupation Zones

COPYRIGHT. GEORGE PHILIP & SON, LTD.

SCANDINAVIA AND THE BALTIC, 1523–1660

Scale 1:12,000,000 (192 miles=1 inch)

Legend:

- Sweden 1523–60 (Gustavus Vasa)
- Acquisitions of Sweden 1560–92 (Eric XIV 1560–68, John III 1568–92)
- Acquisitions of Sweden 1611–54 (Gustavus Adolphus 1611–32, Queen Christina, Chancellor A. Oxenstierna 1632–54)
- Acquisitions of Sweden 1654–60 (Charles X)
- Extent of Swedish colonization in Finland

1645 Date of acquisition or period of possession
- ▲ Iron
- ▲ Copper
- ● Gold
- ○ Silver
- Land over 500m
- Seas and lakes frozen in winter

NORWEGIAN SEA

RUSSIAN EMPIRE

White Sea

Arctic Circle

Lapland

Torne

Luleå

Torneå

Carelia 1617

TRONDHEIM DISTRICT 1658 to Sweden

JÄMTLAND 1645

ÅNGERMAN-LAND

Vasterbotten

Umeå

Gamla karleby (Kokkola)

HÄRJEDALEN

Särna

Vasa

DALECARLIA

Klar

Falun

Gävle

KINGDOM OF SWEDEN

Björneborg (Pori)

Lake Ladoga

Åbo

Northern limit of oak

Vyborg

Kymmene (Kymi)

INGRIA 1583–95 1617

Stolbova

Christiania (Oslo)

Karlstad

Uppsala

Västerås

Åland Is.

Helsingfors

G. of Finland

Area of Swedish Occup.

Narva

Ivangorod

Novgorod 1610–17

NORWAY

Vänern

Stångebro

Stockholm

Revel

1561

1582

Dagö 1582

ESTONIA 1581

Ösel 1645

L. Pskov

Porkhov

Tönsberg

Linköping

Norrköping

Vättern

Gotland

Windau

Dorpat

At the beginning of 1613

Stavanger

Limit of oak

Jönköping

Visby

LIVONIA 1523–61 1621/29–1721

Göteborg

SMÅLAND

Calmar

Öland

Libau

COURLAND

Riga 1621/29 to Sweden

1561 to Pol.

BOHUS-LÄN 1658

HALLAND 1658

Halmstad

Knäred

1645

Düna

United 1380–1814

Frederiksodde (Fredericia)

Odense

Funen

Aalborg

Jutland

SKÅNE

1658 BLEKINGE Brömsebro

Landskrona

Lund

Malmö

Skanör

Bornholm 1658–60 to Sweden

Memel

Niemen

Labiau

Königsberg

Pillau

GR. PR. OF LITHUANIA

K. OF DENMARK

Copenhagen

Zeeland

Schleswig

NORTH SEA

Rügen 1648

1648–1803 Neukloster

Wismar

HITHER POMERANIA

Danzig

Elbing

GR. PR. OF PRUSSIA

BALTIC SEA

Swedish Occup. 1629–35

Oliva

1648–1715/19 ABP. OF BREMEN-VERDEN

Bremen

Wildeshausen 1648–79

Hamburg

Stettin

Elbe

Berlin

Vistula

K. OF POLAND

10   East from Greenwich   15   20   25   30

COPYRIGHT. GEORGE PHILIP & SON. LTD.

150

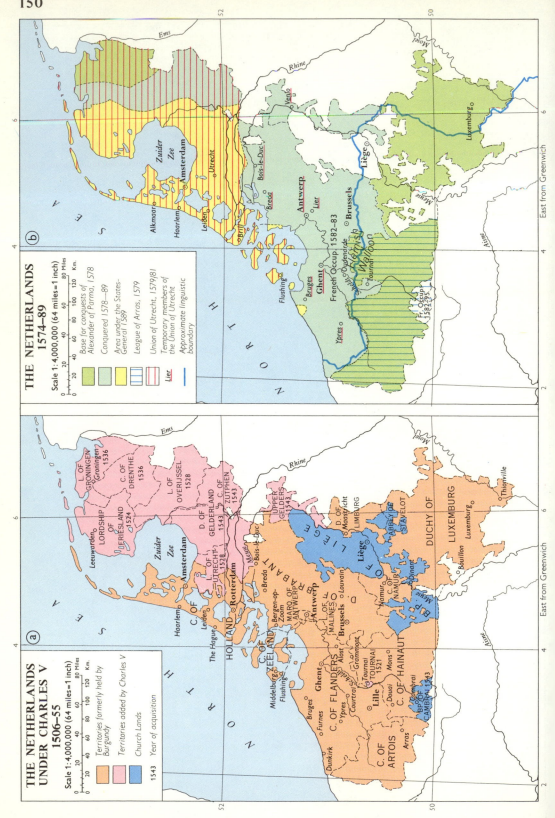

THE NETHERLANDS 1574–89

Scale 1:4,000,000 (64 miles=1 inch)

0 20 40 60 80 Miles
0 20 40 60 80 100 120 Km.

- Base for conquests of Alexander of Parma, 1578
- Conquered 1578—89
- Area under the States-General 1589
- League of Arras, 1579
- Union of Utrecht, 1579/81
- Temporary members of the Union of Utrecht
- Approximate linguistic boundary
- Lier

East from Greenwich

Ems
Rhine
Mosel
Meuse
Aisne

Zuider Zee
Amsterdam
Alkmaar
Haarlem
Leiden
Utrecht
Brill
Bois-le-Duc
Venlo
Luxemburg
Breda
Antwerp
Lier
Brussels
Liège
French Occup. 1582–83
Ghent
Flemish
Walloon
Bruges
Oudenarde
Tournai
Flushing
Ypres
Fr. Occup. 1582–93

NORTH SEA

(b)

THE NETHERLANDS UNDER CHARLES V 1506–55

Scale 1:4,000,000 (64 miles=1 inch)

0 20 40 60 80 Miles
0 20 40 60 80 100 120 Km.

- Territories formerly held by Burgundy
- Territories added by Charles V
- Church Lands
- 1543 Year of acquisition

East from Greenwich

Ems
Rhine
Mosel
Meuse
Aisne

L. OF GRONINGEN 1536
Groningen
C. OF DRENTHE 1536
LORDSHIP OF OVERIJSSEL 1528
OF FRIESLAND 1524
Leeuwarden
D. OF GELDERLAND 1543
ZUTPHEN 1543
UPPER GELDERS 1543
Zuider Zee
Amsterdam
Haarlem
Leiden
Rotterdam
The Hague
C. OF HOLLAND
C. OF ZEELAND
Middelburg
Flushing
Bruges
Furnes
Dunkirk
C. OF ARTOIS
Arras
L. OF UTRECHT 1528
Meuse
Bois-le-Duc
Breda
Bergen-op-Zoom
MARQ. OF ANTWERP
Antwerp
D. OF BRABANT
L. OF MALINES
Brussels
Louvain
Ghent
C. OF FLANDERS
Ypres
Courtrai
Alost
Grammont
Lille
Tournai 1521
TOURNAI
Douai
Mons
C. OF HAINAUT
BP. OF CAMBRAI 1543
Cambrai
D. OF LIMBURG
Maastricht
ABBEY OF STAVELOT
Namur
C. OF NAMUR
Dinant
BP. OF LIÈGE
Liège
Bouillon
Luxemburg
D. OF LUXEMBURG
Thionville

NORTH SEA

(a)

52
50
6
4
2

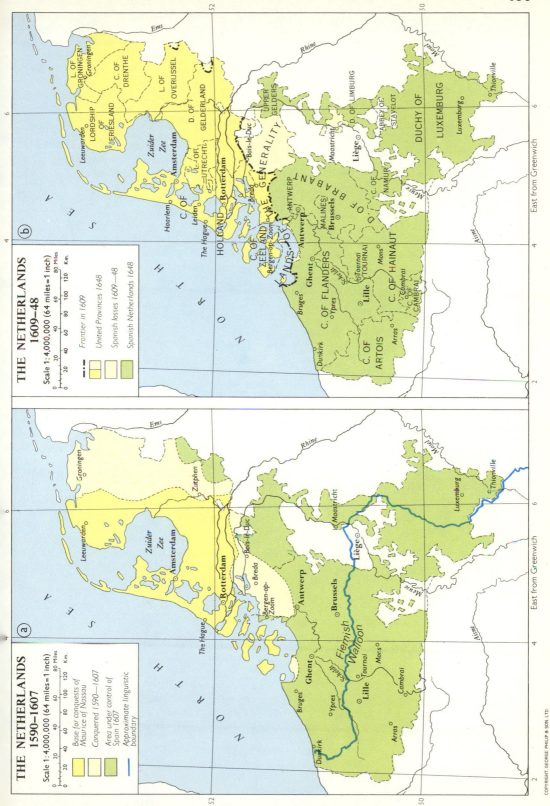

THE NETHERLANDS 1609–48

Scale 1:4,000,000 (64 miles=1 inch)

0 20 40 60 80 Miles
0 20 40 60 80 100 120 Km.

Frontier in 1609
United Provinces 1648
Spanish losses 1609–48
Spanish Netherlands 1648

THE NETHERLANDS 1590–1607

Scale 1:4,000,000 (64 miles=1 inch)

0 20 40 60 80 Miles
0 20 40 60 80 100 120 Km.

Base for conquests of Maurice of Nassau
Conquered 1590—1607
Area under control of Spain 1607
Approximate linguistic boundary

COPYRIGHT GEORGE PHILIP & SON LTD.

THE NETHERLANDS AND BELGIUM
1814–39

Scale 1:3,000,000 (48 miles=1 inch)

Miles

Km.

Losses of the United Netherlands to Prussia 1815/19

Acquisitions of the United Netherlands 1815
(2nd Treaty of Paris)

Kingdom of the United Netherlands 1815-30

Areas under same crown as Netherlands 1839

Kingdom of the Netherlands 1839

Kingdom of Belgium 1839

1830 Date of independence

- - - - Northern boundary of France 1814 (1st Treaty of Paris)

——— Boundary of German Confederation 1815

– – – Boundary changes of German Confederation 1839

——— Approximate linguistic boundary

☆ Fortresses

COPYRIGHT. GEORGE PHILIP & SON, LTD.

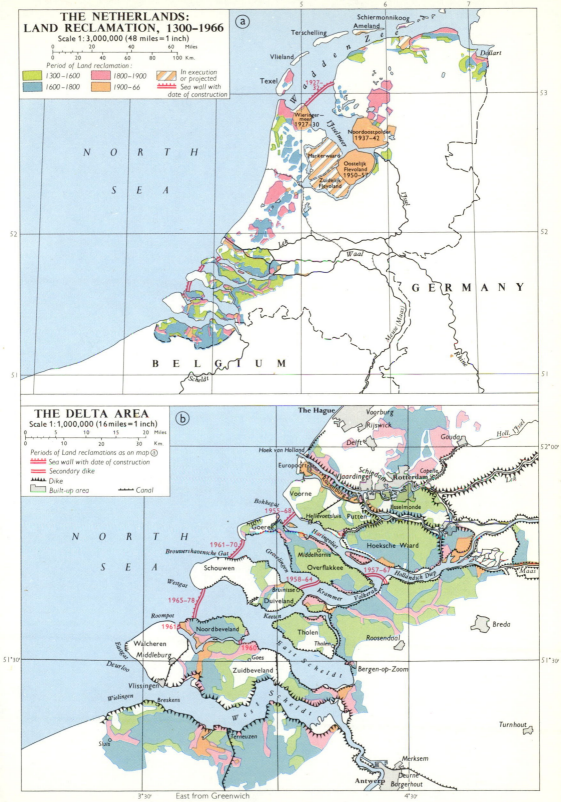

THE NETHERLANDS: LAND RECLAMATION, 1300–1966

Scale 1:3,000,000 (48 miles = 1 inch)

Period of Land reclamation:
- 1300–1600
- 1600–1800
- 1800–1900
- 1900–66
- In execution or projected
- Sea wall with date of construction

Wieringer-meer 1927–30
Noordoostpolder 1937–42
Markerwaard
Oostelijk Flevoland 1950–57
Zuidelijk Flevoland

NORTH SEA

Schiermonnikoog
Ameland
Terschelling
Vlieland
Texel
Dollart
Wadden Zee
IJsselmeer
IJssel

GERMANY

Lek
Waal
Meuse (Maas)
Rhine

BELGIUM

Scheldt

THE DELTA AREA

Scale 1:1,000,000 (16 miles = 1 inch)

Periods of Land reclamations as on map (a)
- Sea wall with date of construction
- Secondary dike
- Dike
- Built-up area
- Canal

The Hague
Voorburg
Rijswick
Delft
Gouda
Holl. IJssel
Hoek van Holland
Europoort
Vlaardingen
Schiedam
Rotterdam
Capelle
Lek
Voorne
Rozenburg
IJsselmonde
Bokkegat 1955–68
Goeree
Hellevoetsluis
Putten
Haringvliet
Hoeksche Waard
Brouwershavensche Gat 1961–70
Greveligen
Middelharnis
Overflakkee
Hollandsch Diep
1957–67
Maas
Westgat
Schouwen
1958–64
Krammer
Volkerak
1965–78
Bruinisse
Duiveland
Roosendaal
Roompot
Keeten
Noordbeveland
Tholen
Tholen
1961
Breda
Walcheren
1960
Goes
Zuidbeveland
East Scheldt
Bergen-op-Zoom
Middleburg
Eastgat
Deurloo
Vlissingen
Breskens
Wielingen
West Scheldt
Terneuzen
Turnhout
Sluis
Merksem
Deurne
Antwerp
Borgerhout

NORTH SEA

3°30'   East from Greenwich   4°30'

COPYRIGHT. GEORGE PHILIP & SON. LTD.

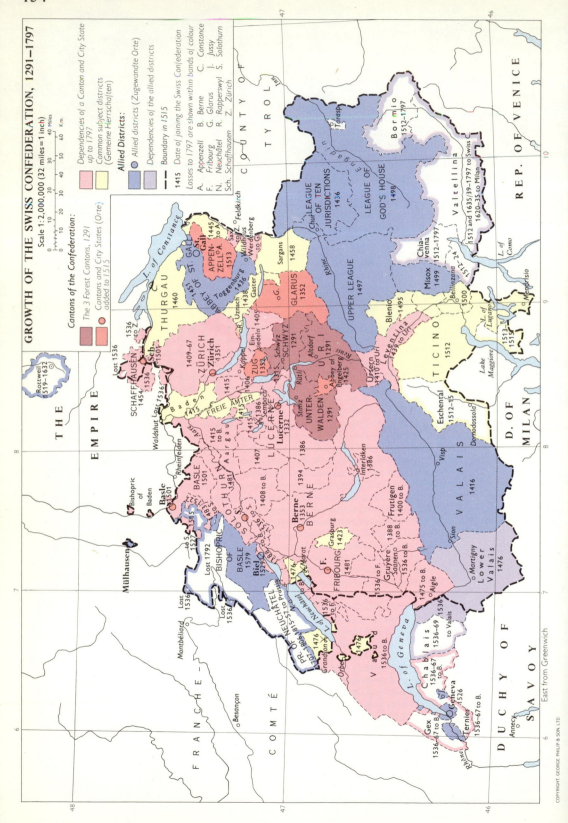

GROWTH OF THE SWISS CONFEDERATION, 1291–1797

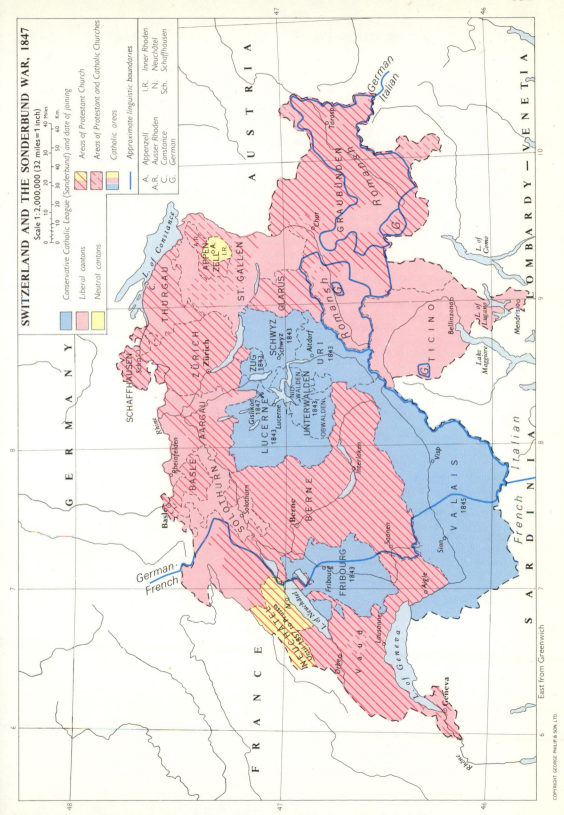

SWITZERLAND AND THE SONDERBUND WAR, 1847

Scale 1:2,000,000 (32 miles=1 inch)

Conservative Catholic League (Sonderbund) and date of joining

Areas of Protestant Church

Areas of Protestant and Catholic Churches

Catholic areas

Approximate linguistic boundaries

Liberal cantons

Neutral cantons

A. Appenzell   I.R.   Inner Rhoden
A.R. Ausser Rhoden   N.   Neuchâtel
C.   Constance   Sch. Schaffhausen
G.   German

G E R M A N Y

A U S T R I A

L O M B A R D Y — V E N E T I A

F R A N C E

S A R D I N I A

German-Italian

L. of Constance

C. of Constance

Tarasp

GRAUBÜNDEN

Romansch

Chur

G.

TICINO

Bellinzona

L. of Como

L. of Lugano

Lake Maggiore

Mendrisio

Italian

SCHAFFHAUSEN

Sch.

THURGAU

APPEN-
ZELL A.R.
I.R.

ST. GALLEN

GLARUS

Rhine

ZÜRICH

Zürich

Rheinfelden

AARGAU

BASLE

Basle

SCHWYZ
1843
Schwyz

Altdorf

URI
1843

ZUG
1843

Gislikon
1847

LUCERNE
1843 Lucerne

NID-
WALDEN
1843

UNTERWALDEN
1843

OBWALDEN

Interlaken

SOLOTHURN

Solothurn

Berne

BERNE

German-
French

NEUCHÂTEL
(Prussia 1851 to Prussia)

N.

L. of Neuchâtel

FRIBOURG
1843

Fribourg

Orbe

Vaud

Lausonne

L. of Geneva

Geneva

Saanen

Aigle

Sion

Visp

VALAIS
1845

Italian

Rhône

French

German-
French

East from Greenwich

COPYRIGHT GEORGE PHILIP & SON LTD.

ITALY, *c.*1500

Scale 1:7,500,000 (120 miles = 1 inch)

| | 0 | 50 | 100 | 150 Miles |

| 0 | 50 | 100 | 150 | 200 | Km. |

Papal States

Lands claimed by the Pope

Smaller independent states

Boundary of the Empire

GROWTH OF FLORENCE TO 1454

Scale 1:5,000,000 (80 miles = 1 inch)

| 0 | 50 | 100 | 150 Miles |

| 0 | 50 | 100 | Km. |

Florentine Lands *c.*1300

Acquisitions 1300–1380

Acquisitions 1381–1454

Protected states

ⓑ

Rocca
S. Casciano
Montecatini
Lucca
MUGELLO
Pistoia
CASENTINO
Pisa
Florence
Campaldino
Sepolcro
S. Miniato
S. Gimignano
Volterra
Poggibonsi
Arezzo
Cortona
Piombino
Elba

ⓐ

THE   EMPIRE

SWISS
CONFEDERATION

Lausanne

Geneva

Domodossola

Locarno

Trent

Belluno
Udine

SAVOY

Aosta

Como

Brescia
Vicenza
Verona

Venice

Trieste

DUCHY OF SAVOY

PIEDMONT

Novara

D. OF MILAN

Milan

Crema

Padua

Este

Fiume

ISTRIA

Pola

K. OF FRANCE

Susa

Turin

MAR. OF ASTI

Marignano

Pavia

Lodi

M. OF MANTUA

Po

D. OF FERRARA

REPUBLIC OF VENICE

MONT-FERRAT

1499–1512,
1515–21 to Fr.

Alessandria

Parma

Mirandola

Modena

D. OF MODENA

Bologna

Ravenna

EMILIA

ROMAGNA

Cesena

Zara

DALMATIA

Spalato

MAR. OF SALUZZO

REP. OF GENOA

Genoa

Pontremoli

1499–1512,
1515–28 to Fr.

Spezia

Massa

Pistoia

Florence

REP. OF SAN MARINO

Urbino

Ancona

Nice

PR. OF MONACO

REP. OF LUCCA

Pisa

REP. OF FLORENCE

1494–1509
indep.

Siena

REP. OF SIENA

PAPAL STATES

Perugia

Assisi

Camerino

ADRIATIC

SEA

Bastia

Piombino

Elba

D. OF PIOMBINO

Orvieto

Viterbo

PATRIMONY

Chieti

REP. OF RAGUSA

Corsica
1284 to Genoa

Ajaccio

Ostia

Tivoli

Rome
OF ST. PETER

Pontecorvo

K. OF NAPLES

Foggia

Barletta

Bari

Capua

Benevento

1504
to Spain

Gaeta

Naples

Salerno

Taranto

Brindisi

Amalfi

Otranto

K. OF SARDINIA

Sassari

Cosenza

T Y R R H E N I A N

S E A

Monte Reale

Cagliari

Catanzaro

Lipari Is.

Seminara

Reggia

Trapani

Palermo

Messina

Egadi Is.

K. OF SICILY
1504 to Spain

Catania

Caltanissetta

Siracusa

Terranova

M E D I T E R R A N E A N

Pantelleria

S E A

Gozo

Malta

8   East from Greenwich   10

12

14

16

COPYRIGHT. GEORGE PHILIP & SON. LTD.

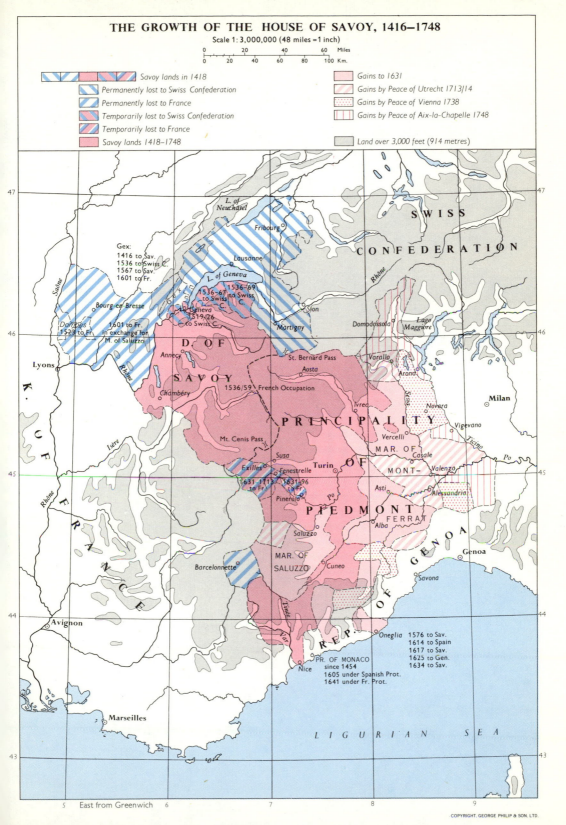

THE GROWTH OF THE HOUSE OF SAVOY, 1416–1748

Scale 1 : 3,000,000 (48 miles =1 inch)

Savoy lands in 1418

Permanently lost to Swiss Confederation

Permanently lost to France

Temporarily lost to Swiss Confederation

Temporarily lost to France

Savoy lands 1418–1748

Gains to 1631

Gains by Peace of Utrecht 1713/14

Gains by Peace of Vienna 1738

Gains by Peace of Aix-la-Chapelle 1748

Land over 3,000 feet (914 metres)

Gex:
1416 to Sav.
1536 to Swiss C.
1567 to Sav.
1601 to Fr.

Dombes
1523 to Fr.
1601 to Fr.
in exchange for
M. of Saluzzo

Oneglia
1576 to Sav.
1614 to Spain
1617 to Sav.
1625 to Gen.
1634 to Sav.

PR. OF MONACO
since 1454
1605 under Spanish Prot.
1641 under Fr. Prot.

COPYRIGHT. GEORGE PHILIP & SON. LTD.

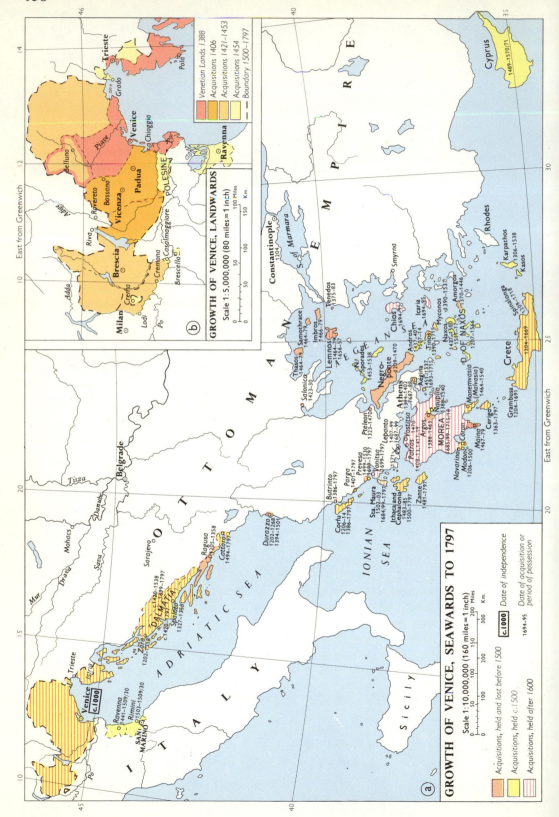

GROWTH OF VENICE, LANDWARDS

Scale 1:5,000,000 (80 miles=1 inch)

Venetian Lands 1388
Acquisitions 1406
Acquisitions 1421–1453
Acquisitions 1454
Boundary 1500–1797

(b)

GROWTH OF VENICE, SEAWARDS TO 1797

Scale 1:10,000,000 (160 miles=1 inch)

c.1000 Date of independence

1694–95 Date of acquisition or period of possession

Acquisitions, held and lost before 1500
Acquisitions, held c.1500
Acquisitions, held after 1600

(a)

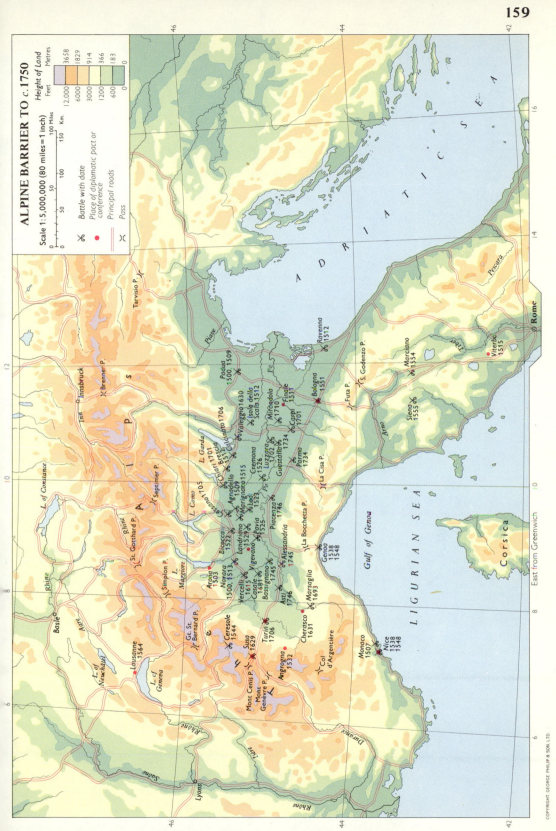
ALPINE BARRIER TO c.1750
Scale 1:5,000,000 (80 miles=1 inch)
0 50 100 Miles
0 50 100 150 Km.
Battle with date
Place of diplomatic pact or conference
Principal roads
Pass
Height of Land
Feet Metres
12,000 3658
6000 1829
3000 914
1200 366
600 183
0 0
The Alps
L. of Constance
Rhine
Basle
Aare
L. of Neuchâtel
Lausanne 1564
L. of Geneva
Saône
Rhône
Lyons
Isère
Durance
St. Gotthard P.
Simplon P.
L. Maggiore
Gt. St. Bernard P.
Septimer P.
L. Como
L. Garda
Inn
Innsbruck
Brenner P.
Tarvisio P.
Piave
Arona 1503
Ceresole 1544
Mont Cenis P.
Susa 1629
Mont Genèvre P.
Turin 1706
Angrogna 1532
Cherasco 1631
Col d'Argentière
Marsaglia 1693
Novara 1500, 1513
Vercelli 1615
Casale 1681
Bassignano 1745
Asti 1746
Alessandria 1745
Vigevano
Bicocca 1522
Landriano 1529
Pavia 1525
Cassano 1705
Agnadello 1509
Marignano 1515
Lodi 1523
Chiari 1701
Brescia 1512
Calcinato 1706
Valeggio 1630
Isola della Scala 1512
Padua 1500, 1509
Cremona 1526
Luzzara 1702
Guastalla 1734
Piacenza 1746
Po
Mirandola 1710
Finale 1511
Carpi 1701
Parma 1734
La Bocchetta P.
La Cisa P.
Genoa 1538 1548
Bologna 1551
Ravenna 1512
Futa P.
S. Godenzo P.
Arno
Siena 1555
Marciano 1554
Tiber
Viterbo 1515
Rome
Pescara
Monaco 1507
Nice 1538 1548
Gulf of Genoa
LIGURIAN SEA
ADRIATIC SEA
Corsica
East from Greenwich
COPYRIGHT. GEORGE PHILIP & SON. LTD.

ITALY, 1713–48

Scale 1: 7,500,000 (120 miles=1 inch)

0   50   100   150 Miles
0 50 100 150 200 Km.

Habsburg Lands
(Austrian Habsburgs extinct 1740;
continued by Habsburg–Lorraine)
Spanish Bourbon Lands

—— Boundary of the Empire

THE EMPIRE

SWISS CONFEDERATION

K. OF FRANCE

Geneva
D. OF SAVOY

K. OF SARDINIA
PR. OF PIEDMONT
Turin
Susa
Vigevano
Po

1713 4 8

1713 to France

Nice
PR. OF MONACO
Oneglia
Finale
Spezia
Pontremoli

REP. OF GENOA

Corsica
to Genoa
Bastia
Ajaccio

K. OF SARDINIA
1714 to Austria, 1717 Spanish Occup.,
1720 to Savoy.
Sassari
Monte Reale
Cagliari

Como
D. OF MILAN
1714 to Aust.
Bergamo
Brescia
Pavia
D. OF MANTUA

D. OF PARMA
1731 to Sp.
1735 to Aust
1748 to Sp.

Guastalla
1748 to Parma

D. OF MODENA

Trent
Belluno
Udine
Rovereto
Vicenza
Padua
Venice

REPUBLIC OF VENICE

Görz
Trieste
Fiume
ISTRIA
Pola

DALMATIA
Zara
Spalato

REP. OF RAGUSA
1718 independent

Ferrara
Bologna
Ravenna
EMILIA
ROMAGNA

Massa
REP. OF LUCCA
Pisa
Florence
Leghorn
GR. DUCHY OF TUSCANY
1737 to Habsburg-
Lorraine
Siena

REP. OF SAN MARINO
Urbino
Ancona

PAPAL STATES
Perugia
Assisi
Spoleto
Orvieto
Viterbo

Piombino
Elba
STATO
DEI PRESIDII
1714 to Aust.
1735 to Spain

PATRIMONY
OF ST. PETER
Rome
Velletri
Gaeta
Capua

Pontecorvo
1512
to Papal States
Benevento

K. OF NAPLES
1714 to Austria, 1735 to Spain
Chieti
Foggia
Barletta
Bari
Naples
Salerno
Amalfi
Taranto
Lecce
Otra
Bri
Cosenza
Catanzaro

ADRIATIC SEA

TYRRHENIAN SEA

MEDITERRANEAN SEA

Lipari Is.
Seminara
Palermo
Messina
Reggio
Trapani
Egadi Is.
K. OF SICILY
1713 to Savoy, 1718 Spanish Occup.,
1720 to Austria, 1735 to Spain
Catania
Terranova
Siracusa
Pantelleria

Gozo
Malta
1530–1798 to Knights of St. John

COPYRIGHT. GEORGE PHILIP & SON LTD.

ITALY, 1815–1924
Scale 1 : 7,500,000 (120 miles=1 inch)

0   50   100   150   200   Km.
0   50   100   150 Miles

K. of Sardinia 1815	Northern boundary of Italy 1914
1860 Dates are those of annexation, first to the K. of Sardinia, and after 1860, to the K. of Italy	Acquisitions 1919/20
Sec. Habsburg secundogeniture	☆ Austrian quadrilateral fortresses (Peschiera, Verona, Legnago, Mantua)

SWITZERLAND

Geneva
1815 Neutral District
1860 to Fr.
Grenoble
Briançon
FRANCE
Nice 1860 to Fr.
PR. OF MONACO 1815-61 under Sardinian Prot. 1861 under French Prot.

K. OF PIEDMONT
Turin
Novara
Magenta
Alessandria
1859
1815-59 to Aust.
LIGURIA
Genoa
SARDINIA

SOUTH TYROL
Bolzano (Bozen)
1919/20
Trento
Belluno
Udine
1866
1815-66 to Aust.
K. OF LOMBARDY AND VENETIA
Milan
Peschiera
Verona
Vicenza
Solferino
Custozza
Goito
Legnago
Mantua
Venice
Trieste
1919/20
Pola
Chenso

Guastalla
1847 to Mod.
D. OF PARMA
1815-47 Sec.
Pontremoli, Tusc.
1847 to Parma
1829 to Mod.
Massa
Pietrasanta
1860
D. OF MODENA
1847-60 Sec.
1860
Fivizzano, Tusc.
1847 to Mod.
D. OF LUCCA
1847 to Tusc.
Florence
1860
GR. DUCHY OF TUSCANY
1815-60 Sec.
Siena
1860
Leghorn
Elba

Ferrara
Bologna
REP. OF SAN MARINO from 1861 under Italian Prot.
Urbino
1860
Ancona
Castelfidardo
PAPAL
Perugia
Assisi
STATES
1870
Mentana
Rome
Velletri
Gaeta
Pontecorvo
Capua
Benevento
Naples
Nola
Salerno

Fiume 1920 Free City 1920 Ital. Occup. 1924 to Italy

Zara 1919/20
Spalato
Lagosta 1919/20

ADRIATIC SEA

Chieti
Foggia
Bari
Taranto
Brindisi
Otranto

1860
K. OF THE TWO SICILIES

Corsica 1768 to Fr.
Ajaccio
Bastia

Sassari
Sardinia
Cagliari

TYRRHENIAN SEA

Cosenza
Lipari Is.
Milazzo
Messina
1862
Aspromonte
Reggio
Palermo
Trapani
Egadi Is.
Calatafimi
Sicily
1860
Catania
Siracusa

MEDITERRANEAN SEA

Pantelleria to Sicily
Gozo
Malta 1814 to Br.

East from Greenwich

COPYRIGHT. GEORGE PHILIP & SON LTD.

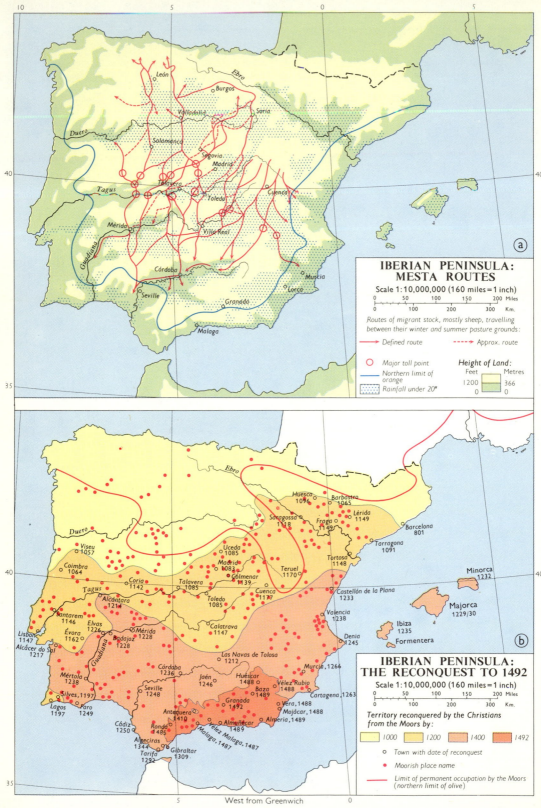

**IBERIAN PENINSULA:
MESTA ROUTES**

Scale 1:10,000,000 (160 miles = 1 inch)

| 0 | 50 | 100 | 150 | 200 Miles |

| 0 | 100 | 200 | 300 | Km. |

*Routes of migrant stock, mostly sheep, travelling
between their winter and summer pasture grounds:*

→ *Defined route*   ⇢ *Approx. route*

○ *Major toll point*   **Height of Land:**

— *Northern limit of
orange*

Feet   Metres

1200   366

0   0

▥ *Rainfall under 20″*

a

**IBERIAN PENINSULA:
THE RECONQUEST TO 1492**

Scale 1:10,000,000 (160 miles = 1 inch)

| 0 | 50 | 100 | 150 | 200 Miles |

| 0 | 100 | 200 | 300 | Km. |

*Territory reconquered by the Christians
from the Moors by:*

| 1000 | 1200 | 1400 | 1492 |

○ *Town with date of reconquest*

● *Moorish place name*

— *Limit of permanent occupation by the Moors
(northern limit of olive)*

b

West from Greenwich

COPYRIGHT. GEORGE PHILIP & SON. LTD.

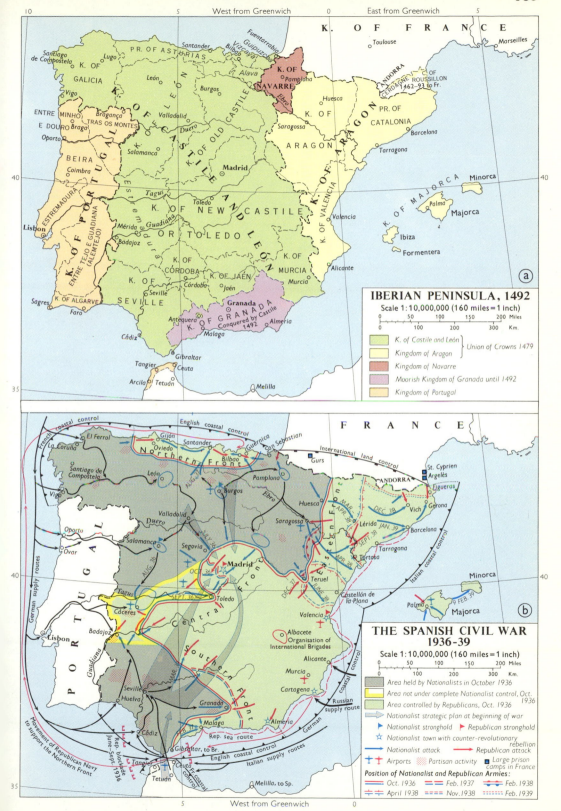

IBERIAN PENINSULA, 1492

Scale 1:10,000,000 (160 miles = 1 inch)

0   50   100   150   200 Miles
0   100   200   300 Km.

- K. of Castile and León   Union of Crowns 1479
- Kingdom of Aragon
- Kingdom of Navarre
- Moorish Kingdom of Granada until 1492
- Kingdom of Portugal

THE SPANISH CIVIL WAR 1936-39

Scale 1:10,000,000 (160 miles = 1 inch)

0   50   100   150   200 Miles
0   100   200   300 Km.

- Area held by Nationalists in October 1936
- Area not under complete Nationalist control, Oct. 1936
- Area controlled by Republicans, Oct. 1936
- Nationalist strategic plan at beginning of war
- ▶ Nationalist stronghold   ▶ Republican stronghold
- ☆ Nationalist town with counter-revolutionary rebellion
- → Nationalist attack   → Republican attack
- Airports   Partisan activity   Large prison camps in France

Position of Nationalist and Republican Armies:
- Oct. 1936   Feb. 1937   Feb. 1938
- April 1938   Nov. 1938   Feb. 1939

COPYRIGHT. GEORGE PHILIP & SON. LTD.

THE EMPIRE
POLA
FRANCE
ITALY
MEDITERRANEAN
Berlin
Elbe
Vistula
Warsaw
Oder
Frankfurt
Prague
Krakow
Paris
Rhine
Danube
GALICIA
Lvov (Lemberg)
Kolomea
Kamene
Chot
Vienna
1683
Nove Zamky
Komarom
Györ
Gran
Erlau
Buda (Ofen)
Pest
STYRIA
St. Gotthard
TRANSYLVANIA
1541
Grosswardein
1664
Gyula
Suce
MOL
Villach
HUNGARY
1541
Milan
Rhône
1664
to Austria 1630
Szigetvar
Venice
Trieste
1526
Mohacs
Szegedin
Temesvar
CROATIA
Peterwardein
1528
Jajce
Sabac
1521
Belgrade
WALLACHI
1393
Bucharest
Barcelona
DALMATIA
BOSNIA
1463
Semendria
Sebenico
Spalato
SERBIA
1459
Adriatic Sea
HERZEGOVINA
1389
Kosovo Polje
Nicopolis
BULGARIA
1393
Sofia
RAGUSA
1526 Ottoman Vassal
MONTENEGRO
Cattaro
Rome
1364
Philippopolis
Üsküb
ALBANIA
1478
Durazzo
RUMELIA
Adrianople
Salonica
Otranto
Ottoman Occup.
1480–81
Gallipoli
Lemnos
1656/57 to Ven.
Canakk
Algiers
1510–29 to Spain
Bugia
1510–55 to Spain
Bona
1535–74 to Spain
Ionian Is.
Prevesa
Lesbos
1462
Lepanto
1499
1571
Negroponte
1470
Chios
1566
Tunis
1535–74 to Spain
MOREA
1458/60
Athens
Samos
1550
ALGIERS
1518
TUNIS
1574
Navarino
Nauplia
Naxos
1566
Modon
1500
Coron
1540
Monemvasia (Malvasia)
Cerigo
Crete
1669
Djerba
Tripoli
Benghazi
TRIPOLI
1551
CYRENAICA
1521
E
0
5
10
15
20
25
50
45
40
35
30
25
East from Greenwich

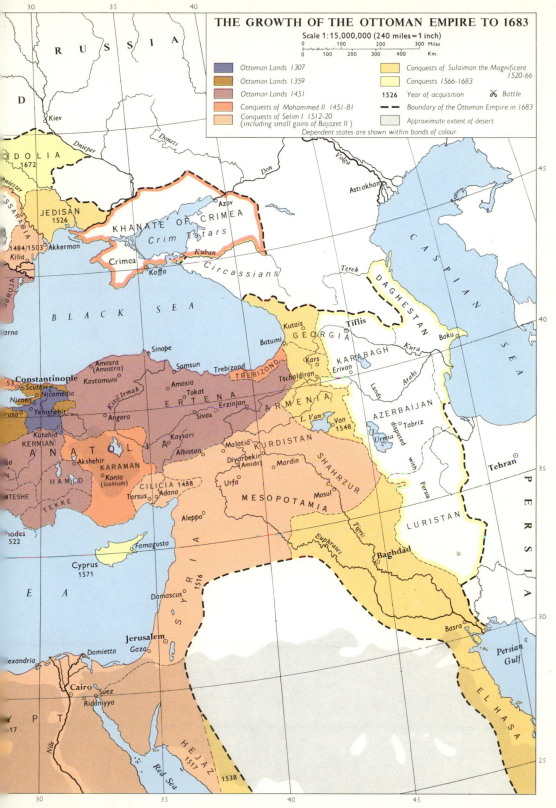

THE GROWTH OF THE OTTOMAN EMPIRE TO 1683

Scale 1:15,000,000 (240 miles=1 inch)

Ottoman Lands 1307	Conquests of Sulaiman the Magnificent 1520-66
Ottoman Lands 1359	Conquests 1566-1683
Ottoman Lands 1451	1526 Year of acquisition �֍ Battle
Conquests of Mohammed II 1451-81	--- Boundary of the Ottoman Empire in 1683
Conquests of Selim I 1512-20 (including small gains of Bajazet II)	Approximate extent of desert

Dependent states are shown within bands of colour

GERMANY

Berlin

POLAND

Warsaw

Paris

Frankfurt

Prague

Krakow

FRANCE

Vistula

Elbe

Oder

Rhine

Danube

SWITZERLAND

AUSTRIA

Vienna

1683

Budapest

BUKOVINA
to Austria
1775

Milan

Venice

Trieste

Agram

Boundary 1683

HUNGARY
to Austria 1699

Grosswardein

MOLD.
1

Barcelona

CROATIA

DALMATIA
to Venice 1699-1797
to Austria 1797 and 1815
to Italy 1805-9
to France 1809-16

Mohacs

Carlowitz

Temesvar

BANAT
1718

TRANSYLVANIA
to Austria 1699

Rome

RAGUSA

1718

Cattaro

BOSNIA
to Austria-Hung.
1878

Belgrade

Sarajevo

Passarowitz

SERBIA
to Austria 1718-39

1817

1878

to Austria
1718-39

Nish

WALLACHIA
1829

Craiova

Bucharest

RU

Plevna

BULGARIA
1878

1908

MONTENEGRO

1878
renewed

Scutari
(Shkodra)

to Serbia
1913

Skopje
(Üsküb)

Sofia

to Bulg.
1913

EAST RUMELI
1878
Philippopo
to Bulg 1885

Algiers

ALBANIA
1913

EPIRUS

MACEDONIA

to Greece
1913

to Bulg.
1913

Salonica

Gallipoli

Ionian Is.
to Ven. until 1797
Fr. 1797-99 and 1807-15
Br. Prot. 1815-63
to Greece 1863

THESSALY
to Greece 1881

Larisa

GREECE

Negroponte
(Euboea)

Chios

ALGIERS

1710
to France 1830/48

Tunis

Missolonghi

1830

MOREA
to Ven.
1685/99
1715/18

Argos

Athens

Samos

Navarino

TUNIS

Nominally Subject
until 1881
Fr. Prot. 1881

Suda

Crete

Spinalon
Turk. 1

Turk. 1718

1898

to Greece 19

Tripoli

Benghazi

TRIPOLI
Ottoman Vassal until 1835.
Ottoman Province 1835-1912.
to Italy 1912

CYRENAICA
Ottoman Vassal until 1835,
Ottoman Province 1835-1912

E

FEZZAN
Ottoman Province 1842-1912

Br.

THE DECLINE OF THE OTTOMAN EMPIRE
1683–1924

Scale 1:15,000,000 (240 miles = 1 inch)

Losses 1683–99 (T. of Carlowitz)	Losses 1916–23 (T. of Lausanne)
Losses 1700–18 (T. of Passarowitz)	Turkey in 1923
Losses 1719–74 (T. of Kutchuk-Kainarji)	1878 Date or period of autonomy
Losses 1775–1812 (T. of Bucharest)	1878 Date of independence
Losses 1813–29/30 (T. of Adrianople)	Boundaries of spheres of influence in Anatolia after the 1914–18 War
Losses 1830–78 (T. of Berlin)	Boundary after T. of Sèvres 1920
Losses 1879–1915 (Ts. of London & Bucharest)	Boundary after T. of Lausanne 1923
	Approximate extent of desert

RUSSIA

Kiev

Vinnitsa
DOLIA
Poland 1699

JEDISAN
to Russia 1792
ARABIA
1812
Ochakov
Kherson
Azov
KHANATE OF CRIMEA
to Russia 1774
Akkerman
1774 ;to Russia 1783
Izmail
Russ. 1829
Turk. 1856
Rum. 1878
Odessa
Kerch
Kuban
Kaffa
Crimea
Circassians
OBRUJA
Rum. 1878
Sevastopol
Constanta
chuk-Kainarji

CASPIAN SEA

Terek
DAGHESTAN
Trib. to 1723
Baku

BLACK SEA

s
g. 1913
Constantinople
Zonguldak
Sinope
Trabzon
Kars
Erivan
Tiflis
GEORGIA
Kura
Batumi
KARABAGH
Trib. to 1730
Araks
AZERBAIJAN
Trib. to 1730
L. Urmia
Izmit
(Nicomedia)
Mudania
Kizil Irmak
Eskisehir
Ankara
ARMENIA
1918–20
L. Van
KURDISTAN
Erzerum
Sivas
French
Kayseri
British
Tehran
Usak
Kütahya
Malatya
ANATOLIA
Italian
Konya
Afyon
to France
1920–21
Urfa
Gaziantep
Mosul
LURISTAN
Antalya
Adana
Silifke
Alexandretta
1939 to Turkey
Aleppo
PERSIA
des
Nicosia
SYRIA
Fr. Mandate 1920
Euphrates
Tigris
Baghdad
Cyprus
Br. Prot. 1878
Annexed by Br. 1914
LEBANON
Fr. Mand. 1920
Beirut
E
A
Damascus
I
R
A
Q
Br. Occup. 1916–20
Br. Mandate 1920
Basra
andria
PALESTINE
Br. Mandate 1920
Amman
KUWAIT
Br. Prot. 1899
Persian
Gulf
Jerusalem
Gaza
TRANS-
JORDAN
Neutral
Zone
Neutral Zone
1920
Cairo
Br. Mandate 1920
1923 Emirate under Br. suzerainty
EL HASA
Suez
PT
r. Prot. 1914
HEJAZ
1916
Nile
Red Sea

COPYRIGHT. GEORGE PHILIP & SON. LTD.

BALKAN PENINSULA
c. 1830

Scale 1:8,000,000 (128 miles=1 inch)

0   50   100   150 Miles
0   50   100   150   200 Km.

Ottoman Lands in 1830

1830 Date of independence

1817 Date of autonomy

Austro–Hungarian military boundary zones, with dates of duration

COPYRIGHT. GEORGE. PHILIP & SON. LTD.

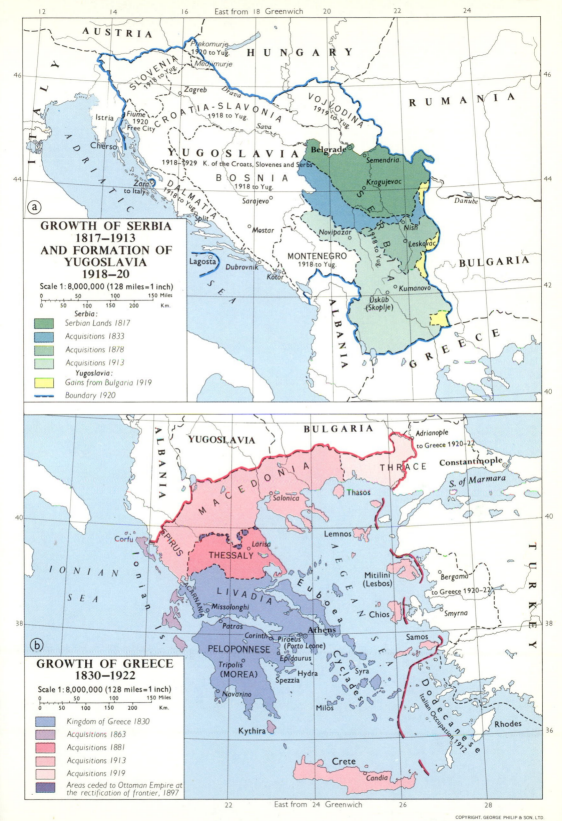

GROWTH OF SERBIA
1817–1913
AND FORMATION OF
YUGOSLAVIA
1918–20

Scale 1:8,000,000 (128 miles=1 inch)

Serbia:
Serbian Lands 1817
Acquisitions 1833
Acquisitions 1878
Acquisitions 1913
Yugoslavia:
Gains from Bulgaria 1919
Boundary 1920

GROWTH OF GREECE
1830–1922

Scale 1:8,000,000 (128 miles=1 inch)

Kingdom of Greece 1830
Acquisitions 1863
Acquisitions 1881
Acquisitions 1913
Acquisitions 1919
Areas ceded to Ottoman Empire at
the rectification of frontier, 1897

COPYRIGHT. GEORGE PHILIP & SON. LTD.

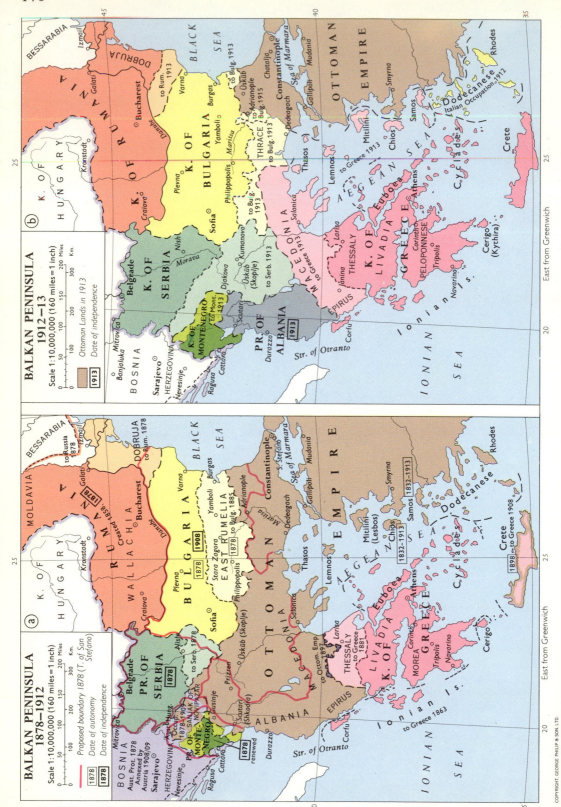

BALKAN PENINSULA 1912–13

Scale 1:10,000,000 (160 miles=1 inch)

Ottoman Lands in 1913

1913 Date of independence

BALKAN PENINSULA 1878–1912

Scale 1:10,000,000 (160 miles=1 inch) (T. of San Stefano)

Proposed boundary 1878 (T. of San Stefano)

1878 Date of autonomy

1878 Date of independence

COPYRIGHT GEORGE PHILIP & SON LTD.

East from Greenwich

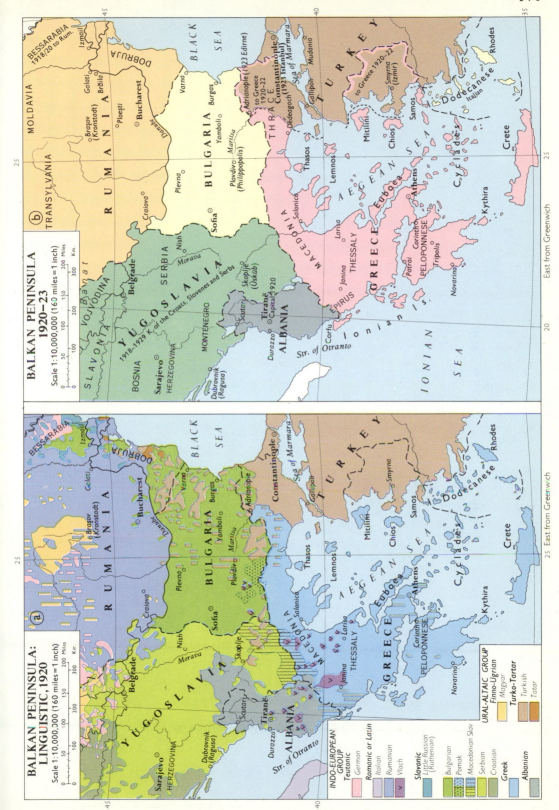

BALKAN PENINSULA 1920–23

Scale 1:10,000,000 (160 miles=1 inch)

b

BESSARABIA
1918/20 to Rum.

MOLDAVIA

TRANSYLVANIA

R U M A N I A

DOBRUJA

Brașov (Kronstadt)
Ploești
Bucharest
Craiova
Galati
Brăila

B L A C K   S E A

Varna

Burgas
Yambol
Plevna
Plovdiv (Philippopolis)

B U L G A R I A

Sofia

SLAVONIA
VOJVODINA

Banat

S E R B I A
Belgrade
Nish
Morava

Y U G O S L A V I A
1918–1929 K. of the Croats, Slovenes and Serbs

BOSNIA
Sarajevo
HERZEGOVINA
Dubrovnik (Ragusa)

MONTENEGRO
Scutari
Durazzo
Tiranë ⊙ Capital 1920
A L B A N I A
Str. of Otranto

Skopje (Üskûb)

M A C E D O N I A
Salonica

EPIRUS
Janina
THESSALY
Larisa

G R E E C E
Corinth
PELOPONNESE
Tripolis
Patrai
Navarino

Adrianople (1923 Edirne)
to Greece 1920–22
T H R A C E
Dedeagach (1923 Istanbul)
Constantinople
Gallipoli
Sea of Marmara
Mudania

T U R K E Y
to Greece 1920–22
Smyrna (Izmir)

Mitilini
Chios
Samos

A E G E A N   S E A
Thasos
Lemnos
Euboea
Athens

Dodecanese
Italian
Rhodes

C y c l a d e s

I O N I A N   S E A
Corfu
Ionian Is.
Kythira
Crete

20   25   East from Greenwich

Scale bar: 0 100 200 300 Miles / 0 100 200 300 Km.

BALKAN PENINSULA: LINGUISTIC, 1920

Scale 1:10,000,000 (160 miles=1 inch)

a

BESSARABIA

R U M A N I A

DOBRUJA
Brașov (Kronstadt)
Bucharest
Craiova
Galati
Izmail

B L A C K   S E A

Varna
Burgas
Yambol
Plevna
Plovdiv
B U L G A R I A
Sofia
Nish
Morava

Y U G O S L A V I A
Belgrade
Sarajevo
HERZEGOVINA
Dubrovnik (Ragusa)
Scutari
Durazzo
Tiranë
A L B A N I A
Str. of Otranto

Skopje
M A C E D O N I A
Salonica

Janina
THESSALY
Larisa
G R E E C E
Corinth
PELOPONNESE
Navarino

Adrianople
Constantinople
Gallipoli
Sea of Marmara
T U R K E Y
Smyrna

Mitilini
Chios
Samos

A E G E A N   S E A
Thasos
Lemnos
Euboea
Athens

Dodecanese
Rhodes

C y c l a d e s

Kythira
Crete

25   East from Greenwich

Scale bar: 0 100 150 200 250 300 Miles / 0 100 200 300 Krr.

Legend

INDO-EUROPEAN GROUP
Teutonic
- German

Romanic or Latin
- Italian
- Rumanian
- Vlach

Slavonic
- Little Russian (Ruthenian)
- Bulgarian
- Pamak
- Macedonian Slav
- Serbian
- Croatian

Greek

Albanian

URAL-ALTAIC GROUP
Finno-Ugrian
- Magyar

Turko-Tartar
- Turkish
- Tatar

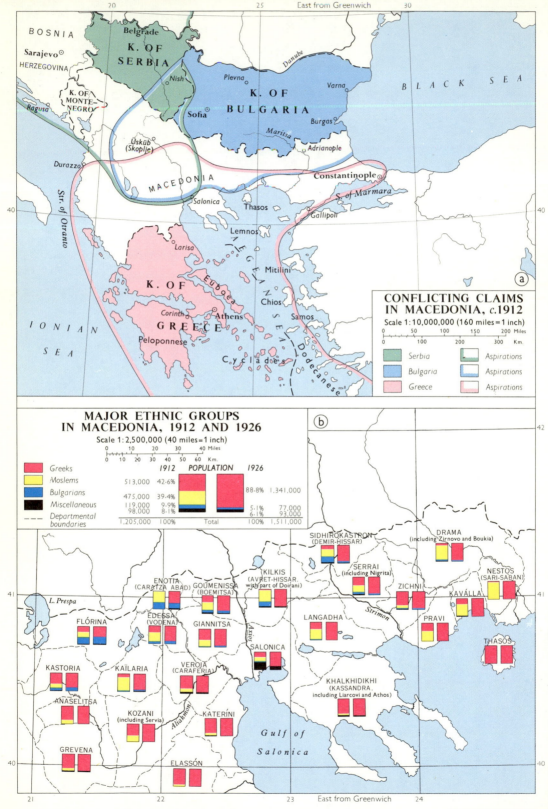

East from Greenwich

BOSNIA

Sarajevo
HERZEGOVINA

K. OF
MONTE-
NEGRO

Ragusa

Str. of Otranto

IONIAN
SEA

Belgrade

K. OF
SERBIA

Nish

Durazzo

MACEDONIA

Salonica

Larisa

K. OF
GREECE

Corinth

Peloponnese

Athens

Euboea

AEGEAN SEA

Cyclades

Plevna

Sofia

K. OF
BULGARIA

Üsküb
(Skoplje)

Danube

Maritsa

Varna

Burgas

Adrianople

BLACK SEA

Constantinople

S. of Marmara

Gallipoli

Thasos

Lemnos

Mitilini

Chios

Samos

Dodecanese

**CONFLICTING CLAIMS
IN MACEDONIA, c.1912**

Scale 1:10,000,000 (160 miles=1 inch)

0   100   200   300 Km.
0   50   100   150   200 Miles

Serbia   Aspirations
Bulgaria   Aspirations
Greece   Aspirations

(a)

(b)

**MAJOR ETHNIC GROUPS
IN MACEDONIA, 1912 AND 1926**

Scale 1:2,500,000 (40 miles=1 inch)

0 10 20 30 40 Miles
0 10 20 30 40 50 60 Km.

Greeks
Moslems
Bulgarians
Miscellaneous
Departmental
boundaries

	1912	POPULATION	1926	
Greeks	513,000	42·6%	88·8%	1,341,000
Moslems	475,000	39·4%		
Bulgarians	119,000	9·9%	5·1%	77,000
Miscellaneous	98,000	8·1%	6·1%	93,000
Total	1,205,000	100%	100%	1,511,000

L. Prespa

FLÓRINA

KASTORIA

ANASELITSA

GREVENA

ENOTIA
(CARATZA ABAD)

GOUMENISSA
(BOEMITSA)

EDESSA
(VODENA)

KAÏLARIA

KOZANI
(including Servia)

GIANNITSA

VEROIA
(CARAFERIA)

ELASSÓN

KILKIS
(AVRET-HISSAR,
with part of Doirani)

SALONICA

KATERÍNI

Axios

Aliakmon

SIDHIROKASTRON
(DEMIR-HISSAR)

SERRAI
(including Nigrita)

LANGADHA

KHALKHIDIKHI
(KASSANDRA,
including Liarcovi and Athos)

Gulf of
Salonica

DRAMA
(including Zirnovo and Boukia)

ZICHNI

PRAVI

Strimon

NESTOS
(SARI-SABAN)

KAVÁLLA

THASOS

East from Greenwich

COPYRIGHT. GEORGE PHILIP & SON. LTD.

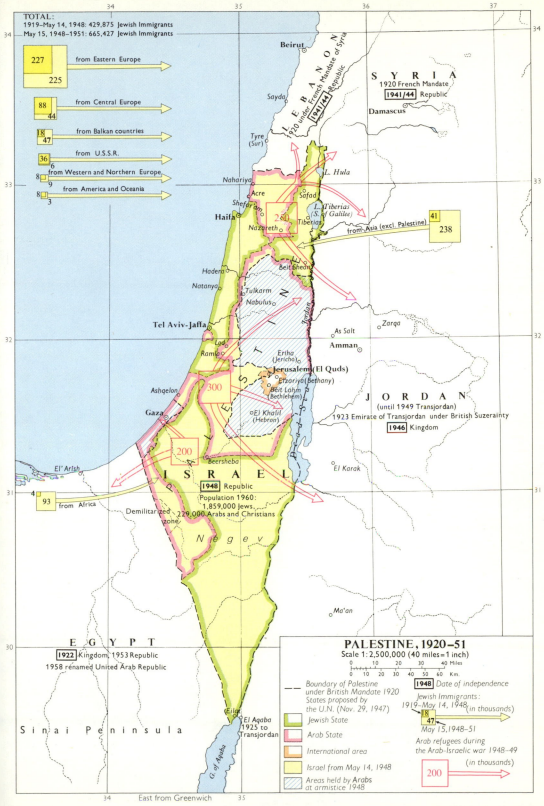

TOTAL:
1919–May 14, 1948: 429,875 Jewish Immigrants
May 15, 1948–1951: 665,427 Jewish Immigrants

227 / 225 — from Eastern Europe

88 / 44 — from Central Europe

18 / 47 — from Balkan countries

36 / 6 — from U.S.S.R.

8 / 9 — from Western and Northern Europe

8 / 3 — from America and Oceania

41 / 238 — from Asia (excl. Palestine)

4 / 93 — from Africa

L E B A N O N
1920 under French Mandate of Syria
1941/44 Republic

S Y R I A
1920 French Mandate
1941/44 Republic

Beirut
Sayda
Damascus
Tyre (Sur)
Nahariya
Acre
Sheferam
Haifa
Nazareth
Safad
L. Hula
L. Tiberias (S. of Galilee)
Tiberias
Beit Shean
Hadera
Natanya
Tulkarm
Nabulus
Tel Aviv-Jaffa
Lod
Ramla
As Salt
Zarqa
Amman
Eriha (Jericho)
Jerusalem (El Quds)
Etzariya (Bethany)
Beit Lahm (Bethlehem)
Ashqelon
Gaza
El Khalil (Hebron)
El Karak
El Arish
Beersheba
Ma'an
Eilat
El Aqaba 1925 to Transjordan

280
300
200

J O R D A N
(until 1949 Transjordan)
1923 Emirate of Transjordan under British Suzerainty
1946 Kingdom

I S R A E L
1948 Republic
Population 1960:
1,859,000 Jews,
229,000 Arabs and Christians

Demilitarized zone

N e g e v

E G Y P T
1922 Kingdom, 1953 Republic
1958 renamed United Arab Republic

S i n a i   P e n i n s u l a

East from Greenwich

G. of Aqaba

PALESTINE, 1920–51
Scale 1:2,500,000 (40 miles=1 inch)

0 10 20 30 40 Miles
0 10 20 30 40 50 60 Km.

—— Boundary of Palestine under British Mandate 1920
States proposed by the U.N. (Nov. 29, 1947)
[green] Jewish State
[pink] Arab State
[orange] International area
[yellow] Israel from May 14, 1948
[hatched] Areas held by Arabs at armistice 1948

1948 Date of independence

Jewish Immigrants:
1919–May 14, 1948 (in thousands)
18 / 47
May 15, 1948–51

Arab refugees during the Arab-Israelic war 1948–49
200 (in thousands)

COPYRIGHT. GEORGE PHILIP & SON. LTD.

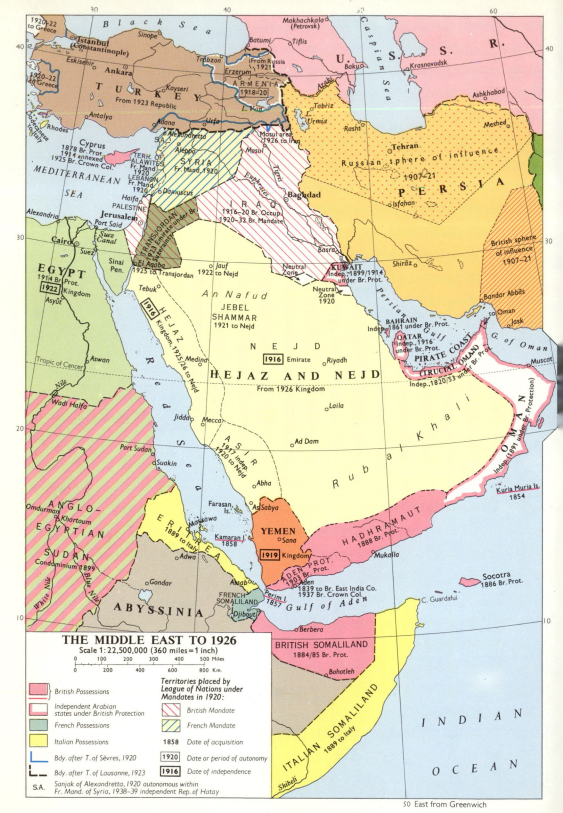

THE MIDDLE EAST TO 1926
Scale 1: 22,500,000 (360 miles = 1 inch)

0	100	200	300	400	500 Miles
0	200	400	600	800 Km.	

British Possessions

Independent Arabian states under British Protection

French Possessions

Italian Possessions

Bdy. after T. of Sèvres, 1920

Bdy. after T. of Lausanne, 1923

S.A. Sanjak of Alexandretta, 1920 autonomous within Fr. Mand. of Syria, 1938–39 independent Rep. of Hatay

Territories placed by League of Nations under Mandates in 1920:

British Mandate

French Mandate

1858 Date of acquisition

1920 Date or period of autonomy

1916 Date of independence

50 East from Greenwich

COPYRIGHT. GEORGE PHILIP & SON, LTD.

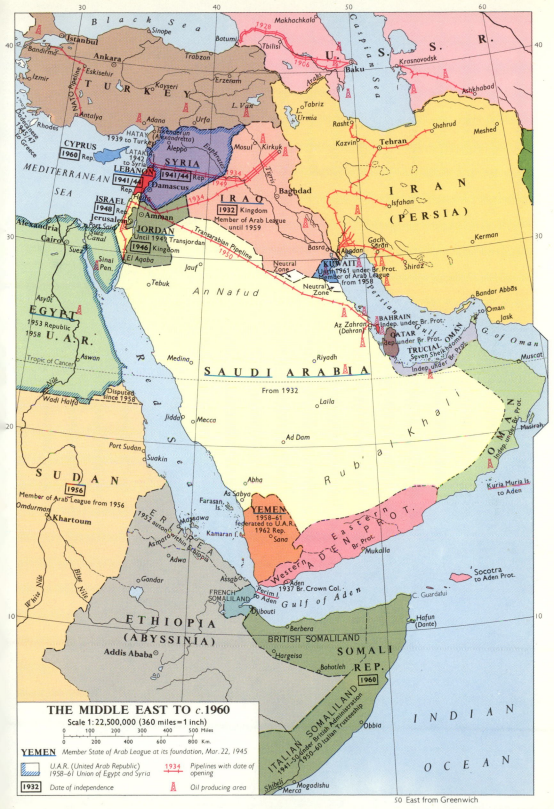

THE MIDDLE EAST TO c.1960

Scale 1 : 22,500,000 (360 miles = 1 inch)

0   100   200   300   400   500 Miles
0   200   400   600   800 Km.

YEMEN *Member State of Arab League at its foundation, Mar. 22, 1945*

U.A.R. (United Arab Republic)
1958-61 Union of Egypt and Syria

1932   *Date of independence*

1934   Pipelines with date of opening

🗼   Oil producing area

50 East from Greenwich

COPYRIGHT. GEORGE PHILIP & SON. LTD.

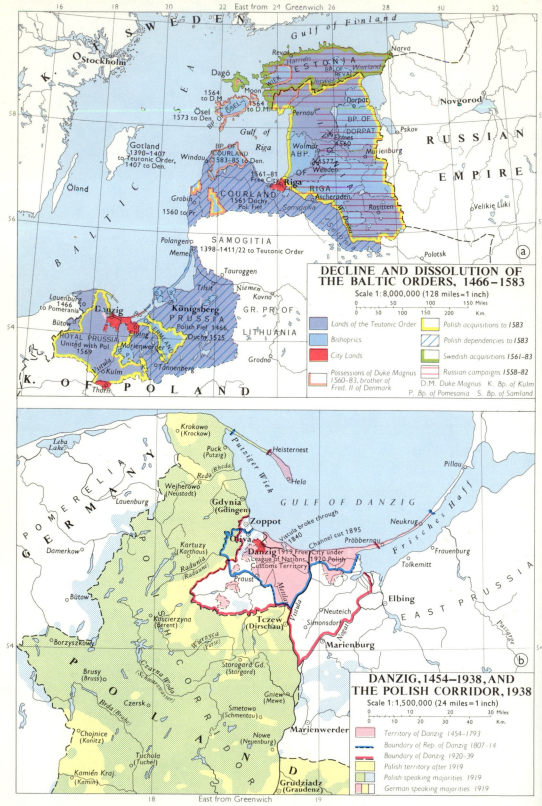

DECLINE AND DISSOLUTION OF THE BALTIC ORDERS, 1466–1583

Scale 1:8,000,000 (128 miles=1 inch)

Lands of the Teutonic Order	Polish acquisitions to 1583
Bishoprics	Polish dependencies to 1583
City Lands	Swedish acquisitions 1561–83
Possessions of Duke Magnus 1560–83, brother of Fred. II of Denmark	Russian campaigns 1558–82

D.M. Duke Magnus K. Bp. of Kulm
P. Bp. of Pomesania S. Bp. of Samland

DANZIG, 1454–1938, AND THE POLISH CORRIDOR, 1938

Scale 1:1,500,000 (24 miles=1 inch)

Territory of Danzig 1454–1793	
Boundary of Rep. of Danzig 1807–14	
Boundary of Danzig 1920–39	
Polish territory after 1919	
Polish speaking majorities 1919	
German speaking majorities 1919	

COPYRIGHT. GEORGE PHILIP & SON, LTD.

POLAND, 1569–1772

Scale 1:12,000,000 (192 miles=1 inch)

K. of Poland before the Union of Lublin, 1569
Boundary of Poland, 1569
Eastern boundary, 1618
Boundary, 1667
Southern boundary, 1672

K. OF SWEDEN

BALTIC SEA

L. Pskov

LIVONIA 1561–1621/29 to Pol.

1585 to Pol.

COURLAND 1561 Duchy, Pol. fief

Riga 1561–81 Free City

1561 to Pol.

Grobin 1560 to Prussia 1609 to Courl.

SAMOGITIA

Memel

W. Dwina

1563–79 to Russia

Sebesh 1678 to Pol.

1678 to Pol.

Polotsk

1637–57/58 to Pol.

Königsberg

D. OF PRUSSIA 1701 Kingdom

Taurogen 1688/90–1795 to Prussia

Kaunas

Vilna

Smolensk

Andrusovo

1618/34–1667/86 to Poland

Oka

Danzig

ROYAL PRUSSIA 1569 united with Pol.

1466–1657/60 Pol. fief 1618

C. OF SERREY 1688/90–1793 to Prussia

Minsk

Mohilev

RUSSIAN

Torun

KUJAWA

PR. OF PLOCK

Grodno

GRAND PRINCIPALITY OF LITHUANIA

WHITE RUTHENIA

1618–44 to Pol.

EMPIRE

Poznan

GREAT POLAND

PR. OF MAZOVIA

Bialystok

Pripet

Gomel

Starodub

Novgorod- Severskiy

1618–34 Pol.

SEVERIA

Putivl

Vistula

Warta

Warsaw

Praga

Bug

PODLESIA

Marshes

Chernigov

Breslau

Czestochowa

Piotrków

Oder

Radom

Lublin

K. OF POLAND

Lutsk

VOLHYNIA

Kiev

1667 to Russia

Kharkov

Sandomir

Zamosc

Union of Lublin from 1569

LITTLE POLAND

Krakow

Przemysl

RED RUSSIA

Lvov

Tarnopol

Buczacz

PODOLIA

Poltava

Dnieper

Vienna

ZIPS 1412–1770/72 to Pol.

Bar

1672–99 to Ottoman Empire

Kamenets-Podolsk

Dniester

Zaporogian Cossacks 1654/67 under Russian sovereignty

K. OF HUNGARY

Buda (Ofen)

PARTITIONS OF POLAND, 1772–95

Scale 1:12,000,000 (192 miles=1 inch)

1st Partition, 1772
To Prussia
To Russia
To Austria
Boundary of Poland, 1772

2nd Partition, 1793
To Prussia
To Russia
Boundary of Poland, 1793

3rd Partition, 1795
To Prussia
To Russia
To Austria

K. OF SWEDEN

BALTIC SEA

LIVONIA

D. OF COURLAND

Riga

Polaga

SAMOGITIA

Memel

Taurogen

W. Dwina

Sebesh

Polotsk

Smolensk

Danzig 1793 to Prussia

ERMLAND

K. OF PRUSSIA

Königsberg

Kovno

Vilna

WEST PRUSSIA

Elbing

NEW EAST PRUSSIA

LITHUANIA

Minsk

NETZE DISTRICT

Bydgoszcz

Torun

Grodno

GREAT POLAND

Poznan

MAZOVIA

Bialystok

BLACK RUSSIA

Gomel

SOUTH PRUSSIA

Praga

Bug

PODLESIA

Pinsk

Pripet

RUSSIAN

Breslau

Czestochowa

Oder

Piotrków

Warsaw

Brest- Litovsk

Marshes

Chernigov

NEW SILESIA

WEST GALICIA

Lublin

Sandomir

LITTLE POLAND

Krakow

VOLHYNIA

Kiev

Kharkov

AUSTRIA

GALICIA AND LODOMERIA

RED RUSSIA

Lvov

Sambor

Kaniow

EMPIRE

UKRAINE

Poltava

Vienna

ZIPS 1770/72 to Hung.

PODOLIA

Dnieper

K. OF HUNGARY

Buda (Ofen)

Dniester

Zaporogian Cossacks 1773/74 entirely under Russian control

East from Greenwich

COPYRIGHT GEORGE PHILIP & SON LTD.

178

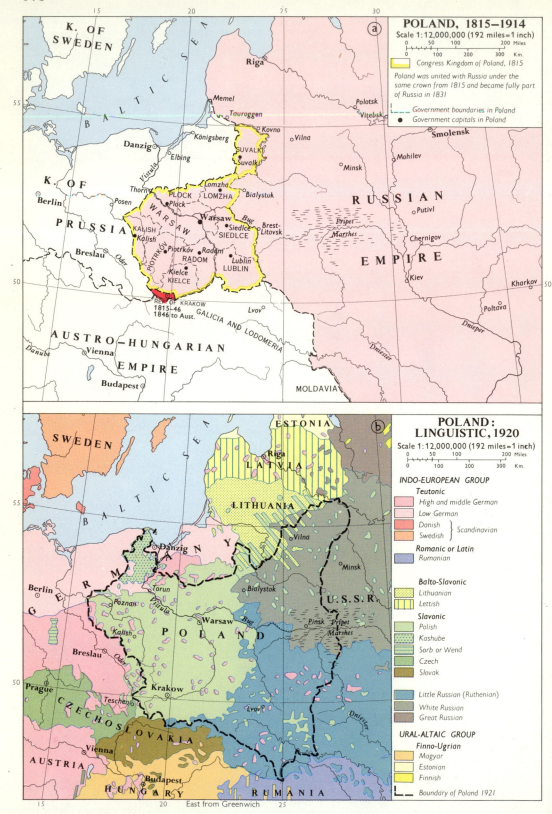

COPYRIGHT. GEORGE PHILIP & SON. LTD.

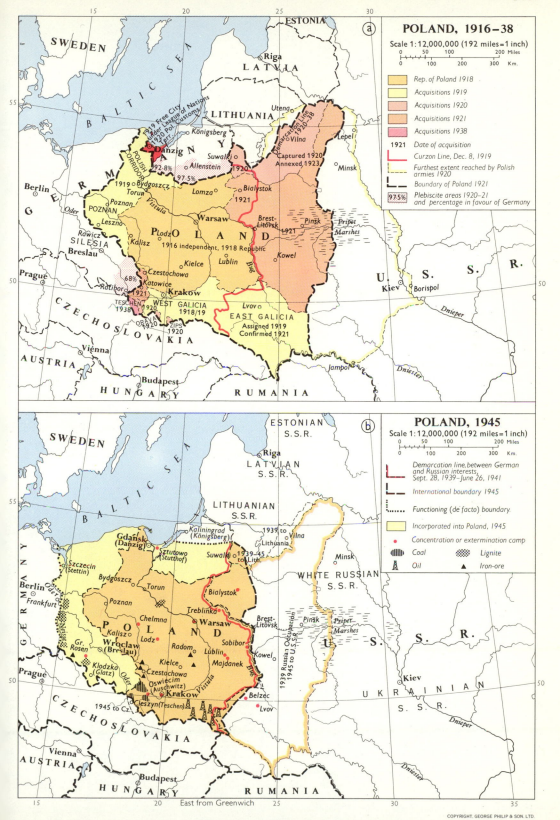

POLAND, 1916–38

Scale 1:12,000,000 (192 miles=1 inch)

	Rep. of Poland 1918
	Acquisitions 1919
	Acquisitions 1920
	Acquisitions 1921
	Acquisitions 1938
1921	Date of acquisition
	Curzon Line, Dec. 8, 1919
	Furthest extent reached by Polish armies 1920
	Boundary of Poland 1921
97.5%	Plebiscite areas 1920–21 and percentage in favour of Germany

SWEDEN

BALTIC SEA

ESTONIA

Riga

LATVIA

LITHUANIA

Königsberg

1919 Free City
under League of Nations
1920 Pol. Customs
terr.

Danzig

POLISH
CORRIDOR

92.8%

97.5%

Suwalki

Allenstein

1920

Uteng

Demarcation line
1920-38

Vilna

Lepel

Minsk

Captured 1920
Annexed 1923

Berlin

G E R M A N Y

Bydgoszcz
1919
Torun

Vistula

Poznan

POZNAN

Leszno

Lomza

Bialystok
1921

Warsaw

Brest-
Litovsk

Pinsk

Pripet
Marshes

Rawicz

SILESIA

Breslau

Kalisz

Lodz
P

O L A N D

1916 independent, 1918 Republic

Kielce

Lublin

Bug

1921

Kowel

Prague

68%

Ratibor
1921

Czestochowa

Katowice

Krakow

WEST
GALICIA
1918/19

Lvov

EAST GALICIA

Assigned 1919
Confirmed 1921

Kiev

Borispol

U. S.

S. R.

Dnieper

TESCHEN
1938

ORAVA
1920

1920

ZIPS
1920

C Z E C H O S L O V A K I A

Vienna

AUSTRIA

Budapest

H U N G A R Y

R U M A N I A

Jampol

Dniester

POLAND, 1945

Scale 1:12,000,000 (192 miles=1 inch)

	Demarcation line between German and Russian interests, Sept. 28, 1939–June 26, 1941
	International boundary 1945
	Functioning (de facto) boundary.
	Incorporated into Poland, 1945
•	Concentration or extermination camp
	Coal
	Lignite
	Oil
	Iron-ore

SWEDEN

BALTIC SEA

ESTONIAN
S.S.R.

Riga

LATVIAN
S.S.R.

LITHUANIAN
S.S.R.

1939 to
Lithuania

Kaliningrad
(Königsberg)

Gdansk
(Danzig)

Sztutowo
(Stutthof)

Suwalki

1939-45
to Lith.

Vilna

Szczecin
(Stettin)

Bydgoszcz

Torun

Bialystok

WHITE RUSSIAN
S.S.R.

Minsk

Berlin

Frankfurt

GERMANY

Oder

Poznan

Chelmna

Treblinka

Warsaw

Brest-
Litovsk

Pinsk

Pripet
Marshes

P O L A N D

Kalisz

Lodz

Radom

Sobibor

Kowel

U. S.

S. R.

Gr.
Rosen

Wrocław
(Breslau)

Oder

Kielce

Lublin

Majdanek

Bug

1939 Russia Occupation
1945 to U.S.S.R.

Prague

Klodzko
(Glatz)

Czestochowa

Oswiecim
(Auschwitz)

Krakow

Vistula

Belzec

Kiev

U K R A I N I A N

S. S. R.

1945 to Cz.

Cieszyn (Teschen)

Lvov

Dnieper

C Z E C H O S L O V A K I A

Vienna

AUSTRIA

Budapest

H U N G A R Y

R U M A N I A

Dniester

East from Greenwich

COPYRIGHT. GEORGE PHILIP & SON. LTD.

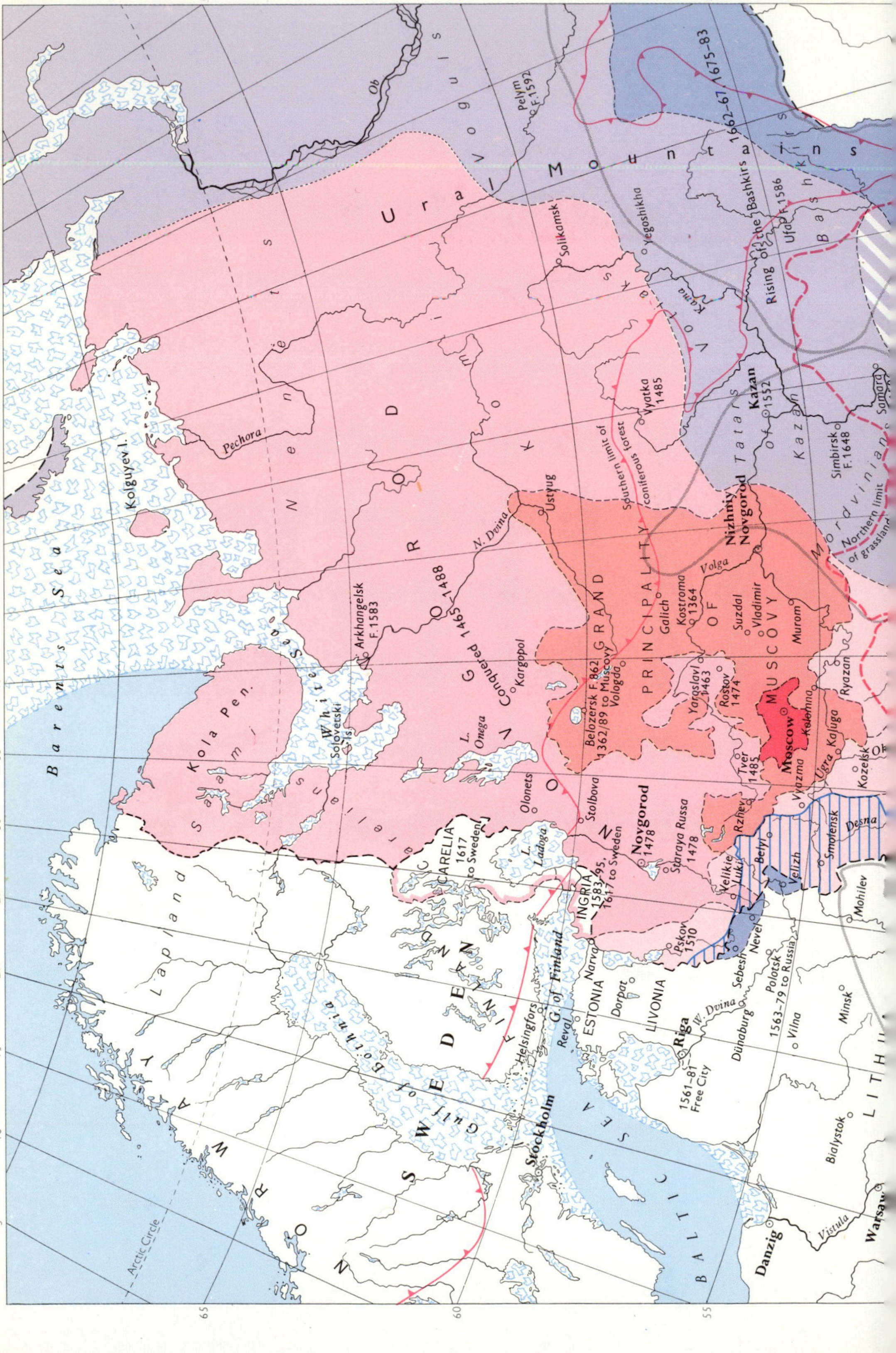
Barents Sea
Kolguyev I.
White Sea
Kola Pen.
Solovetski Is.
Arkhangelsk F.1583
Pechora
N. Dvina
Ob
Ural Mountains
Pelym F.1592
Solikamsk
Yegoshikha
Kama
Vyatka 1485
Southern limit of coniferous forest
Ustyug
Kargopol
L. Onega
Olonets
Stolbova
L. Ladoga
CARELIA 1617 to Sweden
INGRIA 1583–95, 1617 to Sweden
NOVGOROD Conquered 1465–1488
Novgorod 1478
Staraya Russa 1478
GRAND PRINCIPALITY OF MUSCOVY
Belozersk F. 862 1362/89 to Muscovy
Vologda
Galich
Kostroma 1364
Yaroslavl 1463
Rostov 1474
Suzdal
Vladimir
Murom
Nizhniy Novgorod
Volga
Kazan 1552
Tatars of Kazan
Simbirsk F.1648
Samara
Mordvinians
Northern limit of grassland
Rising of the Bashkirs 1662–67, 1675–83
Ufa F.1586
Bashkirs
Moscow
Kolomna
Ryazan
Kaluga
Ugra
Kozelsk
Tver 1485
Rzhev
Vyazma
Smolensk
Desna
Belyi
Velizh
Velikie Luki
Nevel
Pskov 1510
Narva
ESTONIA
Dorpat
LIVONIA
Riga
1561–81 Free City
W. Dvina
Dünaburg
Sebesh
Polotsk 1563–79 to Russia
Vilna
Minsk
Mohilev
Bialystok
LITHU
Warsaw
Vistula
Danzig
Reval
Helsingfors
G. of Finland
FINLAND
Stockholm
SWEDEN
Gulf of Bothnia
Lapland
NORWAY
BALTIC SEA
Arctic Circle
Sami
Karelians
Nentsy
Komi
Votyaks
Voguls

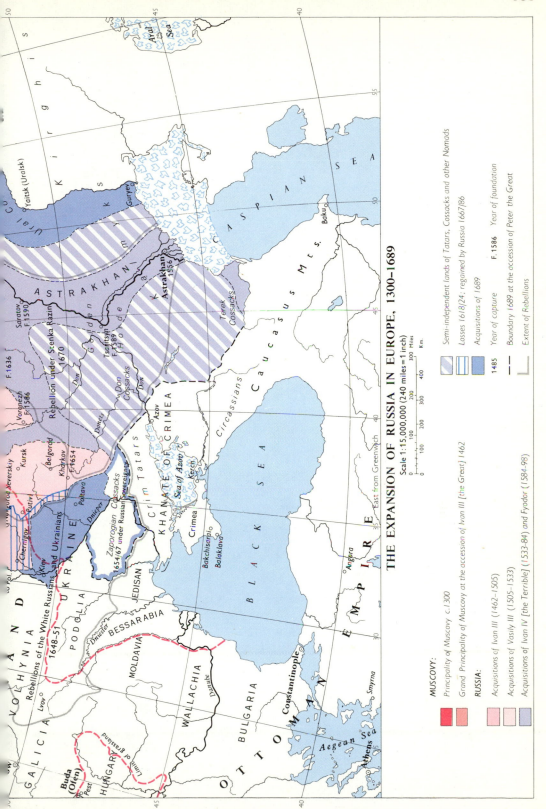

THE EXPANSION OF RUSSIA IN EUROPE, 1300–1689

Scale 1:15,000,000 (240 miles=1 inch)

East from Greenwich

MUSCOVY:

Principality of Muscovy c.1300

Grand Principality of Muscovy at the accession of Ivan III [the Great] 1462

RUSSIA:

Acquisitions of Ivan III (1462–1505)

Acquisitions of Vasily III (1505–1533)

Acquisitions of Ivan IV [the Terrible] (1533–84) and Fyodor (1584–98)

Semi-independent lands of Tatars, Cossacks and other Nomads

Losses 1618/24; regained by Russia 1667/86

Acquisitions of 1689

1485 — Year of capture   F.1586 — Year of foundation

Boundary 1689 at the accession of Peter the Great

Extent of Rebellions

Labels on map:
Aral Sea, CASPIAN SEA, BLACK SEA, Sea of Azov, Aegean Sea, Smyrna, Athens, Angora, Constantinople, Danube, WALLACHIA, BULGARIA, MOLDAVIA, BESSARABIA, PODOLIA, GALICIA, VOLHYNIA, HUNGARY, Buda (Ofen), Pest, Lvov, Dniester, JEDISAN, Limit of grassland, OTTOMAN EMPIRE, KHANATE OF CRIMEA, Crim Tatars, Crimea, Bakhchisarai, Balaklava, Kerch, Azov, Circassians, Caucasus Mts., Baku, Terek Cossacks, ASTRAKHAN, Astrakhan 1556, Kazan, Golden Horde, Don Cossacks, Don, Donets, Zaporogian Cossacks 1654/67 under Russian sovereignty, Dnieper, Poltava, Kiev, Chernigov, Putivl, Novgorod Severskiy, UKRAINE, Rebellions of the White Russians and Ukrainians 1648-51, Kursk, Belgorod, Kharkov F.1654, Voronezh F.1586, F.1636, Rebellion under Stenka Razin 1670, Saratov F.1590, Tsaritsyn F.1589, Guryev, Yaitsk (Uralsk), Ural Cossacks, KIRGHIZ, Kirghiz, S

Scale bar: 0 100 200 300 400 Km. / 0 100 200 300 Miles

COPYRIGHT GEORGE PHILIP & SON LTD

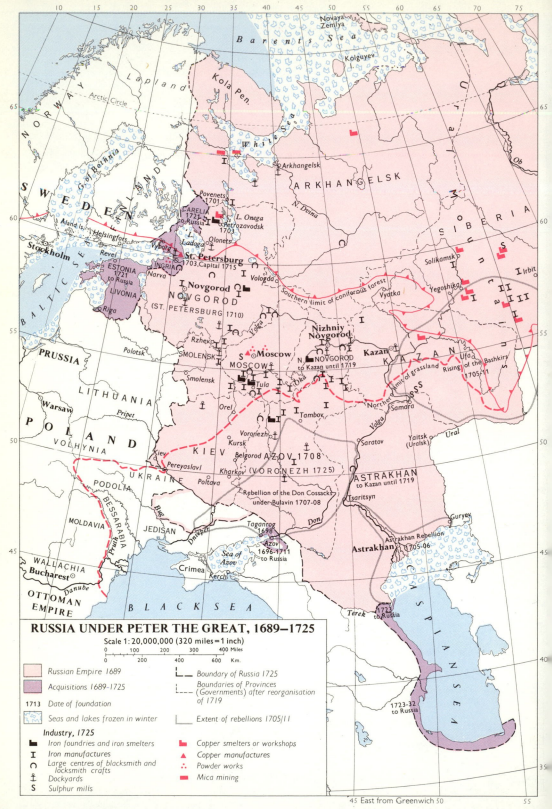

RUSSIA UNDER PETER THE GREAT, 1689–1725

Scale 1: 20,000,000 (320 miles = 1 inch)

0 100 200 300 400 Miles
0 200 400 600 Km.

	Russian Empire 1689
	Acquisitions 1689–1725
1713	Date of foundation
	Seas and lakes frozen in winter

Boundary of Russia 1725
Boundaries of Provinces
(Governments) after reorganisation
of 1719

Extent of rebellions 1705/11

Industry, 1725

Iron foundries and iron smelters
Iron manufactures
Large centres of blacksmith and
locksmith crafts
Dockyards
Sulphur mills

Copper smelters or workshops
Copper manufactures
Powder works
Mica mining

COPYRIGHT: GEORGE PHILIP & SON. LTD.

THE EXPANSION OF RUSSIA IN EUROPE
1725–1855

Scale 1:20,000,000 (320 miles=1 inch)

| 0 | 100 | 200 | 300 | 400 Miles |

| 0 | 200 | 400 | 600 | Km. |

Russian Empire 1725

Acquisitions 1730–1740 (Anna Ivanovna)

Acquisitions 1740–1762 (Elisabeth Petrovna)

Acquisitions 1762–1796 (Catherine II)

Acquisitions 1796–1801 (Paul I)

Acquisitions 1801–1825 (Alexander I)

Acquisitions 1825–1855 (Nicholas I)

1795   Date of acquisition

Boundary of Russia 1855

Bdies. of Provinces (Governments) after reorganisation of 1775

Extent of rebellions 1735–74

Seas and lakes frozen in winter

45 East from Greenwich 50

COPYRIGHT. GEORGE PHILIP & SON. LTD.

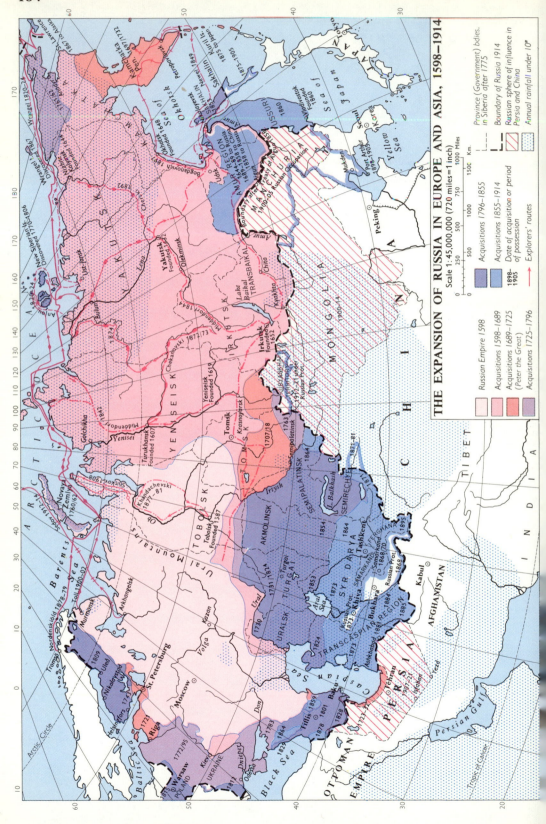

THE EXPANSION OF RUSSIA IN EUROPE AND ASIA, 1598-1914

Scale 1:45,000,000 (720 miles=1 inch)

Russian Empire 1598

Acquisitions 1598-1689

Acquisitions 1689-1725 (Peter the Great)

Acquisitions 1725-1796

Acquisitions 1796-1855

Acquisitions 1855-1914

1898-1905 Date of acquisition or period of possession

Explorers' routes

Province (Government) bodies in Siberia after 1775

Boundary of Russia 1914

Russian sphere of influence in Persia and China

Annual rainfall under 10"

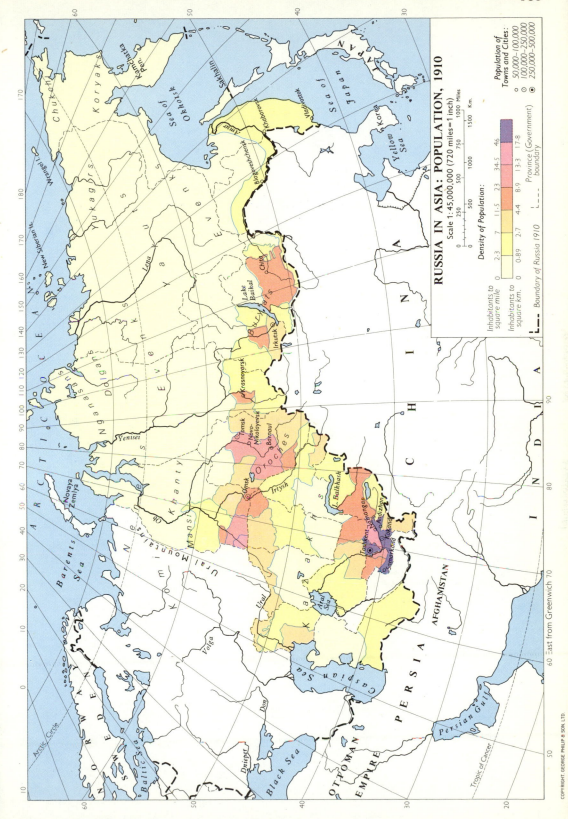

RUSSIA IN ASIA: POPULATION, 1910

Scale 1:45,000,000 (720 miles=1 inch)

0   250   500   750   1000 Miles
0   250   500   750   1000   1500 Km.

Density of Population:

| 0 | 0.89 | 2.7 | 4.4 | 8.9 | 13.3 | 17.8 | Inhabitants to square km. |
| 0 | 2.3 | 7 | 11.5 | 23 | 34.5 | 46 | Inhabitants to square mile |

Province (Government) boundary

Population of Towns and Cities:
50,000–100,000
100,000–250,000
250,000–500,000

Boundary of Russia 1910

COPYRIGHT. GEORGE PHILIP & SON. LTD.

60 East from Greenwich 70

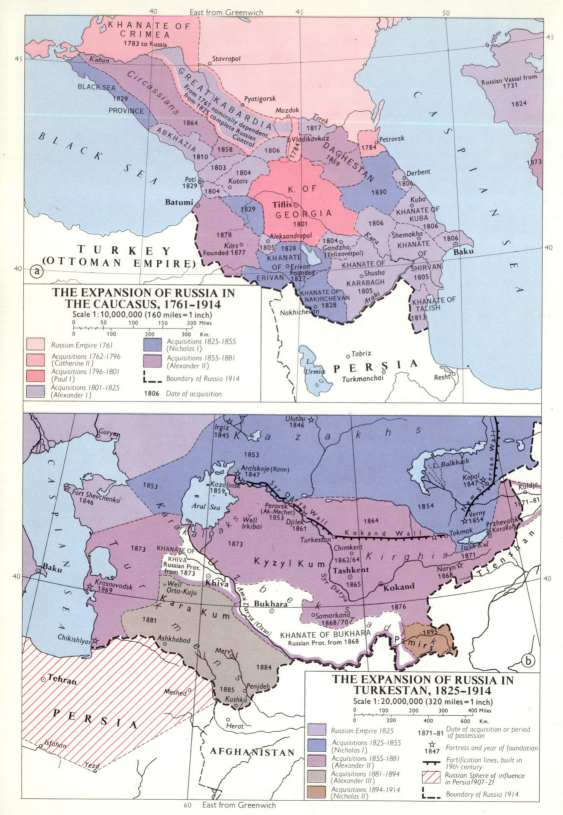

THE EXPANSION OF RUSSIA IN THE CAUCASUS, 1761–1914
Scale 1:10,000,000 (160 miles = 1 inch)

0   50   100   150   200 Miles

0   100   200   300 Km.

- Russian Empire 1761
- Acquisitions 1762–1796 (Catherine II)
- Acquisitions 1796–1801 (Paul I)
- Acquisitions 1801–1825 (Alexander I)
- Acquisitions 1825–1855 (Nicholas I)
- Acquisitions 1855–1881 (Alexander II)
- Boundary of Russia 1914
- **1806** Date of acquisition

THE EXPANSION OF RUSSIA IN TURKESTAN, 1825–1914
Scale 1:20,000,000 (320 miles = 1 inch)

0   100   200   300   400 Miles

0   200   400   600 Km.

- Russian Empire 1825
- Acquisitions 1825–1855 (Nicholas I)
- Acquisitions 1855–1881 (Alexander II)
- Acquisitions 1881–1894 (Alexander III)
- Acquisitions 1894–1914 (Nicholas II)
- **1871–81** Date of acquisition or period of possession
- ☆ 1847 Fortress and year of foundation
- Fortification lines, built in 19th century
- Russian Sphere of influence in Persia 1907–21
- Boundary of Russia 1914

COPYRIGHT. GEORGE PHILIP & SON, LTD.

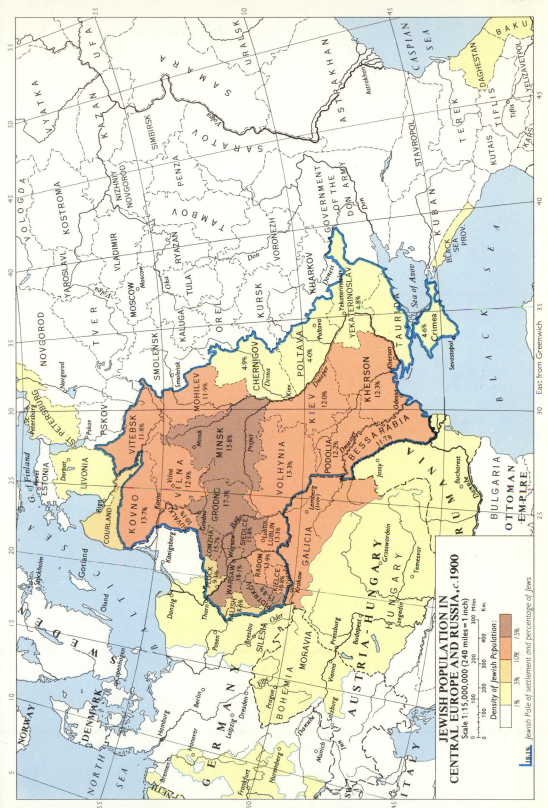

JEWISH POPULATION IN
CENTRAL EUROPE AND RUSSIA, c.1900

Scale 1:15,000,000 (240 miles = 1 inch)

Density of Jewish Population:

1%   5%   10%   15%

18.1% Jewish Pale of settlement and percentage of Jews

COPYRIGHT. GEORGE PHILIP & SON. LTD.

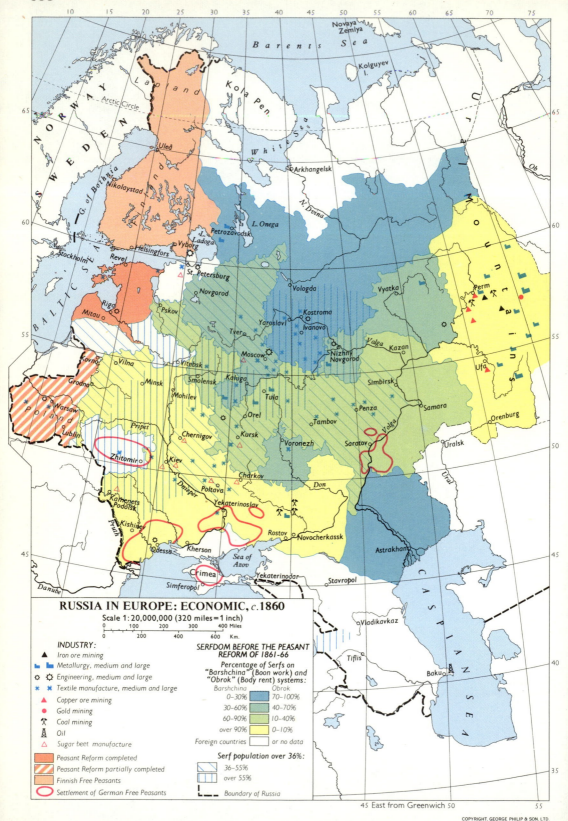

RUSSIA IN EUROPE: ECONOMIC, c.1860

Scale 1:20,000,000 (320 miles=1 inch)

0 100 200 300 400 Miles
0 200 400 600 Km.

INDUSTRY:

▲ Iron ore mining

◪ Metallurgy, medium and large

✿ Engineering, medium and large

✳ Textile manufacture, medium and large

▲ Copper ore mining

● Gold mining

⚒ Coal mining

⚑ Oil

△ Sugar beet manufacture

■ Peasant Reform completed

▨ Peasant Reform partially completed

■ Finnish Free Peasants

◯ Settlement of German Free Peasants

SERFDOM BEFORE THE PEASANT REFORM OF 1861-66

Percentage of Serfs on "Barshchina" (Boon work) and "Obrok" (Body rent) systems:

Barshchina	Obrok
0-30%	70-100%
30-60%	40-70%
60-90%	10-40%
over 90%	0-10%

Foreign countries or no data

Serf population over 36%:

36-55%

over 55%

Boundary of Russia

45 East from Greenwich 50

COPYRIGHT. GEORGE PHILIP & SON. LTD.

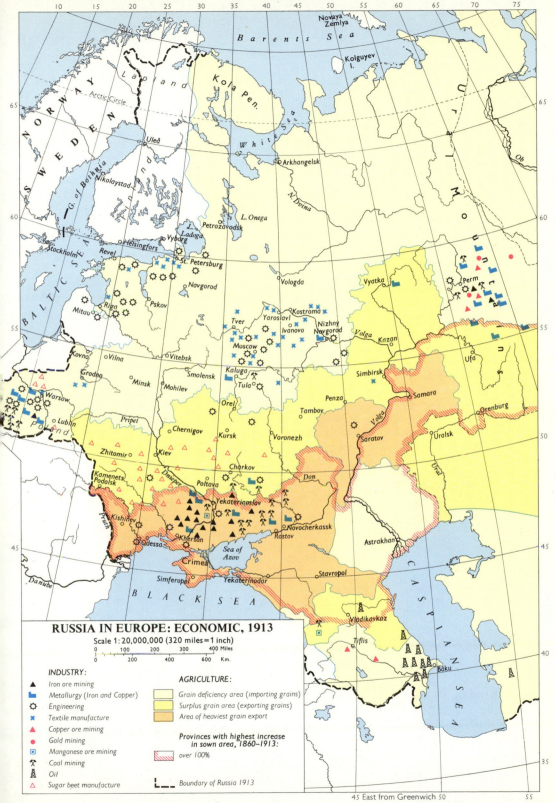

RUSSIA IN EUROPE: ECONOMIC, 1913

Scale 1: 20,000,000 (320 miles = 1 inch)

0   100   200   300   400 Miles
0   200   400   600 Km.

INDUSTRY:

▲ Iron ore mining

▰ Metallurgy (Iron and Copper)

✾ Engineering

✖ Textile manufacture

▲ Copper ore mining

● Gold mining

▣ Manganese ore mining

⚒ Coal mining

⛏ Oil

△ Sugar beet manufacture

AGRICULTURE:

Grain deficiency area (importing grains)

Surplus grain area (exporting grains)

Area of heaviest grain export

Provinces with highest increase in sown area, 1860–1913:

over 100%

⌐ Boundary of Russia 1913

45 East from Greenwich 50

COPYRIGHT. GEORGE PHILIP & SON. LTD.

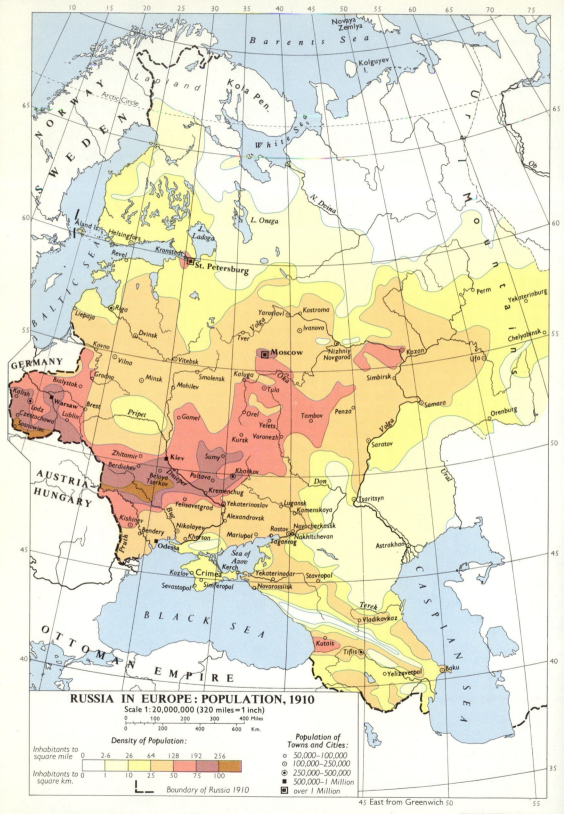

RUSSIA IN EUROPE: POPULATION, 1910

Scale 1:20,000,000 (320 miles=1 inch)

0   100   200   300   400 Miles

0   200   400   600 Km.

Density of Population:

| | 0 | 2·6 | 26 | 64 | 128 | 192 | 256 |
Inhabitants to square mile

| | 0 | 1 | 10 | 25 | 50 | 75 | 100 |
Inhabitants to square km.

Boundary of Russia 1910

Population of Towns and Cities:

○ 50,000–100,000
◎ 100,000–250,000
⊙ 250,000–500,000
■ 500,000–1 Million
▣ over 1 Million

45 East from Greenwich 50

COPYRIGHT. GEORGE PHILIP & SON. LTD.

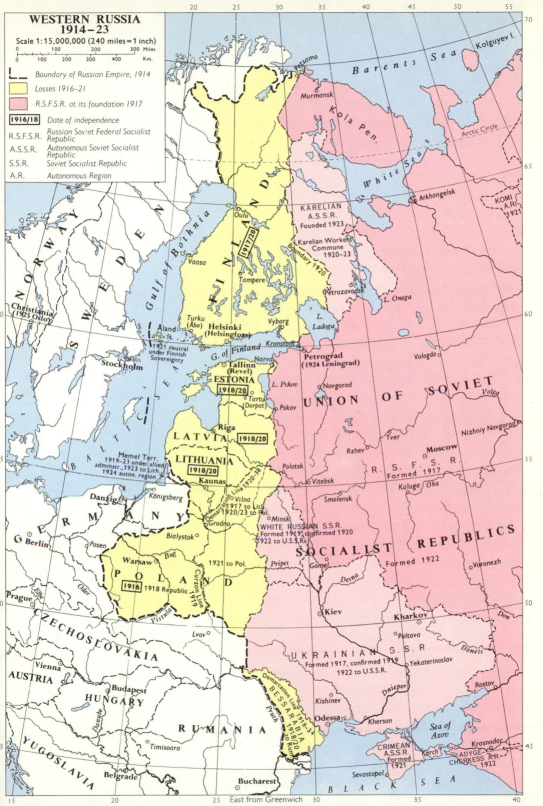

WESTERN RUSSIA
1914–23

Scale 1:15,000,000 (240 miles=1 inch)

| | 0 | 100 | 200 | 300 Miles |

| | 0 | 100 | 200 | 300 | 400 | Km. |

Boundary of Russian Empire, 1914

Losses 1916–21

R.S.F.S.R. at its foundation 1917

1916/18 Date of independence

R.S.F.S.R. Russian Soviet Federal Socialist Republic

A.S.S.R. Autonomous Soviet Socialist Republic

S.S.R. Soviet Socialist Republic

A.R. Autonomous Region

Barents Sea

Kolguyev I.

NORWAY

SWEDEN

Christiania (1925 Oslo)

Stockholm

Murmansk

Kola Pen.

Arctic Circle

White Sea

Arkhangelsk

KOMI A.R. 1921

KARELIAN A.S.S.R. Founded 1923

Karelian Workers' Commune Boundary 1920–23

Oulu

FINLAND

1917/20

Vaasa

Tampere

Turku (Åbo)

Helsinki (Helsingfors)

Vyborg

Petrozavodsk

L. Onega

Aland Is. 1921 neutral under Finnish Sovereignty

G. of Finland

Kronstadt

Narva

Petrograd (1924 Leningrad)

Vologda

Volga

Tallinn (Revel)

ESTONIA 1918/20

Tartu (Dorpat)

L. Pskov

Pskov

Novgorod

UNION OF SOVIET

Riga

LATVIA 1918/20

LITHUANIA 1918/20

Kaunas

Memel Terr. 1919–23 under allied administr., 1923 to Lith. 1924 auton. region

Danzig

Königsberg

Demarcation Line 1920–38

Vilna 1917 to Lith. 1920/23 to Pol.

Grodno

Polotsk

Vitebsk

Rzhev

Tver

Moscow

R. S. F. S. R. Formed 1917

Nizhniy Novgorod

Kaluga

Oka

GERMANY

Berlin

Posen

Bialystok

Smolensk

Minsk

WHITE RUSSIAN S.S.R. Formed 1919, confirmed 1920 1922 to U.S.S.R.

SOCIALIST REPUBLICS

Oder

Warsaw

Bug

1921 to Pol.

POLAND

1916 1918 Republic

Curzon Line 1919

Vistula

Pripet

Gomel

Desna

Formed 1922

Voronezh

Prague

Elbe

Lvov

Kiev

Poltava

Kharkov

Donets

Don

CZECHOSLOVAKIA

Vienna

AUSTRIA

Budapest

HUNGARY

Danube

RUMANIA

Timisoara

UKRAINIAN S.S.R. Formed 1917, confirmed 1919 1922 to U.S.S.R.

Yekaterinoslav

Rostov

Demarcation Line 1918–23

BESSARABIA 1918 to Rum.

Prut

Kishinev

Dnieper

Kherson

YUGOSLAVIA

Belgrade

Bucharest

Odessa

Sea of Azov

Krasnodar

CRIMEAN A.S.S.R. Formed 1921

Sevastopol

Kerch

ADYGE A.R. 1922

CHERKESS A.R. 1922

BLACK SEA

15   20   25 East from Greenwich   30   35   40

45

50

55

60

65

70

COPYRIGHT. GEORGE PHILIP & SON. LTD.

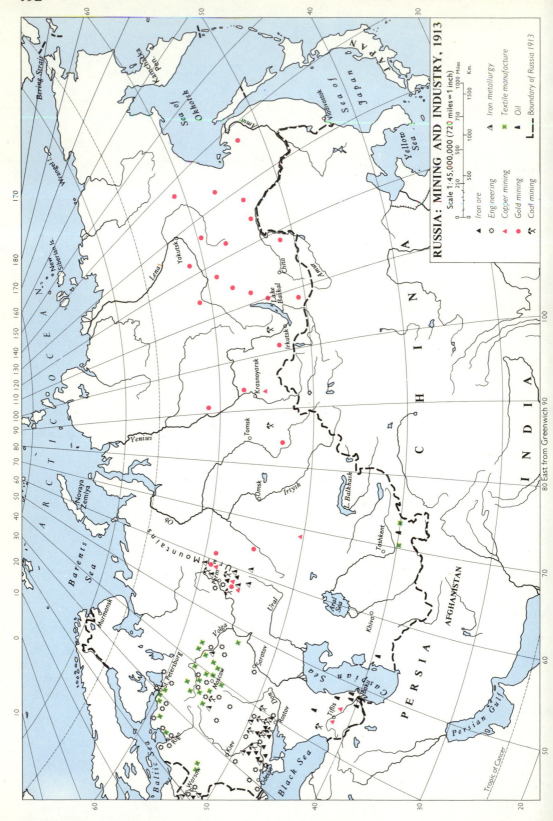

RUSSIA: MINING AND INDUSTRY, 1913

Scale 1:45,000,000 (720 miles=1 inch)

▶ Iron ore   ▲ Iron metallurgy
✿ Engineering ✳ Textile manufacture
▲ Copper mining ▲ Oil
● Gold mining   L— Boundary of Russia 1913
✕ Coal mining

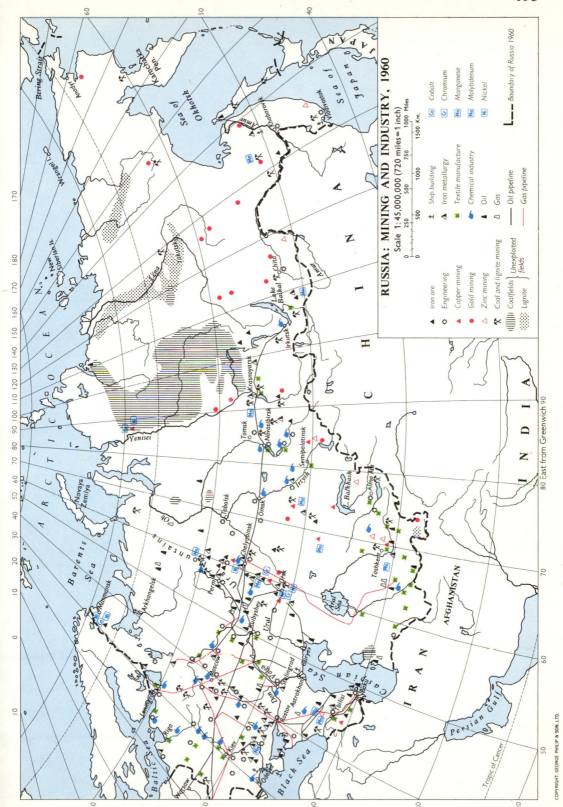

RUSSIA: MINING AND INDUSTRY, 1960

Scale 1:45,000,000 (720 miles=1 inch)

0	250	500	750	1000 Miles
0	500	1000	1500 Km.

Legend

- ◄ Iron ore
- ✿ Engineering
- ▲ Copper mining
- ● Gold mining
- △ Zinc mining
- ▥ Coal and lignite mining
- ⚓ Ship building
- △ Iron metallurgy
- ✳ Textile manufacture
- ♦ Chemical industry
- ▲ Oil
- △ Gas
- ▥ Coalfields ⸬ Unexploited
- ▥ Lignite ⸬ fields

- Co Cobalt
- Cr Chromium
- Mn Manganese
- Mo Molybdenum
- Ni Nickel

- ── Oil pipeline
- ── Gas pipeline
- ⌐ Boundary of Russia 1960

80 East from Greenwich 90

COPYRIGHT. GEORGE PHILIP & SON. LTD.

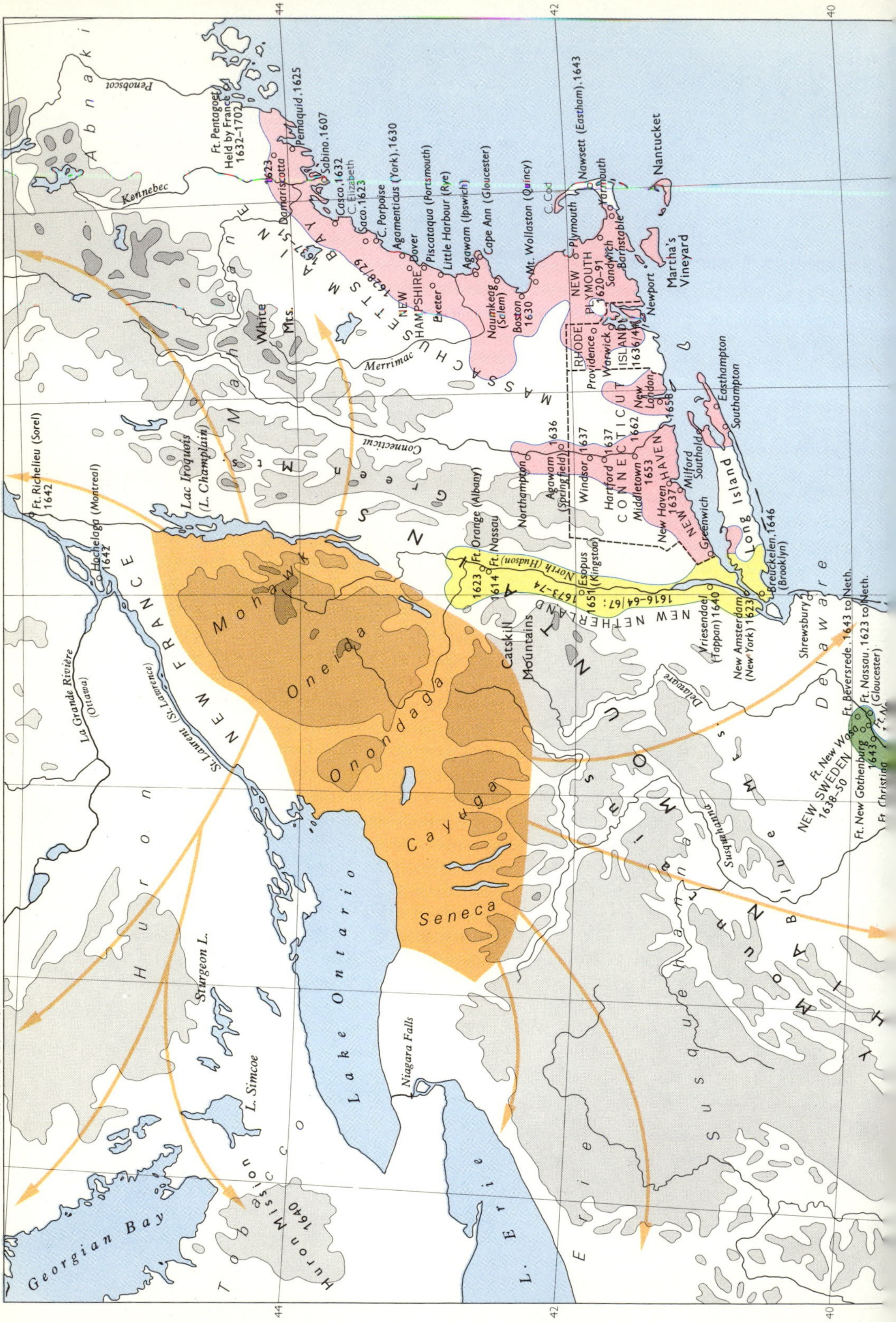
West from Greenwich
80
78
76
74
72
70
68
44
42
40
Georgian Bay
Huron
Sturgeon L.
L. Simcoe
Tobacco
Huron Mission 1640
La Grande Rivière (Ottawa)
St. Laurent (St. Lawrence)
NEW FRANCE
Ft. Richelieu (Sorel) 1642
Hochelaga (Montreal) 1642
Lac Iroquois (L. Champlain)
Lake Ontario
Niagara Falls
L. Erie
Erie
Mohawk
Oneida
Onondaga
Cayuga
Seneca
Catskill Mountains
Susquehanna
Susquehanna
Delaware
Delaware
Blue Mts.
APPALACHIAN MOUNTAINS
Green Mts.
White Mts.
Mahican
Abnaki
Kennebec
Penobscot
Connecticut
Merrimac
Ft. Pentagoet Held by France 1632–1702
1623 Damariscotta
Pemaquid.1625
Sabino.1607
Casco.1632
C. Elizabeth
Saco.1623
C. Porpoise
Agamenticus (York).1630
MAINE 1637–51
MASSACHUSETTS BAY 1628/29
NEW HAMPSHIRE
Dover
Exeter
Piscataqua (Portsmouth)
Little Harbour (Rye)
Agawam (Ipswich)
Cape Ann (Gloucester)
Naumkeag (Salem)
Boston 1630
Mt. Wollaston (Quincy)
C. Cod
NEW PLYMOUTH 1620–91
Plymouth
Nawsett (Eastham).1643
Yarmouth
Sandwich
Barnstable
Nantucket
Martha's Vineyard
Newport
RHODE ISLAND 1636/44
Providence
Warwick
CONNECTICUT
Northampton
Agawam (Springfield) 1636
Windsor 1637
Hartford 1637
Middletown 1662
New London 1658
NEW HAVEN 1653
New Haven 1637
Milford
Southold
Greenwich
Easthampton
Southampton
Long Island
NEW NETHERLAND 1616–64/67; 1673–74
1623 Ft. Orange (Albany)
1614 Ft. Nassau
North (Hudson)
Esopus 1651 (Kingston)
Vriesendael (Tappan) 1640
New Amsterdam (New York) 1623
Breuckelen.1646 (Brooklyn)
Shrewsbury
NEW SWEDEN 1638–50
Ft. New Waso
Ft. Beversrede.1643 to Neth.
Ft. New Gothenburg 1643
Ft. Nassau.1623 to Neth. (Gloucester)
Ft. Christina

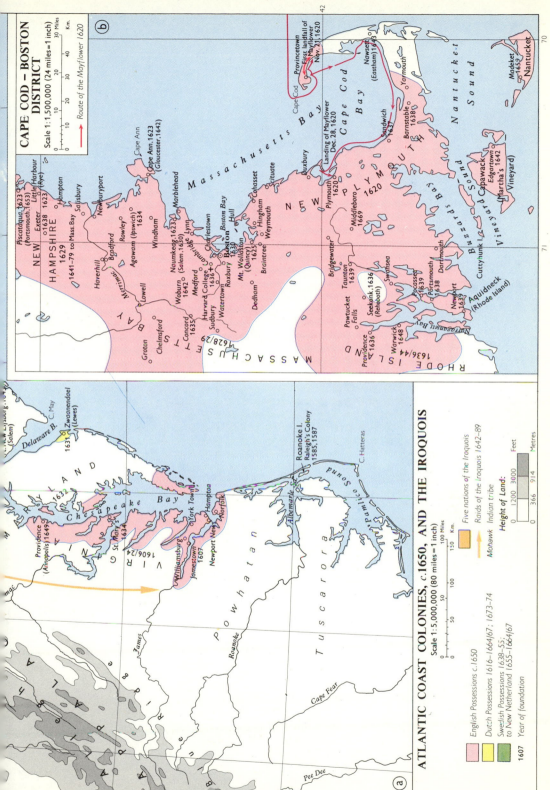

CAPE COD – BOSTON DISTRICT

Scale 1:1,500,000 (24 miles=1 inch)

Route of the Mayflower 1620

ⓑ

First landfall of Mayflower Nov. 21, 1620
Provincetown
Cape Cod
Landing of Mayflower Dec. 28, 1620
Nauset (Eastham) 1643
Yarmouth
Sandwich 1637
Barnstable 1638
Cape Cod Bay
Nantucket Sound
Madeket
Nantucket 1659
Vineyard
Martha's Vineyard
Edgartown
Capawack 1642
Buzzards Bay
Cuttyhunk
Massachusetts Bay

NEW PLYMOUTH
Plymouth 1620
Middleboro 1669
Duxbury
Scituate
Cohasset
Hingham
Weymouth
Bridgewater
Taunton 1639
Swansea
Rehoboth
Seekonk 1636 (Rehoboth)
Dartmouth 1639
Pocasset 1639
Portsmouth 1638
Newport 1639
Aquidneck (Rhode Island)
Narragansett Bay

Cape Ann
Cape Ann 1623 (Gloucester, 1642)
Marblehead
Naumkeag 1623 (Salem, 1630)
Lynn
Charlestown
Boston 1630
Boston Bay
Hull
Mt. Wollaston 1625 (Quincy)
Braintree
Dedham

NEW HAMPSHIRE
Piscataqua 1623 (Portsmouth,1653)
Exeter 1638
Little Harbour (Rye) 1623
Hampton
Salisbury
Newburyport
1629
1641-79 to Mass.Bay
Haverhill
Bradford
Rowley
Agawam (Ipswich) 1634
Windham
Woburn 1642
Medford
Roxbury 1630
Watertown
Harvard College 1636
Sudbury
Concord 1635
Chelmsford
Groton
Lowell
MERRIMAC
MASSACHUSETTS BAY
1628/29

RHODE ISLAND
Providence 1636
Warwick 1648
1636/44
Powtucket Falls

MASSACHUSETTS

ATLANTIC COAST COLONIES, c.1650, AND THE IROQUOIS

Scale 1:5,000,000 (80 miles=1 inch)

ⓐ

C. May
Zwaanendael (Lewes) 1631
Delaware B.
(Salem)
MARYLAND
Annapolis 1649
Providence 1649
St. Mary's 1634
1631
Chesapeake Bay
VIRGINIA
Williamsburg
Jamestown 1607
1606/24
York Town
Newport News
Hampton
Norfolk
Roanoke I. Raleigh's Colony 1585, 1587
Albemarle Sd.
C. Hatteras
Pamlico Sd.
Powhatan
Roanoke
Tuscarora
James
Cape Fear
Pee Dee
Ridge
Blue Ridge

Five nations of the Iroquois
Raids of the Iroquois 1642–89
Mohawk Indian tribe

Height of Land:
Feet
Metres
0 366 914 1200 3000
0 914 1200 3000

English Possessions c.1650
Dutch Possessions 1616–1664/67; 1673–74
Swedish Possessions 1638–55; to New Netherland 1655–1664/67
1607 Year of foundation

COPYRIGHT GEORGE PHILIP & SON LTD

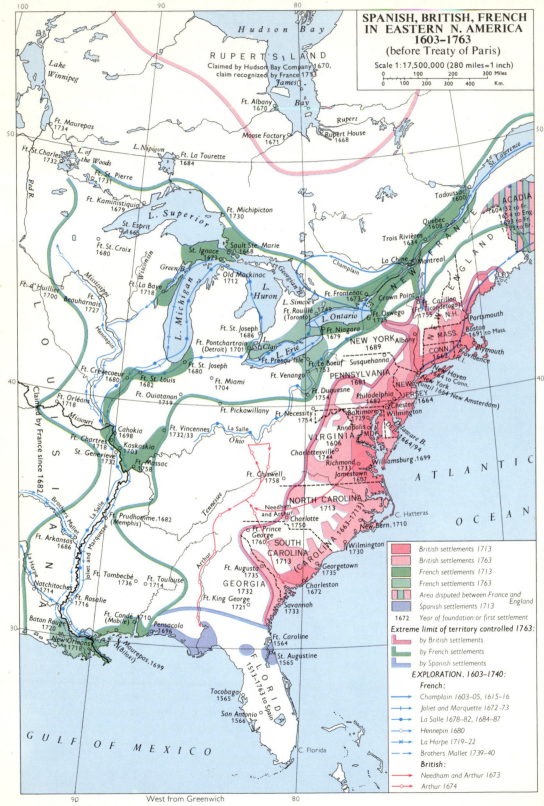

SPANISH, BRITISH, FRENCH IN EASTERN N. AMERICA 1603–1763 (before Treaty of Paris)

Scale 1:17,500,000 (280 miles=1 inch)

0   100   200   300 Miles
0   100   200   300   400 Km.

Hudson Bay

RUPERT'S LAND
Claimed by Hudson Bay Company 1670,
claim recognized by France 1713

James Bay

Ft. Albany 1670

Lake Winnipeg

Ft. Maurepas 1734

Moose Factory 1671

Rupert House 1668

Rupert R.

Ft. St. Charles 1732

L. Nipigon

L. of the Woods

Ft. St. Pierre 1731

Ft. La Tourette 1684

St. Lawrence

ACADIA
1604/32 to Fr.
1654 to Eng.
1670 to Fr.
1713 to Br.

Ft. Kaministiquia 1679

Ft. Michipicton 1730

Tadoussac 1600

Quebec 1608

Ft. d'Huillier 1700

L. Superior

St. Esprit 1665

St. Ignace 1672

Sault Ste. Marie 1668

Trois Rivières 1634

N E W   F R A N C E

N E W   E N G L A N D

Beauharnais 1727

Ft. St. Croix 1680

Wisconsin R.

Green B.

La Baye 1718

Old Mackinac 1712

L. Michigan

Georgian Bay

L. Huron

L. Simcoe

Ft. Rouillé (Toronto)
1749

Ft. Frontenac 1673

Crown Point

Champlain

La Chine

Montreal

Ft. Carillon (Ticonderoga)
1755

N.H.

Portsmouth

Boston 1691 to Mass.

Ft. Maurepas

Ft. Oswego 1726

MASS.

Plymouth

Mississippi R.

Ft. Pontchartrain (Detroit) 1701

Ft. St. Joseph 1686

St. Clair

Ft. Niagara 1679

L. Ontario

NEW YORK 1689

Albany

CONN.

Providence

New Haven 1664 to Conn.

L. Erie

Ft. St. Joseph 1680

Ft. Presqu'Isle 1753

Susquehanna

NEW JERSEY 1664
(New York until 1664 New Amsterdam)

Ft. Crèvecoeur 1680

Ft. St. Louis 1682

Ft. Miami 1704

Ft. Venango

Ft. Le Boeuf 1753

PENNSYLVANIA 1681

Philadelphia 1682

Chester

Wilmington

L O U I S I A N A

Claimed by France since 1682

Missouri R.

Ft. Orléans 1718

Ft. Ouiatanon 1719

Ft. Pickawillany

Ft. Duquesne 1754

Ft. Necessity 1754

Baltimore 1729

MD.

Annapolis 1744

Delaware B. 1664/94

Cahokia 1698

Ft. Vincennes 1732/33

La Salle

Ohio R.

VIRGINIA 1606

Charlottesville 1744

Richmond 1733

Williamsburg 1699

Ft. Chartres 1718

Kaskaskia 1703

St. Genevieve 1732

Ft. Massac 1758

Ft. Chiswell 1758

Jamestown 1607

Tennessee R.

A T L A N T I C   O C E A N

Brothers Mallet

La Salle

Joliet and Marquette

NORTH CAROLINA 1713

Needham and Arthur

Charlotte 1750

C. Hatteras

New Bern 1710

Ft. Prudhomme 1682 (Memphis)

Ft. Prince George 1760

Wilmington 1730

Ft. Arkansas 1686

SOUTH CAROLINA 1713

(CAROLINA 1663–1713)

Georgetown 1735

Arthur

La Harpe

Natchitoches 1714

Ft. Rosalie 1716

Ft. Tombecbé 1736

Ft. Toulouse 1714

Ft. Augusta 1735

GEORGIA 1732

Charleston 1672

Baton Rouge 1720

Ft. Condé 1710 (Mobile)

Pensacola 1696

Ft. King George 1721

Savannah 1733

New Orleans 1718

M. Maurepas, 1699 (Biloxi)

Ft. Caroline 1564

St. Augustine 1565

F L O R I D A
1513–1763 to Spain

G U L F   O F   M E X I C O

Tocobaga 1565

San Antonio 1566

C. Florida

Legend:

- British settlements 1713
- British settlements 1763
- French settlements 1713
- French settlements 1763
- Area disputed between France and England
- Spanish settlements 1713
- 1672 Year of foundation or first settlement

Extreme limit of territory controlled 1763:
- by British settlements
- by French settlements
- by Spanish settlements

EXPLORATION, 1603–1740:

French:
- Champlain 1603–05, 1615–16
- Joliet and Marquette 1672–73
- La Salle 1678–82, 1684–87
- Hennepin 1680
- La Harpe 1719–22
- Brothers Mallet 1739–40

British:
- Needham and Arthur 1673
- Arthur 1674

West from Greenwich

COPYRIGHT. GEORGE PHILIP & SON. LTD.

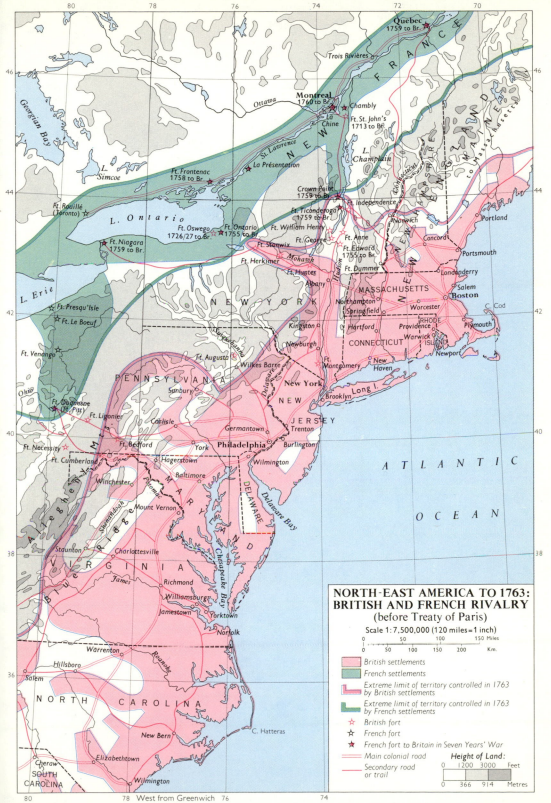

Quebec
1759 to Br.

Trois Rivières

Montreal
1760 to Br.

Chambly

La
Chine

Ft. St. John's
1713 to Br.

Ottawa

N E W

L.
Champlain

St. Lawrence

F R A N C E

N E W   E N G L A N D

to Massachusetts

M A I N E

N E W   H A M P S H I R E

Georgian Bay

L.
Simcoe

Ft. Frontenac
1758 to Br.

La Présentation

Ft. Rouillé
(Toronto)

L. O n t a r i o

Ft. Oswego
1726/27 to Br.

Ft. Ontario
1755 to Br.

Ft. William Henry

Ft. Stanwix

Crown Point
1759 to Br.

Ft. Independence

Ft. Ticonderoga
1759 to Br.

Portland

Ft. Niagara
1759 to Br.

Ft. Herkimer

Mohawk

Ft. George

Ft. Anne

Ft. Edward
1755 to Br.

Concord

Portsmouth

Ft. Hunter

Hudson

Ft. Dummer

Londonderry

L. Erie

Ft. Presqu'Isle

Albany

Northampton

M A S S A C H U S E T T S

Worcester

Salem

Boston

C. Cod

Ft. Le Boeuf

N E W   Y O R K

Springfield

Hartford

Providence

Warwick

R H O D E
I S L A N D

Plymouth

Ft. Venango

Kingston

C O N N E C T I C U T

New
Haven

Newport

Ohio

Susquehanna

Newburgh

Ft. Augusta

Wilkes Barre

Ft. Montgomery

New York

Long I.

Ft. Duquesne
(Ft. Pitt)

P E N N S Y L V A N I A

Sunbury

Delaware

Brooklyn

N E W

Ft. Ligonier

Carlisle

Germantown

J E R S E Y

Trenton

Ft. Necessity

Ft. Bedford

York

Philadelphia

Burlington

A T L A N T I C

Ft. Cumberland

Hagerstown

Wilmington

Allegheny Mts.

Winchester

Baltimore

Potomac

D E L A W A R E

Staunton

Shenandoah

Mount Vernon

M A R Y L A N D

Delaware Bay

O C E A N

Charlottesville

Blue Ridge

V I R G I N I A

James

Richmond

Williamsburg

Jamestown

Yorktown

Chesapeake Bay

Norfolk

Warrenton

Roanoke

Hillsboro

Salem

N O R T H   C A R O L I N A

C. Hatteras

New Bern

Cheraw
SOUTH
CAROLINA

Elizabethtown

Wilmington

**NORTH-EAST AMERICA TO 1763:
BRITISH AND FRENCH RIVALRY**
(before Treaty of Paris)

Scale 1:7,500,000 (120 miles=1 inch)

0   50   100   150 Miles
0   50 100 150 200 Km.

British settlements

French settlements

Extreme limit of territory controlled in 1763
by British settlements

Extreme limit of territory controlled in 1763
by French settlements

☆ British fort

★ French fort

★ French fort to Britain in Seven Years' War

Main colonial road

Secondary road
or trail

Height of Land:

0   1200   3000 Feet

0   366   914 Metres

COPYRIGHT. GEORGE PHILIP & SON. LTD.

80   78 West from Greenwich 76   74

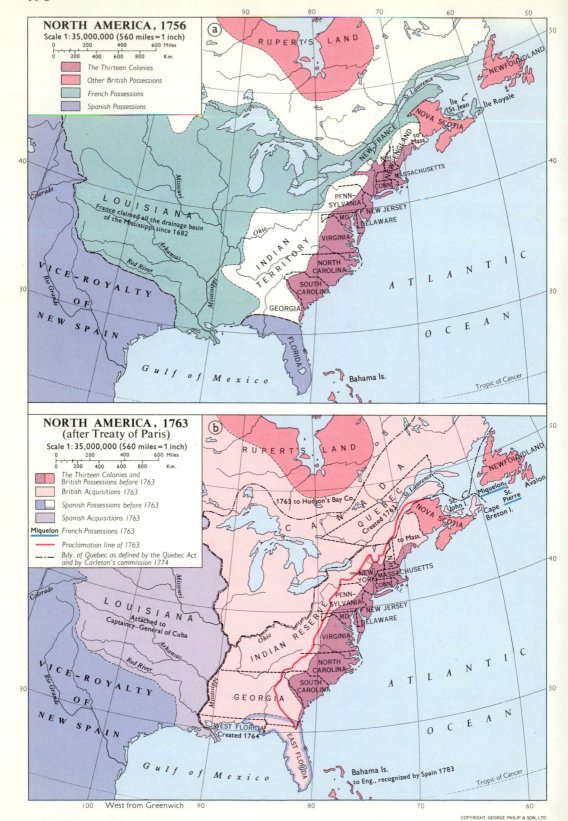

NORTH AMERICA, 1756
Scale 1:35,000,000 (560 miles = 1 inch)

ⓐ

| | 0 | 200 | 400 | 600 Miles |
| | 0 | 200 | 400 | 600 | 800 Km. |

- The Thirteen Colonies
- Other British Possessions
- French Possessions
- Spanish Possessions

RUPERT'S LAND

NEWFOUNDLAND

Ile St. Jean   Ile Royale

NEW-FRANCE

NOVA SCOTIA

St. Lawrence

N.H. NEW ENGLAND
to Mass.
CONN. MASSACHUSETTS

PENN-
SYLVANIA
MD.
DELAWARE
NEW JERSEY

L O U I S I A N A
France claimed all the drainage basin
of the Mississippi since 1682

Missouri

Colorado

Arkansas

Red River

Ohio

INDIAN
TERRITORY

VIRGINIA

NORTH
CAROLINA

SOUTH
CAROLINA

GEORGIA

Mississippi

V I C E - R O Y A L T Y
O F
N E W   S P A I N

Rio Grande

FLORIDA

A T L A N T I C

O C E A N

Gulf of Mexico

Bahama Is.

Tropic of Cancer

NORTH AMERICA, 1763
(after Treaty of Paris)

ⓑ

Scale 1:35,000,000 (560 miles = 1 inch)

| | 0 | 200 | 400 | 600 Miles |
| | 0 | 200 | 400 | 600 | 800 Km. |

- The Thirteen Colonies and British Possessions before 1763
- British Acquisitions 1763
- Spanish Possessions before 1763
- Spanish Acquisitions 1763
- **Miquelon** French Possessions 1763
- Proclamation line of 1763
- Bdy. of Quebec as defined by the Quebec Act and by Carleton's commission 1774

RUPERT'S LAND

NEWFOUNDLAND

1763 to Hudson's Bay Co.

C A N A D A

Miquelon, St. Pierre

Avalon

QUEBEC
Created 1763

St. Lawrence

NOVA SCOTIA

St. John I.

Cape Breton I.

to Mass.

N.Y.
NEW
YORK   MASSACHUSETTS
N.H.
CONN.

L O U I S I A N A
Attached to
Captaincy-General of Cuba

Missouri

Colorado

Arkansas

Red River

Ohio

INDIAN   RESERVE

PENN-
SYLVANIA
MD.
DELAWARE
NEW JERSEY

VIRGINIA

NORTH
CAROLINA

SOUTH
CAROLINA

GEORGIA

Mississippi

V I C E - R O Y A L T Y
O F
N E W   S P A I N

Rio Grande

WEST FLORIDA
Created 1764

EAST FLORIDA

A T L A N T I C

O C E A N

Gulf of Mexico

Bahama Is.
to Eng., recognized by Spain 1783

Tropic of Cancer

100   West from Greenwich   90   80   70   60

COPYRIGHT. GEORGE PHILIP & SON, LTD.

Montgomery killed Dec. 1775 — Quebec

Area disputed with Gt. Br.

CANADA

Ottawa

Georgian Bay

Lake Huron

MONTGOMERY 1775

THOMAS 1777

BURGOYNE 1777

SULLIVAN 1777

ARNOLD SEPT.-DEC. 1775

Montreal

Ft. Chambly
Ft. St. John's

ST. LEGER 1777

St. Lawrence

Lake Ontario

Ft. Oswego

Fort Niagara

BUTLER 1778

Crown Pt.
Ticonderoga

Ft. Stanwix

Freemans Farm Sept. 19, 1777

Oriskany Aug. 6, 1777

Cherry Valley

ARNOLD

Saratoga
Surrender of Burgoyne
Oct. 17, 1777

NEW ENGLAND

Bunker Hill June 16, 1775
Lexington Apr. 19, 1775

Bennington
Aug. 15, 1777

Concord
Cambridge

Boston

D'ESTAING NOV. 1778

Lake Erie

Fort Malden

HAMILTON 1778 to Vincennes

Bemis Heights Oct. 7, 1777

Albany

GATES 1777

Hudson

Hartford

ROCHAMBEAU JUNE 1781

Providence

Newport

UNITED STATES

Newtown

Susquehanna

Wilkes Barre

Wyoming

West Point

New Haven

New London

MAY 1781

Fort Pitt

Redstone Fort

CLARK 1778-79 to Cahokia and Vincennes

Ohio

Germantown Oct.

Valley Forge
Washington's Camp
Dec. 1777–June 1778
Sept. 20, 1777, Paoli

Ft. Washington

1778 WASHINGTON

New York

SIR WILLIAM HOWE JULY 1776 from Halifax

LORD HOWE AUG. 1776 from London

OF

Kanawha

From 1776

Brandywine
Sept. 11, 1777

Wilmington

Mannmouth
Court Ho., June 28, 1778
Princeton, Jan. 3, 1777
Trenton

Philadelphia

JULY 1777

AMERICA

Charlottesville

LAFAYETTE

WASHINGTON/ROCHAMBEAU 1781

ALLIED SEPT 1781

SIR WILLIAM HOWE

DE BARRAS 1781

ATLANTIC

Potomac

Bedford

Richmond

Petersburg

Jamestown July 6, 1781

TARLETON JULY 1781

Yorktown
Surrender of Cornwallis
Oct. 19, 1781

GRASSE

Norfolk

Sept. 5, 1781

D'ESTAING JULY 1778 from Toulon

OCEAN

Roanoke

CORNWALLIS 1781

DE GRASSE 1781 from S. Domingo

British Proclamation Line 1763

Guilford Court House Mar. 15, 1781

Ramsay's Mill

MORGAN GREENE

Charlotte

GATES 1780

GREENE 1781

King's Mtn. Oct. 7, 1780

Cheraw

Cape Fear

Cowpens Jan. 16, 1781

Blackstock Nov. 20, 1780

TARLETON

GREENE

Ninety-six

BALFOUR

Hobkirk's Hill, Apr. 25, 1781
Camden Aug. 16, 1780

CORNWALLIS

Pee Dee

Wilmington

CLINTON/CORNWALLIS JAN. 1780 from New York

CAMPBELL DEC. 1778 from New York

Jan. 29, 1779
Augusta

Eutaw Springs Sept. 8, 1781

LINCOLN 1779

PREVOST

Briar Creek Mar. 3, 1779

Charleston

PREVOST

Dec. 29, 1778
Savannah

THE AMERICAN REVOLUTION
1775–83

Scale 1:8,000,000 (128 miles = 1 inch)

| 0 | 50 | 100 | 150 Miles |
| 0 50 | 100 | 150 | 200 Km |

→ British attack   → U.S. attack

✂ Battle—British victory   ✂ Battle—U.S. victory

British Colonies in North America to 1775

United States 1783

○ U.S. base

→ French advance (from 1778 allied to U.S.)

West from 78 Greenwich   76

COPYRIGHT. GEORGE PHILIP & SON. LTD.

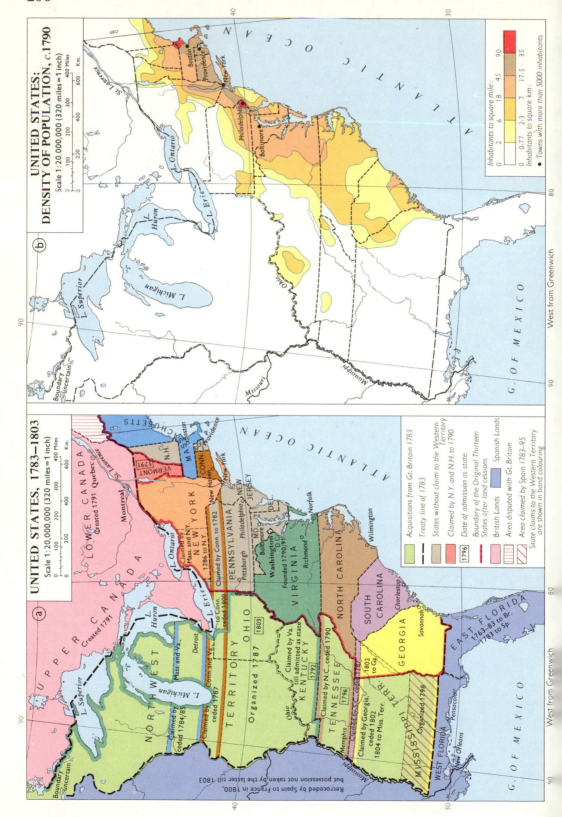

UNITED STATES:
DENSITY OF POPULATION, c.1790
Scale 1:20,000,000 (320 miles=1 inch)

Inhabitants to square mile:
0   2   6   18   45   90
0.77 2-3   7   17.5   35
Inhabitants to square km:
● Towns with more than 5000 inhabitants

UNITED STATES, 1783–1803
Scale 1:20,000,000 (320 miles=1 inch)

Acquisitions from Gt. Britain 1783
Treaty line of 1783
States without claim to the Western Territory
Claimed by N.Y. and N.H. to 1790
Date of admission as state
Boundary of the Original Thirteen
States after land cessions
British Lands   Spanish Lands
Area disputed with Gt. Britain
Area claimed by Spain 1783-95
State claims to the Western Territory
are shown in band colouring

West from Greenwich

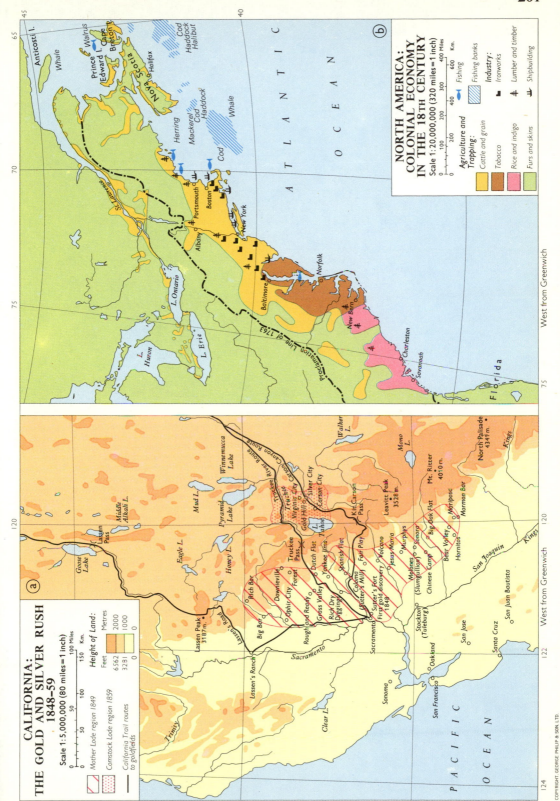

CALIFORNIA: THE GOLD AND SILVER RUSH 1848–59

Scale 1:5,000,000 (80 miles=1 inch)

0   50   100   150 Miles
0   50   100   150 Km.

Height of Land:

Feet	Metres
6562	2000
3281	1000
0	0

Mother Lode region 1849

Comstock Lode region 1859

California Trail routes to goldfields

(a)

PACIFIC OCEAN

Trinity

Sonoma

Clear L.

Santa Cruz

Oakland

San Francisco

San Jose

San Juan Bautista

Stockton (Tuleburg)

Sacramento

San Joaquin

Kings

Lassen's Ranch

Lassen Peak 3187 m.

Lassen Road

Lassen's Road

Goose Lake

Lassen Pass

Middle Alkali L.

Eagle L.

Honey L.

Mud L.

Pyramid Lake

Winnemucca Lake

Carson River Route

Truckee River Route

Truckee Pass

Big Bar

Rich Bar

Downieville

Ophir City

Rough and Ready

Grass Valley

Forest

Rich Dry Diggins

Yankee Jims

Dutch Flat

Spanish Flat

Coloma

Sutter's Mill

Sutter's Fort

First gold discovery 1848

Fair Play

Volcano

Jesus Maria

Murphys

Molelas (Slumgullion)

Chinese Camp

Sonora

Big Oak Flat

Bear Valley

Hornitos

Mariposa

Mormon Bar

Virginia City

Silver City

Gold Hill

Carson City

Truckee

L. Tahoe

Kit Carson Pass

Leavitt Peak 3528 m.

Mt. Ritter 4010 m.

Mono L.

Walker L.

North Palisade 4341 m.

Kings

San Joaquin

West from Greenwich

NORTH AMERICA: COLONIAL ECONOMY IN THE 18TH CENTURY

Scale 1:20,000,000 (320 miles=1 inch)

0   100   200   300   400 Miles
0   200   400   600 Km.

(b)

Agriculture and Trapping:

Cattle and grain

Tobacco

Rice and indigo

Furs and skins

Fishing:

Fishing banks

Industry:

Ironworks

Lumber and timber

Shipbuilding

ATLANTIC OCEAN

Anticosti I.

Whale

Walrus

Prince Edward I.

Cape Breton I.

Nova Scotia

Halifax

Cod

Haddock

Halibut

Whale

Herring

Mackerel

Cod

Haddock

Whale

Cod

Portsmouth

Boston

New York

Albany

L. Ontario

L. Erie

L. Huron

St. Lawrence

Baltimore

Norfolk

New Bern

Charleston

Savannah

Florida

Proclamation Line of 1763

West from Greenwich

COPYRIGHT. GEORGE PHILIP & SON. LTD.

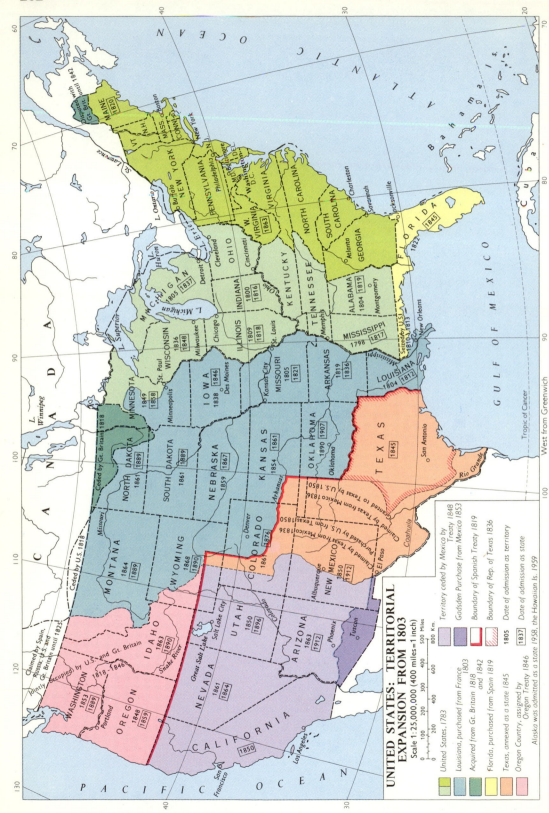

UNITED STATES: TERRITORIAL
EXPANSION FROM 1803

Scale 1:25,000,000 (400 miles=1 inch)

COPYRIGHT GEORGE PHILIP & SON, LTD.

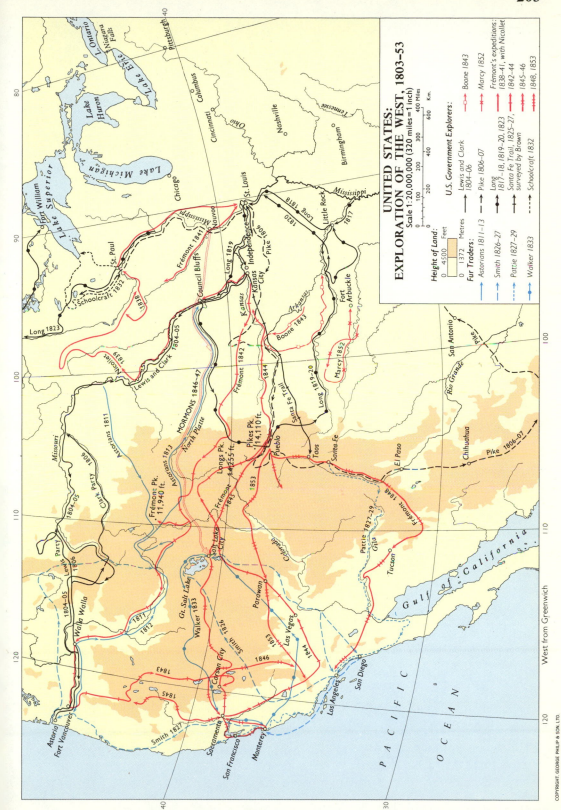

UNITED STATES:
EXPLORATION OF THE WEST, 1803–53
Scale 1:20,000,000 (320 miles=1 inch)

Height of Land:
Feet
4,500
Metres
1,372

U.S. Government Explorers:
Lewis and Clark 1804–06
Pike 1806–07
Long 1817–18, 1819–20, 1823
Santa Fe Trail, 1825–27, surveyed by Brown
Schoolcraft 1832

Fur Traders:
Astorians 1811–13
Smith 1826–27
Pattie 1827–29
Walker 1833

Boone 1843
Marcy 1852
Frémont's expeditions:
1838–41, with Nicollet
1842–44
1845–46
1848, 1853

COPYRIGHT. GEORGE PHILIP & SON, LTD.

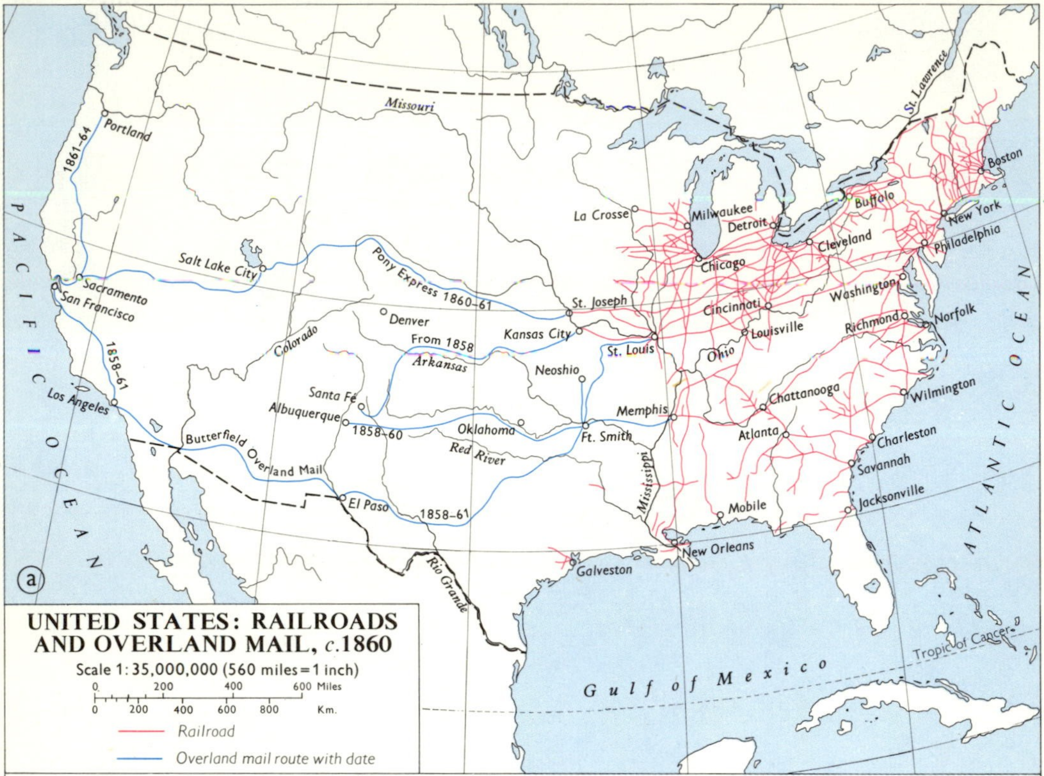

UNITED STATES: RAILROADS AND OVERLAND MAIL, *c.*1860

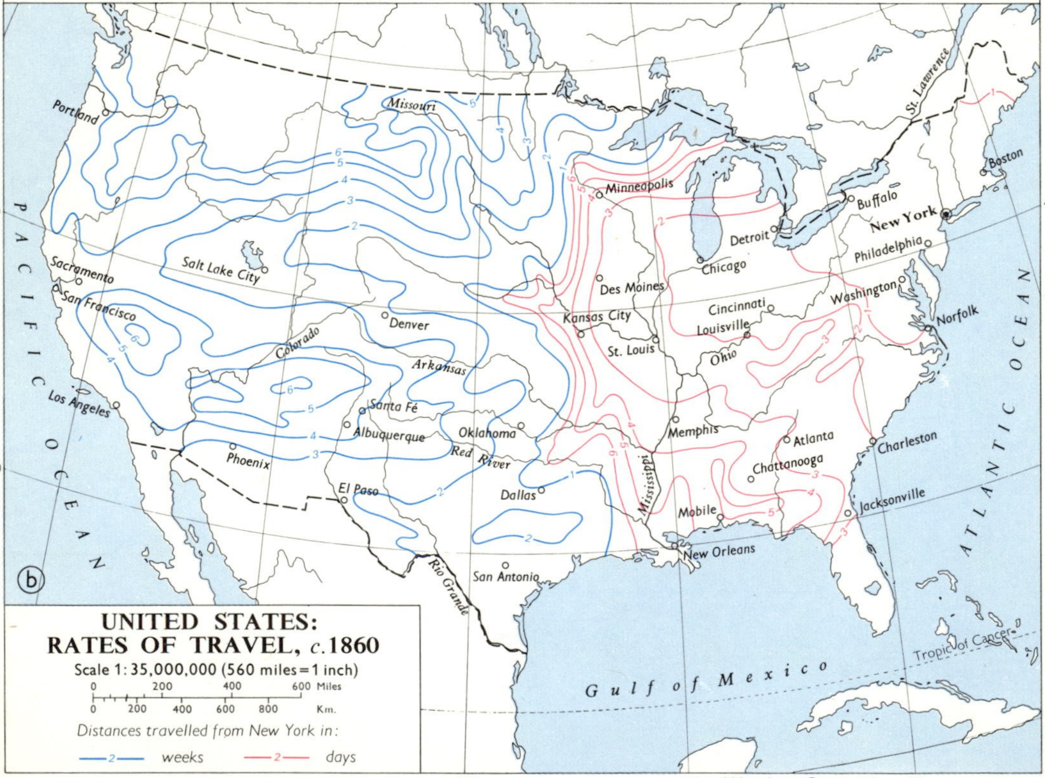

UNITED STATES: RATES OF TRAVEL, *c.*1860

COPYRIGHT. GEORGE PHILIP & SON. LTD.

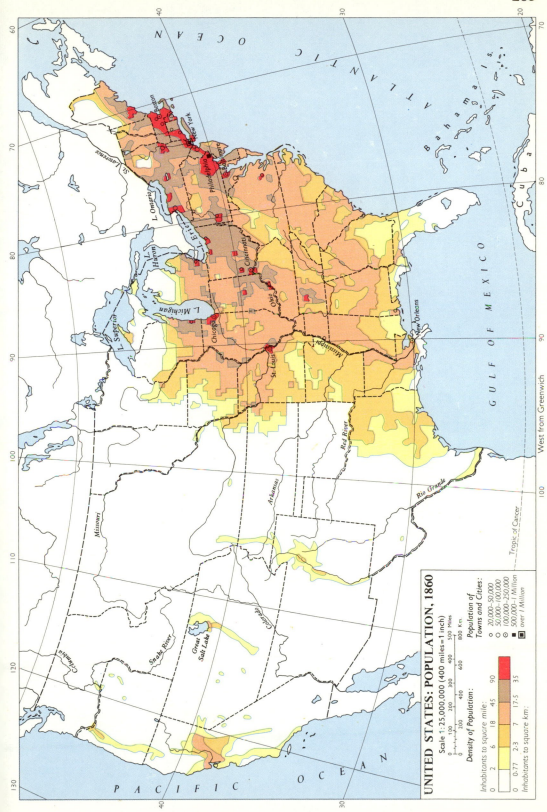

UNITED STATES: POPULATION, 1860

Scale 1:25,000,000 (400 miles = 1 inch)

Population of Towns and Cities:
○ 20,000–50,000
◎ 50,000–100,000
⊙ 100,000–250,000
■ 250,000–1 Million
▣ over 1 Million

Density of Population:

Inhabitants to square mile:
0   2   6   18   45   90   35

Inhabitants to square km:
0   0.77   2.3   7   17.5   35

COPYRIGHT GEORGE PHILIP & SON, LTD.

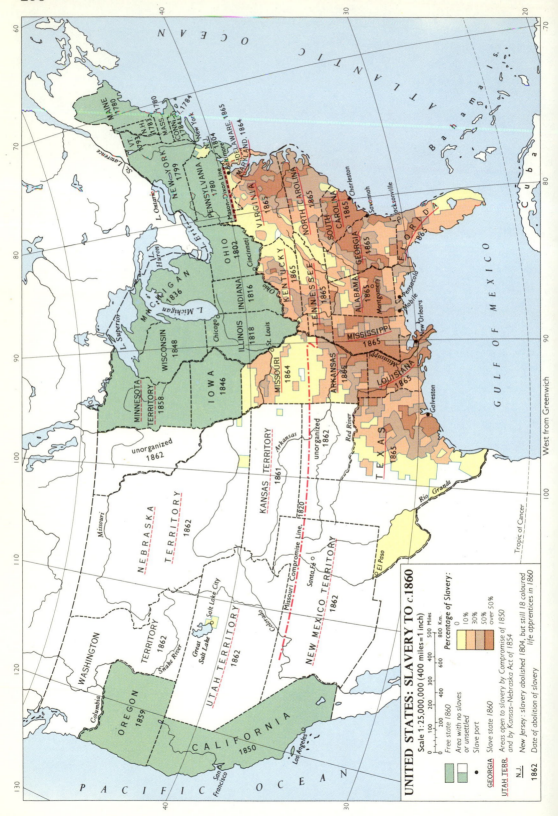

206

UNITED STATES: SLAVERY TO c.1860

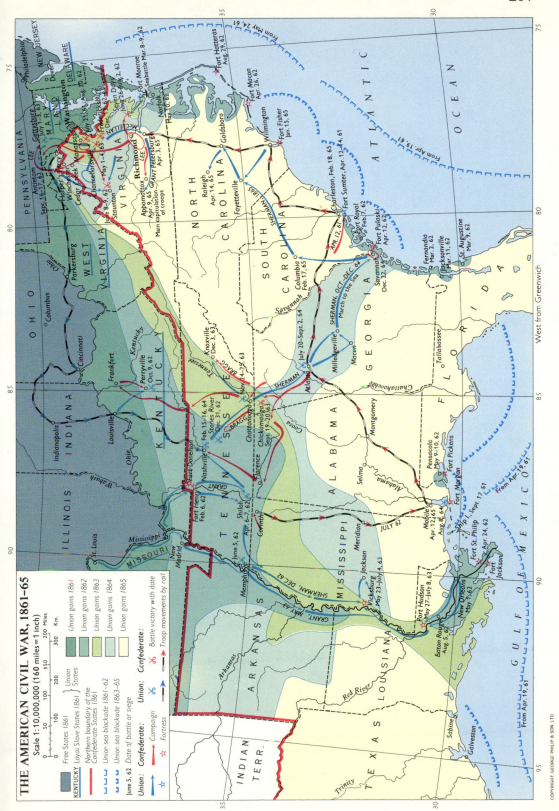

THE AMERICAN CIVIL WAR, 1861–65

Scale 1:10,000,000 (160 miles=1 inch)

KENTUCKY	Free States 1861	Union gains 1861
	Loyal Slave States 1861	Union gains 1862
		Union gains 1863
	Northern boundary of the Confederate States 1861	Union gains 1864
	Union sea blockade 1861–62	Union gains 1865
	Union sea blockade 1863–65	

Confederate:
Troop movements by rail

	Confederate:	Union:
June 5, 62 Date of battle or siege	Campaign	Campaign
	Fortress	Fortress

COPYRIGHT. GEORGE PHILIP & SON, LTD.

West from Greenwich

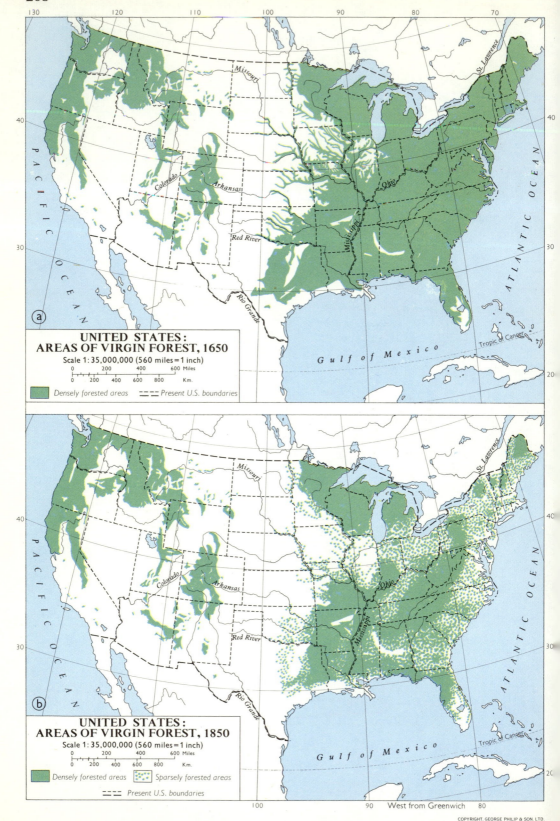

UNITED STATES:
AREAS OF VIRGIN FOREST, 1650
Scale 1:35,000,000 (560 miles = 1 inch)

0   200   400   600 Miles
0   200   400   600   800 Km.

Densely forested areas   Present U.S. boundaries

UNITED STATES:
AREAS OF VIRGIN FOREST, 1850
Scale 1:35,000,000 (560 miles = 1 inch)

0   200   400   600 Miles
0   200   400   600   800 Km.

Densely forested areas   Sparsely forested areas

Present U.S. boundaries

West from Greenwich

COPYRIGHT. GEORGE PHILIP & SON, LTD.

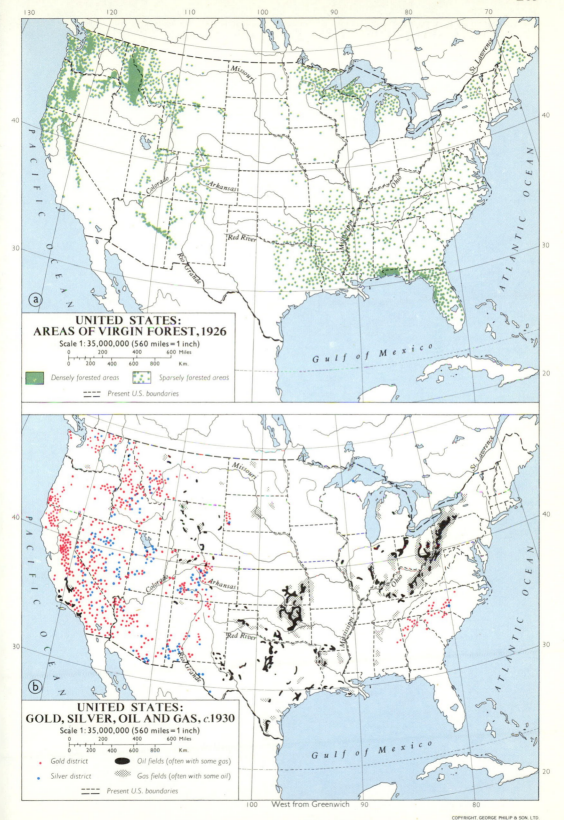

UNITED STATES:
AREAS OF VIRGIN FOREST, 1926

Scale 1:35,000,000 (560 miles=1 inch)

0   200   400   600 Miles
0 200 400 600 800   Km.

Densely forested areas   Sparsely forested areas

- - - Present U.S. boundaries

UNITED STATES:
GOLD, SILVER, OIL AND GAS, c.1930

Scale 1:35,000,000 (560 miles=1 inch)

0   200   400   600 Miles
0 200 400 600 800   Km.

• Gold district   Oil fields (often with some gas)

• Silver district   Gas fields (often with some oil)

- - - Present U.S. boundaries

West from Greenwich

COPYRIGHT. GEORGE PHILIP & SON. LTD.

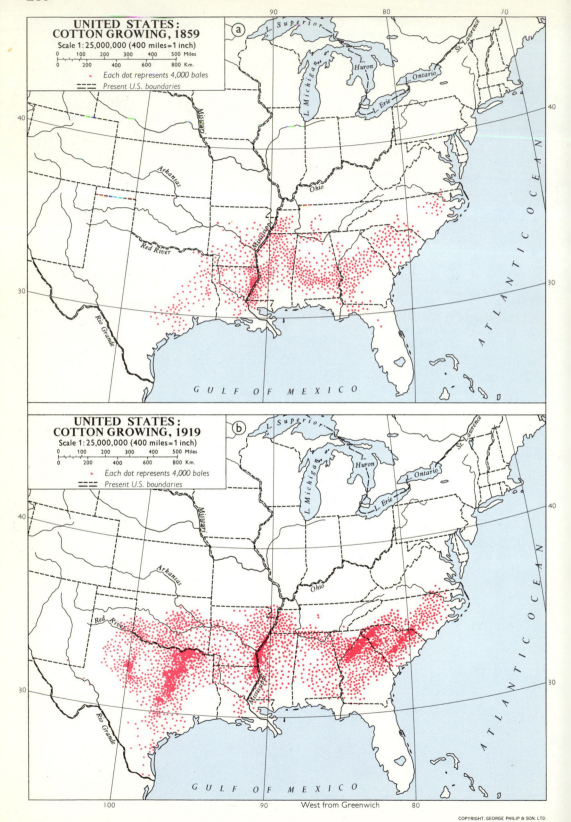

UNITED STATES: COTTON GROWING, 1859
Scale 1:25,000,000 (400 miles=1 inch)
0 100 200 300 400 500 Miles
0 200 400 600 800 Km.
• Each dot represents 4,000 bales
--- Present U.S. boundaries

(a)

L. Superior
St. Lawrence
L. Michigan
L. Huron
L. Ontario
L. Erie

Missouri

Arkansas

Ohio

Red River

Mississippi

Rio Grande

ATLANTIC OCEAN

GULF OF MEXICO

UNITED STATES: COTTON GROWING, 1919
Scale 1:25,000,000 (400 miles=1 inch)
0 100 200 300 400 500 Miles
0 200 400 600 800 Km.
• Each dot represents 4,000 bales
--- Present U.S. boundaries

(b)

L. Superior
St. Lawrence
L. Michigan
L. Huron
L. Ontario
L. Erie

Missouri

Arkansas

Ohio

Red River

Mississippi

Rio Grande

ATLANTIC OCEAN

GULF OF MEXICO
West from Greenwich

COPYRIGHT. GEORGE PHILIP & SON. LTD.

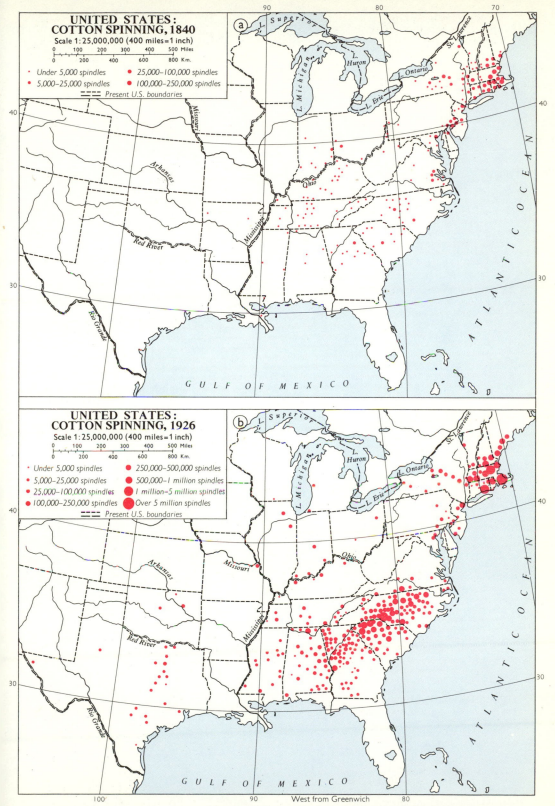

UNITED STATES:
COTTON SPINNING, 1840
Scale 1:25,000,000 (400 miles=1 inch)

- Under 5,000 spindles
- 5,000–25,000 spindles
- 25,000–100,000 spindles
- 100,000–250,000 spindles
- Present U.S. boundaries

UNITED STATES:
COTTON SPINNING, 1926
Scale 1:25,000,000 (400 miles=1 inch)

- Under 5,000 spindles
- 5,000–25,000 spindles
- 25,000–100,000 spindles
- 100,000–250,000 spindles
- 250,000–500,000 spindles
- 500,000–1 million spindles
- 1 million–5 million spindles
- Over 5 million spindles
- Present U.S. boundaries

West from Greenwich

COPYRIGHT. GEORGE PHILIP & SON, LTD.

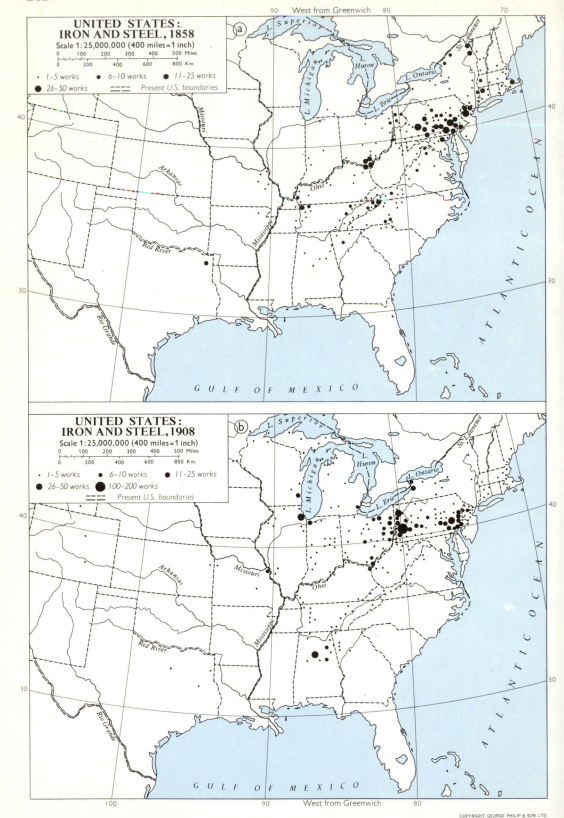

UNITED STATES:
IRON AND STEEL, 1858
Scale 1:25,000,000 (400 miles=1 inch)

1-5 works   6-10 works   11-25 works
26-50 works   Present U.S. boundaries

UNITED STATES:
IRON AND STEEL, 1908
Scale 1:25,000,000 (400 miles=1 inch)

1-5 works   6-10 works   11-25 works
26-50 works   100-200 works
Present U.S. boundaries

COPYRIGHT. GEORGE PHILIP & SON. LTD.

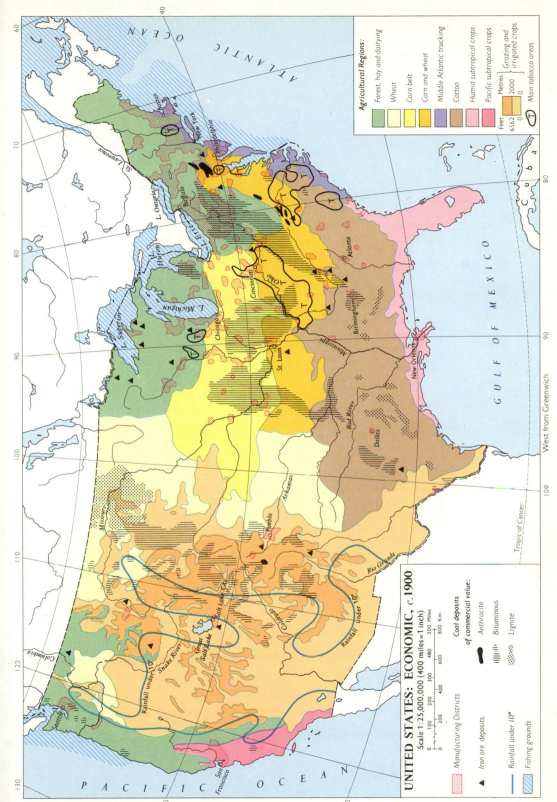

UNITED STATES: ECONOMIC, c.1900

Scale 1:25,000,000 (400 miles=1 inch)

Agricultural Regions:
- Forest, hay and dairying
- Wheat
- Corn belt
- Corn and wheat
- Middle Atlantic trucking
- Cotton
- Humid subtropical crops
- Pacific subtropical crops
- Grazing and irrigated crops
- Main tobacco areas

Manufacturing Districts
Iron ore deposits
Rainfall under 10"
Fishing grounds

Coal deposits of commercial value:
- Anthracite
- Bituminous
- Lignite

COPYRIGHT GEORGE PHILIP & SON, LTD.

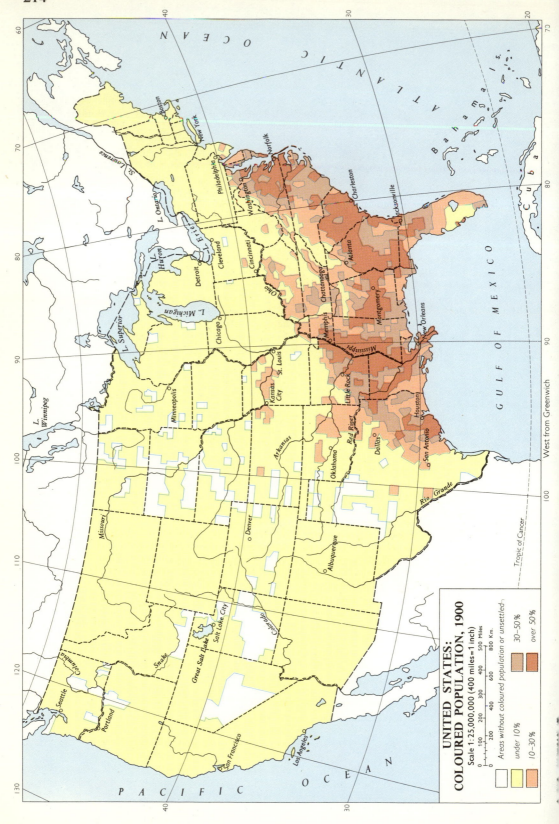

UNITED STATES:
COLOURED POPULATION, 1900

Scale 1:25,000,000 (400 miles=1 inch)

Areas without coloured population or unsettled

under 10%

10-30%

30-50%

over 50%

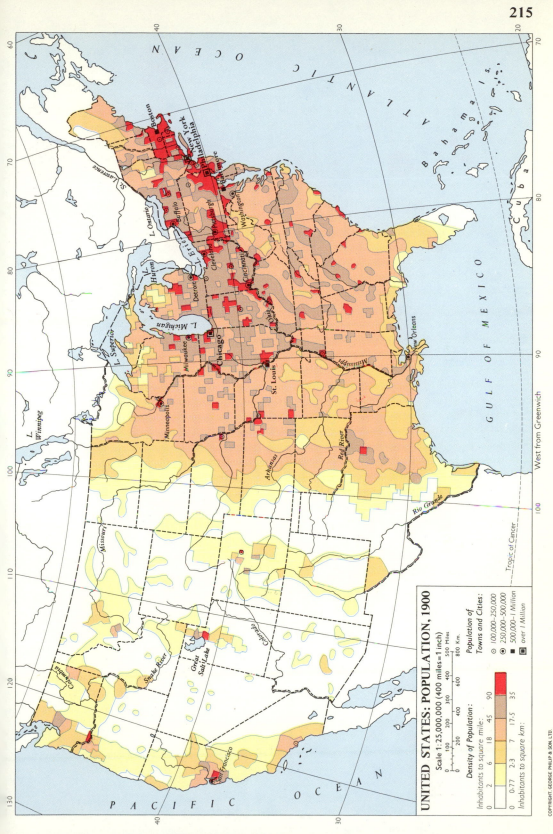

UNITED STATES: POPULATION, 1900
Scale 1:25,000,000 (400 miles=1 inch)

Population of
Towns and Cities:
◎ 100,000–250,000
⊙ 250,000–500,000
■ 500,000–1 Million
□ over 1 Million

Density of Population:
Inhabitants to square mile:
0   2   6   18   45   90
                17.5   35
0   0.77   2.3   7
Inhabitants to square km:

COPYRIGHT. GEORGE PHILIP & SON, LTD.

0   100   200   300   400   500 Miles
0   100   200   300   400   500   600   700   800 Km.

ATLANTIC

OCEAN

Bahama Is.

Cuba

GULF OF MEXICO

West from Greenwich

Tropic of Cancer

PACIFIC   OCEAN

Boston
New York
Philadelphia
Baltimore
Washington
Pittsburgh
Buffalo
Cleveland
Cincinnati
Detroit
Chicago
Milwaukee
Minneapolis
St. Louis
New Orleans
San Francisco

St. Lawrence
L. Ontario
L. Erie
L. Huron
L. Michigan
L. Superior
L. Winnipeg
Ohio
Mississippi
Arkansas
Red River
Rio Grande
Missouri
Colorado
Snake River
Great Salt Lake
Columbia

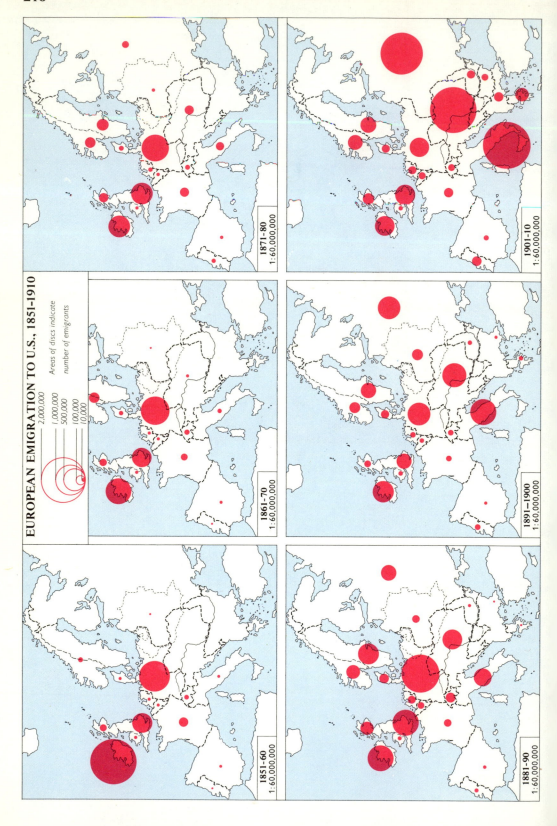

EUROPEAN EMIGRATION TO U.S., 1851-1910

Areas of discs indicate
number of emigrants

2,000,000
1,000,000
500,000
100,000
10,000

1851-60
1:60,000,000

1861-70
1:60,000,000

1871-80
1:60,000,000

1881-90
1:60,000,000

1891-1900
1:60,000,000

1901-10
1:60,000,000

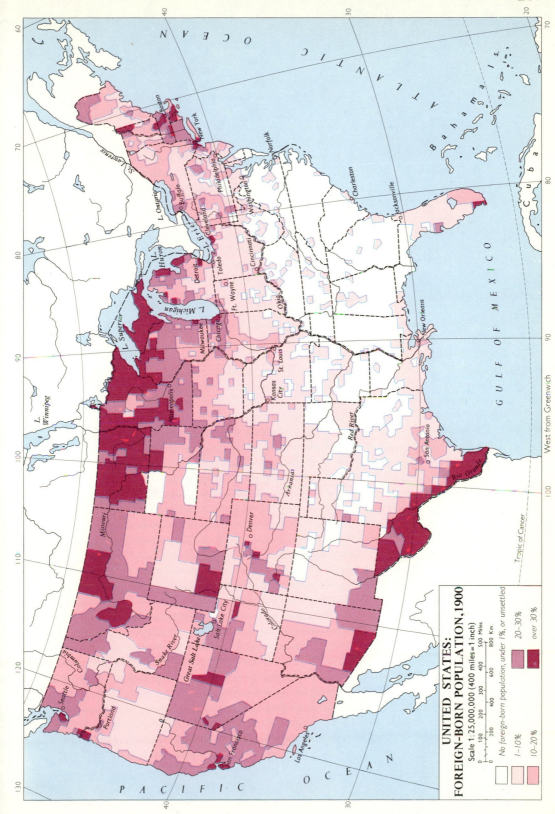

UNITED STATES:
FOREIGN-BORN POPULATION, 1900
Scale 1:25,000,000 (400 miles=1 inch)
0   100   200   300   400   500 Miles
0 200 300 400 500 600 700 800 Km.

No foreign-born population, under 1%, or unsettled

1-10%   20-30%

10-20%   over 30%

COPYRIGHT GEORGE PHILIP & SON, LTD.

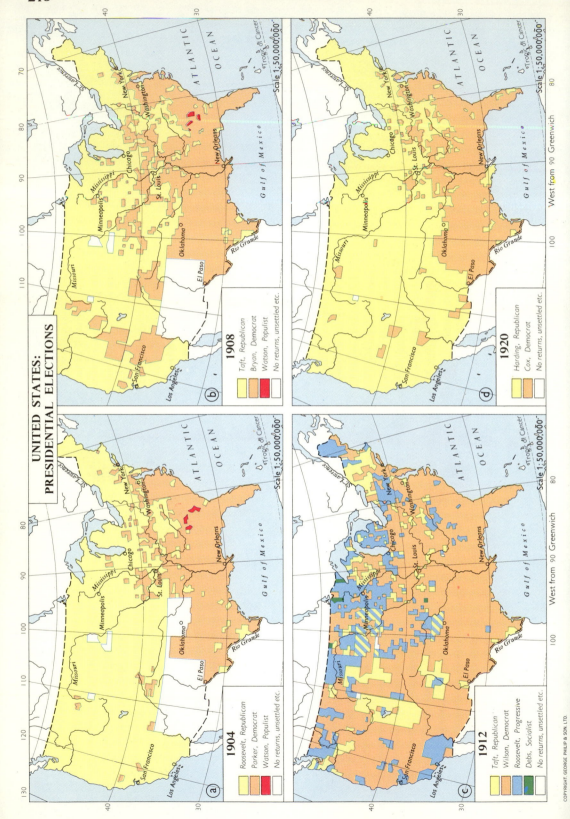

UNITED STATES:
PRESIDENTIAL ELECTIONS

1904

Roosevelt, Republican
Parker, Democrat
Watson, Populist
No returns, unsettled etc.

1908

Taft, Republican
Bryan, Democrat
Watson, Populist
No returns, unsettled etc.

1912

Taft, Republican
Wilson, Democrat
Roosevelt, Progressive
Debs, Socialist
No returns, unsettled etc.

1920

Harding, Republican
Cox, Democrat
No returns, unsettled etc.

Scale 1:50,000,000

West from 90 Greenwich

COPYRIGHT GEORGE PHILIP & SON, LTD.

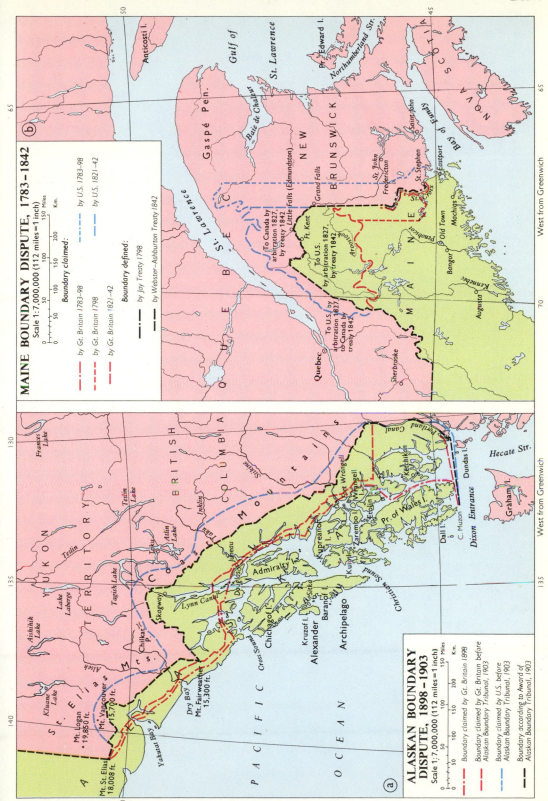

MAINE BOUNDARY DISPUTE, 1783–1842

Scale 1:7,000,000 (112 miles=1 inch)

Boundary claimed:

— · — by Gt. Britain 1783-98
— — — by Gt. Britain 1798
— — — by Gt. Britain 1821-42

— · — · — by U.S. 1783-98
— — — by U.S. 1821-42

Boundary defined:

— · · — by Jay Treaty 1798
— — — by Webster–Ashburton Treaty 1842

ALASKAN BOUNDARY DISPUTE, 1898–1903

Scale 1:7,000,000 (112 miles=1 inch)

— · — · — Boundary claimed by Gt. Britain 1898
— — — Boundary claimed by Gt. Britain before Alaskan Boundary Tribunal, 1903
— — — Boundary claimed by U.S. before Alaskan Boundary Tribunal, 1903
——— Boundary according to Award of Alaskan Boundary Tribunal, 1903

COPYRIGHT. GEORGE PHILIP & SON, LTD.

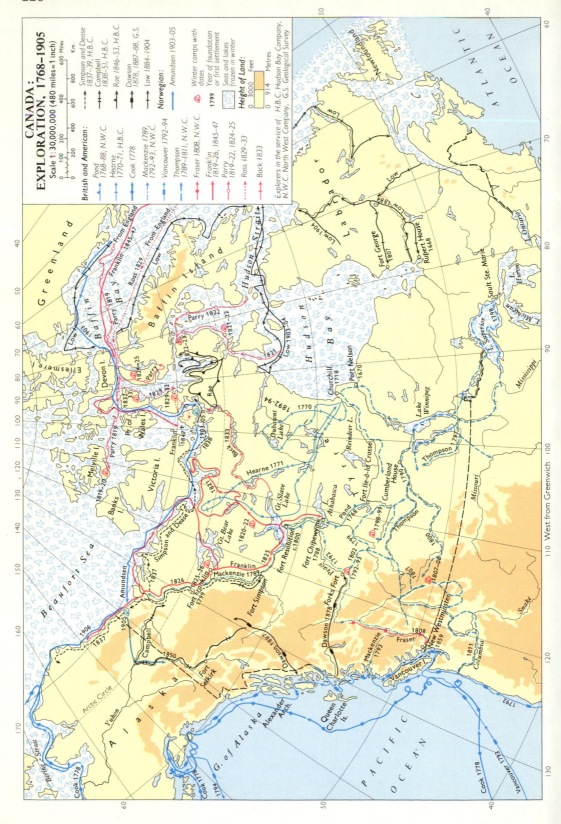

CANADA:
EXPLORATION, 1768–1905

Scale 1:30,000,000 (480 miles=1 inch)

British and American:

Pond 1768–88, N.W.C.
Hearne 1770–71, H.B.C.
Cook 1778
Mackenzie 1789, 1792–93, N.W.C.
Vancouver 1792–94
Thompson 1789–1811, N.W.C.
Fraser 1808, N.W.C.
Franklin 1819–26, 1845–47
Parry 1819–22, 1824–25
Ross 1829–33
Back 1833

Simpson and Dease 1837–39, H.B.C.
Campbell 1838–51, H.B.C.
Rae 1846–53, H.B.C.
Dawson 1878, 1887–88, G.S.
Low 1884–1904

Norwegian:

Amundsen 1903–05

Winter camps with dates
1799 Year of foundation or first settlement
Seas and lakes frozen in winter

Height of Land:
Metres 0 914
Feet 0 3000

Explorers in the service of: H.B.C. Hudson Bay Company, N.W.C. North West Company, G.S. Geological Survey

0 100 200 300 400 500 600 Miles
0 200 400 600 800 Km.

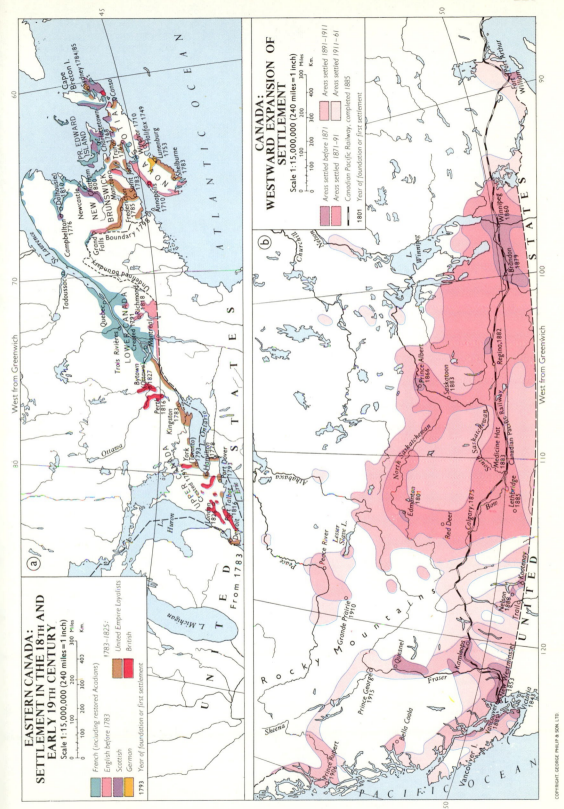

(a) EASTERN CANADA: SETTLEMENT IN THE 18TH AND EARLY 19TH CENTURY

Scale 1:15,000,000 (240 miles=1 inch)

0 100 200 300 Miles
0 100 200 300 400 Km.

French (including restored Acadians)

English before 1783

Scottish

German

1783–1825:
United Empire Loyalists
British

1793 Year of foundation or first settlement

(b) CANADA: WESTWARD EXPANSION OF SETTLEMENT

Scale 1:15,000,000 (240 miles=1 inch)

0 100 200 300 400 Miles
0 100 200 300 Km.

Areas settled before 1871
Areas settled 1871–91
Areas settled 1891–1911
Areas settled 1911–61
Canadian Pacific Railway, completed 1885

1801 Year of foundation or first settlement

COPYRIGHT. GEORGE PHILIP & SON, LTD.

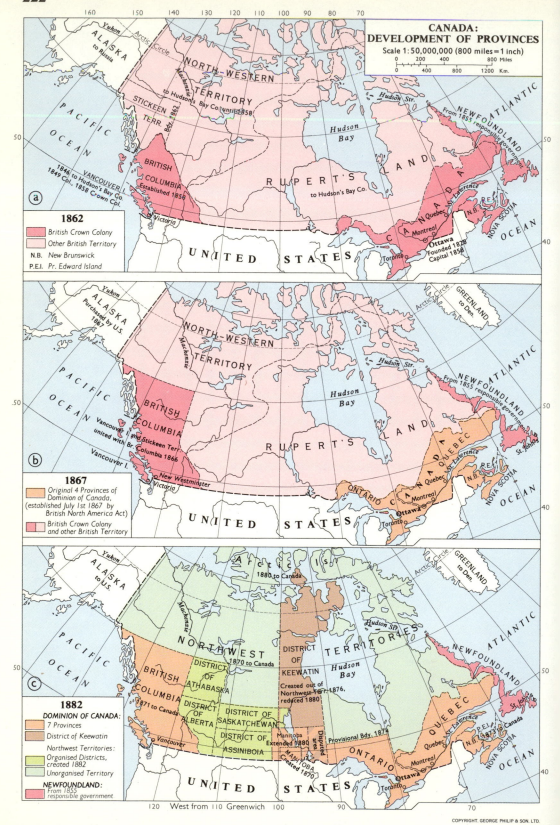

**CANADA:
DEVELOPMENT OF PROVINCES**

Scale 1:50,000,000 (800 miles=1 inch)

0   200   400   600   800 Miles
0   400   800   1200 Km.

1862

British Crown Colony
Other British Territory
N.B.   New Brunswick
P.E.I. Pr. Edward Island

1867

Original 4 Provinces of
Dominion of Canada,
(established July 1st 1867 by
British North America Act)
British Crown Colony
and other British Territory

1882
DOMINION OF CANADA:
7 Provinces
District of Keewatin
Northwest Territories:
Organised Districts,
created 1882
Unorganised Territory
NEWFOUNDLAND:
From 1855
responsible government

COPYRIGHT. GEORGE PHILIP & SON. LTD.

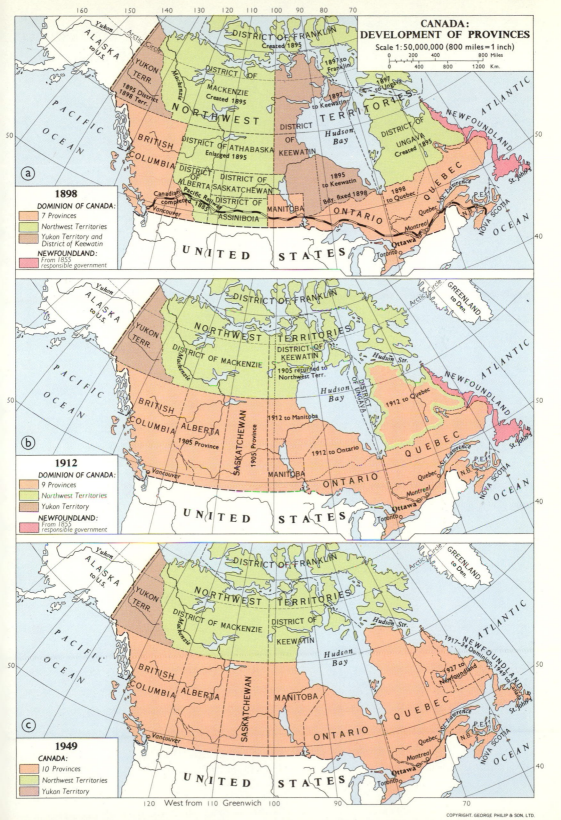

CANADA:
DEVELOPMENT OF PROVINCES

Scale 1:50,000,000 (800 miles=1 inch)

0 200 400 800 Miles
0 400 800 1200 Km.

(a) 1898

DOMINION OF CANADA:
7 Provinces
Northwest Territories
Yukon Territory and District of Keewatin

NEWFOUNDLAND:
From 1855 responsible government

(b) 1912

DOMINION OF CANADA:
9 Provinces
Northwest Territories
Yukon Territory

NEWFOUNDLAND:
From 1855 responsible government

(c) 1949

CANADA:
10 Provinces
Northwest Territories
Yukon Territory

West from 110 Greenwich

COPYRIGHT. GEORGE PHILIP & SON, LTD.

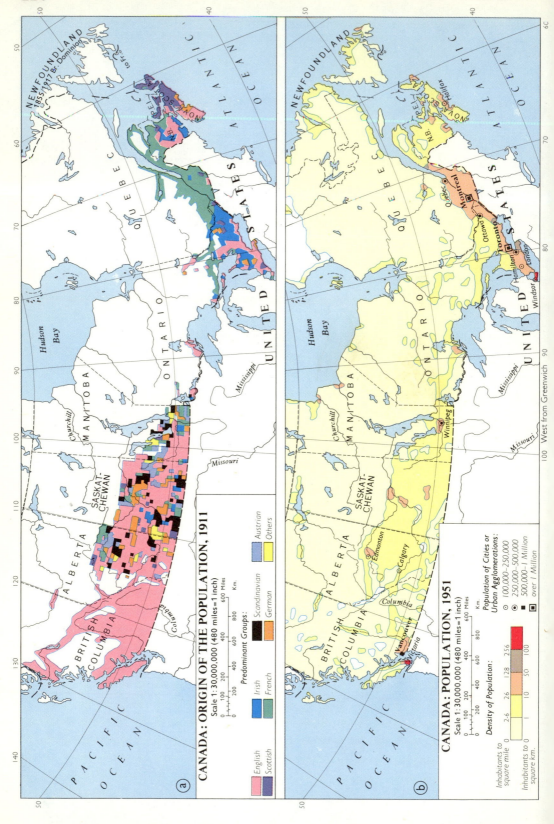

CANADA: ORIGIN OF THE POPULATION, 1911

Scale 1 : 30,000,000 (480 miles = 1 inch)

0 100 200 400 600 Miles
0 200 400 600 800 Km.

Predominant Groups:

English
Scottish
Irish
French
Scandinavian
German
Austrian
Others

(a)

CANADA: POPULATION, 1951

Scale 1 : 30,000,000 (480 miles = 1 inch)

0 100 200 400 600 Miles
0 200 400 600 800 Km.

Density of Population:

Inhabitants to square mile: 2·6 26 128 256
Inhabitants to square km.: 1 10 50 100

Population of Cities or Urban Agglomerations:

○ 100,000–250,000
◎ 250,000–500,000
■ 500,000–1 Million
□ over 1 Million

(b)

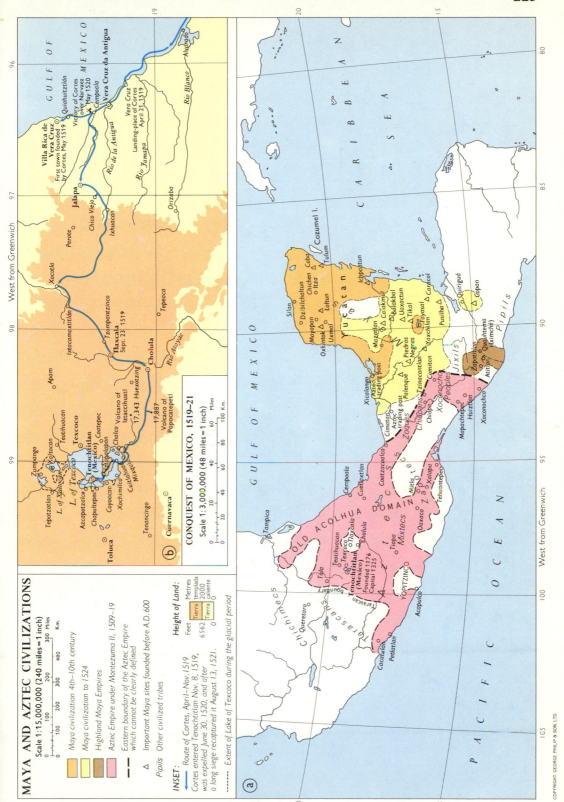

MAYA AND AZTEC CIVILIZATIONS

Scale 1:15,000,000 (240 miles=1 inch)

0 100 200 300 400 Km.

0 100 200 300 Miles

Maya civilization 4th–10th century

Maya civilization to 1524

Highland Maya Empires

Aztec Empire under Montezuma II, 1509–19

Eastern boundary of the Aztec Empire which cannot be clearly defined

△ Important Maya sites founded before A.D. 600

Pipils Other civilized tribes

Height of Land:

Feet	Metres
6562	Tierra templada 2000
0	Tierra caliente 0

INSET:

Route of Cortes, April–Nov. 1519. Cortes entered Tenochtitlan Nov. 8, 1519, was expelled June 30, 1520, and after a long siege recaptured it August 13, 1521.

‑‑‑‑ Extent of Lake of Texcoco during the glacial period

(b) CONQUEST OF MEXICO, 1519–21

Scale 1:3,000,000 (48 miles=1 inch)

0 20 40 60 80 100 Km.

0 20 40 60 Miles

GULF OF MEXICO

Villa Rica de Vera Cruz
First town founded by Cortes, May 1519

Quiahuitztlan

Victory of Cortes over Narvaez May 1520

Cempoala

Vera Cruz da Antigua

Vera Cruz Landing-place of Cortes April 21 1519

Rio de la Antigua

Rio Jamapa

Rio Blanco

Alvarado

Orizaba

Jalapa

Perote

Chico Viejo

Ixhuacan

Xocotla

Izompontzinco

Tepeaca

Tlaxcala Sept. 23 1519

Itzcamaxtitlan

Cholula

Rio Atoyac

Apam

Teotihuacan

Texcoco

Chalco Volcano of Iztaccíhuatl 17,343

Volcano of Popocatepetl 17,887

Huexotzinco

Zumpango

Xaltocan

L. of Xaltocan

Tepotzotlan

Tenochtitlan (Mexico)

L. of Texcoco

Azcapotzalco

Chapultepec

Coatepec

Coyoacan

Xochimilco

Chalco

Cuitlahuac

Mizqui

Cuernavaca

Tenancingo

Toluca

West from Greenwich

96 97 98 99

(a)

CARIBBEAN SEA

GULF OF MEXICO

PACIFIC OCEAN

Yucatan

Cozumel I.

Tulum

Coba

Chichen Itza

Dzibilchaltun

Mayapan

Uxmal

Oxintok

Loltun

Ichpaatun

Calakmul

Balakbal

Uaxactun

Tikal

Naranjo

Caracol

Quirigua

Copan

Mazatan

Piedras Negras

Yaxchilan

Palenque

Pusilha

Xicalango Aztec trading post

Cintapec Aztec trading post

Comitan

Tzinacantlan

Quen Santo Quiché

Atitlan

Zapotitlan

Pipils

Mixes

Zoques

Chiapas

Xoconocho

Mapachtepec

Huiztlan

Xoconochco

Tampico

Cempoala

Coatzacoalco

Cuetlaxtlan

Mitla

Oaxaca

Zapotecs

Tehuantepec

Teotihuacan

Tula

Texcoco

Tlaxcala

Cholula

Tenochtitlan (Mexico) Founded 1176 Capital 1325

YOPITZINCO

Tlapa

Mixtecs

OLD ACOLHUA DOMAIN

Tarascan boundary

Chichimecs

Queretaro

Tarascans

Tula

Acapulco

Cacatulan

Pedatlan

West from Greenwich

105 100 95 90 85 80

20 15

COPYRIGHT GEORGE PHILIP & SON, LTD.

NORTH AMERICA: THE EXPLORATION OF THE SOUTH-WEST TO 1618

Scale 1:15,000,000 (240 miles=1 inch)

Height of Land

Feet	Metres
6562	2000
3281	1000

Legend:
- Narvaez–de Vaca 1528-36
- de Soto 1539-42
- de Moscoso 1542-43
- de Coronado 1540-42 (principal route)
- Diaz 1540 (subsidiary expedition to Coronado)
- de Alarcón 1540
- Beltran-Espejo 1582-83
- Oñate 1596-1605
- Ute Indian tribe

ANNUAL RAINFALL

Rainfall: see inset

Inches	Cms.
20	50.8
10	25.4

Kern River, Serrano, Diegueño, Yavapai, Navaho, Ute, Colorado, Hopi, Tusayan (Hopi), Pueblos (Zuni), Cibola (Zuni), Zuñi, Jemez, Taos, Santa Fé, Albuquerque, Pecos (Cicuye), Keres, Tewa, Apache (Puebloans), Chiricahua, Tarahumare, Opata, Pima, Seri, Urés, Guaymas, Yaqui, Mayo, Alamos, Acaxee, Tepehuane, Chihuahua, Santa Barbara, Culiacán, Mazatlan, Durango, Zacatecas, Zacateco, Cora, Tepic, San Blas, Compostela, Guadalajara, Querétaro, Guanajuato, Tenochtitlán (Mexico), Tampico, Tamaulipeco, Pame, Lagunero, Coahuilteco, Toboso, Concho, Rio Grande, El Paso, Yuma, Cochimi, Waicuri, Gulf of California, Pacific Ocean, Gulf of Mexico, Mississippi, Chickasaw, Choctaw, Mobila, Osage, Wichita, Tawakoni, Kichai, Caddo, Atakapa, Tonkawan Tribes, Natchez, Pacaha, Brazos

Route annotations:
- Narvaez 1528
- Narvaez wrecked, de Vaca continued
- de Soto 1539-42
- de Moscoso 1542-43
- de Coronado 1540-42
- de Vaca 1535-36
- Beltran-Espejo 1582-83
- Oñate 1596-1605
- de Alarcón 1540
- Diaz 1540
- de Vaca
- de Moscoso
- Guachoya, de Soto died, de Moscoso took command
- Anilco, de Moscoso built seven pinnaces

Tropic of Cancer
West from Greenwich

Santa Fé, El Paso, Mazatlan, Tenochtitlán (inset)

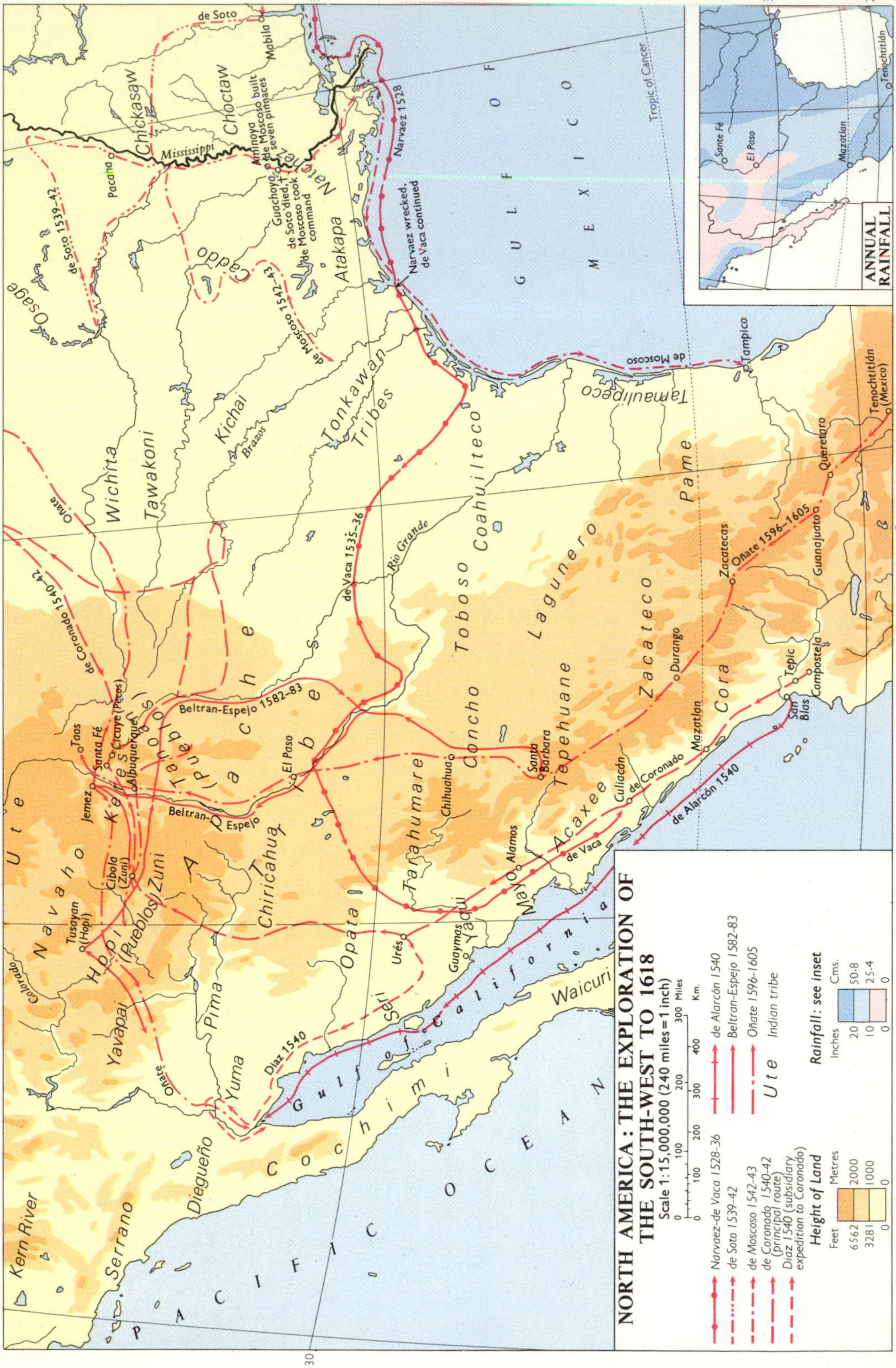

COPYRIGHT GEORGE PHILIP & SON LTD

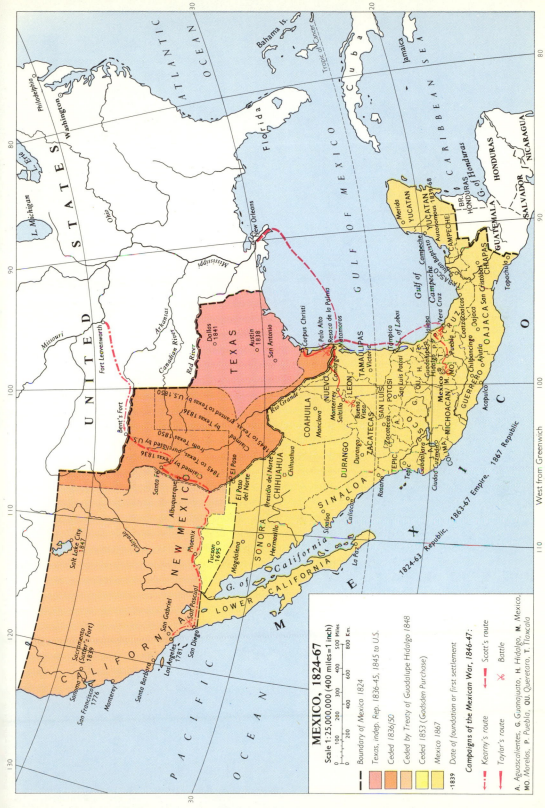

MEXICO, 1824-67
Scale 1:25,000,000 (400 miles=1 inch)

0 100 200 300 400 500 Miles
0 200 400 600 800 Km.

--- Boundary of Mexico 1824
Texas, indep. Rep. 1836-45, 1845 to U.S.
Ceded by Treaty of Guadalupe Hidalgo 1848
Ceded 1853 (Gadsden Purchase)
Mexico 1867
Date of foundation or first settlement

-1839

Campaigns of the Mexican War, 1846-47:
─·─·─ Kearny's route ────── Scott's route
────── Taylor's route ✗ Battle

A. Aguascalientes, G. Guanajuato, H. Hidalgo, M. Mexico,
MO. Morelos, P. Puebla, QU. Queretaro, T. Tlaxcala

COPYRIGHT GEORGE PHILIP & SON LTD.

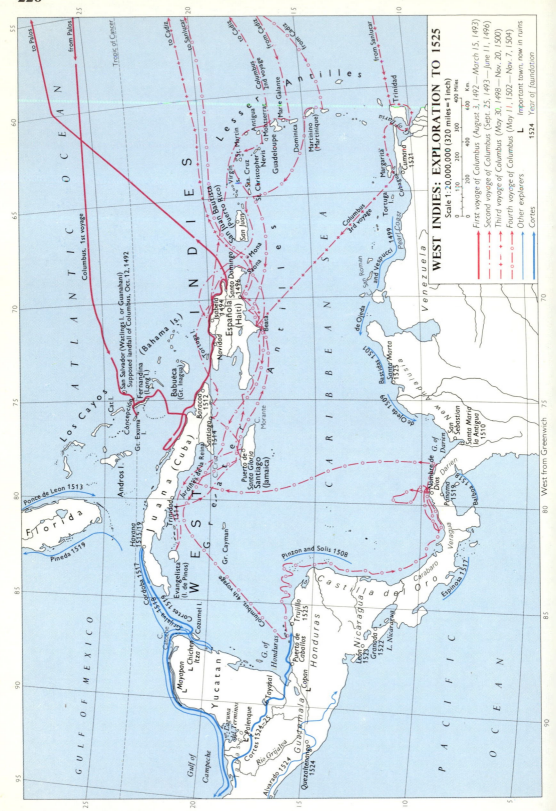

WEST INDIES: EXPLORATION TO 1525

Scale 1:20,000,000 (320 miles = 1 inch)

First voyage of Columbus (August 3, 1492 — March 15, 1493)
Second voyage of Columbus (Sept. 25, 1493 — June 11, 1496)
Third voyage of Columbus (May 30, 1498 — Nov. 20, 1500)
Fourth voyage of Columbus (May 11, 1502 — Nov. 7, 1504)
Other explorers
Cortes

L   Important town, now in ruins
1524   Year of foundation

0   100   200   300   400 Miles
0   200   400   600   Km.

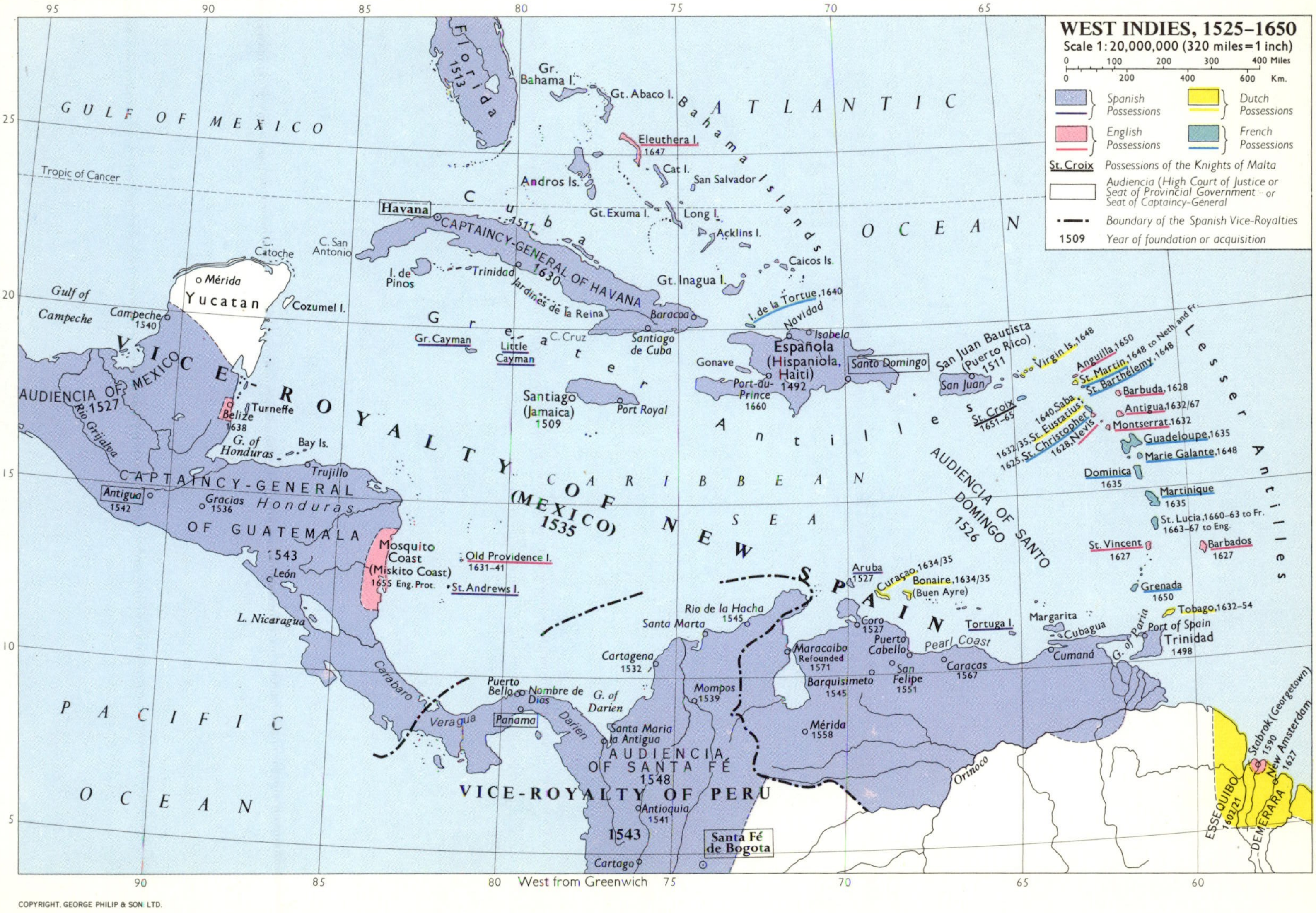
WEST INDIES, 1525–1650
Scale 1:20,000,000 (320 miles = 1 inch)
0 100 200 300 400 Miles
0 200 400 600 Km.
Spanish Possessions
Dutch Possessions
English Possessions
French Possessions
St. Croix Possessions of the Knights of Malta
Audiencia (High Court of Justice or Seat of Provincial Government or Seat of Captaincy-General
Boundary of the Spanish Vice-Royalties
1509 Year of foundation or acquisition
GULF OF MEXICO
ATLANTIC OCEAN
PACIFIC OCEAN
CARIBBEAN SEA
Tropic of Cancer
Florida 1513
Gr. Bahama I.
Gt. Abaco I.
Bahama Islands
Eleuthera I. 1647
Cat I.
Andros Is.
San Salvador
Gt. Exuma I.
Long I.
Acklins I.
Caicos Is.
Gt. Inagua I.
Havana
Cuba 1511
CAPTAINCY-GENERAL OF HAVANA 1630
Trinidad
Jardines de la Reina
I. de Pinos
C. San Antonio
C. Catoche
Mérida
Yucatan
Cozumel I.
Gulf of Campeche
Campeche 1540
Baracoa
Santiago de Cuba
C. Cruz
Greater Antilles
Gr. Cayman
Little Cayman
Santiago (Jamaica) 1509
Port Royal
I. de la Tortue, 1640
Navidad
Isabela
Española (Hispaniola, Haiti) 1492
Gonave
Port-au-Prince 1660
Santo Domingo
San Juan Bautista (Puerto Rico) 1511
San Juan
St. Croix 1651–65
Virgin Is., 1648
Anguilla, 1650
St. Martin, 1648 to Neth. and Fr.
St. Barthélemy, 1648
Barbuda, 1628
1640 Saba
1632/35 St. Eustatius
1625 St. Christopher
1628 Nevis
Antigua, 1632/67
Montserrat, 1632
Guadeloupe, 1635
Marie Galante, 1648
Dominica 1635
Martinique 1635
St. Lucia, 1660–63 to Fr. 1663–67 to Eng.
St. Vincent 1627
Barbados 1627
Grenada 1650
Tobago, 1632–54
Port of Spain
Trinidad 1498
Lesser Antilles
AUDIENCIA OF SANTO DOMINGO 1526
VICE-ROYALTY OF NEW SPAIN (MEXICO) 1535
AUDIENCIA OF MEXICO 1527
Rio Grijalva
Belize 1638
Turneffe
G. of Honduras
Bay Is.
Trujillo
CAPTAINCY-GENERAL OF GUATEMALA 1543
Antigua 1542
Gracias 1536
Honduras
León
L. Nicaragua
Mosquito Coast (Miskito Coast) 1655 Eng. Prot.
Old Providence I. 1631–41
St. Andrews I.
Carabaro
Veragua
Puerto Bello
Nombre de Dios
Panama
Darien
G. of Darien
Santa Maria la Antigua
Cartagena 1532
Santa Marta
Rio de la Hacha 1545
Mompos 1539
AUDIENCIA OF SANTA FÉ 1548
VICE-ROYALTY OF PERU 1543
Antioquia 1541
Cartago
Santa Fé de Bogota
Aruba 1527
Curaçao, 1634/35
Bonaire, 1634/35 (Buen Ayre)
Coro 1527
Maracaibo Refounded 1571
Barquisimeto 1545
Mérida 1558
Puerto Cabello
San Felipe 1551
Pearl Coast
Caracas 1567
Tortuga I.
Margarita
Cubagua
Cumaná
G. of Paria
Orinoco
ESSEQUIBO 1602/21
DEMERARA
Stabrok (Georgetown) 1590
New Amsterdam 1627
West from Greenwich
COPYRIGHT. GEORGE PHILIP & SON LTD.

WEST INDIES, 1650–1763

Scale 1:20,000,000 (320 miles=1 inch)

			Km.
0	200	400	600
0	100	200	300	400 Miles

Spanish Possessions

British Possessions

Portuguese Possessions

Dutch Possessions

French Possessions

Danish Possessions

Audiencia (High Court of Justice or Seat of Provincial Government)

Seat of Captaincy-General

Boundary of the Span. Vice-Royalties

Year of acquisition or period of possession

1688

A T L A N T I C   O C E A N

Lesser Antilles

Windward Islands

Anguilla 1650 now Fr.
St. Martin
St. Barthélemy
Saba
Barbuda
St. Eustatius
St. Christopher
Nevis
Antigua
English Harbour
Montserrat
Guadeloupe
Marie Galante
Dominica 1748–63 neutral, 1763 to Br.
Martinique
St. Lucia 1748–63 neutral, 1763 to Br.
Barbados
St. Vincent 1748–63 neutral, 1763 to Br.
Grenada 1763–79
Tobago (1677 to Fr., 1748–63 neutral, 1763 to Br.)
Trinidad

L e e w a r d   I s.

Leeward Is.

Margarita

Tortuga
Aruba 1688
Bonaire
Curaçao
Coro
San Felipe

Pearl Coast

Caracas

Orinoco

CAPTAINCY-GENERAL AND PRESIDENCY OF CARACAS 1742/86
Until 1739 to Vice-Royalty of New Spain

VICE-ROYALTY OF NEW GRANADA 1717/39–1819

Puerto Rico
San Juan
Mona
Saona

CAPTAINCY-GENERAL OF SANTO DOMINGO

Santo Domingo
Santiago de la Vega
Española (Hispaniola)
Cap-Français
Port-au-Prince
SAINT-DOMINGUE (HAITI) 1665/92
la Torue

G r e a t e r   A n t i l l e s

C A R I B B E A N   S E A

Barracoa
Santiago de Cuba
Trinidad
Jardines de la Reina
Sta. Cruz
Santa Marta
a C. Cruz de la Reina
Kingston (Port Royal)
Santiago (Jamaica) 1655/70

Little Cayman
Gr. Cayman 1655/70

CAPTAINCY-GENERAL OF CUBA
1762–63 Br. Occupation

Havana
I. de Pinos
C. San Antonio

Maracaibo
Barquisimeto
Mérida
Rio de la Hacha
Mompos
Cartagena
Santa Marta

VICE-ROYALTY OF NEW GRANADA

CAPTAINCY-GENERAL OF NEW GRANADA

Santa Fé de Bogota

Cartago

Rio Hacha

Puerto Bello
Nombre de Dios
G. of Darien
Panamá

B a h a m a   I s l a n d s

Gr. Bahama I.
Gr. Abaco I.
Eleuthera I.
Cat I.
San Salvador
Long I.
Cat I.
Acklins I.
Caicos Is.
Gt. Exuma I.
Andros Is.
Gt. Inagua I.
Bahamas 1670 to Eng.

Florida 1763

G U L F   O F   M E X I C O

Tropic of Cancer

C. Catoche
Cozumel I.
C. San Antonio
Yucatan
Mérida
Campeche
Gulf of Campeche
Rio Grijalba

AUDIENCIA OF MEXICO

VICE-ROYALTY OF NEW SPAIN

CAPTAINCY-GENERAL OF GUATEMALA

Antigua

Trujillo
Gracias á Dios
Honduras
León
L. Nicaragua
Belize
Turneffe
G. of Honduras

Mosquito Coast (Miskito Coast)
Old Providence I.
St. Andrews I.

P A C I F I C   O C E A N

West from Greenwich

to Portugal

DEMERARA
ESSEQUIBO
Stabroek (Georgetown)
New Amsterdam

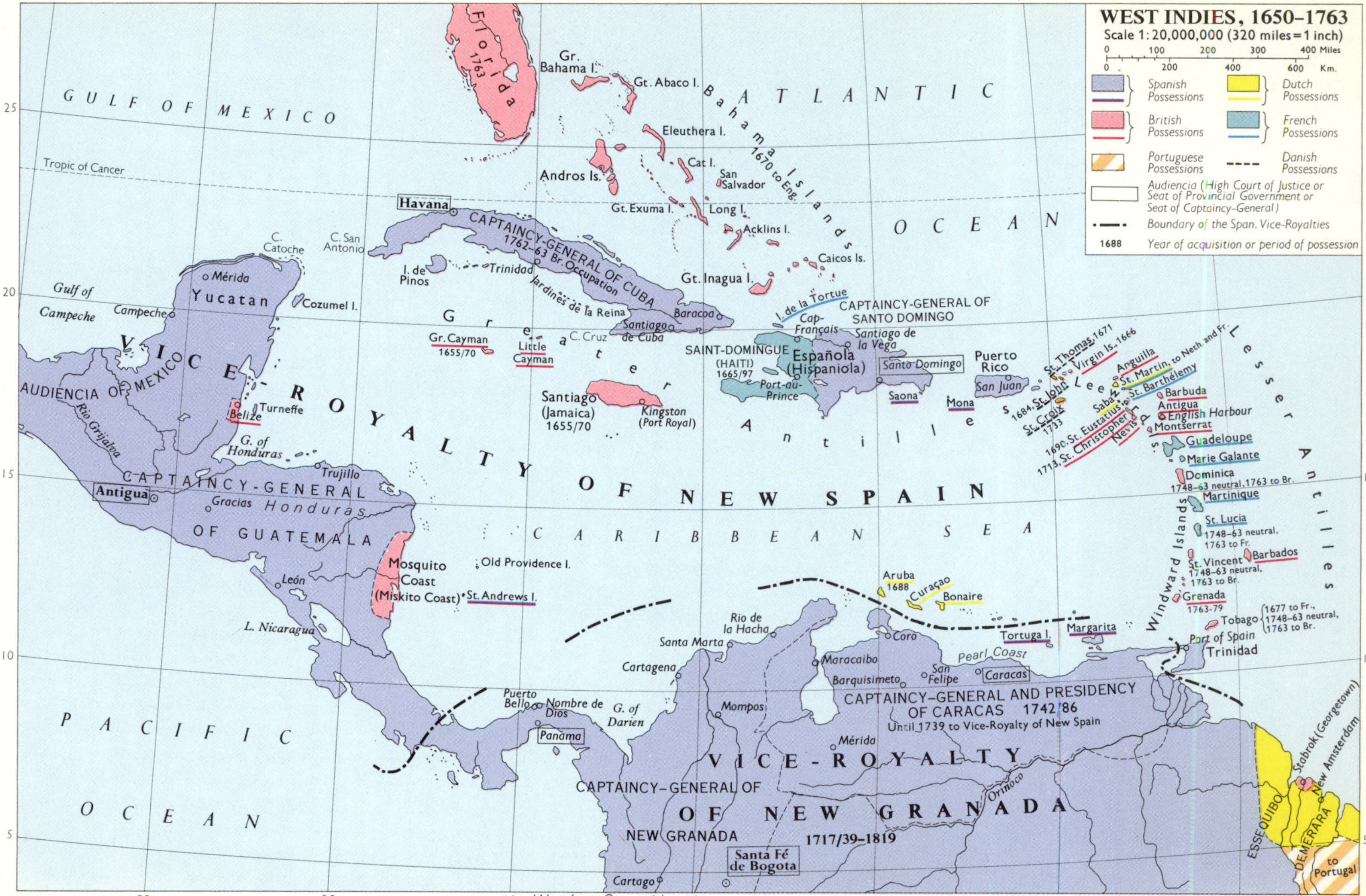

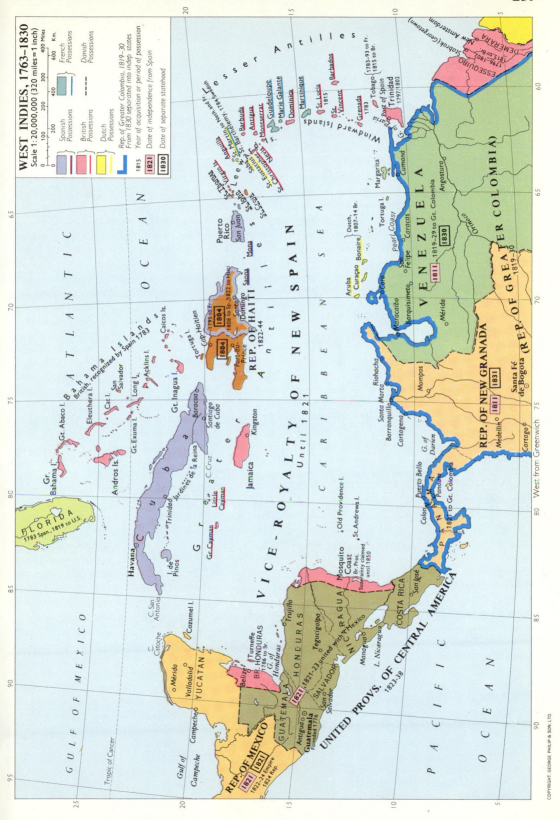
WEST INDIES, 1763–1830
Scale 1:20,000,000 (320 miles=1 inch)
Spanish Possessions
British Possessions
Dutch Possessions
French Possessions
Danish Possessions
Rep. of Greater Colombia, 1819–30 From 1830 separated into indep states
1815 Year of acquisition or period of possession
1821 Date of independence from Spain
1830 Date of separate statehood
GULF OF MEXICO
ATLANTIC OCEAN
CARIBBEAN SEA
PACIFIC OCEAN
VICE-ROYALTY OF NEW SPAIN
Until 1821
Greater Antilles
Lesser Antilles
Leeward Is.
Windward Islands
FLORIDA
1783 Span., 1819 to U.S.
Tropic of Cancer
Gr. Bahama I.
Gt. Abaco I.
Bahama Islands
British, recognized by Spain 1783
Eleuthera I.
Andros Is.
Cat I.
San Salvador
Gt. Exuma I.
Long I.
Acklins I.
Caicos Is.
Gt. Inagua I.
Havana
Cuba
C. San Antonio
I. de Pinos
Trinidad
Jardines de la Reina
Baracoa
Santiago de Cuba
Gr. Cayman
Little Cayman
C. Cruz
Jamaica
Kingston
Tortuga I.
Cap-Haïtien
1795 to Fr.
1804
1808 to Sp., 1822 to Haiti
Port-au-Prince
Santo Domingo
REP. OF HAITI
1822-44
Saona
Mona
Puerto Rico
San Juan
St. Thomas
Virgin Is.
St. John
St. Croix
Anguilla
St. Martin, to Neth. and Fr.
St. Barthélemy, 1784 Swedish
Saba
St. Eustatius
St. Christopher
Nevis
Barbuda
Antigua
Montserrat
Guadeloupe
Marie Galante
Dominica
Martinique
St. Lucia
1815
St. Vincent
Barbados
Grenada
1783
Tobago
1783–93 to Fr.
1815 to Br.
Port of Spain
Trinidad
1797/1802
G. of Paria
Margarita
Tortuga I.
Aruba
Curaçao
Bonaire
Dutch, 1807–14 Br.
Pearl Coast
Coro
Maracaibo
Barquisimeto
San Felipe
Caracas
Cumaná
VENEZUELA
1811
1819–29 to Gt. Colombia
1830
Mérida
Angostura
Orinoco
ESSEQUIBO
1796–1802
1815 to Br.
DEMERARA
Stabrok (Georgetown)
New Amsterdam
(REP. OF GREATER COLOMBIA)
1819–30
REP. OF NEW GRANADA
1811
1831
Medellín
Santa Fé de Bogota
Cartago
Mompos
Riohacha
Santa Marta
Barranquilla
Cartagena
G. of Darien
Puerto Bello
Colon
Panama
PANAMA
1821 to Gt. Colombia
Old Providence I.
St. Andrews I.
Mosquito Coast
Br. Prot.
Suzerainty claimed until 1850
COSTA RICA
San José
NICARAGUA
1821-23 united with Mexico
Managua
L. Nicaragua
HONDURAS
Tegucigalpa
Trujillo
SALVADOR
San Salvador
GUATEMALA
1821
Antigua
Guatemala
Founded 1776
UNITED PROVS. OF CENTRAL AMERICA
1823-38
Belize
BR. HONDURAS
1786 to Br.
Turneffe
G. of Honduras
Cozumel I.
C. Catoche
Mérida
Valladolid
YUCATAN
Campeche
Gulf of Campeche
REP. OF MEXICO
1821
1821
1822–24 Empire
1824 Rep.
West from Greenwich

COPYRIGHT. GEORGE PHILIP & SON. LTD.

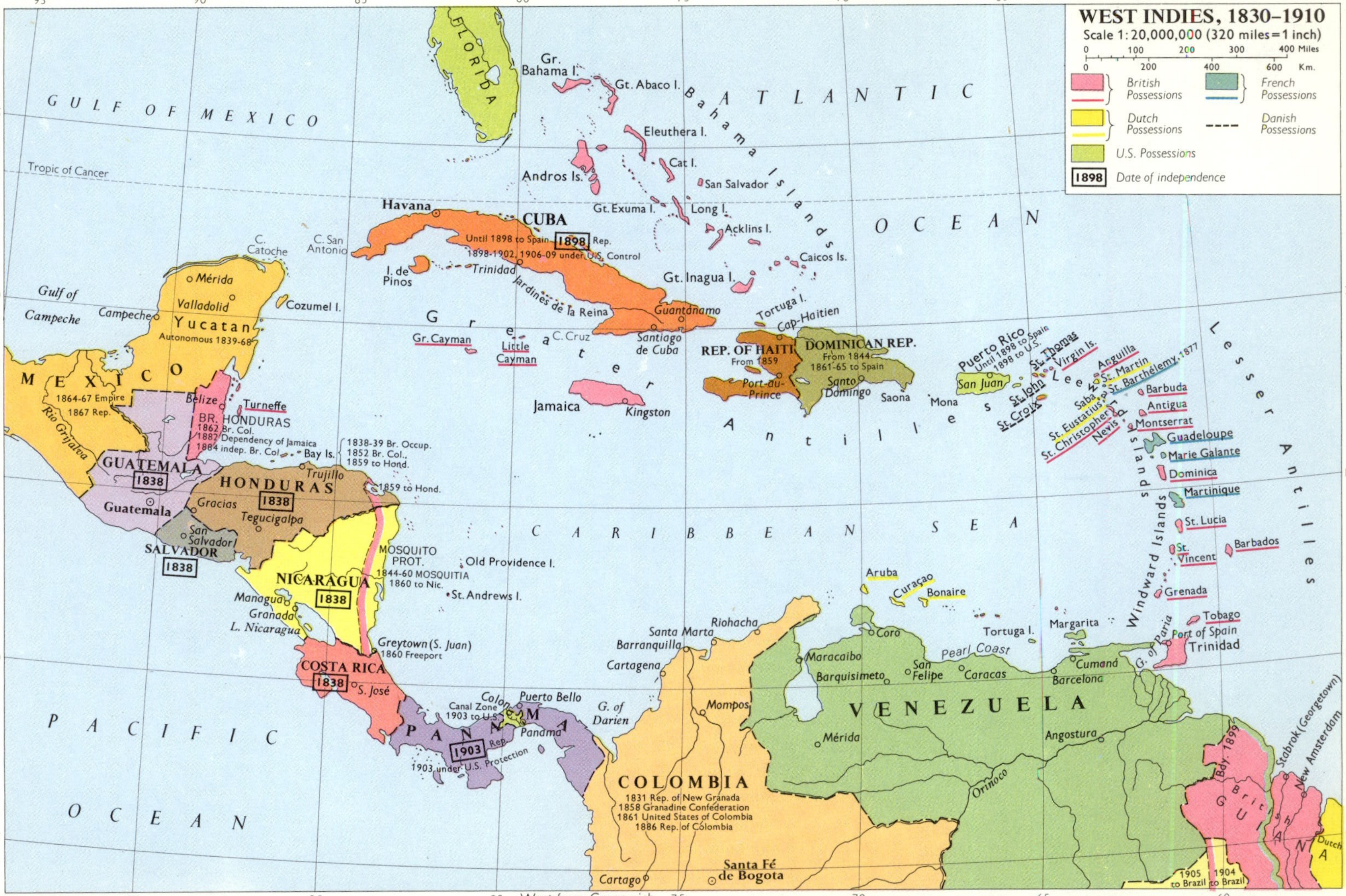
WEST INDIES, 1830–1910
Scale 1:20,000,000 (320 miles=1 inch)
0 100 200 300 400 Miles
0 200 400 600 Km.
British Possessions
French Possessions
Dutch Possessions
Danish Possessions
U.S. Possessions
1898 Date of independence
G U L F O F M E X I C O
A T L A N T I C O C E A N
Tropic of Cancer
FLORIDA
Gr. Bahama I.
Gt. Abaco I.
Bahama Islands
Eleuthera I.
Cat I.
Andros Is.
San Salvador
Gt. Exuma I.
Long I.
Acklins I.
Caicos Is.
Gt. Inagua I.
Havana
CUBA
Until 1898 to Spain 1898 Rep.
1898-1902, 1906-09 under U.S. Control
C. Catoche
C. San Antonio
I. de Pinos
Trinidad
Jardines de la Reina
Guantánamo
Santiago de Cuba
Tortuga I.
Cap-Haïtien
REP. OF HAITI
From 1859
Port-au-Prince
DOMINICAN REP.
From 1844
1861-65 to Spain
Santo Domingo
Saona
Mona
Puerto Rico
Until 1898 to Spain
1898 to U.S.
San Juan
St. Thomas
Virgin Is.
St. John
St. Croix
Anguilla
St. Martin
St. Barthélemy, 1877
Saba
St. Eustatius
St. Christopher
Nevis
Leeward Islands
Barbuda
Antigua
Montserrat
Guadeloupe
Marie Galante
Dominica
Martinique
St. Lucia
St. Vincent
Barbados
Grenada
Windward Islands
Tobago
Port of Spain
Trinidad
G. of Paria
Lesser Antilles
Greater Antilles
Gr. Cayman
Little Cayman
C. Cruz
Jamaica
Kingston
Gulf of Campeche
Campeche
Mérida
Valladolid
Yucatan
Autonomous 1839-68
Cozumel I.
MEXICO
1864-67 Empire
1867 Rep.
Rio Grijalva
Belize
Turneffe
BR. HONDURAS
1862 Br. Col.
1882 Dependency of Jamaica
1884 indep. Br. Col.
Bay Is.
1838-39 Br. Occup.
1852 Br. Col.,
1859 to Hond.
GUATEMALA
1838
Guatemala
HONDURAS
1838
Trujillo
Gracias
Tegucigalpa
1859 to Hond.
San Salvador
SALVADOR
1838
MOSQUITO PROT.
1844-60 MOSQUITIA
1860 to Nic.
NICARAGUA
1838
Managua
Granada
L. Nicaragua
Old Providence I.
St. Andrews I.
Greytown (S. Juan)
1860 Freeport
COSTA RICA
1838
S. José
Colon
Canal Zone
1903 to U.S.
Puerto Bello
Panamá
PANAMA
1903 Rep.
1903 under U.S. Protection
G. of Darien
C A R I B B E A N S E A
Aruba
Curaçao
Bonaire
Tortuga I.
Margarita
Riohacha
Santa Marta
Barranquilla
Cartagena
Mompos
COLOMBIA
1831 Rep. of New Granada
1858 Granadine Confederation
1861 United States of Colombia
1886 Rep. of Colombia
Cartago
Santa Fé de Bogota
Coro
Maracaibo
Barquisimeto
San Felipe
Caracas
Pearl Coast
Cumaná
Barcelona
VENEZUELA
Mérida
Angostura
Orinoco
BRITISH GUIANA
Bdy. 1899
Stabrok (Georgetown)
New Amsterdam
Dutch
1905 to Brazil
1904 to Brazil
P A C I F I C O C E A N
West from Greenwich
95
90
85
80
75
70
65
60
25
20
15
10
5

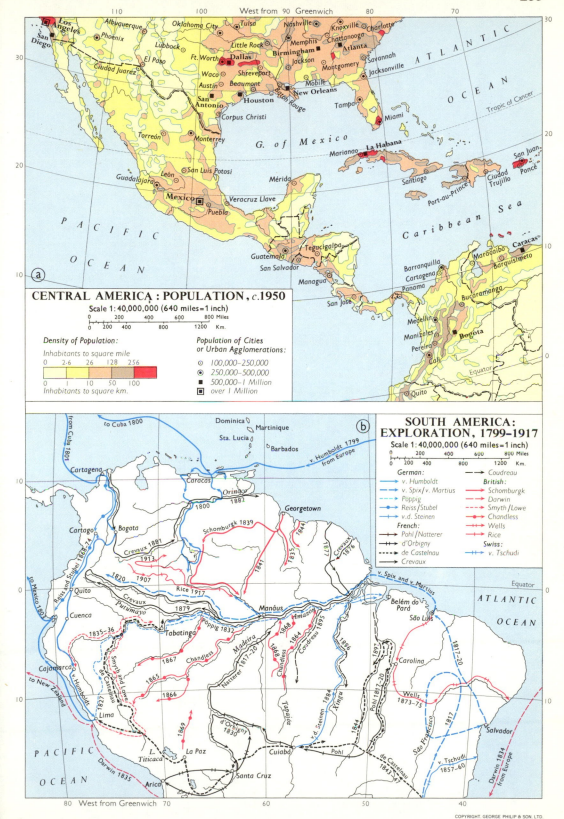

CENTRAL AMERICA : POPULATION, c.1950

Scale 1: 40,000,000 (640 miles = 1 inch)

0   200   400   600   800 Miles
0   200   400   600   800 Km.

Density of Population:

Inhabitants to square mile
0   2·6   26   128   256

0   1   10   50   100
Inhabitants to square km.

Population of Cities or Urban Agglomerations:

⊙ 100,000–250,000
◉ 250,000–500,000
■ 500,000–1 Million
▣ over 1 Million

SOUTH AMERICA: EXPLORATION, 1799–1917

Scale 1: 40,000,000 (640 miles = 1 inch)

0   200   400   600   800 Miles
0   200   400   600   800   1200 Km.

German:
— v. Humboldt
— v. Spix/v. Martius
— Pöppig
— Reiss/Stubel
— v.d. Steinen

French:
— Pohl/Natterer
— d'Orbigny
— de Castelnau
— Crevaux

— Coudreau

British:
— Schomburgk
— Darwin
— Smyth/Lowe
— Chandless
— Wells
— Rice

Swiss:
— v. Tschudi

COPYRIGHT. GEORGE PHILIP & SON. LTD.

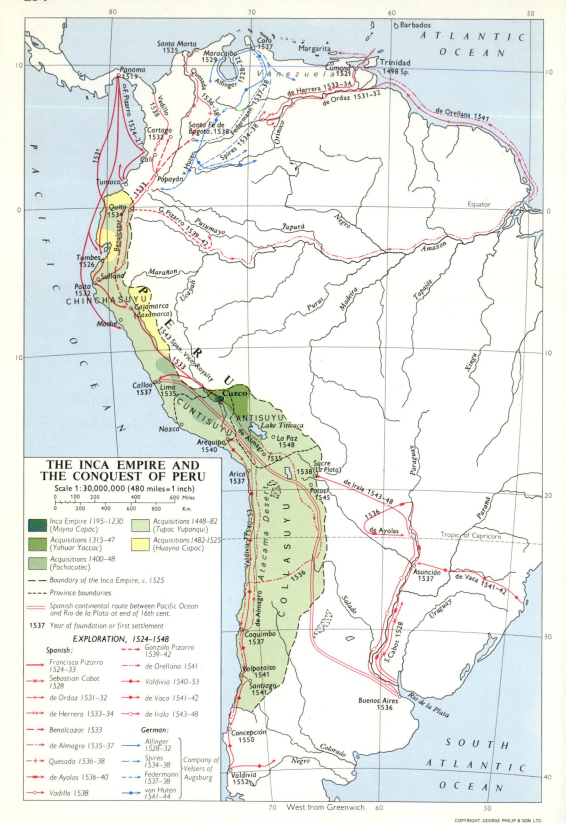

THE INCA EMPIRE AND
THE CONQUEST OF PERU

Scale 1:30,000,000 (480 miles=1 inch)

0 100 200   400   600 Miles

0 200 400   800 Km.

Inca Empire 1195–1230 (Mayna Capac)

Acquisitions 1448–82 (Tupac Yupanqui)

Acquisitions 1315–47 (Yahuar Yaccac)

Acquisitions 1482–1525 (Huayna Capac)

Acquisitions 1400–48 (Pachacutec)

— — Boundary of the Inca Empire, c. 1525

····· Province boundaries

Spanish continental route between Pacific Ocean and Rio de la Plata at end of 16th cent.

1537 Year of foundation or first settlement

EXPLORATION, 1524–1548

Spanish:

Francisco Pizarro 1524–33

Sebastian Cabot 1528

de Ordaz 1531–32

de Herrera 1533–34

Benalcazar 1533

de Almagro 1535–37

Quesada 1536–38

de Ayolas 1536–40

Vadillo 1538

Gonzalo Pizarro 1539–42

de Orellana 1541

Valdivia 1540–53

de Vaca 1541–42

de Irala 1543–48

German:

Alfinger 1528–32

Spires 1534–38

Federmann 1537–38

von Huten 1541–44

Company of Velsers of Augsburg

COPYRIGHT. GEORGE PHILIP & SON. LTD.

VICE-ROYALTY OF NEW SPAIN
1535

Dominica
1635 Fr.
Martinique, 1635 Fr.
St. Lucia, 1627–60 Eng.
St. Vincent
1627 Eng.
Barbados, 1627 Eng.

Rio de la Hacha
Santa Marta
Cartagena 1532
Mómpos
Tobago, 1632–54 Dutch
Trinidad
1498 Span.

Maracaibo
Coro
Puerto
Cabello
Caracas
1567
Cumaná

ATLANTIC

Panama
1519
1538
Barquisimeto
Mérida

AUDIENCIA
Santa Fé de
Bogotá

Antioquia
Cartago
OF
SANTA FÉ
1538
1548

Cali

Pasto
Popayán
Ibarra
PRESIDENCIA
Quito
1534
Portoviejo
OF QUITO
1563
Guayaquil
Cuenca

ESEQUIBO 1602/21 Dutch
DEMERARA
Stabrok, 1590 Eng.
(Georgetown)
New Amsterdam, 1627 Dutch
SURINAM, 1650 Eng.
Paromoribo, 1613 Dutch
Cayenne 1635

GUIANA
1596 Span.

Spanish
Portuguese
1494

Equator

DUTCH BRAZIL
1630–1654

Belém do Pará
1616
Gurupá
C. OF PARÁ
1616
Maranhão
(São Luis)
Port.
Ceará Port.
C. OF CEARÁ
1613
C. OF
MARANHÃO
1615
Natal 1597
C. OF PARAIBA
1532
Paraiba
Port.
Olinda Port.
C. OF PERNAMBUCO
1532
Recife Port.
1631
C. OF SERGIPE
1532
Ft. Maurits
Sergipe
del Rey
C. OF
BAHIA
1532
Bahia
Capital 1549–1763
Ilhéus 1534
C. OF
PORTO &
SEGURO
1532
Santa Cruz
Porto Seguro
C. OF
ESPIRITO
SANTO
1532
C. OF
RIO DE JANEIRO
1532
Rio de Janeiro
1565
Santos 1545

Túmbes
1526
Piura
Cajamarca
Trujillo
AUDIENCIA
Huánuco

VICE

Lima
1535
Huancavelica
Callao
Cuzco

L. Titicaca
Arequipa
La Paz

Putumayo
Japurá
Negro
Amazon
Amazon
Madeira
Purús
Marañón
Ucayali
Juruá
Tapajós
Xingú
Tocantins
São Francisco

1618

OF LIMA
1543

ROYALTY

PRESIDENCIA
OF
CHARCAS
1559

Santa Cruz

La Plata
1538
Potosí
1545
Arica

OF PERU
1543

CAPTAINCY-
GENERAL
AND
PRESIDENCIA
OF CHILE
1606

Jujuy
Salta
Tucumán
Santiago
del Estero
Catamarca
La Rioja
Córdoba 1573
Santa Fé

Mendoza
San Juan
1536
La Serena
Valparaiso
Santiago
1541
Chillán
Concepción
Ft. Arauco
Valdivia
1552
Osorno
Chiloé I.

San Luis

Buenos Aires
1536

Fort Olimpo

Paraguay
Paraná
Uruguay
Paraná

1609–31

1630
Asunción
1537
Ciudad Real
São Paulo 1532
São
Vicente
C. OF
SANTA CATARINA
1532
Santa Catarina I.
Destêrro
1640

DESERT
Atacama

Juan Fernandez Is.
1563

Magellan's Str.

PACIFIC OCEAN

Tropic of Capricorn

OCEAN

SOUTH AMERICA, c.1650

Scale 1:40,000,000 (640 miles = 1 inch)

0   200   400   600   800 Miles
0   200   400   600   800   1200 Km.

Spanish Lands		Dutch Lands
Portuguese Lands		French Lands
English Lands		

Jesuit mission states with dates

Demarcation line according to the
Treaty of Tordesillas, 1494

Division between Spanish and
Portuguese influence at the end of the
16th cent.

Audiencia (High Court of Justice or
Seat of Provincial Government or
Seat of Captaincy-General)

1511 Year of foundation of an Audiencia,
a Captaincy-General, or a Captaincy

1535 Year of foundation or first settlement

C. Captaincy

90   West from 80 Greenwich   70   60   50

COPYRIGHT. GEORGE PHILIP & SON. LTD.

SOUTH AMERICA IN THE 18TH CENTURY

Scale 1: 40,000,000 (640 miles = 1 inch)

0   200   400   600   800 Miles
0   200   400   800   1200 Km.

Possessions up to 1650 and later acquisitions:

Spanish Lands
Portuguese Lands
British Lands
Dutch Lands
French Lands

Jesuit mission states (until 1767)

Boundary of the Spanish Vice-Royalties 1777

Audiencia (High Court of Justice or Seat of Provincial Government or Seat of Captaincy-General)

1709 Year of foundation of an Audiencia, a Captaincy-General, or a Captaincy

1726 Year of foundation or first settlement

C. Captaincy

COPYRIGHT. GEORGE PHILIP & SON. LTD.

SOUTH AMERICA
1800–30

Scale 1 : 40,000,000 (640 miles=1 inch)

0   200   400   600   800 Miles
0 200 400 600 800 1000 1200 Km.

Rep. of Greater Colombia, 1819–30,
from 1830 separated into indep. states

1811 Date of independence from Spain

1811 Date of separate statehood

☆ Last Spanish fortresses 1826

⚔ Battle in the wars of independence
1810–27

COPYRIGHT. GEORGE PHILIP & SON. LTD.

SOUTH AMERICA
1830–1956

Scale 1 : 40,000,000 (640 miles=1 inch)

0	200	400	600 800 Miles
0	200 400	800	1200 Km.

Confederation of Peru and Bolivia 1836–39

Battle of the War of the Pacific 1879–84

Sea battle of World War I or II with date

1903 Date of independence

1907 Boundary with date of final agreement

Lima Seat of Pan-American Congress with date
1938

Essequibo, Demerara and Berbice were
united to form British Guiana from 1831

COPYRIGHT. GEORGE PHILIP & SON. LTD.

Caribbean Sea

Barranquilla
Cartagena
Maracaibo
Barquisimeto ■ Caracas
A T L A N T I C

Orinoco

Medellín
Bucaramanga
Manizales
Pereira ■ Bogotá
Cali

Quito
Guayaquil
Putumayo *Japurá* *Negro*
Amazon Belém
Equator

Marañón
Amazon
Ucayali
Madeira
Purus
Tapajós
Xingu
Tocantins
Fortaleza

Recife

São Francisco

Lima
Callão
L. Titicaca
La Paz
Salvador

Arequipa

Belo Horizonte

P A C I F I C   O C E A N

Tropic of Capricorn

Tucumán
Asunción
Paraguay
Paraná
Uruguay
São Paulo Niterói
Santos Rio de Janeiro
Curitiba

Porto Alegre
O C E A N

Santa Fé
Córdoba
Rosario
Mendoza
Buenos Aires
Valparaíso
Santiago
Avellaneda La Plata
Montevideo
Concepción
Salado
Mar del Plata
Negro Bahía Blanca

SOUTH AMERICA : POPULATION, *c.*1950

Scale 1 : 40,000,000 (640 miles = 1 inch)

| 0 | 200 | 400 | 600 | 800 Miles |

| 0 | 200 | 400 | 800 | 1200 | Km. |

Density of Population:

Inhabitants to square mile

| Unpopulated | 0 | 2·6 | 26 | 128 | 256 |

| | 0 | 1 | 10 | 50 | 100 |

Inhabitants to square km.

Population of Cities or Urban Agglomerations:

⊙ *100,000 – 250,000*
◉ *250,000 – 500,000*
■ *500,000 – 1 Million*
▣ *over 1 Million*

90   West from 80 Greenwich   70

COPYRIGHT. GEORGE PHILIP & SON. LTD.

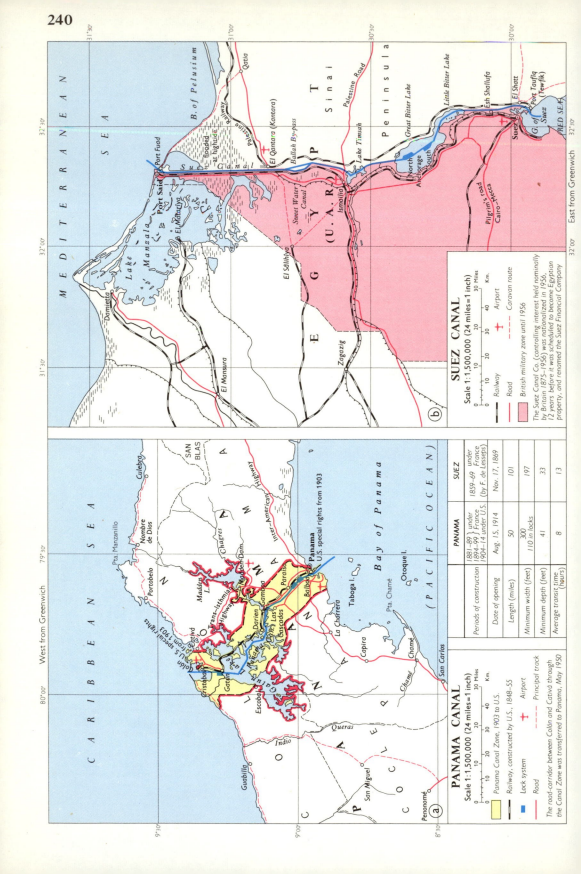

West from Greenwich · East from Greenwich

PANAMA CANAL
Scale 1:1,500,000 (24 miles=1 inch)
0 10 20 30 40 50 Km.
0 10 20 30 Miles

Panama Canal Zone, 1903 to U.S.
Railway, constructed by U.S., 1848–55
Lock system
Road
Airport
Principal track

The road-corridor between Colón and Cativá through the Canal Zone was transferred to Panama, May 1950

SUEZ CANAL
Scale 1:1,500,000 (24 miles=1 inch)
0 10 20 30 40 Km.
0 10 20 30 Miles

Railway
Road
Airport
Caravan route
British military zone until 1956

The Suez Canal Co. (controlling interest held nominally by Britain 1875–1956) was nationalized in 1956, 12 years before it was scheduled to become Egyptian property, and renamed the Suez Financial Company

	PANAMA	SUEZ
Periods of construction	1881–89 } under France 1894–99 } France 1904–14 under U.S.	1859–69 under France (by F. de Lesseps)
Date of opening	Aug. 15, 1914	Nov. 17, 1869
Length (miles)	50	101
Minimum width (feet)	300 110 in locks	197
Minimum depth (feet)	41	33
Average transit time (hours)	8	13

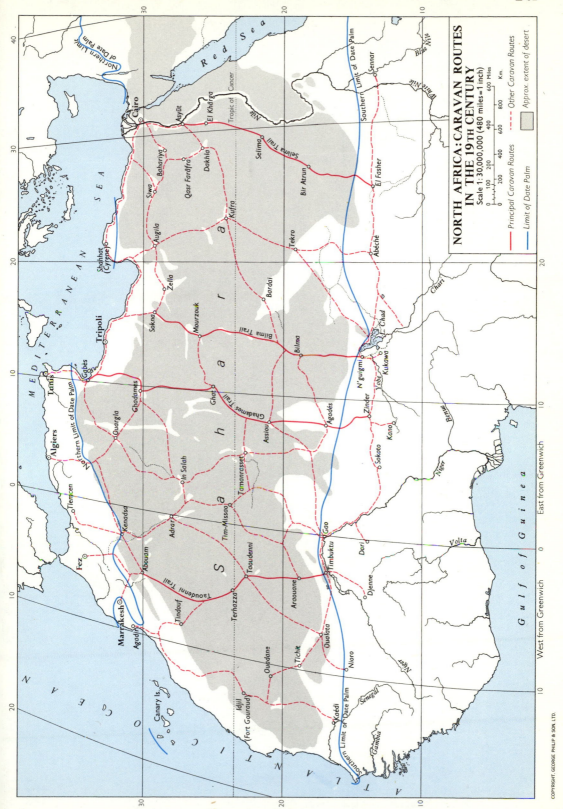

NORTH AFRICA: CARAVAN ROUTES
IN THE 19TH CENTURY
Scale 1:30,000,000 (480 miles=1 inch)

Principal Caravan Routes
Other Caravan Routes
Approx. extent of desert.
Limit of Date Palm

COPYRIGHT. GEORGE PHILIP & SON. LTD.

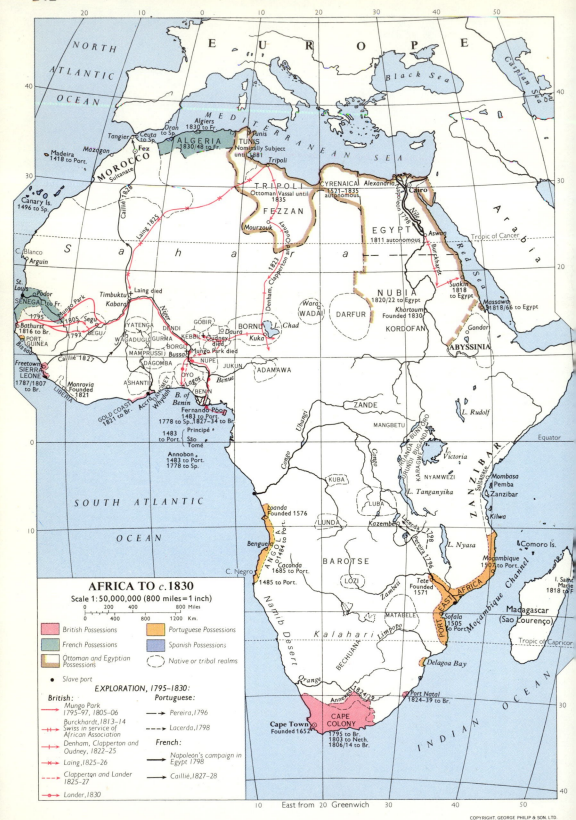

AFRICA TO c.1830

Scale 1:50,000,000 (800 miles = 1 inch)

0 200 400 800 MILES
0 400 800 1200 Km.

British Possessions
French Possessions
Ottoman and Egyptian Possessions
Portuguese Possessions
Spanish Possessions
Native or tribal realms

- Slave port

EXPLORATION, 1795–1830:

British:
— Mungo Park 1795–97, 1805–06
↦ Burckhardt, 1813–14
↦ Swiss in service of African Association
↦ Denham, Clapperton and Oudney, 1822–25
↦ Laing, 1825–26
--- Clapperton and Lander 1825–27
↦ Lander, 1830

Portuguese:
→ Pereira, 1796
--- Lacerda, 1798

French:
→ Napoleon's campaign in Egypt 1798
→ Caillié, 1827–28

East from Greenwich

COPYRIGHT, GEORGE PHILIP & SON. LTD.

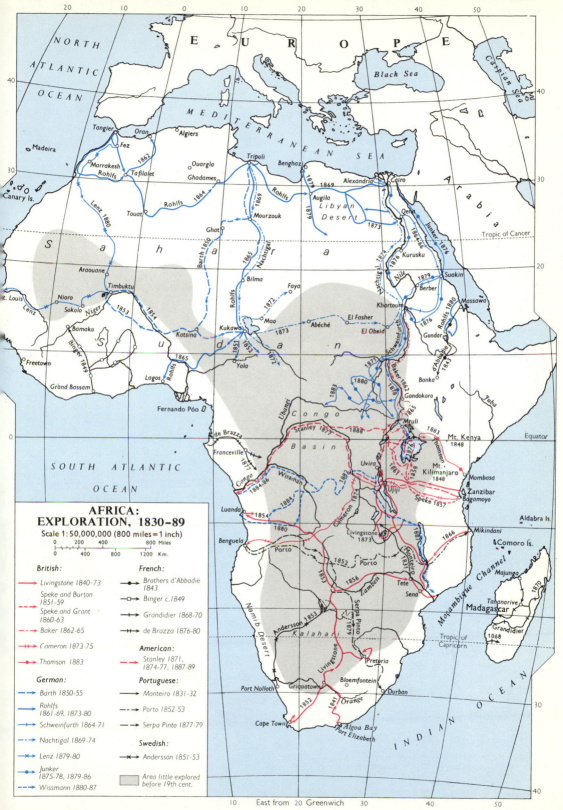

AFRICA:
EXPLORATION, 1830–89

Scale 1:50,000,000 (800 miles=1 inch)

0   200   400   600   800 Miles
0   400   800   1200 Km.

British:
Livingstone 1840–73
Speke and Burton 1851–59
Speke and Grant 1860–63
Baker 1862–65
Cameron 1873–75
Thomson 1883

German:
Barth 1850–55
Rohlfs 1861–69, 1873–80
Schweinfurth 1864–71
Nachtigal 1869–74
Lenz 1879–80
Junker 1875–78, 1879–86
Wissmann 1880–87

French:
Brothers d'Abbadie 1843
Binger c.1849
Grandidier 1868–70
de Brazza 1876–80

American:
Stanley 1871, 1874–77, 1887–89

Portuguese:
Monteiro 1831–32
Porto 1852–53
Serpa Pinto 1877–79

Swedish:
Andersson 1851–53

Area little explored before 19th cent.

COPYRIGHT. GEORGE PHILIP & SON. LTD.

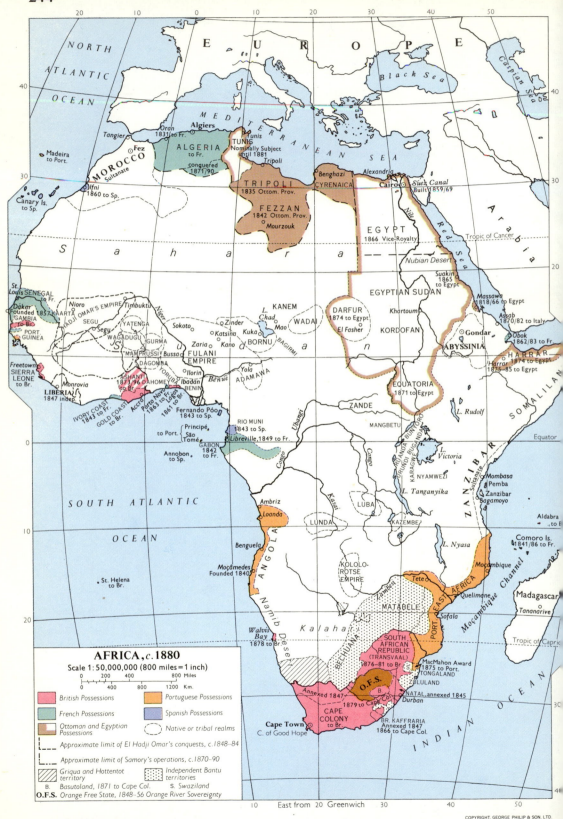

AFRICA, *c.*1880

Scale 1 : 50,000,000 (800 miles = 1 inch)

0   200   400   800 Miles
0   400   800   1200 Km.

British Possessions

French Possessions

Ottoman and Egyptian Possessions

Portuguese Possessions

Spanish Possessions

Native or tribal realms

Approximate limit of El Hadji Omar's conquests, c.1848–84

Approximate limit of Samory's operations, c.1870–90

Griqua and Hottentot territory

Independent Bantu territories

B. Basutoland, 1871 to Cape Col.   S. Swaziland

O.F.S. Orange Free State, 1848–56 Orange River Sovereignty

COPYRIGHT. GEORGE PHILIP & SON. LTD.

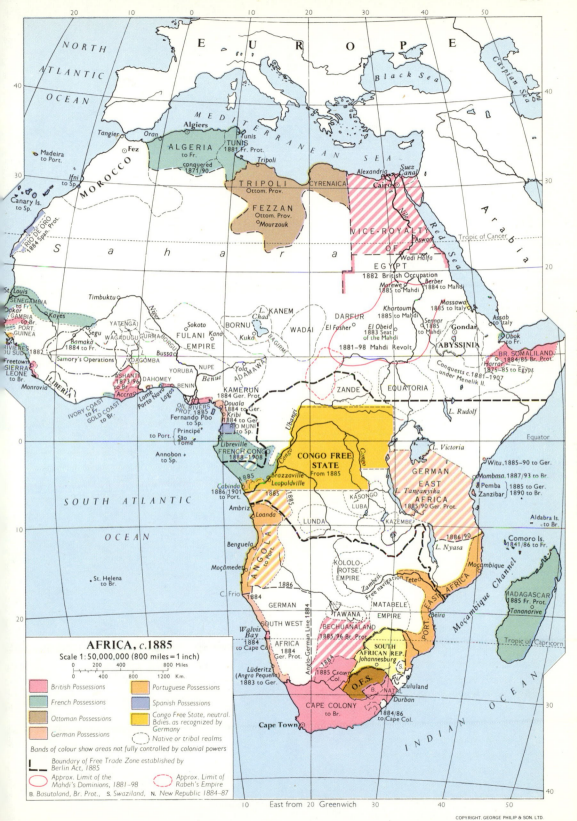

NORTH

ATLANTIC

OCEAN

EUROPE

Black Sea

Caspian Sea

Madeira
to Port.

Canary Is.
to Sp.

Tangier
Oran

MOROCCO

Fez

Algiers

MEDITERRANEAN SEA

ALGERIA
to Fr.
conquered
1871/90

TUNIS
1881 Fr. Prot.

Tripoli

TRIPOLI
Ottom. Prov.

CYRENAICA

Alexandria
Cairo

Suez
Canal

RIO DE ORO
1884 Span.Prot.

Ifni
to Fr.

FEZZAN
Ottom. Prov.
Mourzouk

Sahara

VICE-ROYALTY
OF
EGYPT

Nile

Red Sea

Arabia

Tropic of Cancer

St. Louis
SENEGAMBIA
to Fr.
Dakar
GAMBIA
to Br.
PORT.
GUINEA

Kayes

RIVIERES
DU SUD 1882

Freetown
SIERRA
LEONE
to Br.

Monrovia
LIBERIA

Timbuktu

Bamako
1884 to Fr.

Segu

WAGADUGU

YATENGA

GURMA

Samory's Operations

DAGOMBA

ASHANTI
1873/96
to Br.
Accra

IVORY COAST
to Fr.
GOLD COAST
to Br.

Niger

L. KANEM

Sokoto

BORNU

Kano
Kuka

FULANI

EMPIRE

Bussa

NUPE

YORUBA

DAHOMEY
Lome
Porto Novo
Lagos

Benue

Yola

BENIN

Wadi Halfa

Marewe
1885 to Mahdi

Berber
1884 to Mahdi

1882 British Occupation

Khartoum
1885 to Mahdi

El Obeid
1883 Seat
of the Mahdi

Sennar
1885
to Mahdi

Massawa
1885 to Italy

Assab
to Italy

DARFUR

El Fasher

WADAI

1881-98 Mahdi Revolt

Gondar

ABYSSINIA

Obok
to Fr.

BR. SOMALILAND
1884/85 Br. Prot.

Harrar
1875-85 to Egypt

Conquests c.1881-1907
under Menelik II.

ADAMAWA

ZANDE

EQUATORIA

KAMERUN
1884 Ger. Prot.
Douala
1884 to Ger.
Kribi
1884 to Ger.

OIL RIVERS
PROT. 1885

Fernando Póo
to Sp.

Príncipe
to Port.
São
Tomé

RIO MUNI
to Sp.

Annobon
to Sp.

Libreville
FRENCH CONGO
1888-1908

CONGO FREE
STATE
From 1885

Congo

L. Rudolf

L. Victoria

Equator

GERMAN
EAST
AFRICA
1885/90 Ger. Prot.

L. Tanganyika

Witu 1885-90 to Ger.

Mombasa 1887/93 to Br.

Pemba
Zanzibar
1885 to Ger.
1890 to Br.

Cabinda
1886/1901
to Port.

Brazzaville
Leopoldville

1885

SOUTH ATLANTIC

OCEAN

Ambriz

Loanda

Benguela

Moçamedes

ANGOLA
to Port.

St. Helena
to Br.

C. Frio

1884

1886

KASONGO

LUBA

LUNDA

KAZEMBE

KOLOLO-
ROTSE
EMPIRE

Zambezi

L. Nyasa

1886/90

Mocambique

EAST AFRICA

Tete

Free navigation

Beira

Aldabra Is.
to Br.

Comoro Is.
1841/86 to Fr.

MADAGASCAR
1885 Fr. Prot.
Tananarive

Mozambique Channel

Tropic of Capricorn

GERMAN
SOUTH
WEST
AFRICA
1884 Ger. Prot.

Walvis
Bay
1884
to Cape Col.

Lüderitz
(Angra Pequena)
1883 to Ger.

Anglo-German Line 1884

1884

1885 Crown
Col.

MATABELE
EMPIRE

TAWANA

BECHUANALAND
1885/96 Br. Prot.

SOUTH
AFRICAN
REP.
Johannesburg

S.

B.
O.F.S.

N.

Zululand

1884/86
to Cape Col.

NATAL
Durban

CAPE COLONY
to Br.

Cape Town

INDIAN
OCEAN

AFRICA, c.1885

Scale 1:50,000,000 (800 miles = 1 inch)

0   200   400   800 Miles

0   200   400   600   800   Km.

British Possessions
French Possessions
Ottoman Possessions
German Possessions

Portuguese Possessions
Spanish Possessions
Congo Free State, neutral.
Bdies. as recognized by
Germany

Native or tribal realms

Bands of colour show areas not fully controlled by colonial powers

Boundary of Free Trade Zone established by
Berlin Act, 1885

Approx. Limit of the
Mahdi's Dominions, 1881-98

Approx. Limit of
Rabeh's Empire

B. Basutoland, Br. Prot.,   S. Swaziland,   N. New Republic 1884-87

East from 20 Greenwich

COPYRIGHT. GEORGE PHILIP & SON. LTD.

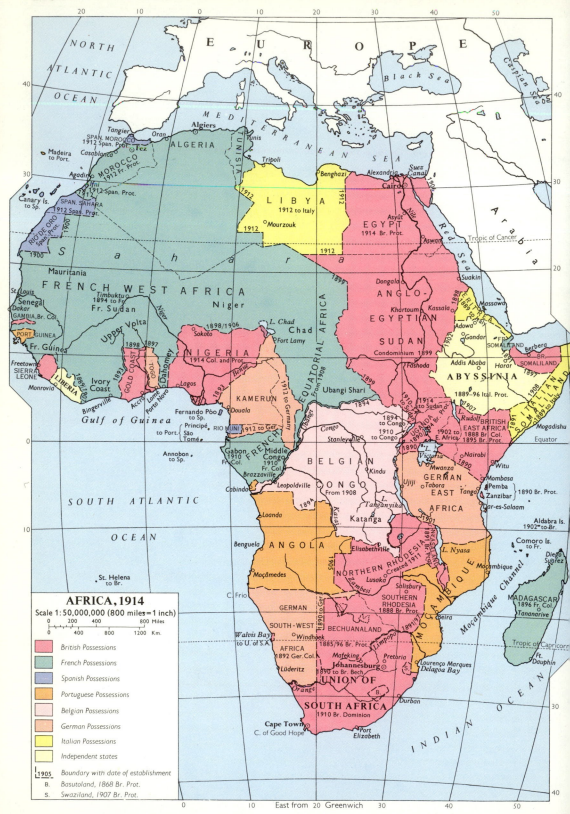

AFRICA, 1914

Scale 1:50,000,000 (800 miles=1 inch)

	British Possessions
	French Possessions
	Spanish Possessions
	Portuguese Possessions
	Belgian Possessions
	German Possessions
	Italian Possessions
	Independent states

1905 Boundary with date of establishment
B. Basutoland, 1868 Br. Prot.
S. Swaziland, 1907 Br. Prot.

COPYRIGHT. GEORGE PHILIP & SON. LTD.

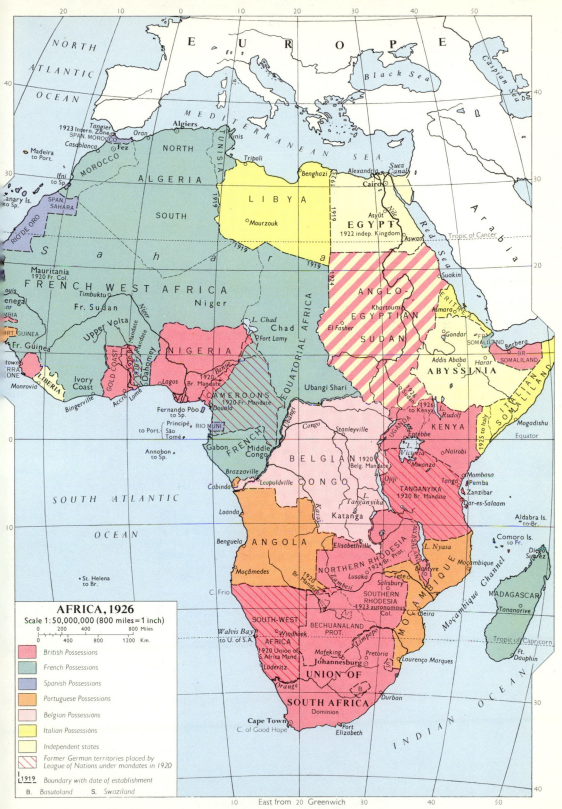

AFRICA, 1926

Scale 1:50,000,000 (800 miles=1 inch)

0	200	400		800 Miles
0	400	800	1200	Km.

British Possessions

French Possessions

Spanish Possessions

Portuguese Possessions

Belgian Possessions

Italian Possessions

Independent states

Former German territories placed by
League of Nations under mandates in 1920

1919 Boundary with date of establishment

B. Basutoland   S. Swaziland

East from 20 Greenwich

COPYRIGHT. GEORGE PHILIP & SON. LTD.

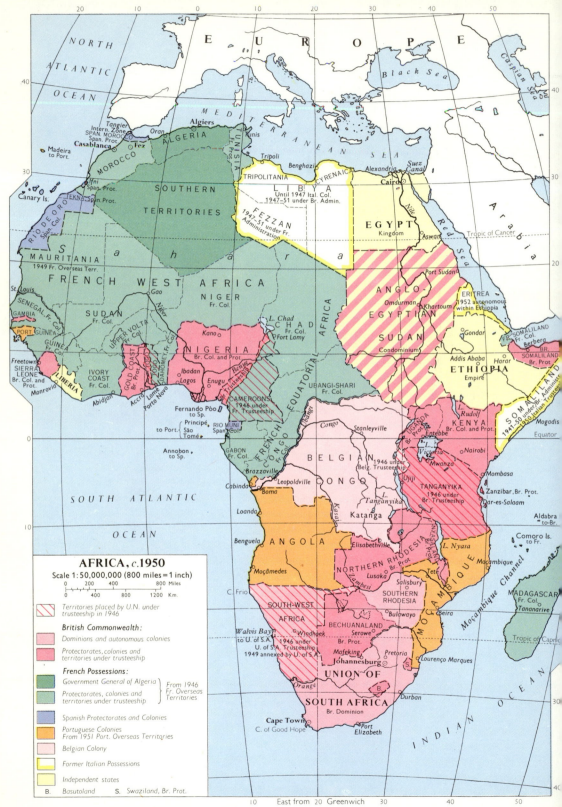

NORTH

ATLANTIC

OCEAN

40

30

Madeira
to Port.

Canary Is.

AFRICA, c.1950

Scale 1:50,000,000 (800 miles = 1 inch)

| 0 | 200 | 400 | | 800 Miles |
| 0 | 400 | 800 | 1200 | Km. |

Territories placed by U.N. under
trusteeship in 1946

British Commonwealth:

Dominions and autonomous colonies

Protectorates, colonies and
territories under trusteeship

French Possessions:

Government General of Algeria — From 1946

Protectorates, colonies and
territories under trusteeship — Fr. Overseas
Territories

Spanish Protectorates and Colonies

Portuguese Colonies
From 1951 Port. Overseas Territories

Belgian Colony

Former Italian Possessions

Independent states

B. Basutoland. S. Swaziland, Br. Prot.

EUROPE

MEDITERRANEAN SEA

Black Sea

Caspian Sea

Tangier
Intern. Zone
SPAN. MOROCO
Span. Prot.
MOROCCO
Casablanca
Fez
Oran
Algiers
Tunis
ALGERIA
TUNISIA
Tripoli
Benghazi
CYRENAICA
Alexandria
Cairo
Suez Canal

Ifni Span. Prot.
TEKNA Span. Prot.
SOUTHERN

TERRITORIES

TRIPOLITANIA
LIBYA
Until 1947 Ital. Col.
1947–51 under Br. Admin.
FEZZAN
1947–51 under Fr.
Administration

EGYPT
Kingdom
Aswan
Tropic of Cancer

Arabia
Red Sea

RIO DE ORO
Span. Col.
MAURITANIA
1949 Fr. Overseas Terr.
S a h a r a

Port Sudan
ANGLO-
EGYPTIAN

SUDAN
Omdurman
Khartoum
Condominium

ERITREA
1952 autonomous
within Ethiopia
Gondar
FR. SOMALILAND Fr. Col.
Berbera
BR. SOMALILAND Br. Prot.

St. Louis
SENEGAL Fr. Col.
GAMBIA
PORT. GUINEA
GUINEA Fr. Col.
Freetown
SIERRA LEONE
Br. Col. and Prot.
Monrovia
LIBERIA

FRENCH WEST AFRICA

SUDAN
Fr. Col.
UPPER VOLTA
IVORY
COAST
Fr. Col.
Abidjan
Gao
Niger
NIGER
Fr. Col.
GOLD COAST Br. Prot.
TOGO Br. Trusteeship
DAHOMEY Fr. Col.
Accra
Porto Novo
Kano
L. Chad
CHAD
Fr. Col.
Fort Lamy
NIGERIA
Br. Col. and Prot.
Ibadan
Lagos
Enugu
Benue
CAMEROONS
1946 under
Trusteeship

FRENCH EQUATORIAL AFRICA

UBANGI-SHARI
Fr. Col.

Addis Ababa
Harar
ETHIOPIA
Empire

SOMALILAND
1941–50 Br. Administ.
1950 Italian Col.

Fernando Pòo
to Sp.
Principé
to Port.
São
Tomé
RIO MUNI
Span. Col.
GABON
Fr. Col.
Brazzaville
FRENCH CONGO
Congo
Ubangi
Stanleyville
UGANDA Br. Prot.
L. Rudolf
KENYA
Br. Col. and Prot.
L. Victoria
Nairobi
Mombasa
Equator

Annobon
to Sp.

SOUTH ATLANTIC

OCEAN

Cabinda

Loanda
Boma
Leopoldville
BELGIAN CONGO
1946 under
Belg. Trusteeship
Katanga
L. Tanganyika
Ujiji
Mwanza
L. Kivu
TANGANYIKA
1946 under
Br. Trusteeship
Dar-es-Salaam
Zanzibar, Br. Prot.
Aldabra
to Br.

Comoro Is.
to Fr.

Benguela
ANGOLA
Moçamedes
Elisabethville
NORTHERN RHODESIA
Lusaka
L. Nyasa
NYASALAND Br. Prot.
Tete
Zambezi
Salisbury
SOUTHERN
RHODESIA
Bulawayo
Beira
MOÇAMBIQUE
Moçambique

MADAGASCAR
Fr. Col.
Tananarive
Moçambique Channel

C. Frio
SOUTH-WEST
AFRICA
1946 under
U. of S.A. Trusteeship
1949 annexed by U. of S.A.
Walvis Bay
to U. of S.A.
Windhoek
BECHUANALAND
Br. Prot.
Serowe
Mafeking
Pretoria
Johannesburg
UNION OF
SOUTH AFRICA
Br. Dominion
Orange
Cape Town
C. of Good Hope
Port
Elizabeth
Durban
Lourenço Marques
Tropic of Capricorn

INDIAN

OCEAN

East from Greenwich

COPYRIGHT. GEORGE PHILIP & SON LTD.

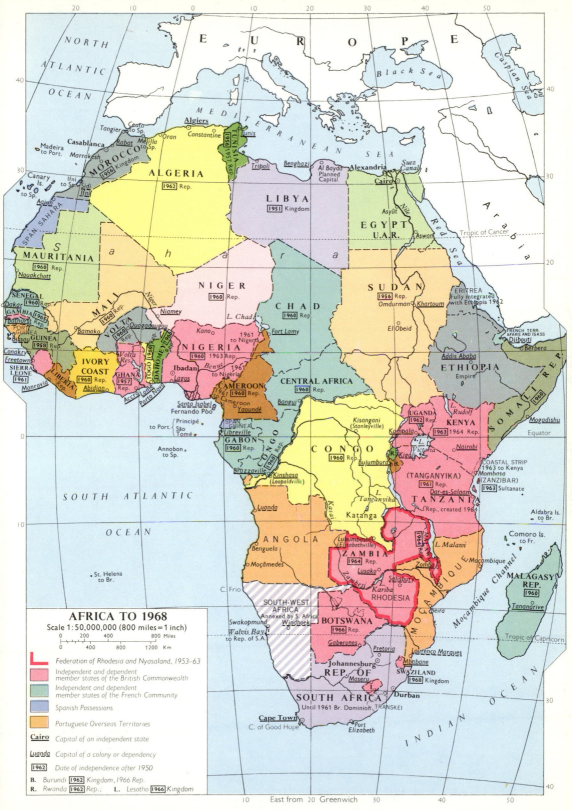
AFRICA TO 1968
Scale 1:50,000,000 (800 miles = 1 inch)
0 200 400 800 Miles
0 400 800 1200 Km
Federation of Rhodesia and Nyasaland, 1953–63
Independent and dependent member states of the British Commonwealth
Independent and dependent member states of the French Community
Spanish Possessions
Portuguese Overseas Territories
Cairo Capital of an independent state
Luanda Capital of a colony or dependency
1962 Date of independence after 1950
B. Burundi 1962 Kingdom, 1966 Rep.
R. Rwanda 1962 Rep.; L. Lesotho 1966 Kingdom
E U R O P E
NORTH ATLANTIC OCEAN
SOUTH ATLANTIC OCEAN
INDIAN OCEAN
MEDITERRANEAN SEA
Black Sea
Caspian Sea
Red Sea
Arabia
Tropic of Cancer
Tropic of Capricorn
Equator
Sahara
Madeira to Port.
Canary Is. to Sp.
Casablanca
Tangier
Ceuta to Sp.
Melilla to Sp.
Rabat
Marrakesh
MOROCCO 1956 Kingdom
Ifni to Sp.
Sidi Ifni
Aaiun
SPAN. SAHARA
Algiers
Oran
Constantine
ALGERIA 1962 Rep.
Tunis
TUNISIA 1956 1957 Rep.
Tripoli
Benghazi
Al Bayda Planned Capital
LIBYA 1951 Kingdom
Alexandria
Suez Canal
Cairo
Asyût
Nile
Aswan
EGYPT U.A.R.
MAURITANIA 1960 Rep.
Nouakchott
SENEGAL 1960 Rep.
Dakar
GAMBIA 1965
Bathurst
PORT. GUINEA
Bissau
GUINEA 1958 Rep.
Conakry
Freetown
SIERRA LEONE 1961
Monrovia
LIBERIA Rep.
IVORY COAST 1960 Rep.
Abidjan
MALI 1960 Rep.
Bamako
Niger
Niamey
VOLTA 1960 Rep.
Ouagadougou
GHANA 1957 Rep.
Accra
TOGO 1960 Rep.
Lomé
DAHOMEY 1960 Rep.
Porto Novo
NIGER 1960 Rep.
L. Chad
Kano
NIGERIA 1960 1963 Rep.
Ibadan
Lagos
Benue
1961 to Nigeria
CHAD 1960 Rep.
Fort Lamy
CAMEROON 1960 Rep.
1961 to Cameroon
Yaoundé
Santa Isabel
Fernando Póo
to Port. Principé São Tomé
SPAN. GUINEA
Libreville
GABON 1960 Rep.
Annobon to Sp.
CONGO 1960 Rep.
Brazzaville
CENTRAL AFRICA 1960 Rep.
Bangui
SUDAN 1956 Rep.
Omdurman
Khartoum
El Obeid
ERITREA Fully integrated with Ethiopia 1962
FRENCH TERR. AFARS AND ISASS
Djibouti
Berbera
Addis Ababa
ETHIOPIA Empire
SOMALI REP. 1960
Mogadishu
L. Rudolf
UGANDA 1962 Rep.
Kampala
KENYA 1963 1964 Rep.
Nairobi
L. Victoria
Kigali
Bujumbura
Kisangani (Stanleyville)
CONGO 1960 Rep.
Kinshasa (Léopoldville)
Kasai
L. Tanganyika
Katanga
COASTAL STRIP 1963 to Kenya
Mombasa
(ZANZIBAR) 1963 Sultanate
(TANGANYIKA) 1961 Rep.
Dar-es-Salaam
TANZANIA Rep., created 1964
Aldabra Is. to Br.
Luanda
ANGOLA
Benguela
Moçâmedes
Lubumbashi (Elisabethville)
ZAMBIA 1964 Rep.
Lusaka
Zambesi
MALAWI 1964 Rep.
L. Malawi
Zomba
Moçambique
Moçambique Channel
MOÇAMBIQUE
Comoro Is. to Fr.
MALAGASY REP. 1960
Tananarive
St. Helena to Br.
C. Frio
SOUTH-WEST AFRICA Annexed by S. Africa
Windhoek
Swakopmund
Walvis Bay to Rep. of S.A.
Salisbury
Kariba
RHODESIA
Beira
BOTSWANA 1966 Rep.
Gaberones
Pretoria
Johannesburg
Lourenço Marques
Mbabane
SWAZILAND 1968 Kingdom
REP. OF SOUTH AFRICA Until 1961 Br. Dominion
Maseru
L.
Durban
TRANSKEI
Cape Town
C. of Good Hope
Port Elizabeth
East from Greenwich

COPYRIGHT. GEORGE PHILIP & SON. LTD.

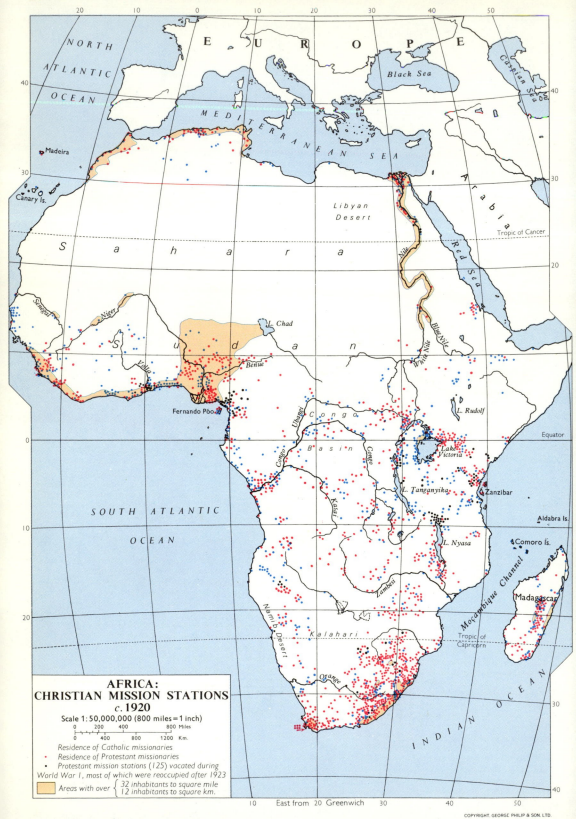

AFRICA:
CHRISTIAN MISSION STATIONS
*c.*1920

Scale 1:50,000,000 (800 miles=1 inch)

Residence of Catholic missionaries
Residence of Protestant missionaries
Protestant mission stations (125) vacated during
World War I, most of which were reoccupied after 1923
Areas with over { 32 inhabitants to square mile
                  12 inhabitants to square km.

COPYRIGHT. GEORGE PHILIP & SON. LTD.

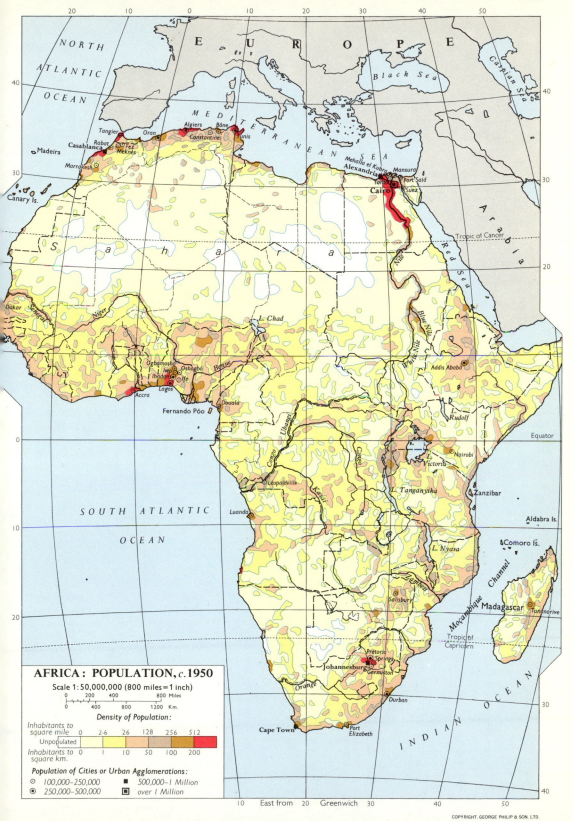

AFRICA: POPULATION, c.1950

Scale 1:50,000,000 (800 miles=1 inch)

0 200 400 800 Miles
0 400 800 1200 Km.

Density of Population:

Inhabitants to square mile: 0 2·6 26 128 256 512

Unpopulated

Inhabitants to square km.: 0 1 10 50 100 200

Population of Cities or Urban Agglomerations:

⊙ 100,000–250,000   ■ 500,000–1 Million
◉ 250,000–500,000   ▣ over 1 Million

COPYRIGHT. GEORGE PHILIP & SON. LTD.

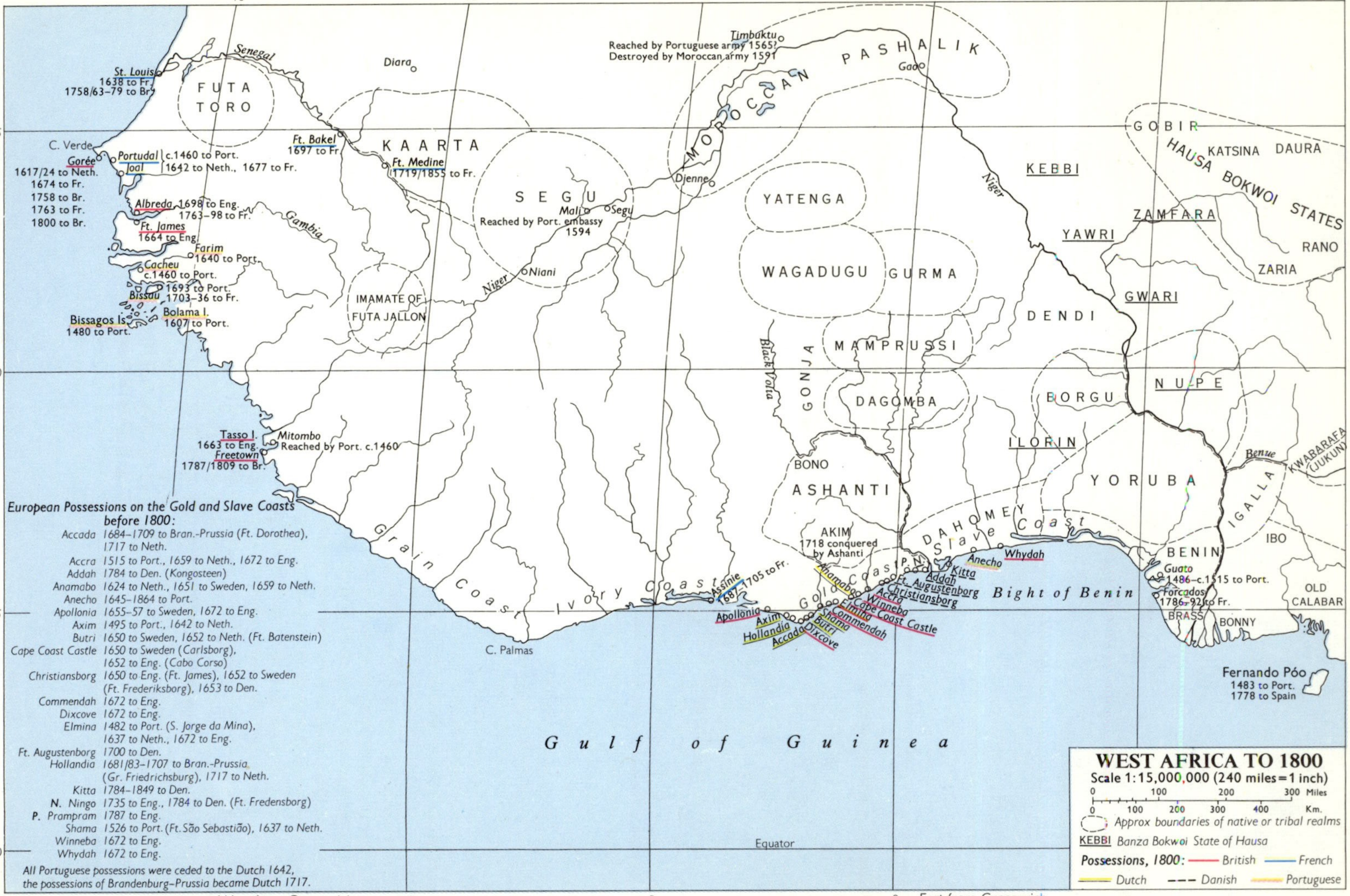
WEST AFRICA TO 1800
Scale 1:15,000,000 (240 miles=1 inch)
0 100 200 300 Miles
0 100 200 300 400 Km.
Approx boundaries of native or tribal realms
KEBBI Banza Bokwoi State of Hausa
Possessions, 1800: British French Dutch Danish Portuguese
European Possessions on the Gold and Slave Coasts before 1800:
Accada 1684–1709 to Bran.-Prussia (Ft. Dorothea), 1717 to Neth.
Accra 1515 to Port., 1659 to Neth., 1672 to Eng.
Addah 1784 to Den. (Kongosteen)
Anamabo 1624 to Neth., 1651 to Sweden, 1659 to Neth.
Anecho 1645–1864 to Port.
Apollonia 1655–57 to Sweden, 1672 to Eng.
Axim 1495 to Port., 1642 to Neth.
Butri 1650 to Sweden, 1652 to Neth. (Ft. Batenstein)
Cape Coast Castle 1650 to Sweden (Carlsborg), 1652 to Eng. (Cabo Corso)
Christiansborg 1650 to Eng. (Ft. James), 1652 to Sweden (Ft. Frederiksborg), 1653 to Den.
Commendah 1672 to Eng.
Dixcove 1672 to Eng.
Elmina 1482 to Port. (S. Jorge da Mina), 1637 to Neth., 1672 to Eng.
Ft. Augustenborg 1700 to Den.
Hollandia 1681/83–1707 to Bran.-Prussia (Gr. Friedrichsburg), 1717 to Neth.
Kitta 1784–1849 to Den.
N. Ningo 1735 to Eng., 1784 to Den. (Ft. Fredensborg)
P. Prampram 1787 to Eng.
Shama 1526 to Port. (Ft. São Sebastião), 1637 to Neth.
Winneba 1672 to Eng.
Whydah 1672 to Eng.
All Portuguese possessions were ceded to the Dutch 1642, the possessions of Brandenburg–Prussia became Dutch 1717.
St. Louis 1638 to Fr. 1758/63–79 to Br.
C. Verde
Gorée 1617/24 to Neth. 1674 to Fr. 1758 to Br. 1763 to Fr. 1800 to Br.
Portudal c.1460 to Port.
Joal 1642 to Neth., 1677 to Fr.
Albreda 1698 to Eng. 1763–98 to Fr.
Ft. James 1664 to Eng.
Farim 1640 to Port.
Cacheu c.1460 to Port.
Bissau 1693 to Port. 1703–36 to Fr.
Bolama I. 1607 to Port.
Bissagos Is. 1480 to Port.
Ft. Bakel 1697 to Fr.
Ft. Medine 1719/1855 to Fr.
Tasso I. 1663 to Eng.
Freetown 1787/1809 to Br.
Mitombo Reached by Port. c.1460
Senegal
Gambia
Niger
Black Volta
Benue
FUTA TORO
KAARTA
Diara
SEGU
Mali
Segu
Reached by Port. embassy 1594
Niani
IMAMATE OF FUTA JALLON
Djenne
Timbuktu
Reached by Portuguese army 1565?
Destroyed by Moroccan army 1591
MOROCCAN PASHALIK
Gao
YATENGA
WAGADUGU
GURMA
MAMPRUSSI
DAGOMBA
GONJA
BONO
ASHANTI
AKIM 1718 conquered by Ashanti
DENDI
BORGU
ILORIN
YORUBA
DAHOMEY
KEBBI
YAWRI
ZAMFARA
GWARI
NUPE
GOBIR
KATSINA
DAURA
HAUSA BOKWOI STATES
RANO
ZARIA
KWARARAFA (JUKUN)
IGALLA
IBO
BENIN
Guato 1486–c.1515 to Port.
Forcados 1786–92 to Fr.
BRASS
BONNY
OLD CALABAR
Fernando Póo 1483 to Port. 1778 to Spain
Grain Coast
Ivory Coast
Gold Coast
Slave Coast
Assinie 1687–1705 to Fr.
C. Palmas
Bight of Benin
Gulf of Guinea
Equator
West from Greenwich
East from Greenwich

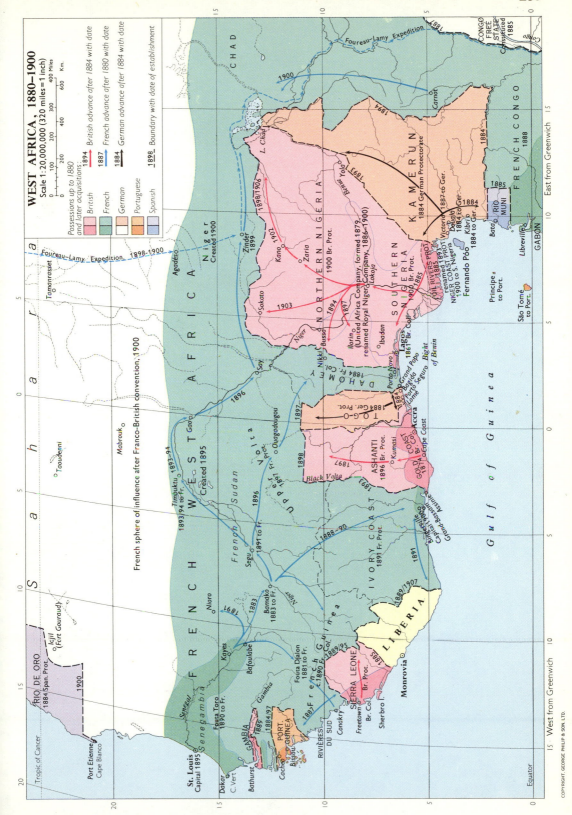
WEST AFRICA, 1880–1900
Scale 1: 20,000,000 (320 miles = 1 inch)
Possessions up to 1880 and later acquisitions:
British
French
German
Portuguese
Spanish
1894 British advance after 1884 with date
1887 French advance after 1880 with date
1884 German advance after 1884 with date
1898 Boundary with date of establishment
S a h a r a
Tropic of Cancer
RIO DE ORO
1884 Span. Prot.
1900
Icjil (Fort Gouraud)
Taoudenni
Tamanrasset
Mabrouk
Port Etienne
Cape Blanco
French sphere of influence after Franco-British convention, 1900
Foureau-Lamy Expedition, 1898-1900
Agadés
FRENCH WEST AFRICA
Created 1895
Niger
Created 1900
St. Louis
Capital 1895
Senegal
Senegambia
Dakar
C. Vert
Fouta Toro
1890 to Fr.
Kayes
Nioro
1891
Bafoulabe
1883
Timbuktu
1893/94 to Fr.
1893–94
Gao
French Sudan
Segu
1891 to Fr.
1896
Bamako
1883 to Fr.
Upper Volta
1897 Fr. Prot.
Ouagadougou
Say
Zinder
1899
CHAD
Bathurst
GAMBIA
1889
1884/97
Gambia
PORT. GUINEA
Cacheo
Bissau
Fouta Djalon
1881 to Fr.
1887
French Guinea
c.1890 Fr. Col.
1889/95
RIVIÈRES DU SUD
Conakry
SIERRA LEONE
Br. Prot.
Freetown
Br. Col.
Sherbro I.
1885
LIBERIA
1889/1907
Monrovia
Niger
1888–90
IVORY COAST
1891 Fr. Prot.
1891
Bingerville
Capital 1900
Grand-Bassam
Assinie
1893
1898
Black Volta
1897
ASHANTI
1896 Br. Prot.
Kumasi
GOLD COAST
1874 Br. Col.
Accra
Cape Coast
TOGO
1884 Ger. Prot.
1884
Lomé
Bagida
Porto Seguro
Grand Popo
DAHOMEY
1884 Fr. Col.
Porto Novo
Nikki
Lagos
1861 Br. Col.
Bight of Benin
Gulf of Guinea
Sokoto
1903
Kano
1902
Zaria
1898/1906
L. Chad
NORTHERN NIGERIA
1900 Br. Prot.
Bussa
1894
1897
Ilorin
(United Africa Company, formed 1879, renamed Royal Niger Company, 1886–1900)
Lokoja
Ibadan
Benue
Yola
SOUTHERN NIGERIA
1900 Br. Prot.
1885
OIL RIVERS PROT. 1885
renamed 1893
NIGER COAST PROT.
1900 to S. Nigeria
Fernando Póo
Principe to Port.
São Tomé to Port.
1893
KAMERUN
1884 German Protectorate
Victoria
1887 to Ger.
Douala
1884 to Ger.
Kibri
1884 to Ger.
1884
1894
Carnot
1900
Foureau-Lamy Expedition
1887
CONGO FREE STATE
Constituted 1885
Congo
Bata
RIO MUNI
1885
Libreville
FRENCH CONGO
1888
GABON
Equator
West from Greenwich
East from Greenwich

COPYRIGHT. GEORGE PHILIP & SON, LTD.

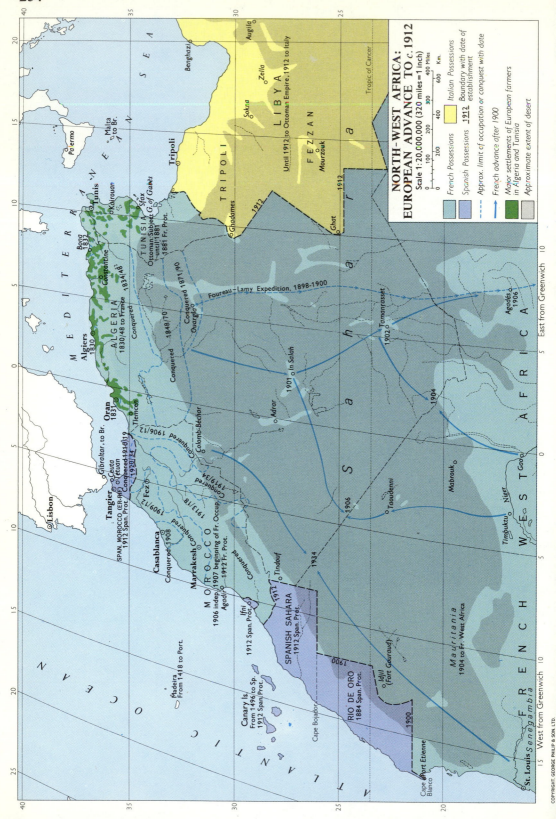

NORTH-WEST AFRICA:
EUROPEAN ADVANCE TO c. 1912

Scale 1:20,000,000 (320 miles=1 inch)

	French Possessions	Italian Possessions
	Spanish Possessions	1912 Boundary with date of establishment
		Approx. limit of occupation or conquest with date
		French advance after 1900
		Major settlements of European farmers in Algeria and Tunisia
		Approximate extent of desert

LIBYA

TRIPOLI

FEZZAN

Benghazi
Auglia
Zella
Sokra
Tripoli
Mourzouk
Ghadames
Ghot
Until 1912 to Ottoman Empire, 1912 to Italy

MEDITERRANEAN SEA

Palermo
Malta to Br.
Tunis
Kairouan
Sfax
G. of Gabes
Bona 1837
Constantine 1834/48
Algiers 1830
Oran 1831
Gibraltar, to Br.
Ceuta
Tetuan
Tlemcen

TUNISIA
Subject to Ottoman Empire until 1881
1881 Fr. Prot.

ALGERIA
1830/48 to France

Conquered 1871/90
Conquered 1848/70
Ouargla
Conquered
Adrar
In Salah
Tamanrasset
1902
Agadés 1906

Foureau–Lamy Expedition, 1898-1900

SAHARA

WEST AFRICA

Colomb-Béchar
Conquered 1906/12
Fez
Conquered 1909/12
Marrakesh
Conquered 1919/34
Conquered 1913/18
Agadir 1912 Fr. Prot.

MOROCCO
1906 indep, 1907 beginning of Fr. Occup.
1912 Fr. Prot.

Casablanca
Conquered 1908

Tangier
SPAN. MOROCCO (ER-RIF) Tetuan
1912 Span. Prot.
Conquered 1920/34

Ifni
1912 Span. Prot.

SPANISH SAHARA
1912 Span. Prot.

RIO DE ORO
1884 Span. Prot.

Mauritania
1904 to Fr. West Africa

Tindouf
1912
Taudenni
Mabrouk
Timbuktu
Niger
Gao
Mbrouk
Idjil (Fort Gouraud)
1900

FRENCH

Lisbon

ATLANTIC OCEAN

Madeira
From 1418 to Port.

Canary Is.
From 1496 to Sp.
1912 Span. Prot.

Cape Bojador

Cape Blanco
Port Etienne

St. Louis
Senegambia

Tropic of Cancer

East from Greenwich

West from Greenwich

COPYRIGHT, GEORGE PHILIP & SON, LTD.

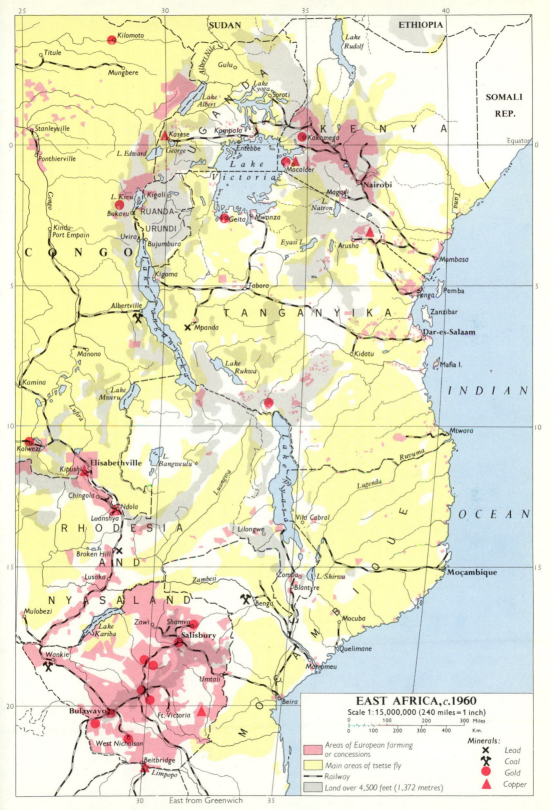

EAST AFRICA, c.1960

Scale 1:15,000,000 (240 miles = 1 inch)

0   100   200   300 Miles
0 100 200 300 400 Km.

Areas of European farming or concessions
Main areas of tsetse fly
Railway
Land over 4,500 feet (1,372 metres)

Minerals:
✕ Lead
⚒ Coal
⬤ Gold
▲ Copper

COPYRIGHT. GEORGE PHILIP & SON. LTD.

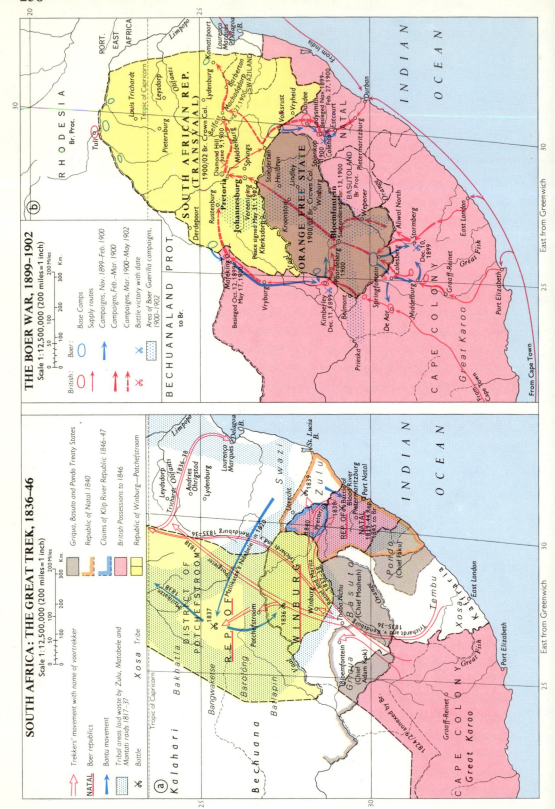

SOUTH AFRICA: THE GREAT TREK, 1836-46

Scale 1:12,500,000 (200 miles=1 inch)

	Griqua, Basuto and Pondo Treaty States
	Republic of Natal 1840
	Claims of Klip River Republic 1846-47
	British Possessions to 1846
	Republic of Winburg—Potche/stroom

Trekkers' movement with name of voortrekker

Boer republics

Bantu movement

Tribal areas laid waste by Zulu, Matabele and
Mantati raids 1817-37

✗ Battle

Xosa Tribe

THE BOER WAR, 1899–1902

Scale 1:12,500,000 (200 miles=1 inch)

	Base Camps
	Supply routes
	Campaigns, Nov. 1899–Feb. 1900
	Campaigns, Feb.–Mar. 1900
	Campaigns, Mar. 1900–May 1902
	Battle victory with date
	Area of Boer Guerilla campaigns, 1900–1902

Boer:

British:

SOUTH AFRICA, 1854-1910
Scale 1:12,500,000 (200 miles=1 inch)

Cape Colony and Natal 1854				
" " acquisitions 1854-95				
Orange Free State 1854				
" " acquisitions 1854-84				
South African Republic 1854				
" " acquisitions 1854-95				

1910 united as
Union of South Africa,
British Dominion

Boundary of Union of South Africa 1900

1858 Date of acquisition or period of possession

Lyd. Lydenburg. O.F.S. Orange Free State, S.A.R. South African Republic.

COPYRIGHT GEORGE PHILIP & SON, LTD.

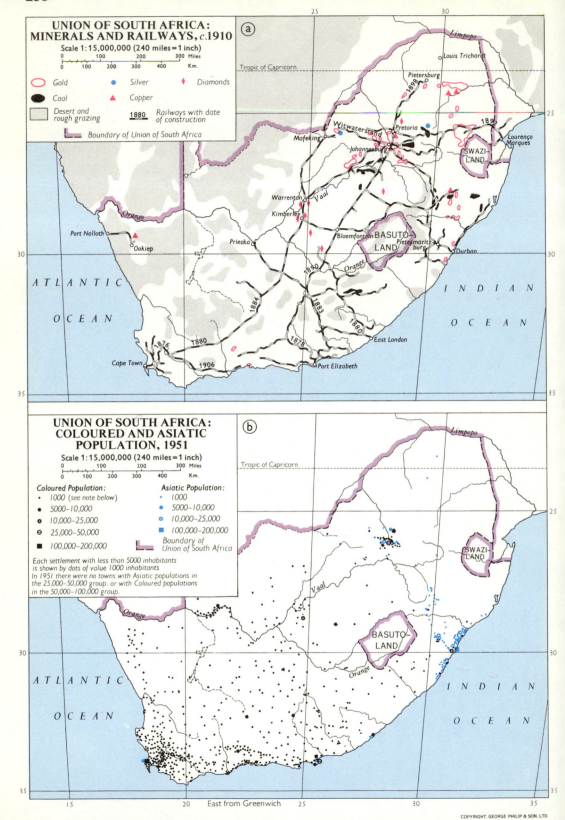

UNION OF SOUTH AFRICA: MINERALS AND RAILWAYS, c.1910
(a)

Scale 1:15,000,000 (240 miles=1 inch)

0   100   200   300 Miles

0   100   200   300   400 Km.

Gold
Coal
Silver
Copper
Diamonds

Desert and rough grazing

1880 — Railways with date of construction

Boundary of Union of South Africa

Tropic of Capricorn

Louis Trichardt
Pietersburg
1898
Witwatersrand
Mafeking
Pretoria
Johannesburg
SWAZI-LAND
Lourenço Marques
1895

Warrenton
Vaal
Kimberley
Prieska
Bloemfontein
BASUTO-LAND
Pietermaritzburg
Durban

Port Nolloth
Ookiep
Orange

ATLANTIC OCEAN

INDIAN OCEAN

1884
1890
Orange
1883
1880
East London

1876
1880
1878
Cape Town
1906
Port Elizabeth

UNION OF SOUTH AFRICA: COLOURED AND ASIATIC POPULATION, 1951
(b)

Scale 1:15,000,000 (240 miles=1 inch)

0   100   200   300 Miles

0   100   200   300   400 Km.

Coloured Population:
· 1000 (see note below)
• 5000–10,000
◦ 10,000–25,000
⊖ 25,000–50,000
■ 100,000–200,000

Asiatic Population:
· 1000
• 5000–10,000
◦ 10,000–25,000
■ 100,000–200,000

Boundary of Union of South Africa

Each settlement with less than 5000 inhabitants is shown by dots of value 1000 inhabitants
In 1951 there were no towns with Asiatic populations in the 25,000–50,000 group. or with Coloured populations in the 50,000–100,000 group.

Tropic of Capricorn

Limpopo

SWAZI-LAND

Vaal

BASUTO-LAND

Orange

ATLANTIC OCEAN

INDIAN OCEAN

East from Greenwich

COPYRIGHT. GEORGE PHILIP & SON. LTD.

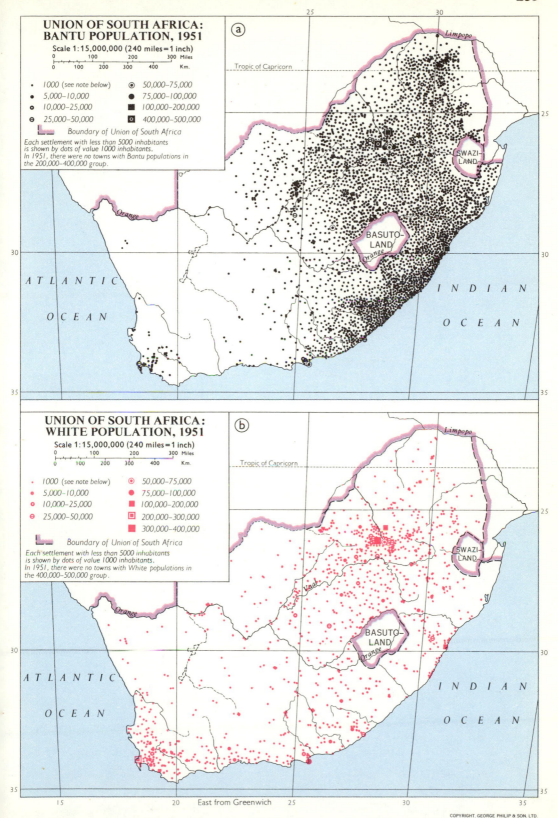

UNION OF SOUTH AFRICA: BANTU POPULATION, 1951

Scale 1:15,000,000 (240 miles=1 inch)

0   100   200   300 Miles
0   100   200   300   400   500 Km.

- 1000 (see note below)
- 5,000–10,000
- 10,000–25,000
- 25,000–50,000
- 50,000–75,000
- 75,000–100,000
- 100,000–200,000
- 400,000–500,000

▭ Boundary of Union of South Africa

Each settlement with less than 5000 inhabitants is shown by dots of value 1000 inhabitants. In 1951, there were no towns with Bantu populations in the 200,000–400,000 group.

Tropic of Capricorn

Limpopo

ATLANTIC OCEAN

Orange

SWAZILAND

BASUTOLAND

Orange

INDIAN OCEAN

UNION OF SOUTH AFRICA: WHITE POPULATION, 1951

Scale 1:15,000,000 (240 miles=1 inch)

0   100   200   300 Miles
0   100   200   300   400 Km.

- 1000 (see note below)
- 5,000–10,000
- 10,000–25,000
- 25,000–50,000
- 50,000–75,000
- 75,000–100,000
- 100,000–200,000
- 200,000–300,000
- 300,000–400,000

▭ Boundary of Union of South Africa

Each settlement with less than 5000 inhabitants is shown by dots of value 1000 inhabitants. In 1951, there were no towns with White populations in the 400,000–500,000 group.

Tropic of Capricorn

Limpopo

Vaal

ATLANTIC OCEAN

Orange

SWAZILAND

BASUTOLAND

Orange

INDIAN OCEAN

East from Greenwich

COPYRIGHT. GEORGE PHILIP & SON. LTD.

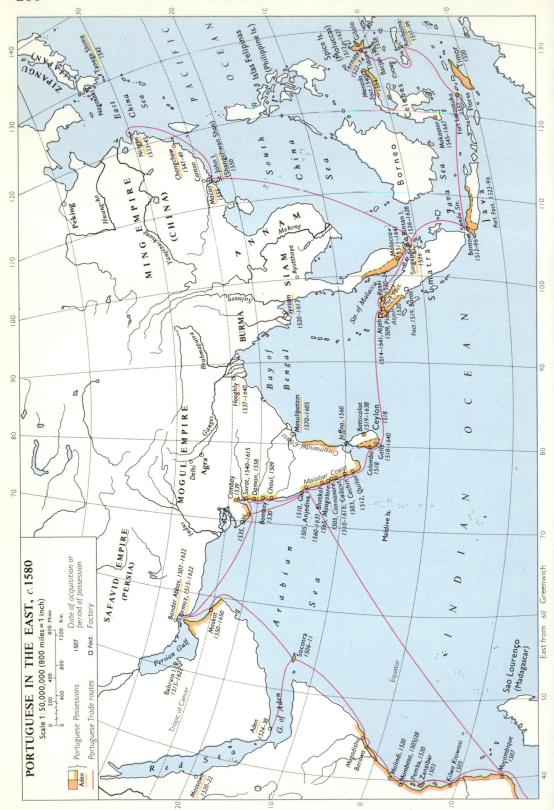

PORTUGUESE IN THE EAST, *c.*1580

Scale 1:50,000,000 (800 miles=1 inch)

| 0 | 200 | 400 | 600 | 800 Miles |

| 0 | 400 | 800 | 1200 Km. |

1507   Date of acquisition or period of possession

☐ Fact.   Factory

Portuguese Possessions
Portuguese Trade routes

Aden

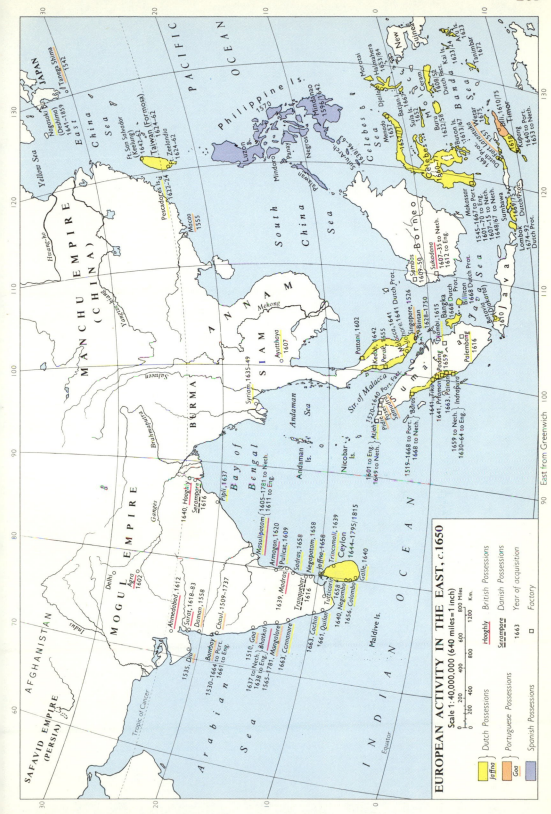
EUROPEAN ACTIVITY IN THE EAST, c.1650
Scale 1: 40,000,000 (640 miles=1 inch)
0 200 400 600 800 Miles
0 200 400 800 1200 Km.
Jaffna Dutch Possessions
Goa Portuguese Possessions
Spanish Possessions
Hooghly British Possessions
Serampore Danish Possessions
1663 Year of acquisition
Factory
SAFAVID EMPIRE (PERSIA)
AFGHANISTAN
MOGUL EMPIRE
MANCHU EMPIRE (CHINA)
BURMA
SIAM
ANNAM
JAPAN
Arabian Sea
Bay of Bengal
Andaman Sea
South China Sea
East China Sea
Yellow Sea
Celebes Sea
Banda Sea
Java Sea
PACIFIC OCEAN
INDIAN OCEAN
Tropic of Cancer
Equator
Indus
Ganges
Brahmaputra
Salween
Mekong
Yangtze-kiang
Hwang-ho
Delhi
Agra 1602
Ahmedabad, 1612
1535, Diu
Surat, 1618–83
Daman, 1558
Bombay 1530–1664 to Port. 1661 to Eng.
Chaul, 1509–1737
1510, Goa
Bhatkal 1637 to Neth. 1638 to Eng.
1565–1781, Mangalore
1663, Cannanore
1663, Cochin
1661, Quilon
Tutticorin 1658
1640, Negombo
1656, Colombo
Galle, 1640
Ceylon 1644–1795/1815
Trincomali, 1639
Jaffna, 1658
Negapatam, 1658
Sadras, 1658
Tranquebar 1616
1639, Madras
Pulicat, 1609
Armagon, 1620
Masulipatam 1605–1781 to Neth. 1611 to Eng.
Pipli, 1637
1640, Hooghly
Serampore 1616
Maldive Is.
Andaman Is.
Nicobar Is.
Syriam, 1635–49
Ayutthaya 1607
Str. of Malacca
Atjeh 1601 to Eng. 1649 to Neth.
Pidie Paser Samudra 1520–1640 Port. Fact.
Baros 1519–1668 to Port. 1668 to Neth.
1641, Tiku
1641, Priaman
1663, Painan
Indrapura 1659 to Neth. 1630–64 to Eng.
Padang 1659
Djambi, 1615
Palembang 1616
Sumatra
Pattani, 1602
Kedah, 1642
Perak, 1655
Malacca, 1641
Johore, 1641 Dutch Prot.
Singapore, 1526
Bintan 1628–1750
Bangka 1668 Dutch Prot.
Billiton 1668 Dutch Prot.
Batavia (Djakarta) 1610
Java
Sambas 1609–50
Sukadana 1607–35 to Neth. 1612 to Eng.
Borneo
Makassar 1545–1667 to Port. 1601–70 to Eng. 1607–15 to Neth. 1648/67 to Neth.
Lombok 1674–92 Dutch Prot.
Sumbawa 1669/75 Dutch Prot.
Fort Larantuka 1557
1667 Dutch Prot.
Wetar 1675
Dili, 1610/75
Timor
1618 Kupang 1640 to Port. 1653 to Neth.
Celebes 1660–77
Menado 1657
1657/77
Buton Is. 1613/67
Buru 1622/58
Sula Is. 1652
Batjan I. 1667
Djailolo
Morotai
Halmahera 1653/84
Moluccas
Ceram
1608/52 Dutch Fact.
Kai Is. 1623/24
Aru Is. 1623
Tanimbar 1672
New Guinea
Sulu Arch. 1638/46–63
Palawan
Mindoro
Panay
Negros
Mindanao 1596/1642
Luzon
Philippine Is. 1570
Macao 1555
Pescadores Is. 1622–24
Ft. San Salvador (Keelung) 1642–62
Taiwan (Formosa) 1624–62
Ft. Zeelandia 1624–62
Nagasaki (Deshima) 1641–1859
Tanega Shima 1542
East from Greenwich

COPYRIGHT, GEORGE PHILIP & SON, LTD.

262

MANCHU EMPIRE (CHINA)

Canton

BURMA
From 1769 Chin. Trib.

Tongking

Gulf of Tongking

Macao to Port.

Hainan

Irrawaddy

Rangoon

Andaman Is.
1789–96 to Br.

Andaman Sea

Ten Degree Channel

SIAM

Ayutthaya
Bangkok

Tourane
1787 to Fr.

SOUTH

Nicobar Is.
1756 to Den.
Gt. Nicobar

Gulf of Siam

Phnom Penh

CHINA

Poulo Condore
1787 to Fr.

SEA

Palawan
(Paragua)

Atjeh
1649 to Neth.
1810 to Br.

Pidie

Pasei

Pattani, 1795 to Br.
1814/17 to Neth.

Kedah
1718–95 Dutch Prot.
1786 to Br.

Penang I.

Wellesley Prov.1800 to Br.

Perak, 1655 to Neth.
1795 to Br.

Brunei

West Sumatra
1811–19 to Br.

Samadura

Strait of Malacca

Malay Peninsula

Natuna Is.

Sarawak

Nias
1693

Baros
1668

1649

West Coast

Malacca 1641 to Neth.,1795–1802 to Br.
1814/17 to Neth.

Johore
1641–1795 Dutch Prot.

Singapore, 1526 to Port.
1795/1819 to Br.

Borneo

Tiku

1641

Sambas
1795 to Br.

Mambava
1787 Dutch Prot.

1659 to Neth., 1795 to Br., Padang
1816 to Neth.

Priaman

Indragiri
1619–79

Rîouw Arch.

Sukadana
1699

1685 to Eng., 1663, Painan
1630–64 to Eng., 1659 to Neth., Indrapura

Batang Kapas

Sukadana

Bandjarmasin
1756–1809, 1816 to Neth.

Minangkabau

Djambi
1615

Lingga Arch.
1795 to Br.

Bangka
1668 Dutch Prot., 1806 to Neth.
1812 to Br., 1816 to Neth.

Martapura

1684 to Eng., Benkulen
1685 to Eng., Silebar

1684

Dutch Fact.

Palembang
1616 to Neth.
1812–16 to Br.

Billiton
1668 Dutch Prot.
1812 to Br.

Bandjarmasin
1745–1809 to Neth.
1812 to Br., 1816 to Neth.

1648/67 to Neth.
1812 to Br.
1816 to Neth.

1753

Sunda Str.

Batavia
(Djakarta)

Java Sea

Str. of Makassar

1628 to Br., Bantam
1684 to Neth.

1809

1619

1677/1813

Chirebon
1681

Tegal,1677

Semarang
1746

Japara, 1677
Demak, 1651

Rembang
1671/1743

Gresik, 1651

Madura
1743
1705

1813

1684

1705

MATARAM
1755 Neth. Prot.

Surabaja

1811

1743

Bali
1814–16 to Br.

Sumbawa
1669/75 Dutch Pre

INDIAN

Java

1811–16 to Br.

1812

1743
1777

Lombok
1674–92 Dutch Prot.

Bima
1680

EAST INDIES, 1700–1820
Scale 1:22,500,000 (360 miles = 1 inch)
0   100   200   300   400   500 Miles
0   200   400   600   800 Km.

OCEAN

Native states or unsettled areas

Dutch Possessions in 17th cent.

Dutch acquisitions to 1820

Spanish Possessions

Portuguese Possessions

Acquisitions of Dutch East India Company, from 1795 Dutch East Indies

British Possessions

Danish Possessions

1797   Date of acquisition or period of possession

□ Dutch factory
■ English factory

The colours also include protectorates and areas of privileged factories

110

East from Greenwich

Formosa
1683 to China

Tropic of Cancer

Tunas

M a r i a n a   o r   L a d r o n e   I s.
1668 to Spain

Saypan
Tinian

Guam
S. Rosa

P A C I F I C

Babuyan Is.

P
h
i
l
i
p
p
i
n
e   I s.
Spanish, 1762-64 to Br.

Luzon

Manila

Mindoro

Samar

Panay

Leyte

Negros

Bohol

Mindanao

Jolo

Sulu Arch.

Ulithi Atoll   Feis
Yap   C a r o l i n e   I s.
1696 to Spain
Gulu   Uleai

Palau Is.
(Pelew Is.)

O C E A N

Equator

Talaud Is.

C e l e b e s   S e a

Sangihe Is.
1677/84

Morotai

Menado
1657 to Neth.
1797 to Br.

Djailolo
Ternate
1801 to Br.
Tidore
1797 to Br.

Halmahera
1653/84

1657/77

G. of
Tomini

Batjan Is.

Obi Is.
1682

Peleng
1667

Sula Is.
1652

M
o
l
u
c
c
a
s

Celebes

0 to Br.   1817 to Neth.

Makassar

Butung Is.
1613/67 Dutch Prot.

Ceram
1796-1802

1810-17 to Br.

Ceram   S e a

1608/52 Dutch Fact.

Buru
1622/58

Amboina
1605 to Neth.
1796 to Br.
1817 to Neth.

Banda Is.

Kai Is.
1632/34

Aru Is.
1623

N e w   G u i n e a

Salajar
1675

B a n d a   S e a

F l o r e s   S e a

Wetar
1675

Damar
1646

Tanimbar Is.
1672

A r a f u r a   S e a

Flores
1667 Dutch
Prot.

Alor Is.

Dili
1610/75 to Port.

Solor
1613

Babar
1671
Moa
1668

Timor
1811-16 to Br.

1655

S a w u   S e a

Sumba

1662

Kupang
1653

T i m o r   S e a

A u s t r a l i a

20

130

140

20

10

10

0

0

10

10

120

130

COPYRIGHT. GEORGE PHILIP & SON. LTD.

EAST INDIES, 1820–1914
Scale 1:22,500,000 (360 miles = 1 inch)

| 0 | 100 | 200 | 300 | 400 | 500 Miles |
| 0 | 200 | 400 | 600 | 800 Km. |

British Possessions

British sphere of influence 1896

Straits Settlements, established
1826 by Br. East India Co.,
1867 Br. Crown Col.

Malay States under Br. Prot.:

Federated from 1895

Unfederated

Malay Provinces:

1824 Year of acquisition or
period of possession

J. Johore, K. Kedah, KE. Kelantan,
N.S. Negri Sembilan, PA. Pahang, PE. Perak, P. Perlis, S. Selangor, T. Trengganu

Dutch Possessions

French Possessions

French sphere of influence 1898

Portuguese Possessions

German Possessions

United States Possessions

East from Greenwich

110

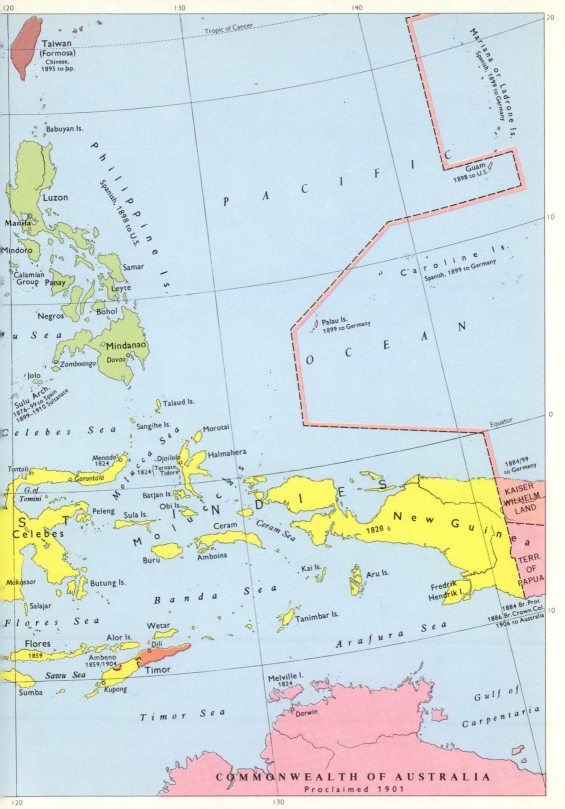

Taiwan
(Formosa)
Chinese,
1895 to Jap.

Tropic of Cancer

Mariana or Ladrone Is.
Spanish, 1899 to Germany

P A C I F I C

Babuyan Is.

Luzon

Guam
1898 to U.S.

Manila

Mindoro

Caroline Is.
Spanish, 1899 to Germany

Calamian
Group Panay   Samar

Leyte

Negros   Bohol

Palau Is.
1899 to Germany

u Sea

Mindanao

O C E A N

Zamboango   Davao

Jolo

Sulu Arch.
1876-99 to Spain
1899–1910 Sultanate

Talaud Is.

Celebes Sea

Equator

Sangihe Is.

Menado
1824   Djailolo
1824   Halmahera   Morotai

1884/99
to Germany

Tontoli   Gorontalo   Ternate
Tidore

KAISER
WILHELM
LAND

G. of
Tomini   Batjan Is.

S T   N   D   I   E   S

Peleng   Obi Is.   New Guinea

S   Sula Is.

Celebes   Ceram   1828

Ceram Sea

TERR.
OF
PAPUA

Buru   Amboina

Makassar   Butung Is.

Kai Is.   Aru Is.

Fredrik
Hendrik I.

1884 Br. Prot.
1886 Br. Crown Col.
1906 to Australia

Salajar

Banda Sea

Flores Sea

Tanimbar Is.

Wetar

Arafura Sea

Alor Is.   Dili

Flores
1859   Ambeno
1859/1904   Timor

Melville I.
1824

Gulf of

Sawu Sea   Kupang

Sumba

Carpentaria

Timor Sea

Darwin

COMMONWEALTH OF AUSTRALIA
Proclaimed 1901

COPYRIGHT. GEORGE PHILIP & SON, LTD.

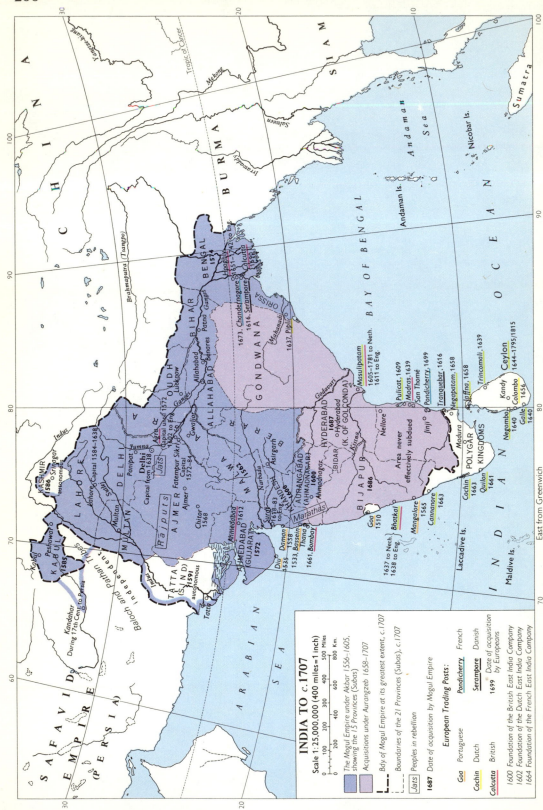

INDIA TO c.1707

Scale 1:25,000,000 (400 miles=1 inch)

The Mogul Empire under Akbar 1556–1605,
showing the 15 Provinces (Subas)

Acquisitions under Aurangzeb 1658–1707

Bdy of acquisition by Mogul Empire

Boundaries of the 21 Provinces (Subas), c.1707

Jats Peoples in rebellion

1687 Date of acquisition by Mogul Empire

European Trading Posts:

Goa Portuguese   Pondicherry French

Cochin Dutch   Serampore Danish

Calcutta British   1699 Date of acquisition
by Europeans

1600 Foundation of the British East India Company
1602 Foundation of the Dutch East India Company
1664 Foundation of the French East India Company

0 100 200 300 400 500 Miles
0 200 400 600 800 Km.

COPYRIGHT GEORGE PHILIP & SON. LTD.

East from Greenwich

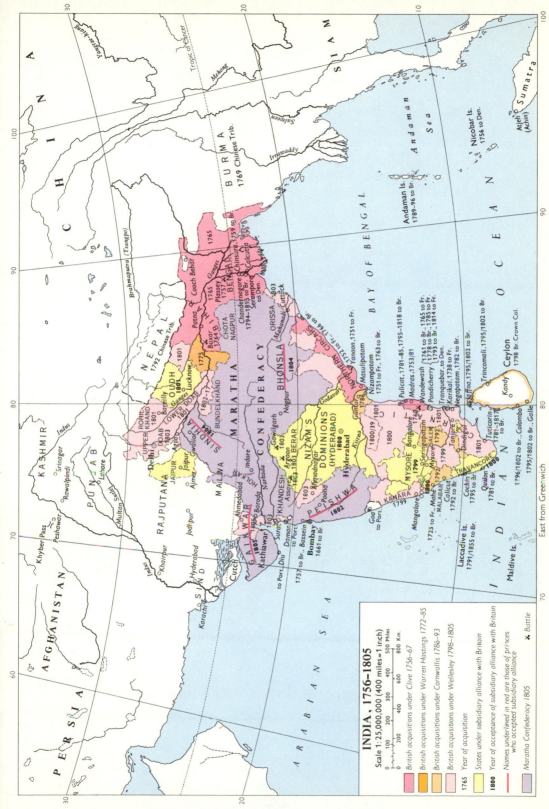

INDIA, 1756–1805
Scale 1:25,000,000 (400 miles=1 inch)

| | | 100 200 300 400 500 Miles |
| | | 100 200 300 400 600 800 Km. |

British acquisitions under Clive 1756–67
British acquisitions under Warren Hastings 1772–85
British acquisitions under Cornwallis 1786–93
British acquisitions under Wellesley 1795–1805
1765   Year of acquisition
States under subsidiary alliance with Britain
1800   Year of acceptance of subsidiary alliance with Britain
        Names underlined in red are those of princes
        who accepted subsidiary alliance
⚔ Battle
Maratha Confederacy 1805

COPYRIGHT. GEORGE PHILIP & SON LTD.

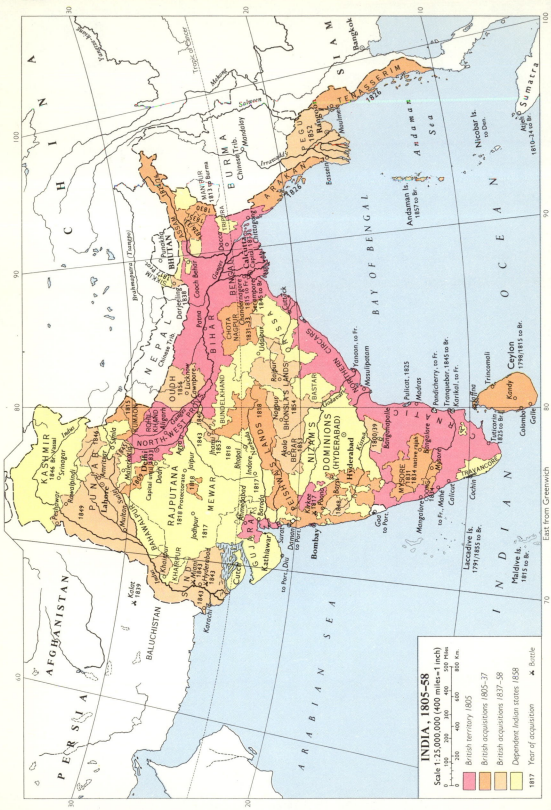

INDIA, 1805-58
Scale 1:25,000,000 (400 miles=1 inch)

British territory 1805
British acquisitions 1805-37
British acquisitions 1837-58
Dependent Indian states 1858
1817 Year of acquisition ✕ Battle

COPYRIGHT. GEORGE PHILIP & SON, LTD.

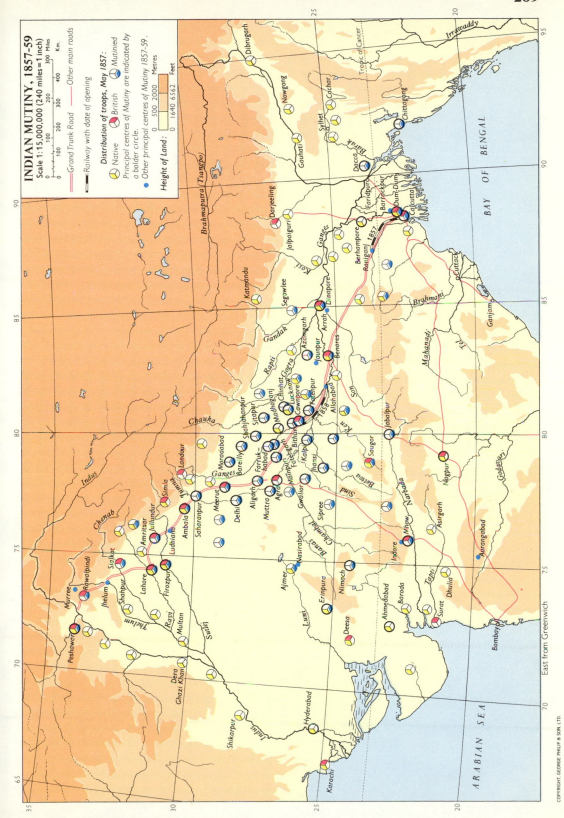

INDIAN MUTINY, 1857–59

Scale 1:15,000,000 (240 miles=1 inch)

0 100 200 300 Miles

0 100 200 300 400 Km.

Grand Trunk Road — Other main roads

Railway with date of opening

Distribution of troops, May 1857:
Native — British — Mutinied

Principal centres of Mutiny are indicated by a bolder circle.

Other principal centres of Mutiny 1857–59.

Height of Land: Metres — Feet
500 2000
1640 6562

BAY OF BENGAL

ARABIAN SEA

COPYRIGHT. GEORGE PHILIP & SON, LTD.

East from Greenwich

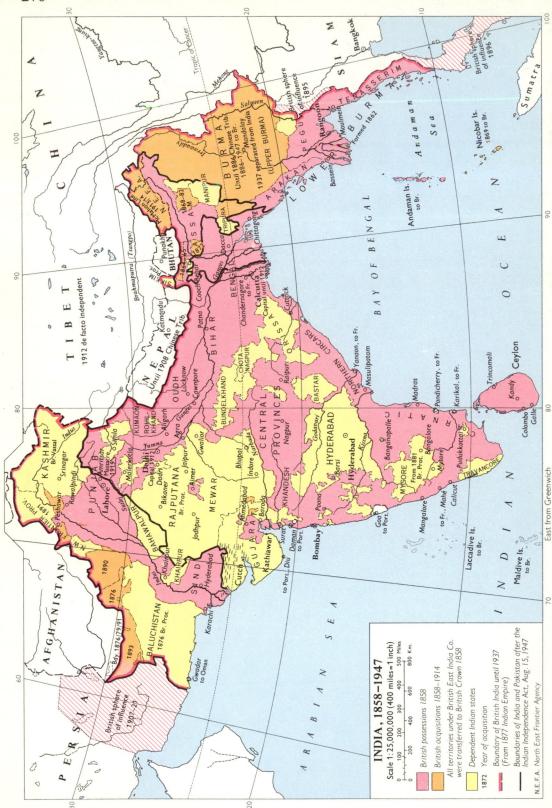

INDIA, 1858–1947

Scale 1:25,000,000 (400 miles=1 inch)

Miles 100 200 300 400 500 Miles
Km. 200 400 600 800 Km.

Br. possessions 1858

British acquisitions 1858–1914

All territories under British East India Co. were transferred to British Crown 1858

Dependent Indian states

1872 Year of acquisition

Boundary of British India until 1937 (From 1877 Indian Empire)

Boundaries of India and Pakistan after the Indian Independence Act, Aug. 15, 1947

N.E.F.A. North East Frontier Agency

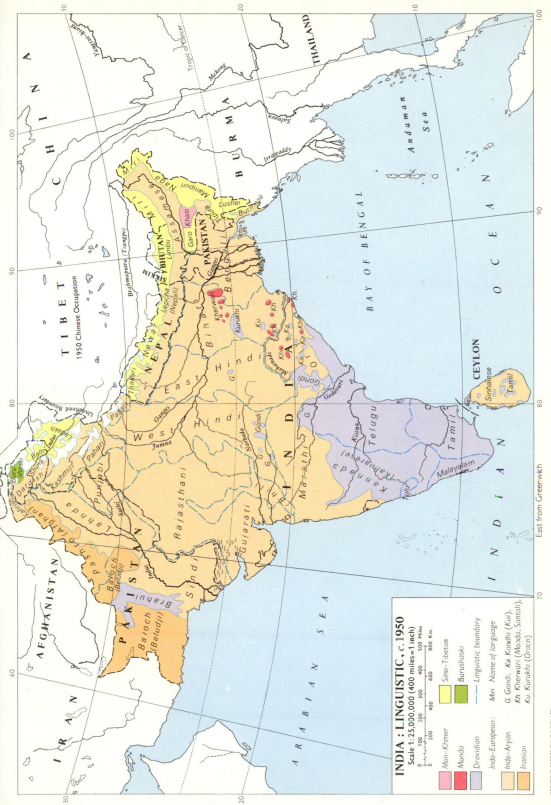

INDIA: LINGUISTIC, c. 1950
Scale 1:25,000,000 (400 miles=1 inch)

Mon-Khmer		Sino-Tibetan	Miri Name of language
Munda		Burushaski	
Dravidian		Linguistic boundary	G. Gondi, Ka Kandhi (Kui),
Indo-European:			Kh. Kherwari (Mo̱nda, Santali),
Indo-Aryan			Ku. Kurukhi (Oraon)
Iranian			

COPYRIGHT. GEORGE PHILIP & SON LTD.

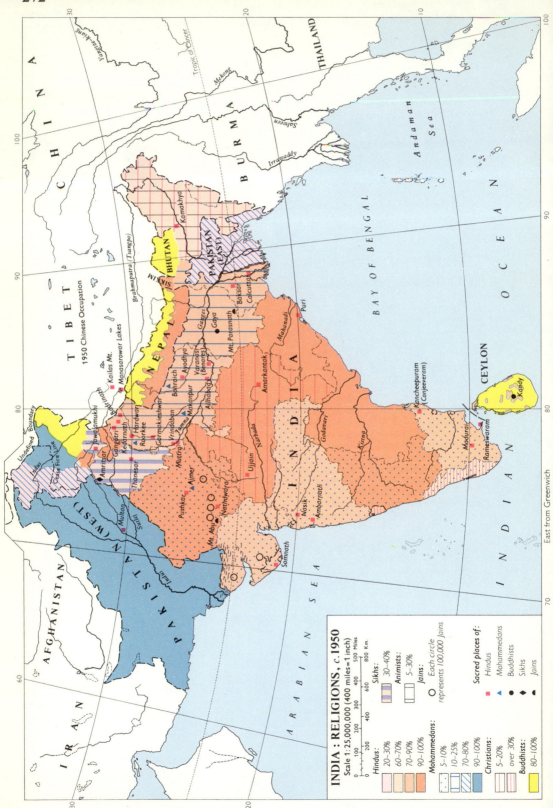

INDIA: RELIGIONS, c.1950

Scale 1:25,000,000 (400 miles=1 inch)

0 100 200 300 400 500 Miles

0 200 400 600 800 Km.

Hindus:
20–30%
60–70%
70–90%
90–100%

Mohammedans:
5–10%
10–25%
70–80%
90–100%

Christians:
5–20%
over 30%

Buddhists:
80–100%

Sikhs:
30–40%

Animists:
5–30%

Jains:
O Each circle
represents 100,000 Jains

Sacred places of:
Hindus
Mohammedans
Buddhists
Sikhs
Jains

East from Greenwich

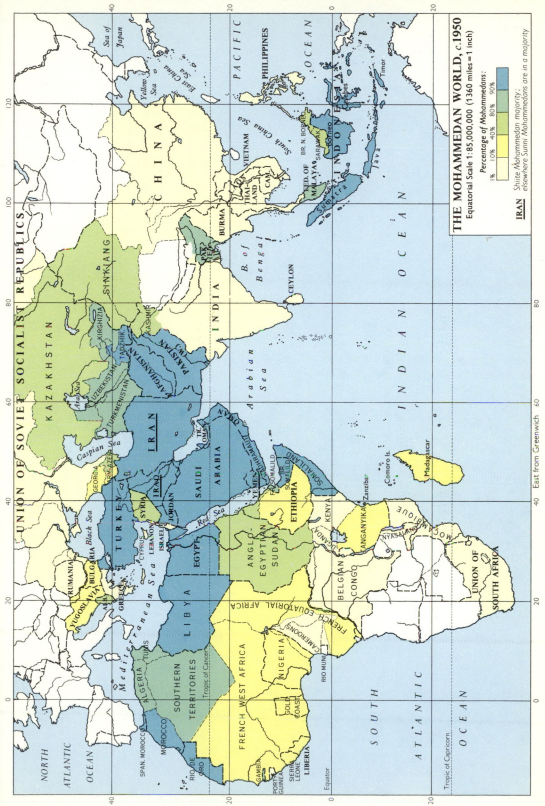

THE MOHAMMEDAN WORLD, *c.*1950

Equatorial Scale 1:85,000,000 (1360 miles = 1 inch)

Percentage of Mohammedans:

1% 10% 40% 80% 90%

IRAN *Shiite Mohammedan majority;*
elsewhere Sunni Mohammedans are in a majority

COPYRIGHT. GEORGE PHILIP & SON. LTD.

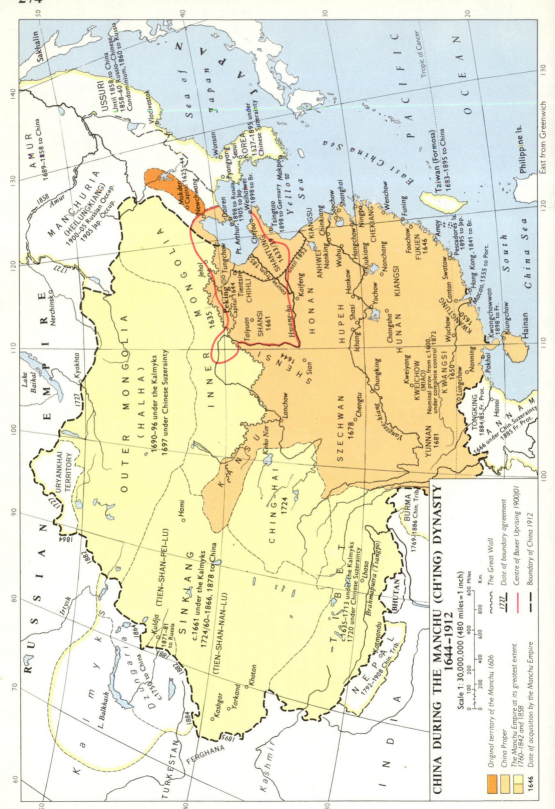

CHINA DURING THE MANCHU (CH'ING) DYNASTY 1644–1912

Scale 1:30,000,000 (480 miles=1 inch)

0	100	200	300	400	500	600 Miles
0	200	400	600	800		Km.

Original territory of the Manchu 1606

China Proper

The Manchu Empire at its greatest extent
1760–1842 and 1858

1646   Date of acquisition by the Manchu Empire

——— The Great Wall

1772   Date of boundary agreement

——— Centre of Boxer Uprising 1900/01

--- Boundary of China 1912

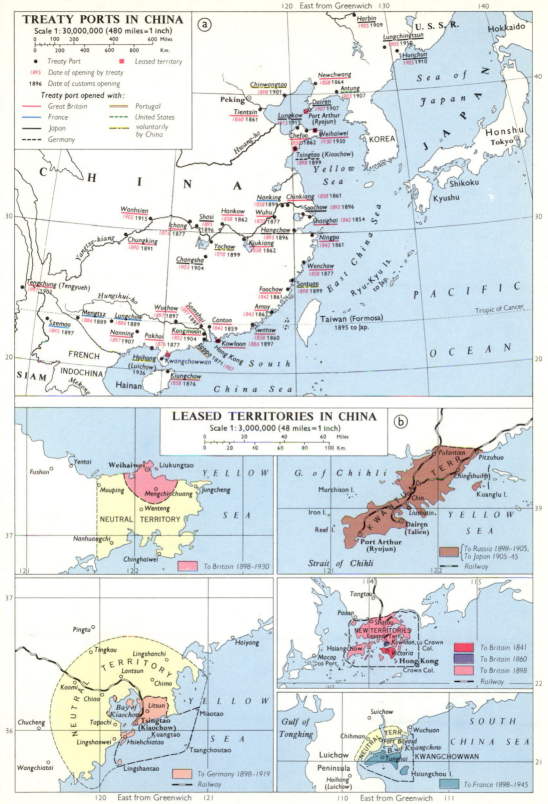

TREATY PORTS IN CHINA
Scale 1:30,000,000 (480 miles=1 inch)

0 100 200 400 600 Miles		
0 200 400 600 800 Km.		

• Treaty Port   ■ Leased territory

1895 Date of opening by treaty

1896 Date of customs opening

Treaty port opened with:
— Great Britain   — Portugal
— France   --- United States
— Japan   -·-· voluntarily by China
--- Germany

LEASED TERRITORIES IN CHINA
Scale 1:3,000,000 (48 miles=1 inch)

0 20 40 60 Miles		
0 20 40 60 80 100 Km.		

To Britain 1898–1930

To Russia 1898–1905, To Japan 1905–45
— Railway

To Germany 1898–1919
— Railway

NEW TERRITORIES Leased Terr.
Kowloon, to Crown Col.
Macao to Port.
Hong Kong
Crown Col.

To Britain 1841
To Britain 1860
To Britain 1898
— Railway

NEUTRAL TERR.
Fort Bayard
B. of Kwangchow
KWANGCHOWWAN

To France 1898–1945

COPYRIGHT. GEORGE PHILIP & SON, LTD.

276

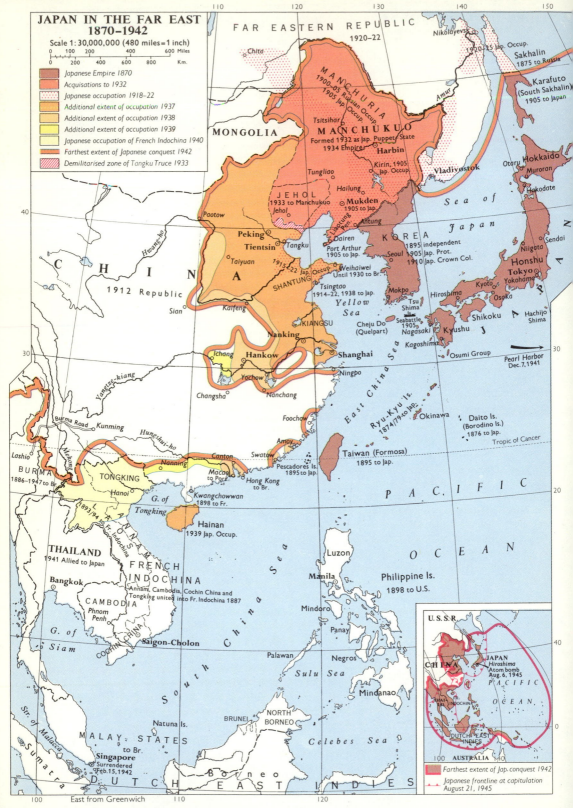

JAPAN IN THE FAR EAST
1870–1942
Scale 1 : 30,000,000 (480 miles = 1 inch)

0 100 200 400 600 Miles	
0 200 400 600 800 Km.	

- Japanese Empire 1870
- Acquisitions to 1932
- Japanese occupation 1918–22
- Additional extent of occupation 1937
- Additional extent of occupation 1938
- Additional extent of occupation 1939
- Japanese occupation of French Indochina 1940
- Farthest extent of Japanese conquest 1942
- Demilitarised zone of Tangku Truce 1933

COPYRIGHT. GEORGE PHILIP & SON. LTD.

THE FAR EAST UNTIL c.1939

Scale 1:40,000,000 (640 miles=1 inch)

British Possessions
French Possessions
U.S. Possessions
Extent of Japanese Occupation in China 1939
Portuguese Possessions
Netherlands Possessions
Japanese Possessions

THE MARCHES OF THE RED ARMY IN CHINA:
Revolutionary centres 1933–34
1st March: The Long March (Oct. 1934–Oct. 1935)
2nd March (Nov. 1935–Nov. 1936)
4th March (Mar. 1935–Oct. 1936)
Area of the Regime of Yenan 1937

U. S. S. R.

Chita
Blagoveshchensk
Amur
Khabarovsk
Nikolayevsk
Kamchatka Pen.
Petropavlovsk
Sakhalin

MONGOLIA
1924 People's Rep.

MANCHUKUO
Formed 1932 as Jap. Puppet-State
1934 Empire
Tsitsihar
Hailung
Kirin
Harbin
Vladivostok
Paronaisk
Karafuto
(South Sakhalin)
Otaru
Muroran
Hokkaido
Hakodate

JEHOL
1933 to Manchukuo
Jehol
Mukden
Antung
Dairen
Pt. Arthur
KOREA
Seoul
Pusan
Weihaiwei 1910 Jap. Crown Col.
Until 1930 to Br.
Mokpo

Sea of Japan

Sendai
Niigata
Honshu
Tokyo
Kyoto
Yokohama
Osaka
Hiroshima
Shikoku
Nagasaki
Kyushu

Paotow
Kao-t'ai
Sining
TIBET
Lhasa
Paiyu
Claimed by China
Sadiya

Hwang-ho
Yenan
(Fushih)
Peking
Tientsin
Taiyuan
Kaifeng
Sian
MAO-TSE-TUNG
AUG. 1935
MAY 1935
Chengtu
1912 Republic
C H I N A

Tsingtao
1938 to Jap.
Nanking
KIANGSU
Shasi
Hankow
Shanghai
Yellow Sea

East China Sea

Tsinan
Weihaiwei
Okinawa
Ryu-Kyu Is.
Tropic of Cancer

Chungking
Yangtse-kiang
Changsha
JAN. 1935
Mekong
Kunming
Tali
Kweilin
Nanning
Canton
Swatow
Amoy
Foochow
Nanchang
Taipeh
Taiwan (Formosa)
Tainan

Chittagong
Mandalay
BURMA
Rangoon
Moulmein
Tavoy
Surat Thani
TONGKING
Hanoi
Luang Prabang
Vientiane
LAOS
Hué
Tourane
Macao
to Port.
Hong Kong
to Br.
Kwangchowwan
to Fr.
Hainan
1939 Jap. Occup.

South China Sea

Laoag
Luzon
Manila
Philippine Is.
to U.S.
Iloilo
Cebu
Mindanao
Davao

PACIFIC
OCEAN

Guam
to U.S.

Yap
Caroline Is.
Jap. Mandate

THAILAND
Bangkok
ANNAM
CAMBODIA
Phnom Penh
Phan Rang
FRENCH
INDOCHINA
Saigon–Cholon
COCHIN CHINA

Kutaraja
Medan
Padang
Kuala Lumpur
MALAY STATES
Malacca
Singapore
Pontianak
Bangka
Palembang
Teluk Betung

Jesselton
Brunei
BRUNEI
NORTH
BORNEO
SARAWAK
Kuching
Borneo
Sandakan
Menado
Halmahera
Celebes Sea
Celebes
Buru
Ceram
Fakfak
NEW GUINEA

Sumatra
DUTCH EAST INDIES
Bandjarmasin
Makassar
Banda Sea
Equator

Batavia
Bandung
Java
Semarang
Jogjakarta
Surabaja
Java Sea
Sumbawa
Flores
Sumba
Timor
Dili
Darwin
AUSTRALIA

INDIAN OCEAN

100   East from Greenwich   110
120
130
140

COPYRIGHT. GEORGE PHILIP & SON. LTD.

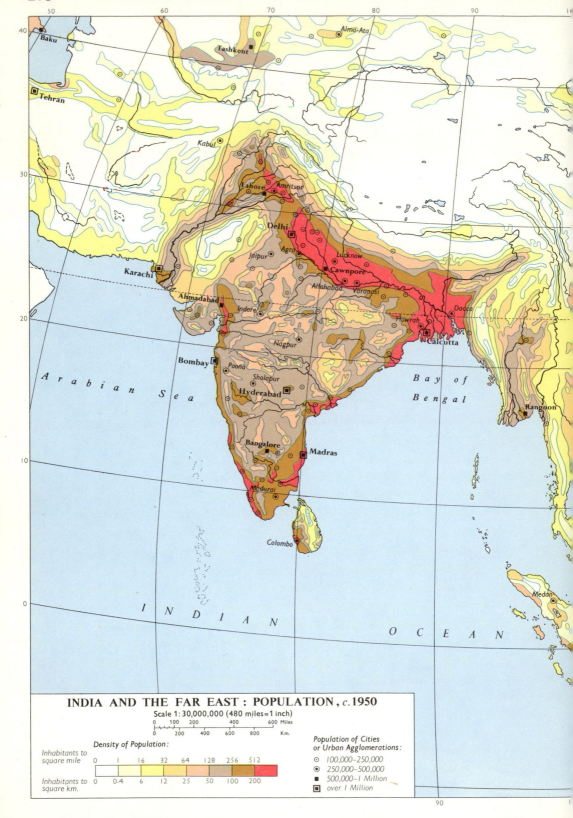
Baku
Tehran
Tashkent
Alma-Ata
Kabul
Lahore
Amritsar
Delhi
Agra
Jaipur
Lucknow
Cawnpore
Karachi
Allahabad
Varanasi
Ahmadabad
Indore
Dacca
Howrah
Calcutta
Nagpur
Bombay
Poona
Sholapur
Hyderabad
Bangalore
Madras
Madurai
Colombo
Rangoon
Medan
Arabian Sea
Bay of Bengal
INDIAN OCEAN

INDIA AND THE FAR EAST : POPULATION, *c.* 1950

Scale 1: 30,000,000 (480 miles = 1 inch)

Density of Population:									
Inhabitants to square mile	0	1	16	32	64	128	256	512	
Inhabitants to square km.	0	0·4	6	12	25	50	100	200	

Population of Cities or Urban Agglomerations:

- *100,000–250,000*
- *250,000–500,000*
- *500,000–1 Million*
- *over 1 Million*

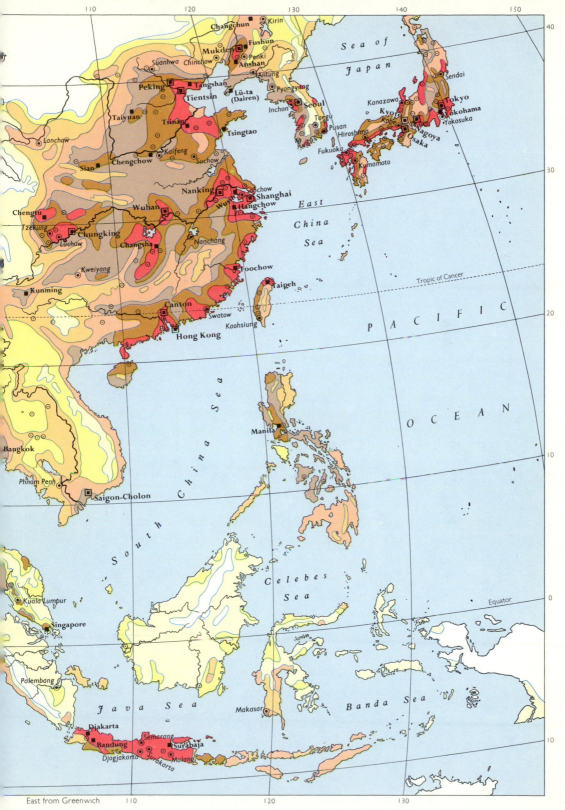
Sea of Japan
East China Sea
South China Sea
Celebes Sea
Java Sea
Banda Sea
PACIFIC OCEAN
Tropic of Cancer
Equator
Changchun
Kirin
Mukden
Fushun
Penki
Anshan
Suanhwa
Chinchow
Antung
Peking
Tangshan
Tientsin
Lü-ta (Dairen)
Pyongyang
Seoul
Inchon
Taegu
Pusan
Taiyuan
Tsinan
Tsingtao
Lanchow
Kaifeng
Chengchow
Suchow
Sian
Nanking
Soochow
Shanghai
Wusih
Hangchow
Wuhan
Chengtu
Tzekung
Chungking
Luchow
Changsha
Nanchang
Kweiyang
Foochow
Kunming
Taipeh
Canton
Swatow
Kaohsiung
Hong Kong
Sendai
Kanazawa
Tokyo
Kyoto
Yokohama
Kobe
Yokosuka
Nagoya
Hiroshima
Osaka
Fukuoka
Kumamoto
Manila
Bangkok
Phnom Penh
Saigon-Cholon
Kuala Lumpur
Singapore
Palembang
Makasar
Djakarta
Bandung
Semarang
Surabaja
Djogjakarta
Surakarta
Malang
110
120
130
140
150
40
30
20
10
0
East from Greenwich

COPYRIGHT, GEORGE PHILIP & SON, LTD.

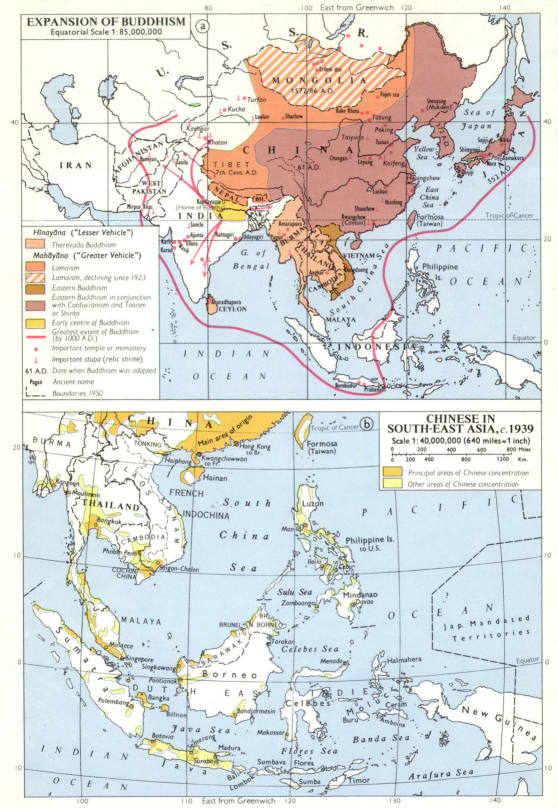

EXPANSION OF BUDDHISM
Equatorial Scale 1:85,000,000

a

Hinayāna ("Lesser Vehicle")

Therevada Buddhism

Mahāyāna ("Greater Vehicle")

Lamaism

Lamaism, declining since 1923

Eastern Buddhism

Eastern Buddhism in conjunction with Confucianism and Taoism or Shinto

Early centre of Buddhism

Greatest extent of Buddhism (by 1000 A.D.)

■ Important temple or monastery

⊥ Important stupa (relic shrine)

61 A.D. Date when Buddhism was adopted

Pagan Ancient name

⌐⌐⌐ Boundaries 1950

CHINESE IN SOUTH-EAST ASIA, *c.*1939

Scale 1:40,000,000 (640 miles=1 inch)

b

Principal areas of Chinese concentration

Other areas of Chinese concentration

COPYRIGHT. GEORGE PHILIP & SON. LTD.

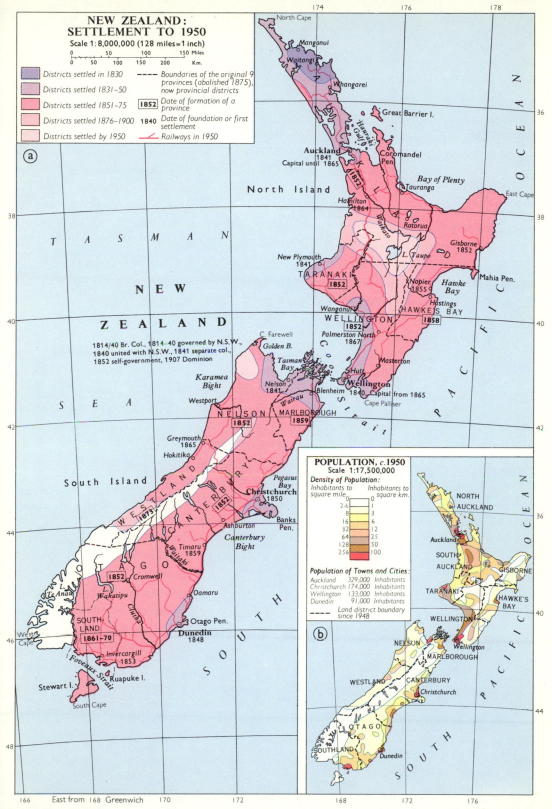

**NEW ZEALAND:
SETTLEMENT TO 1950**

Scale 1:8,000,000 (128 miles = 1 inch)

	Miles
0	50 100 150 Miles
0	50 100 150 200 Km.

Districts settled in 1830

Districts settled 1831–50

Districts settled 1851–75

Districts settled 1876–1900

Districts settled by 1950

— — — Boundaries of the original 9 provinces (abolished 1875), now provincial districts

1852 Date of formation of a province

1840 Date of foundation or first settlement

Railways in 1950

North Cape

Mangonui

Waitangi

Whangarei

Great Barrier I.

Hauraki Gulf

Coromandel Pen.

Auckland 1841
Capital until 1865

Bay of Plenty

Tauranga

East Cape

North Island

Hamilton 1864

Waikato

Rotorua

L. Taupo

Gisborne 1852

New Plymouth 1841

TARANAKI 1852

Napier 1855

Hawke Bay

Mahia Pen.

Wanganui

WELLINGTON 1852

Palmerston North 1867

HAWKE'S BAY 1858

Hastings

Masterton

NEW

ZEALAND

1814/40 Br. Col., 1814–40 governed by N.S.W.,
1840 united with N.S.W., 1841 separate col.,
1852 self-government, 1907 Dominion

C. Farewell

Golden B.

Tasman Bay

Hutt

Wellington 1840 Capital from 1865

Nelson 1841

Blenheim

Cape Palliser

Westport

Wairau

NELSON 1852

MARLBOROUGH 1859

Karamea Bight

T A S M A N

S E A

Greymouth 1865

Hokitika

CANTERBURY

Pegasus Bay

Christchurch 1850

Banks Pen.

South Island

WESTLAND 1873

1852

Ashburton

Canterbury Bight

OTAGO

Timaru 1859

Waitaki

1852

Cromwell

Oamaru

L. Te Anau

L. Wakatipu

Clutha

SOUTH LAND 1861–70

Dunedin 1848

West Cape

Invercargill 1853

Otago Pen.

Foveaux Strait

Ruapuke I.

Stewart I.

South Cape

East from Greenwich

POPULATION, c.1950

Scale 1:17,500,000

Density of Population:

Inhabitants to square mile	Inhabitants to square km.
0	0
2·6	1
8	3
16	6
32	12
64	25
128	50
256	100

Population of Towns and Cities:

Auckland 329,000 Inhabitants
Christchurch 174,000 Inhabitants
Wellington 133,000 Inhabitants
Dunedin 91,000 Inhabitants

— — — Land district boundary since 1948

NORTH AUCKLAND

SOUTH AUCKLAND

Auckland

GISBORNE

TARANAKI

HAWKE'S BAY

WELLINGTON

NELSON

MARLBOROUGH

Wellington

WESTLAND

CANTERBURY

Christchurch

OTAGO

SOUTHLAND

Dunedin

P A C I F I C   O C E A N

S O U T H   P A C I F I C   O C E A N

COPYRIGHT. GEORGE PHILIP & SON, LTD.

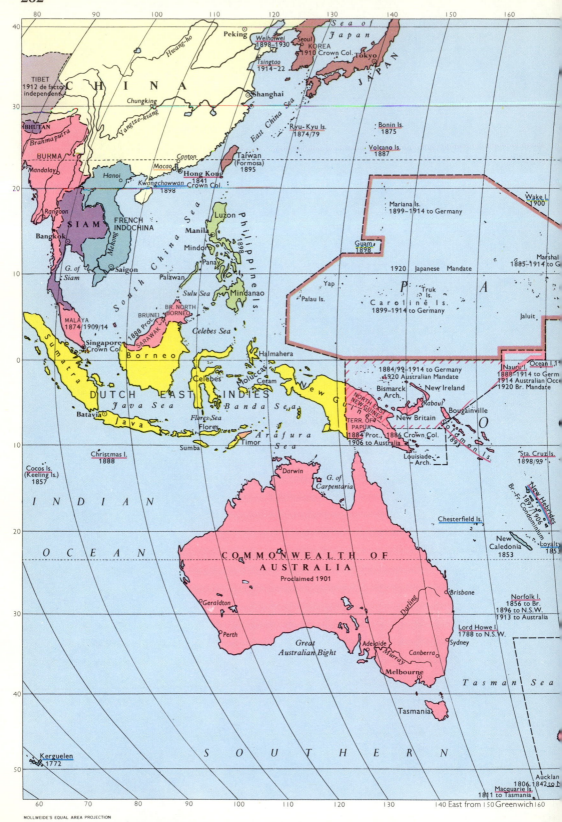
CHINA
TIBET 1912 de facto independent
BHUTAN
BURMA
Mandalay
Rangoon
SIAM
Bangkok
FRENCH INDOCHINA
Hanoi
Saigon
G. of Siam
MALAYA 1874/1909/14
Singapore Crown Col.
Peking
Weihaiwei 1898–1930
Tsingtao 1914–22
Shanghai
Chungking
Canton
Macao
Hong Kong 1841 Crown Col.
Kwangchowwan 1898
Taiwan (Formosa) 1895
KOREA 1910 Crown Col.
Seoul
Tokyo
JAPAN
Sea of Japan
East China Sea
Ryu-Kyu Is. 1874/79
Bonin Is. 1875
Volcano Is. 1887
Mariana Is. 1899–1914 to Germany
Guam 1898
Wake I. 1900
1920 Japanese Mandate
Yap
Palau Is.
Truk Is.
Caroline Is. 1899–1914 to Germany
Marshal 1885–1914 to G
Jaluit
Luzon
Manila
Mindoro
Panay
Palawan
Mindanao
Philippine Is. 1898
South China Sea
Sulu Sea
Celebes Sea
BR. NORTH BORNEO
BRUNEI
SARAWAK 1888 Prot.
Borneo
Sumatra
DUTCH EAST INDIES
Java Sea
Batavia
Java
Celebes
Halmahera
Moluccas
Ceram
Banda Sea
Flores Sea
Flores
Sumba
Timor
Arafura Sea
New Guinea
1884/99–1914 to Germany 1920 Australian Mandate
NORTH EAST NEW GUINEA
TERR. OF PAPUA 1884 Prot., 1886 Crown Col. 1906 to Australia
Bismarck Arch.
New Ireland
Rabaul
New Britain
Bougainville
Solomon Is. 1893
Louisiade Arch.
Nauru I. 1888–1914 to Germ 1914 Australian Occ 1920 Br. Mandate
Ocean I.
Sta. Cruz Is. 1898/99
New Hebrides 1897/1906 Br.-Fr. Condominium
Christmas I. 1888
Cocos Is. (Keeling Is.) 1857
INDIAN OCEAN
Darwin
G. of Carpentaria
Chesterfield Is.
New Caledonia 1853
Loyalty 1853
COMMONWEALTH OF AUSTRALIA
Proclaimed 1901
Geraldton
Perth
Brisbane
Darling
Great Australian Bight
Adelaide
Murray
Canberra
Sydney
Melbourne
Norfolk I. 1856 to Br. 1896 to N.S.W. 1913 to Australia
Lord Howe I. 1788 to N.S.W.
Tasman Sea
Tasmania
SOUTHERN
Kerguelen 1772
Aucklan 1806, 1842 to N
Macquarie Is. 1811 to Tasmania
140 East from 150 Greenwich 160

MOLLWEIDE'S EQUAL AREA PROJECTION

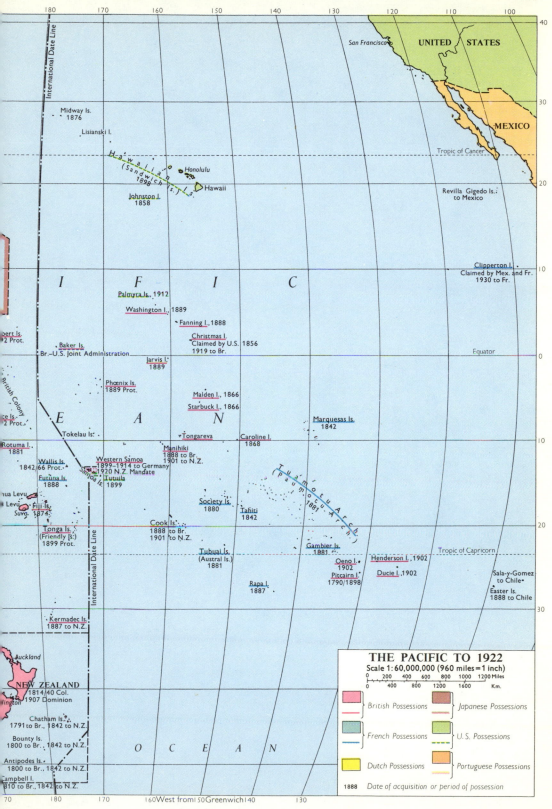

International Date Line

180 170 160 150 140 130 120 110 100

40

San Francisco

UNITED STATES

30

Midway Is.
1876

Lisianski I.

Tropic of Cancer

MEXICO

20

Hawaiian
(Sandwich
1898
Honolulu

Johnston I.
1858

Ls.

Hawaii

Revilla Gigedo Is.
to Mexico

10

Clipperton I.
Claimed by Mex. and Fr.
1930 to Fr.

I F I C

Palmyra Is. 1912

Washington I. 1889

Fanning I., 1888

Christmas I.
Claimed by U.S. 1856
1919 to Br.

Equator

0

pert Is.
2 Prot.

Baker Is.
Br.–U.S. Joint Administration

Jarvis I.
1889

British Colony

ce Is.
2 Prot.

Phœnix Is.
1889 Prot.

Maiden I., 1866

Starbuck I., 1866

Marquesas Is.
1842

E A N

Tokelau Is.

Tongareva

Caroline I.
1868

10

Rotuma I.
1881

Manihiki
1888 to Br.
1901 to N.Z.

Wallis Is.
1842/66 Prot.

Western Samoa
1899–1914 to Germany
1920 N.Z. Mandate

Futuna Is.
1888

Tutuila
1899

Tuamotu Arch
(Paumotu) 1881

nua Levu

Society Is.
1880

e Levu

Fiji Is.

Suva. 1874

Tahiti
1842

Tonga Is.
(Friendly Is.)
1899 Prot.

Cook Is.
1888 to Br.
1901 to N.Z.

20

Gambier Is.
1881

Tubuai Is.
(Austral Is.)
1881

Oeno I.
1902

Pitcairn I.
1790/1898

Henderson I., 1902

Ducie I., 1902

Tropic of Capricorn

Sala-y-Gomez
to Chile

Rapa I.
1887

Easter Is.
1888 to Chile

30

Kermadec Is.
1887 to N.Z.

International Date Line

Auckland

NEW ZEALAND
1814/40 Col.
ington 1907 Dominion

Chatham Is.
1791 to Br., 1842 to N.Z.

Bounty Is.
1800 to Br. 1842 to N.Z.

Antipodes Is.
1800 to Br., 1842 to N.Z.

Campbell I.
810 to Br., 1842 to N.Z.

O C E A N

70 180 170 160West from 150Greenwich140 130

THE PACIFIC TO 1922
Scale 1:60,000,000 (960 miles = 1 inch)

0 200 400 600 800 1000 1200 Miles
0 400 800 1200 1600 Km.

British Possessions	Japanese Possessions
French Possessions	U.S. Possessions
Dutch Possessions	Portuguese Possessions

1888 Date of acquisition or period of possession

COPYRIGHT. GEORGE PHILIP & SON. LTD.

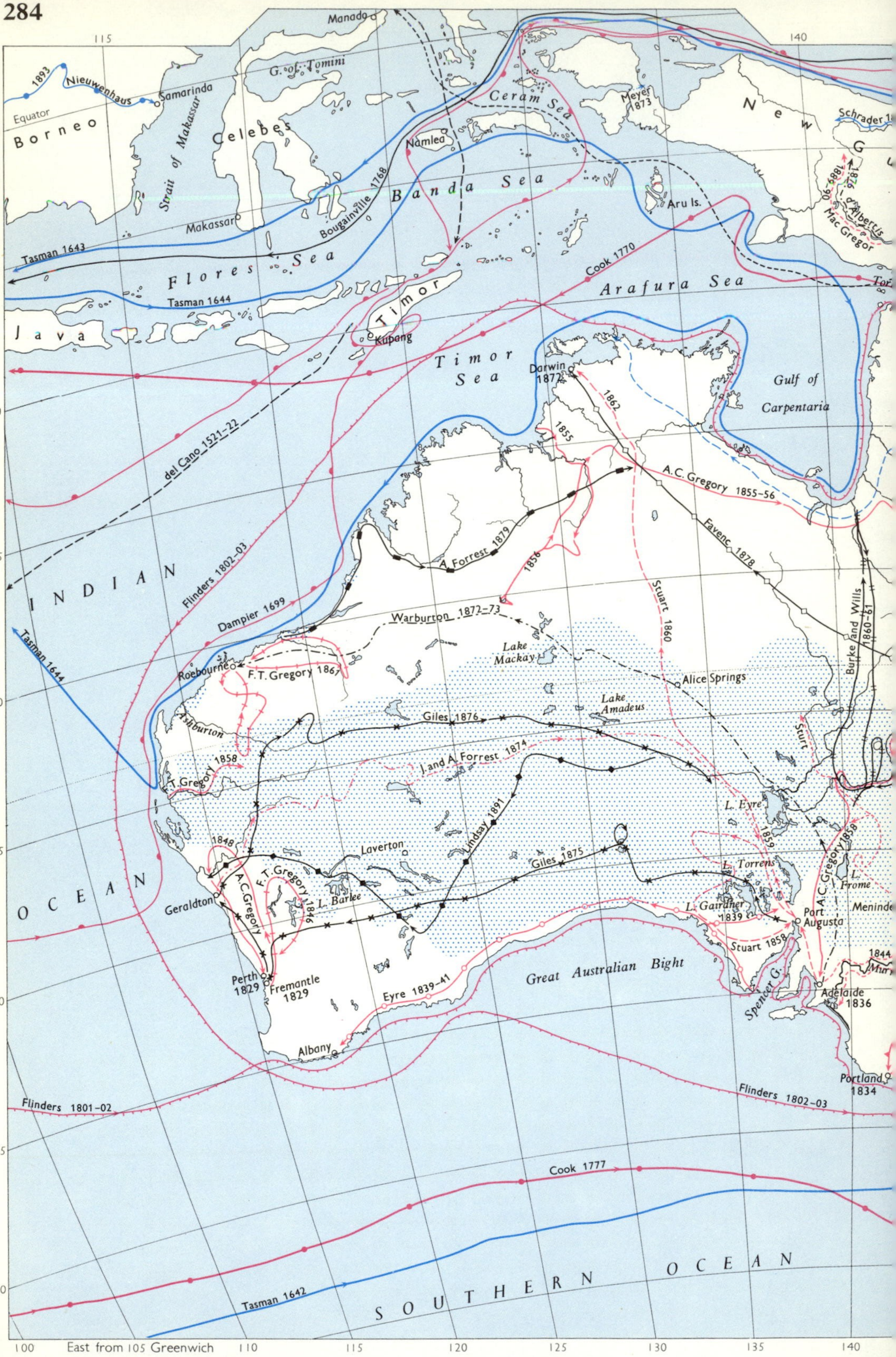

Manado

1893
Nieuwenhaus
Samarinda
Equator
Borneo
Celebes
G. of Tomini
Ceram Sea
Meyer 1873
Schrader 18
New
G
Namlea
Banda Sea
Strait of Makassar
Makassar
Bougainville 1768
Flores Sea
Tasman 1643
Tasman 1644
Aru Is.
Cook 1770
Arafura Sea
Albert
1875-76
Mac Gregor
Java
Kupang
Timor
Sea
Darwin 1872
Gulf of Carpentaria
Tor
A. C. Gregory 1855-56
del Cano 1521-22
1862
1855
Flinders 1802-03
Favenc 1878
INDIAN
A. Forrest 1879
1856
Dampier 1699
Warburton 1872-73
Stuart 1860
Burke and Wills 1860-61
Roebourne
F. T. Gregory 1867
Lake Mackay
Alice Springs
Giles 1876
Lake Amadeus
Ashburton
J. and A. Forrest 1874
L. Eyre
Sturt
1858
Giles 1875
F. T. Gregory 1858
Lindsay 1891
T. Gregory
Laverton
L. Torrens
A. C. Gregory 185
1848
F.T.Gregory 1846
L. Barlee
L. Frome
Meninde
Geraldton
A. C. Gregory
L. Gairdner 1839
Stuart 1858
Perth 1829
Fremantle 1829
Eyre 1839-41
Great Australian Bight
Part Augusta
1844
Mur
Spencer G.
Adelaide 1836
Albany
Portland 1834
Flinders 1801-02
Flinders 1802-03
OCEAN
Cook 1777
Tasman 1642
SOUTHERN OCEAN
East from Greenwich

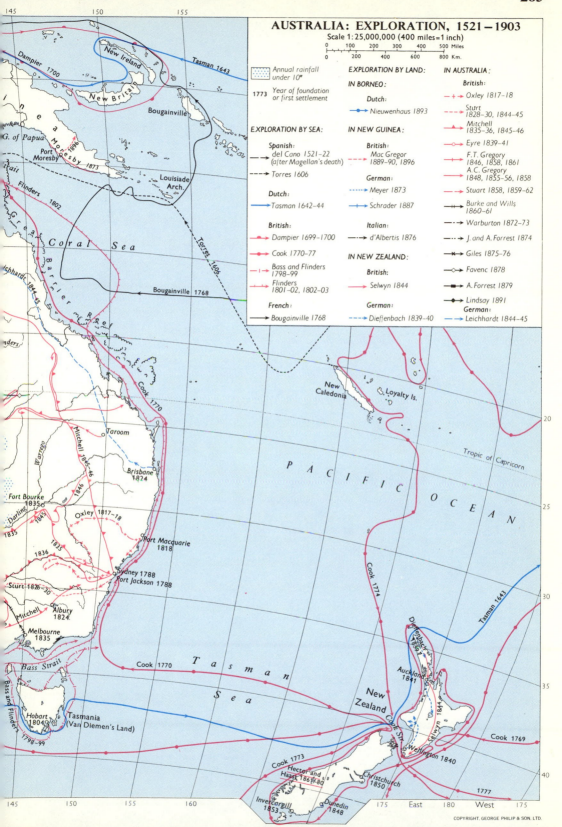

AUSTRALIA: EXPLORATION, 1521–1903
Scale 1:25,000,000 (400 miles=1 inch)

0 100 200 300 400 500 Miles
0   200   400   600   800 Km.

Annual rainfall under 10″

1773 Year of foundation or first settlement

EXPLORATION BY SEA:

Spanish:
→ del Cano 1521–22 (after Magellan's death)
⇢ Torres 1606

Dutch:
— Tasman 1642–44

British:
● Dampier 1699–1700
● Cook 1770–77
↳ Bass and Flinders 1798–99
→ Flinders 1801–02, 1802–03

French:
→ Bougainville 1768

EXPLORATION BY LAND:

IN BORNEO:

Dutch:
● Nieuwenhaus 1893

IN NEW GUINEA:

British:
– – Mac Gregor 1889–90, 1896

German:
····· Meyer 1873
+–+ Schrader 1887

Italian:
–·– d'Albertis 1876

IN NEW ZEALAND:

British:
→ Selwyn 1844

German:
– – Dieffenbach 1839–40

IN AUSTRALIA:

British:
–+– Oxley 1817–18
— Sturt 1828–30, 1844–45
▲ Mitchell 1835–36, 1845–46
◇ Eyre 1839–41
→ F. T. Gregory 1846, 1858, 1861
→ A. C. Gregory 1848, 1855–56, 1858
→ Stuart 1858, 1859–62
— Burke and Wills 1860–61
–·→ Warburton 1872–73
–··→ J. and A. Forrest 1874
✕–✕ Giles 1875–76
◇–◇ Favenc 1878
■–■ A. Forrest 1879
◆–◆ Lindsay 1891

German:
→ Leichhardt 1844–45

COPYRIGHT. GEORGE PHILIP & SON. LTD.

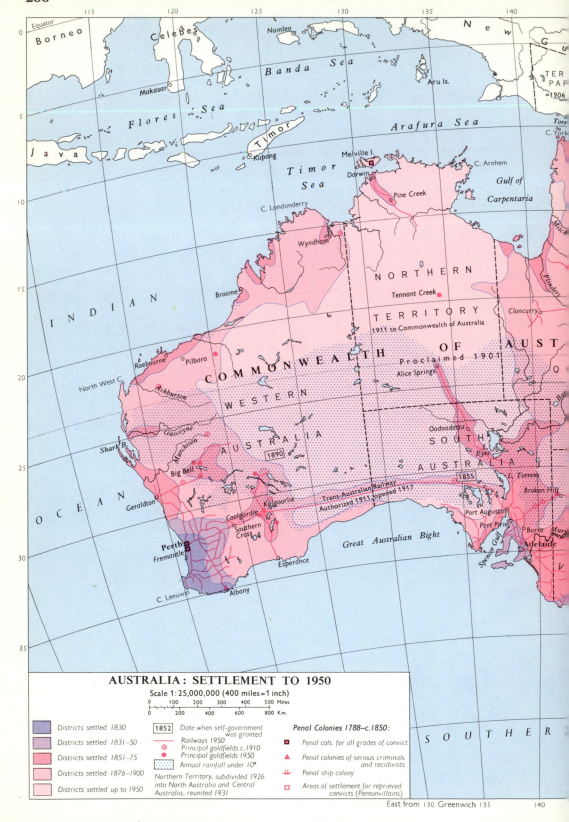

AUSTRALIA: SETTLEMENT TO 1950

Scale 1:25,000,000 (400 miles = 1 inch)

0 100 200 300 400 500 Miles

0 200 400 600 800 Km.

Districts settled 1830

Districts settled 1831–50

Districts settled 1851–75

Districts settled 1876–1900

Districts settled up to 1950

1852 Date when self-government was granted

Railways 1950

⊕ Principal goldfields c.1910

● Principal goldfields 1950

Annual rainfall under 10″

Northern Territory, subdivided 1926 into North Australia and Central Australia, reunited 1931

Penal Colonies 1788–c.1850:

■ Penal cols. for all grades of convict

▲ Penal colonies of serious criminals and recidivists

⚓ Penal ship colony

□ Areas of settlement for reprieved convicts (Pentonvillains)

East from 130 Greenwich 135   140

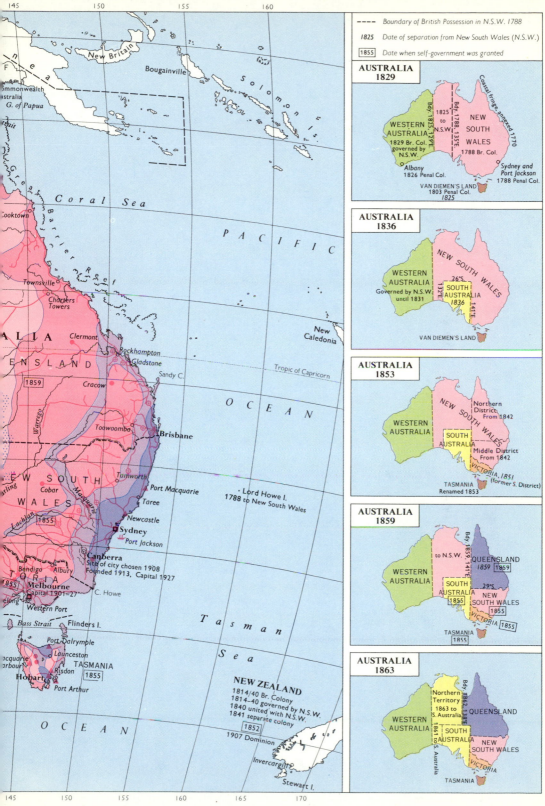

Boundary of British Possession in N.S.W. 1788
1825 Date of separation from New South Wales (N.S.W.)
1855 Date when self-government was granted

AUSTRALIA 1829

WESTERN AUSTRALIA
1829 Br. Col.
governed by N.S.W.

Bdy. 1825, 129°E

1825 to N.S.W.

Bdy. 1788, 135°E

NEW SOUTH WALES
1788 Br. Col.

Coastal fringe annexed 1770

Albany 1826 Penal Col.

Sydney and Port Jackson 1788 Penal Col.

VAN DIEMEN'S LAND 1803 Penal Col. 1825

AUSTRALIA 1836

WESTERN AUSTRALIA
Governed by N.S.W. until 1831

132°E

NEW SOUTH WALES

26°S

SOUTH AUSTRALIA 1836

141°E

VAN DIEMEN'S LAND

AUSTRALIA 1853

WESTERN AUSTRALIA

NEW SOUTH WALES

SOUTH AUSTRALIA

Northern District From 1842

Middle District From 1842

VICTORIA, 1851 (former S. District)

TASMANIA Renamed 1853

AUSTRALIA 1859

WESTERN AUSTRALIA

to N.S.W.

Bdy. 1859, 141°E

SOUTH AUSTRALIA 1855

QUEENSLAND 1859 1859

29°S

NEW SOUTH WALES 1855

VICTORIA 1855

TASMANIA 1855

AUSTRALIA 1863

WESTERN AUSTRALIA

Northern Territory 1863 to S. Australia

Bdy. 1862, 138°E

1861 to S. Australia

SOUTH AUSTRALIA

QUEENSLAND

NEW SOUTH WALES

VICTORIA

TASMANIA

New Britain

Bougainville

Solomon Is.

Commonwealth
Australia
G. of Papua

New Guinea

Coral Sea

PACIFIC OCEAN

Cooktown

Townsville

Charters Towers

Great Barrier Reef

Clermont

Rockhampton
Gladstone
Sandy C.

Tropic of Capricorn

New Caledonia

Cracow

QUEENSLAND

1859

Warrego

Toowoomba

Brisbane

NEW SOUTH WALES

1855

Darling

Cobar

Tamworth

Macquarie

Port Macquarie

Lachlan

Taree

Lord Howe I.
1788 to New South Wales

Newcastle

Sydney
Port Jackson

Canberra
Site of city chosen 1908
Founded 1913, Capital 1927

Bendigo Albury

VICTORIA

1855

Melbourne
Capital 1901-27

C. Howe

Geelong
Western Port

Bass Strait   Flinders I.

Macquarie Harbour

Port Dalrymple
Launceston

TASMANIA

Risdon

Hobart

Port Arthur

1855

Tasman Sea

OCEAN

NEW ZEALAND
1814/40 Br. Colony
1814-40 governed by N.S.W.
1840 united with N.S.W.
1841 separate colony
1852
1907 Dominion

Invercargill

Stewart I.

COPYRIGHT. GEORGE PHILIP & SON. LTD.

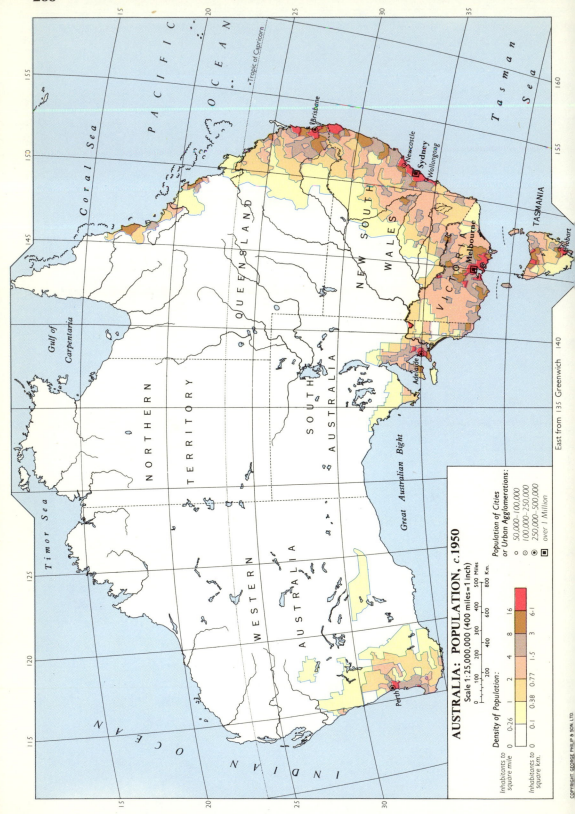

AUSTRALIA: POPULATION, c.1950

Scale 1:25,000,000 (400 miles=1 inch)

Density of Population:

Inhabitants to square mile	0	0.26	1	2	4	8	16
Inhabitants to square km.	0	0.1	0.38	0.77	1.5	3	6.1

Population of Cities or Urban Agglomerations:

○ 50,000–100,000
◎ 100,000–250,000
◉ 250,000–500,000
◼ over 1 Million

COPYRIGHT GEORGE PHILIP & SON, LTD.

East from 135 Greenwich

SUBJECT INDEX

For abbreviations, see pages xxiii–xxiv

Abyssinia, *see* Ethiopia
Acadia
  17–18C.: 196
Acarnania
  19C.: 168, 169b
Adam Kok's Land
  19C.: 257
Adams–Onis Treaty or Spanish Treaty
  (1819), 202
Aden Prot.
  16C.: 2, 5, 260
  19–20C.: 15–21, 62, 174, 175
Adrianople (1829), T. of, 166–7
Adwalton Moor (1643), B. of, 96a
Affane (1565), B. of, 94a
Afghanistan
  20C.: 273, 280
Africa
  16C.: 2, 4–6a
  17C.: 6b
  18C.: 7a, 8–11, 41b, 43b, 252
  19C.: 7b, 12–15, 47b, 241–5
  20C.: 16–23, 55a, 62, 246–51
Agnadello (1509), B. of, 159
Agriculture, *see* Economy
Ahmadnagar
  15–16C.: 3, 266
Aix-la-Chapelle (1668), T. of, 33b, 108–9
Aix-la-Chapelle (1748), T. of, 39, 42
Akhaltsikhe (1853), B. of, 51a
Åland Is.
  20C.: 56, 83, 191
Alaska
  18C.: 10, 220
  19C.: 12, 14, 219a, 220, 222, 223a
  20C.: 16–20, 26, 223b, c
Alawites, Terr. of
  20C.: 174
Albania
  15C.: 164
  16–18C.: 71–5
  19C.: 77–9, 168, 170a
  20C.: 53, 57–61, 81, 83, 85, 166, 169,
    170a, 171, 273
Alberta
  19C.: 222c, 223a
  20C.: 223b, c, 224a, b
  See Canada
Alcantara (1706), B. of, 34
Alessandria (1745), B. of, 159
Alexandretta, Sanjak of
  20C.: 174
Alexandria (1798), B. of, 45b

Algeria, Algiers
  16C.: 70, 164
  17C.: 72
  18C.: 74, 166
  19C.: 76–9, 241–5
  20C.: 22–3, 58, 80, 82, 84, 246–51, 254,
    273
Allerheim (1645), B. of, 31b
Almansa (1707), B. of, 34
Almenara (1710), B. of, 34
Alsace
  15C.: 106
  17C.: 108–9, 111
  18C.: 113a, 115a, 132
  19C.: 117, 141a, b
  20C.: 57, 58, 80, 82
Amboina (E. Indies)
  16C.: 260
  17C.: 263
  18C.: 263
  19C.: 265
  20C.: 265, 279, 280
Amiens (1870), B. of, 117
Amiens (1802), T. of, 48, 50b
Amritsar (1809), T. of, 50b
Amur
  17–19C.: 184, 274
Anatolia
  15C.: 164–5
  16C.: 71
  17C.: 73
  18C.: 75
  20C.: 166–7
  See Ottoman Empire, Turkey
Ancona (1798), B. of, 44
Andaman Is.
  18–19C.: 262, 267
  19–20 C.: 264, 268, 270
Andorra
  16C.: 70
  17C.: 72
  18C.: 74
  19C.: 76–9
  20C.: 52, 58, 80, 82, 84, 90, 91
Anglo-Egyptian Sudan, *see* Sudan
Anguilla (W. Indies)
  17–20C.: 22, 229–32
Annam, *see* Indochina
Ansbach
  15C.: 122–3, 138a
  16C.: 124–5
  17C.: 129a, 130–1
  18C.: 134, 139a

Northwest Territories (*cont.*)
  20C.: 223b, c
  See Canada
Norway
  16C.: 2, 70, 118, 120
  17C.: 36a, b, 72, 149
  18C.: 37a, 74
  19C.: 26, 49, 52, 56, 58, 76, 78, 86, 93
  20C.: 80, 82, 84, 90–3
Novara (1500, 1513), B. of, 159
Nova Scotia
  18C.: 43a, 198
  19C.: 221a, 222, 223a
  20C.: 223b, c, 224
  See Canada
Novgorod
  15–17C.: 180
  18C.: 182, 183
  19C.: 183
  20C.: 187
Novi (1799), B. of, 44
Novipazar, Sanjak of
  19C.: 146, 170a
Nubia
  19C.: 242
Nuremberg (1632), B. of, 31a
Nuremberg (1538), Catholic League of, 128
Nuremberg Globe (c. 1530), 1
Nyasaland
  20C.: 246–51, 255, 273
Nystad (1721), T. of, 37b

Ohio
  18C.: 200
  19C.: 202, 206, 207
  See United States
Oil fields
  Middle East: 175
  Poland: 179b
  Russia in Asia: 192, 193
  Russia in Europe: 188, 189
  United States: 209b
Oil Rivers Prot.
  19C.: 245, 253
Oirat, Khanate of the
  16C.: 3
Oldenburg
  16C.: 122, 124
  17C.: 130
  18C.: 132–4
  19C.: 49, 78, 135, 136, 140, 141
Old Providence I.
  17–20C.: 229–32
Oliva (1660), T. of, 36b
Oman
  20C.: 174, 175, 273

Ontario
  19C.: 222b, c, 223a
  20C.: 223b, c, 224
  See Canada
Orange, Pr. of
  16C.: 107
  18C.: 35, 74, 111
Orange Free State
  19C.: 244, 245
  20C.: 256b, 257
Oregon
  19C.: 202, 206
  See United States
Oregon Treaty (1846), 202
Oriskany (1777), B. of, 199
Orissa
  16C.: 3
  18C.: 266, 267
  19C.: 268
  20C.: 270
Orléans (1870), B. of, 117
Osnabrück, Bp. of
  16C.: 122, 124
  17C.: 32a, 129, 130
Otricoli (1798), B. of, 44
Ottoman Empire
  16C.: 2, 66–7, 71, 164–5
  17C.: 73, 164–5
  18C.: 38, 42, 75, 166–7
  19C.: 77, 79, 86–7, 166–9a
  20C.: 53, 81, 166–7, 169b
Oudenaarde (1708), B. of, 34
Oudh
  18C.: 50b, 266
  19C.: 267, 268
  20C.: 270

Pacific Ocean
  16C.: 4–5
  17C.: 6b
  18C.: 7a, 8–11
  19C.: 7b, 12–15
  20C.: 16–23, 55b, 63, 282–3
Padua (1500, 1509), B. of, 159
Pakistan
  20C.: 23, 270–3, 289
  See India
Palamos (1694), B. of, 33a
Palatinate, Lower
  16C.: 120, 122–6, 128
  17C.: 127, 130
  19C.: 49, 140–1
Palatinate, Upper
  16C.: 123, 125
  17C.: 32a, 131

Albert D. Kirwan

JOHN J. CRITTENDEN

The Struggle for the Union

UNIVERSITY OF KENTUCKY
PRESS

COPYRIGHT © 1962 BY THE UNIVERSITY OF KENTUCKY PRESS
MANUFACTURED IN THE UNITED STATES OF AMERICA
LIBRARY OF CONGRESS CATALOG CARD
NO. 62-19380

The publication of this book has been aided by a grant from
The Ford Foundation.

E
340
.C9
K5

6/1/63 McClurg 6.93

SEVERAL decades ago James G. Randall indicated that in John Jordan Crittenden biographers were overlooking one of the important figures of nineteenth century America. More recently the works of Allan Nevins, David Potter, Kenneth Stampp, and others, in disclosing more sharply Crittenden's role in the great secession crisis, have confirmed Randall's earlier judgment. Despite this growing recognition of his significance and despite the fact (or perhaps because of it) that Crittenden's long and complex career of a half century affected most of the great issues of American political life of this period, he has remained relatively unstudied by historians.

Crittenden's service in the United States Senate began on the day of Monroe's inaugural, before Calhoun, Webster, or Benton had yet entered that chamber; and he died, still a member of the Congress, more than a dozen years after they had passed from the scene. His path also crossed those of Adams, Jackson, Van Buren, Harrison, Tyler, Polk, Taylor, Fillmore, Pierce, Buchanan, Lincoln, Seward, Douglas, and Jefferson Davis. With all of them he was intimately associated, and there is hardly a major political event in the three decades prior to the Civil War in which he did not figure. No other American was nominated for the Supreme Court by Presidents as far separated in time as Quincy Adams and Lincoln. Few Americans have served in the cabinets of three different Presidents. But it was not so much the length of his career as his vital involvement in so many portentous events and crises that has demanded some fullness in development; to condense these pages more than has been done would, I think, sacrifice too much in the way of an understanding of Crittenden and his times.

Perhaps the most complex of Crittenden's involvements was his

Alma College Library
Alma, Michigan

relationship to Henry Clay. For more than three decades Crittenden was Clay's devoted lieutenant, and this tended both to shroud Crittenden's early career in relative obscurity and also to make extremely difficult the biographer's task of disentanglement. Such a relationship was not unusual in the early years of the nineteenth century, for the idea of party as a well-organized, cohesive, and permanent association did not make its appearance in America at least until the advent of Jackson or even later. Political leadership at that time was personal, and political associations were held together by ties sometimes of affection but always of individual interest. So long as a leader was able to maintain his leadership, the only avenue to political advancement was to serve in a subaltern position until time or changing fortunes created a vacancy.

But even in an era of personal leadership, Henry Clay overshadowed more than others the younger subordinates who surrounded him. By the end of the War of 1812 Clay had become a figure of such stature and importance that he controlled and directed the political destiny of his state in a manner rarely equaled. He was not a party boss like Thurlow Weed or, later, Mark Hanna, who operated slyly behind the scenes to outwit or outmaneuver opponents. Clay was the beau ideal of a statesman—a champion who stood in the front line of battle himself, baring his own bosom to the cannonading of the political wars. His magnetic personality, his flights of impassioned oratory, and his unmatchable charm, when he chose to use it, would hold fast his friends; and these qualities, together with his fiery belligerence and his sarcasm, would drive his enemies before him. Opposition from Kentuckians he would not brook, as Felix Grundy, Blair, Kendall, and the Wickliffe clan learned to their sorrow.

It was all but inevitable, therefore, that an accomplished and ambitious young attorney like Crittenden should at the outset of his career attach himself to Clay, and it was equally logical that Clay should welcome so promising a young man. For three decades their careers were inextricably intertwined. But Clay as the leader of his party was unmistakably the senior member of the partnership. The course he followed either in national or local affairs, his spectacular utterances, and above all the letters he wrote were of vital significance both to Crittenden's political fortunes and to his development as a statesman. To try to understand Crittenden without